P.G.Wodehouse

A LITERARY BIOGRAPHY

P.G.Wodehouse

A LITERARY BIOGRAPHY

Benny Green

PAVILION
MICHAEL JOSEPH

for Norman and Grete

The author wishes to thank
A. P. Watt Limited for their permission
to quote from the works of P. G. Wodehouse.

Photoset by
Rowland Phototypesetting Limited
Bury St Edmunds, Suffolk

Printed by
Hollen Street Press, Slough

Green, Benny
P.G. Wodehouse.
I. Wodehouse, P.G. – Biography
2. Authors, English – 20th century – Biography
I. Title
823'.912   PR6045.053Z/
ISBN 0-907516-04-1

Contents

List of illustrations   6

Prologue   7

1 Schoolboy at Dulwich   11

2 Bank clerk in Lombard Street   37

3 Free-lance in New York   64

4 Lyricist on Broadway   95

5 Novelist in the stalls   124

6 Scriptwriter in Hollywood   153

7 Novelist in a padded cell   181

8 Knight in exile   213

Epilogue   236

Notes to the text   239

Chronology   247

Bibliography   249

Index   251

List of illustrations

Jacket collage – Barry Phelps, Irene Editions, London sw6

Between pages 64 and 65
Dulwich College First xi 1899 – photo by Eileen Tweedy
Mike – photo by Eileen Tweedy
The Captain – photo by Eileen Tweedy
The Swoop – photo by Eileen Tweedy
PGW *c*.1904 – Culver Pictures
PGW at Hunstanton Hall – bbc Hulton Picture Library
Oh Joy! – The Raymond Mander and Joe Mitchenson Theatre Collection
PGW and Gertrude Lawrence – The Raymond Mander and Joe
Mitchenson Theatre Collection
PGW in Ian Hay's car – bbc Hulton Picture Library
PGW with his wife Ethel and daughter Leonora – Associated Press

Between pages 112 and 113
PGW in Hollywood – Culver Pictures
PGW being interviewed in internment camp – Associated Press
PGW in Berlin – United Press International
Notes for a Jeeves novel – photo by Eileen Tweedy
'Jeeves and the Song of Songs' – photo by Eileen Tweedy
Jeeves in the Offing – photo by Eileen Tweedy
Very Good, Jeeves – photo by Eileen Tweedy
PGW with dog – Camera Press (photo Tom Blau)
PGW reading Perry Mason novel – Camera Press (photo Tom Blau)
PGW in Long Island woodlands – Camera Press (photo Tom Blau)

6

Prologue

'I must tell you about this wonderful, charming man Wodehouse'

IRA GERSHWIN

BY 1867 IMPERIAL TRAFFIC WAS BRISK, as the British wandered the surface of the planet in search of either divine missions or increased dividends, or, better still if it could be arranged, both at the same time. Off they sailed down the sea lanes of the world, out from Liverpool, into Southampton Water, down the Bristol Channel, away from Tilbury, unwittingly parodying with a thousand variations the scenario of Ford Madox Brown's 'The Last of England': the brevet colonels flushed with the proud apoplexy of a recent mention in dispatches; horse-faced subalterns whose toothy sibilance would soon be whistling across the promontories of the North-west Frontier; staff majors grimly pursuing the carrot of a KCIE; ruddy adjutants whose leaden gallantries might before long be rattling the teacups of some half-forgotten hill station; reverend gentlemen dedicated to the export of their religion to areas which had known their own when the English were still daubing their rumps with berry juice; smooth-cheeked young men who had prepared themselves to serve as Assistant District Commissioners and dispense justice over tracts of land half as big as Wales by serving for a term or two as House Captain – all these men resolved to reconciling somehow the opposing ideals of playing the game and pinching someone else's property, and miraculously succeeding, at least in part. Off they galumphed, across the spacious and still unpolluted plains of the nineteenth century, carrying with them not only pistols but polo mallets, not only prayer-books but score-books, proselytizers of the ideal embodied in the Clarenden Report, that curious document which built into the code of Empire the idea of formalized team games as the expression of gentlemanly culture.[1]

In that year a young Civil Servant called Henry Ernest Wodehouse took the boat for the Crown Colony of Hong Kong, armoured against fate by the assurances of the Repton crammers who had guided him, if not quite to wisdom, then at least through the labyrinth of the Indian Civil Service examinations. The colony had been acquired by the British in 1841, with the purpose of expediting the dispatch of opium to China, a noble imperial enterprise which proved so congenial to the natives as to require the presence of no more than some Indian soldiers, Sikh policemen, two battalions of the British army plus the usual mass of camp followers, scholars, scriveners, bishops, engineers, clerks and restaurateurs, that familiar horde of Victorian petty functionaries trained in the necessity of making the world not only safe but also reasonably comfortable for business investment. Wodehouse, who had been equipped for his duties of dispensing justice to the Chinese by a thorough grounding in the love life of Dido and the ruminations of Marcus Aurelius, was untroubled by the realization that a posting to Hong Kong was rather like being awarded your Second Eleven colours; for the First Eleven always went to India, leaving the lesser colonies to those in whom character, it was said, was more evident than brainpower. Young Wodehouse was an exemplar of the type required in a place like Hong Kong, sober, conscientious, honest, and quite without that vaulting ambition which might so easily tempt a man to cast covetous eyes on the fleshpots of Delhi and Simla.

A public-school education and distant hints of nobility in his family tree would have made him instantly acceptable to the British colony perched on the slopes of the Peak, a tribal enclave whose occupants remained studiously aloof from the locals and patronized them terrifically. The Chinese returned the compliment, referring to the Governor, John Pope-Hennessy, as 'Number One Good Friend' while privately puzzling over the riddle which so exercised the mind of Sun Yat Sen: 'I began to wonder how it was that England could do such things as they have done with the barren rock of Hong Kong within seventy or eighty years, while in four thousand the Chinese have achieved nothing like it.' Wodehouse soon became a respected magistrate, and in a mere ten years had married a member of the Fishing Fleet, that group of acceptable young English lady anglers whose parents, having perceived that so many of the big matrimonial fish seemed to go East, sent their daughters after them in the hope of landing one. In 1877 Ernest married Eleanor Deane, a Somerset parson's daughter, and later that year she gave birth to the first English child to be born on the Peak, a confluence of events irresistibly evoking thoughts of Sir Walter Scott; the baby was christened Philip Peveril. Two years later Ernest Armine followed, but when on 15 October 1881 the third child arrived, Eleanor was back in the old country visiting friends in Guildford, Surrey. Soon she and the infant Pelham Grenville sailed back to Hong Kong, where by 1883 both she and her husband had become acutely aware of that most painful portion of the White Man's Burden, how to reconcile an affectionate parental solicitude with a desirably English upbringing.

Fortunately for the Wodehouses, the English by this time had perfected the ideal answer to the problem, a series of juvenile hotels and boarding houses staffed by groups of educational ladies and gentlemen who would, for a small consideration, perform willingly enough many of the more onerous duties of parenthood. In 1884, mother and children returned to England, where Eleanor rented a house in Bath and placed her three most priceless possessions in the charge of a perfect stranger called Miss Roper, an unbending character who appears to have proceeded on the assumption that godliness is next to cleanliness but a long way behind. She then returned to Hong Kong, a parting which proved freakishly brief, only two short years elapsing before Ernest and Eleanor were back, although this apparently reckless display of parental concern was due less to their passion for their sons than to the need for Ernest's presence at Buckingham Palace, where he was to be made a Companion of the Order of St Michael and St George in recognition of his outstanding work in the planning and execution of the Chinese section of the Great Exposition. His work in the planning and exposition of the Wodehouse section of the British Empire was rather less auspicious for, like Mrs Jellyby with regard to Africa, Ernest's eyes had a curious habit of seeming to look a long way off. He and his wife were soon away again, leaving the boys at a small school in Croydon, where Pelham Grenville, by this time generally addressed as Plum, composed his first literary work, an essay in pastoral concerning a thrush and some worms, a dramatic narrative so inconclusive that its author was obliged to inform his readers in a closing cadence, 'Now my story is ended'. It was at Croydon also that Wodehouse began to develop a partiality for domestic servants in preference to their employers.

Every summer holiday the boys would be farmed out to the Worcestershire home of their paternal grandmother, whose simian aspect and status as superannuated martinet possibly explains Ernest's eagerness to get out of the country. After three years at Croydon, Peveril developed a weak chest and had to bow to the prevailing medical theory that Guernsey was a sure cure. So the three boys were packed off to yet another educational boarding house at Elizabeth College, where they lived with the headmaster, and in the holidays were delivered to the homes of assorted aunts. After two years of the Guernsey idyll, one of these aunts, Edith, persuaded the absent Ernest to send Plum to sea, on the undeniably logical assumption that as a naval education had not noticeably impaired her husband's character, it would have no ill effects on the nephew's. So Wodehouse went off to a naval preparatory school in Kent where he was bored by a curriculum which lacked any organized games. During one holiday he went off to visit his beloved elder brother Armine, by now a boarder at Dulwich College, and found the environment so superior to anything promised by the Royal Navy that he begged his father to be allowed to go there too. 'My father was very indulgent,' explains Wodehouse. In the autumn term of 1894 he took up residence in Ivyholme house, where his status as boarder seemed more preferable than any other he could imagine because 'it offered much more opportunity for making friendships and generally feeling that one was part of the life of the school'.

He was now experienced in the subtle gradations of preparatory and public school hierarchies, was embarked on the nebulous art of literary composition, had encountered in his own father those frailties of temperament against which neither civic honours nor aristocratic connections are altogether proof, had perceived certain ironies of the status of the domestic servant, had found a geographical location which seemed to him quite perfect, and had tasted the mixed pleasures of surrogate parentage within the family. His raw materials were to hand.

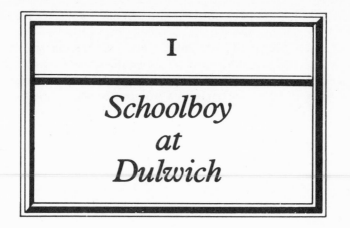

I

Schoolboy at Dulwich

ANY DOUBT THAT DULWICH DID NOT serve as the model for Wodehouse's first considerable literary invention is dispelled by his best friend at school, studymate William Townend:

> Wrykyn is Dulwich, a Dulwich not situated in a London suburb but in the country. But whereas the boys of Wrykyn are practically all boarders, Dulwich, like Bedford and St Paul's, though with four large boarding houses, now increased to five, is in the main a day school; nevertheless, elderly men who were at Dulwich between the years 1895 and 1901 will recognize and appreciate Plum's masterly delineation of the life we lived so long ago.

From the attitudes of the boys in the school stories it is clear that Wodehouse considered the status of boarder highly desirable; a mere day boy was hardly a participant in school life at all. However, after one year as a Dulwich boarder he was suddenly reduced to the indignity of day boy by the reappearance in the district of his parents. This interlude lasted less than a year, after which the family moved north and returned Wodehouse to the bosom of his only true family, the adolescent community of the college:

> It was what you would call a middle-class school. We were all the sons of reasonably solvent but certainly not wealthy parents, and we all had to earn our living later on. Compared with Eton, Dulwich would be something like an American State University compared with Harvard

or Princeton. Bertie Wooster's parents would never have sent him to Dulwich, but Ukridge could very well have been there. . . . Some farseeing parents, knowing that their sons would have to go into business later, put them on the Modern side, where they learned French and German and mathematics; but the average parent chose the Classical, where they learned Latin and Greek, presumably with a vague idea that if all went well they would go to Oxford or Cambridge. In my day, to the ordinary parent, education meant Classics. I went automatically on the Classical side and, as it turned out, it was the best form of education I could have had as a writer.

Middle-class or not, Wodehouse's companions in the Classical Sixth included a subsequent High Commissioner for South Africa, a Provost of King's College, Cambridge, an Archbishop of Cape Town, a Deputy Keeper of Public Records, and the polar explorer Sir Ernest Shackleton.

If any of these men had been asked at the time to foresee some way in which Wodehouse might distinguish himself, their thoughts might well have winged their way to the playing field. It was as an outstanding cricketer as much as anything else that Wodehouse became known at Dulwich. Both Classical and Modern sides strained every nerve and sinew to excel at what they took to be the real business of public-school life, team games:

We were a great all-round school in those days. In my last year, the captain of football and three of the team got university scholarships, and another passed into Sandhurst in the first three. The brainless athlete was quite a rarity. We might commit mayhem on the football field, but after the game was over we trotted off to our houses and wrote Latin verse.

At the end of 1899 Wodehouse's headmaster, a terrifying apparition called Gilkes, who stood six feet six and sported a long white beard, gave his verdict on Wodehouse. Years later, Wodehouse remembered him as 'a man who was always trying to damp people, to keep them from getting above themselves', appending a pastiche of the sort of thing he had in mind:

'So you made a century against Tonbridge, did you my boy? Well, always remember that you will soon be dead, and in any case, the bowling was probably rotten.'

Wodehouse retained considerable affection for Gilkes, whose determination to 'damp' people overcame his perceptions as a published novelist and caused him to score nought out of a hundred in assessing the most remarkable pupil ever to come under his care; the 1899 verdict read:

He is a most impractical boy . . . often forgetful; he finds difficulty in the most simple things and asks absurd questions, whereas he can understand the more difficult things. . . . He has the most distorted ideas about wit and humour; he draws over his books in a most distressing way, and writes foolish rhymes in other people's books. One is obliged to like him in spite of his vagaries.

These vagaries were almost invariably of a literary kind. According to Townend, Wodehouse

> worked, if he worked at all, supremely fast, writing Latin and Greek verses as rapidly as he wrote English. . . . We talked incessantly, about books and writing. Plum's talk was exhilarating. I had never known such talk. Even at the age of seventeen he could discuss lucidly writers of whom I had never heard. I was impressed by his knowledge. He was an omnivorous reader. Some authors were Barry Pain and James Payn, Rudyard Kipling and W. S. Gilbert. But it is impossible to say who were his favourite authors. He liked so many and all kinds. And from the first time I met him, he had decided to write. He never swerved.

Wodehouse became an author in the autumn of 1902 with the publication of *The Pothunters*, in which one Jim Thomson, a boy at St Austin's School, is wrongly suspected of breaking into the sports pavilion and stealing the trophies stored there. Thomson has indeed broken into the pavilion but for a perfectly innocent reason, and is unlucky enough to have disturbed the real burglar; it takes eighteen short chapters occupying one term in the life of the school for Thomson's innocence to be established and the identity of the real thief discovered. St Austin's is so civilized and pleasant a sort of place as to create the illusion of laughter and good weather even under the shadow of felonious suspicions. The pupils are at least as judicious as their instructors and often a great deal more worldly; when a detective arrives on the premises to investigate the mystery of the missing cups, one of the boys remarks, in defiance of the frequent Holmes–Watson references which Wodehouse was in the habit of scattering about his school texts, 'I don't think detectives are much class'. The local grandee, Sir Alfred Venner, MP, is derided as a brainless lout. Boys spend their time reading *Punch* and *The Sportsman* and playing selections from Gilbert and Sullivan on the banjo. The most revealing moment comes when two of the hero's friends are pretending to accuse one Welch of the purloining of the cups:

> 'It looks to me', said Charteris, 'as if Welch, thinking his chances of the quarter rather rocky, hired one of his low acquaintances to steal the cup for him.'
>
> 'Shouldn't wonder. Welch knows some jolly low characters.'
>
> 'Welch is a jolly low character himself,' said Tony judicially. 'I wonder you associate with him, Alderman.'
>
> 'Stand in loco parentis. Aunt of his asked me to keep an eye on him. "Dear George is so wild," she said.'

Before Welch could find words to refute this hideous slander, Tony cut in once more. 'The only reason he doesn't drink gin and play billiards at the Blue Lion is that gin makes him ill and his best break at pills is six, including two flukes.'

'As a matter of fact,' said Welch, changing the conversation with a jerk, 'I don't much care if the cups are stolen. One doesn't only run for the sake of the pot.'

Charteris groaned. 'Oh, well,' he said, 'if you're going to take the high moral standpoint and descend to brazen platitudes like that, I give you up.'

Although this is a first novel, written by a young sprig still too young to vote, the signs are ominous. Deep derision is being flung at the conventions of school fiction, and the modern reader cannot help wondering if, while writing such passages, it occurred to Wodehouse that his days as a specialist in public-school yarns were numbered. Here he was, an absolute beginner, and already he was laughing at the genre.

During the thirty years before Wodehouse published *The Pothunters*, the propagation of public-school fiction had been the exclusive reserve of certain proselytizing interests resolved on converting the classroom into an arena for the struggle between God and the Devil, a misuse of an innocent genre which was not only pernicious but ridiculous. In the quintessential example, *Eric, or Little by Little*, one of the most idiotic books of the nineteenth century, the hero begins his bathetic slide down the slippery slope to perdition by using the word 'devil', although how a child was expected to swallow the obscenity of hell without reference to its chairman of the board is one of several questions to which Frederick Farrar, the book's author, appears never to have addressed himself. The theologians of the period had discovered for themselves the rules of a most convenient moral determinism which proved that the uttering of the word 'devil' leads to the blasphemy of smoking as inevitably as the confluence of fire and gunpowder leads to an explosion, and that smoking leads just as inevitably to the consumption of wines and spirits, which causes the purloining of pigeons, which causes drunkenness at prayers, which causes the stealing of sovereigns, which leads to a career in the Merchant Navy. This last curious and delightfully incongruous link in the chain of causal reaction turns out to be the death of poor Eric, who, having proceeded crime by crime through Farrar's litany of the damned, proves to be deficient in those qualities of physical hardihood which are the exotic fruits of a refusal to make audible references to the devil. At one point the hero attempts to save a schoolmate from drowning. Being Eric, he fails, and the dying drownee's last gurgled words are 'Dear Eric, don't smoke'. Later, when through Eric's neglect his young brother falls over a conveniently adjacent cliff, Eric writes, 'Oh, how my whole soul yearns towards him. I *must* be a better boy. I *will* be better than I have been.' Considering that he has already helped to dispatch two people, this ambition does not seem to be excessively immodest, but it is still too much for the dreadful Eric, who runs away to sea, comes home and dies, lingering just long enough to learn that his mother, whose knowledge of a life on the ocean wave would seem to be sketchy, has died of distress at the thought of his nautical exploits.

Farrar, the lunatic responsible for this cheapskate misappropriation of the Christian ethic, was one of the leaders of that quaint Fundamentalist army which marched so staunchly up the garden path of the nineteenth century, and which so persistently confused the issues of education and salvation as to transmute its schoolmasters into divines and its divines into schoolmasters. He himself was the exemplar of the type, becoming headmaster of Marlborough and finally Dean of Canterbury, delaying his departure for the plains of paradise just long enough to be contemporaneous with the chaste blasphemies of Wodehouse's schoolboy fictions. That they were indeed blasphemies is confirmed when seen in the light of the reaction to Eric of one of Farrar's Nonconformist opponents, E. E. Kellett:

> If Mr Farrar has been in the habit of meeting such boys as he describes, we can only say that a most kind and indulgent fate has not permitted us the same advantage. Young gentlemen who do nothing but walk about their school playgrounds with their arms round one another's necks, discussing the various responsibilities of a Christian's duty, deserve to be caged and kept for public exhibition. Boys and girls who are perpetually stopping in the middle of their play to say prayers and sing hymns are simply nauseating. And boys and girls who bristle with texts, quote long passages of Scripture, refreshing themselves at frequent intervals by reference to Dr Watts, are specimens of juvenile humanity whose society would be unbearable.[1]

Unbearable or not, Farrar's became the accepted style of school fiction, until by 1879 the greatest fraud of all had become commerically viable. In that year there appeared the first issue of *The Boy's Own Paper*, a highly successful organ of religious propaganda passing itself off as a secular diversion. In fact it was published by the Religious Tract Society, an organization whose adherence to the teachings of the Sermon on the Mount did not inhibit its administrators from telling a pretty lie regarding their ownership of *The Boy's Own Paper*. This lie consisted of pretending that the paper was nothing to do with them; ostensibly the magazine was issued from the 'Leisure Hour' offices in Paternoster Row. Its editors were often harangued by their paymasters for failing to give enough prominence to 'Christian truth and influence', a neat enough paraphrase of Farrar's modest confession that with *Eric* he had attempted 'the vivid inculcation of moral purity'.

But *The Boy's Own Paper*, dubious though its moral bona fides may have been, was fortunate enough to recruit to the cause a writer of school stories whose talent was so considerable that it could not be stifled by even the twaddling pietism of his religious ethic. Talbot Baines Reed, the most influential writer of school fiction between Thomas Hughes[2] and Wodehouse, and an interesting example of a hereditary prig, was a religious huckster who, under an assumed name, sold sermons to schoolboys who thought they were buying tips about camp fires and yarns about bats and balls. By buttering the biblical pill with liberal quantities of football and feasts in the dorm, Reed achieved a curious halfway house between the Christian Socialism of F. D. Maurice[3] and the jockstrap jocosities of Edwardian public-school fiction, a quaint hybrid which might best be defined as Musclebound Christianity. Reed's grandfather had salved his own conscience by endowing an asylum 'for Idiots' and a hospital 'for the Incurable'; his father belonged to the British and Foreign Bible Society; his brother was secretary of that society. Reed himself was a deacon in the Congregational Church and an active partner in the family printing business. He had never attended a boarding school; he had never been a schoolmaster; he was not a professional writer, and indeed had so little interest in the commercial possibilities of his school stories that he virtually gave away their copyright to the Religious Tract Society.

Handicapped in this multiplicity of ways, he was ideally equipped to write a book even funnier than *Eric*. But heavily influenced though he was by Farrar, and demented though he appears to have been regarding God's distaste for beer, billiards and the working classes, Reed possessed a genuine narrative gift and a thorough grasp of the atmosphere of life at a boarding school. Unlike Farrar, he could still remember what it was like to be a boy, and had not allowed his subsequent evangelical maunderings to repress the evidence. If the modern public-school romance can be said to have a beginning, then Reed's *The Fifth Form at St Dominic's* (1887) is that beginning. Some of the boys and masters at St Dominic's enjoy an existence independent of the school, and one or two of the characters even bear a vestigial resemblance to real people. But the plot leans heavily on the same narrative crutch of daft determinism which sustained Farrar so well.

It is tempting for a less devout age to dismiss the likes of Farrar and Reed as hypocrites making a tidy living out of the religious susceptibilities of innocent young men. But Farrar and Reed were very far from being hypocrites, although it would have spoken much better for them if they had been. It is one thing to write pietistic garbage for money and fame, quite another to write it out of moral megalomania. Nor should it be thought that St Dominic's disappeared with the modern era. Far into the Twenties and Thirties, novels of public-school life for juvenile consumption were being produced which propagated the same cold-bath theology. None of Reed's disciples, however, remotely approached him in his talent for telling a story and describing the groupings of school life.[4]

It has been one of the ironies of Reed's fate to be remembered for his second-best book. After *The Fifth Form at St Dominic's*, he published a novel of a richer texture, *The Willoughby Captains*, in which all the tensions of the plot are created by the appointment of an unfashionable boy as school captain and his struggle to win the allegiance of his fellows. In spite of its comparative obscurity, *The Willoughby Captains*, understandably eclipsed by the symbolic fame of its predecessor as the first of its kind, was destined to become one of the most influential of all school stories. Wodehouse would certainly have known of it, and in *The Head of Kay's* (1905) deployed a variation of its theme of an unpredictable appointee winning through. But by the time *The Head of Kay's* was published, Wodehouse was already an experienced public-school novelist who, after five volumes in quick succession, was beginning to outgrow the limitations of the genre.

Each of Wodehouse's school books represents a considerable advance on the one before, in manipulation of plot, mastery of dialogue, psychological shrewdness regarding the contents of boys' heads, above all in originality of language. *The Pothunters* was followed in 1903 by *A Prefect's Uncle*, which displays a continuing preoccupation with the Savoy operas and *Punch*; when a young cricketer is dropped from the school team, he accepts an invitation to practise with lesser players, for, 'like Mr Phil May's lady when she was ejected with perfect justice by a barman, he went somewhere where he would be respected'.[5] This time the story concerns the mixed fortunes of Gethryn, a senior boy at Beckford College, who is instructed to meet an uncle he has never seen off the London train. This uncle is smaller and younger than his nephew, and is destined to be one of the most disruptive forces ever to collide with the routine of Beckford. While the incongruity of the situation evokes Anstey's *Vice Versa*,[6] 'there are other, more disconcerting elements to the story. Farnie, Gethryn's small uncle, is a genuine original, a prematurely finished cynic mildly amused by the childish protocol of the public-school system.[7] At first he is patient with the bewildered Gethryn: 'Your mater was my elder sister. You'll find it works out all right. Look here. A, the daughter of B and C, marries. No, look here. I was born when you were four. See?'

But Gethryn does not see, especially when he begins to realize that Farnie is the spokesman for an unthinkable intellectual lobby which simply cannot take the idea of a public school with any seriousness. At first Gethryn tries to muster the conventional sympathy of the veteran for the raw recruit:

> 'By the way, I forgot to ask. Have you ever been to school before?'
> 'Yes,' said Farnie, in the dreamy voice of one who recalls memories from the misty past. 'I was at Harrow before I came here, and at Wellington before I went to Harrow, and at Clifton before I went to Wellington.'
> Gethryn gasped. 'Anywhere before you went to Clifton?'
> 'Only private schools.'
> 'Why did you leave Harrow?'
> 'Sacked,' was the laconic reply.
> 'Why did you leave Wellington?'
> 'Sacked,' said Farnie again.

Later Farnie offers the additional information that he has experienced life at four other private schools: 'I worked off those in a year and a half.' It is not very long before he has worked off Beckford, too, which is a pity because, from the moment that Farnie runs away never to return, understandably convinced that to stay on to be flogged for playing billiards would be ridiculous, the narrative subsides into the conventional catalogue of sporting contests won and lost. But the intermittent barrage of mockery against the Farrar–Reed battalions never flags. There is, for instance, a brief discussion on how to behave towards uncles:

> 'We should strive to be kind, even to the very humblest. On the off chance, you know. The unknown may have struck it rich in sheep or something out in Australia. Most uncles come from Australia.'

Sometimes the attacks are more specific, as when Norris, the captain of cricket, wins the toss against the MCC and elects to bat first:

> Tom Brown, we read, in a similar position, 'with the usual liberality of young hands', put his opponents in first. Norris was not so liberal. He may have been young, but he was not so young as all that.

It is typical of Wodehouse that he should deploy Gilbert to deflate Thomas Hughes.[8]

But in his third book, *Tales of St Austin's* (1903), a collection of reprinted pieces, the oblique jibe develops into a dashing frontal assault. In a mock-serious disquisition called 'The Tom Brown Question', which opens with a side-swipe at Samuel Butler's theory that the author of *The Iliad* was a woman, Wodehouse toys with the idea that the brio of the first half of Hughes' book is so contradicted by the cant of the second that the novel must be the work of two hands. As a possible scenario, he suggests that soon after completing his book, Hughes was visited by representatives of an organization known to itself as the S.S.F.P.W.L.W.T.R.O.E.B.A.S.T.H.G.I. and to others as the Secret Society for Putting Wholesome Literature Within the Reach of Every Boy and Seeing That He Gets It:

> 'We have come to speak to you about your book. Our representative has read Part One and reports unfavourably. It contains no moral. There are scenes of violence, and your hero is far from perfect.'
> 'I think you mistake my object,' said Mr Hughes. 'Tom is a boy, not a patent medicine. In other words, he is not supposed to be perfect.'

Hughes, threatened with assassination, then agrees to let the Society rewrite the second half of *Tom Brown* to conform to the pattern of morally uplifting literature, which exercise creates the flawed work familiar to schoolboys of Wodehouse's generation. But it is in an extended essay entitled 'Work' that Wodehouse launches the heaviest of all his attacks, on the type of classical education to which every public school was committed. In the course of advising readers that *Rodney Stone*, *Vice Versa* and *Many Cargoes* are much to be preferred to the histories of Thucydides, he flings down a gauntlet:

What, I ask, does the scholar gain, either morally or physically, or in any other way, by knowing who was tribune of the people in 284 BC, or what is the precise difference between the various constructions of 'cum'? It is not as if ignorance of the tribune's identity caused him any mental unrest. In short, what excuse is there for the student? Our children are being led to ruin by this system. They will become Dons and think in Greek. The victim of the craze stops at nothing. He puns in Latin. He quips and quirks in Ionic and Doric. In the worst stages of the disease he will edit Greek plays and say that Merry quite misses the fun of the passage, or that Jebb is mediocre. Think, I beg of you, paterfamilias, and you, mater ditto, what your feelings would be were you to find Henry or Archibald Cuthbert correcting proofs of the *Agamemnon* and inventing 'nasty ones' for Mr Sidgwick. Very well then, be warned. Our bright-eyed lads are taught insane constructions in Greek and Latin from morning till night, and they come for their holidays, in many cases, without the merest foundation of a batting style. They will read Herodotus without a dictionary for pleasure, but ask them to translate the childishly simple sentence: 'Trott was soon in his timber-yard with a length'un that whipped across from the off',[9] and they'll shrink abashed and swear they have not skill at that, as Gilbert says.

Accompanying this spirited attack on the acquirement of the very skills which Wodehouse himself possessed are an epistolary sequence called 'L'Affaire Uncle John', which demonstrates the desirability of procuring the kind of sinecure enabling a man to spend all his time playing cricket, and a chapter called 'A Shocking Affair', which the author describes in his brief preface as 'one of our failures', the story having been rejected by the editors to whom it had been offered, and which probably explains the remark: 'There are three things which anyone thinks he can do better than anyone else, namely poking a fire, writing a novel and opening a door.' There are also references to Wilde, Browning, Shakespeare, and one or two mild jibes at the German Emperor.

The next novel in the school sequence, *The Gold Bat* (1904), continues to trade in counters which must by now have become familiar to Wodehouse's schoolboy readers: W. S. Gilbert, team games and the popular arts. One boy's study wall is festooned with photographs of Irving, Little Tich, Dan Leno, Martin-Harvey, Mrs Pat and Herbert Campbell; there are passing references to Conan Doyle, Jerome, Anstey, Stevenson and Rider Haggard; one senior boy incorporates into his smalltalk a recognizable imitation of Mrs Micawber expressing her loyalty to her husband, and there are intermittent displays of that political nihilism which remained with Wodehouse throughout his life and prevented him from ever taking any politicians at their own evaluation. The plot of *The Gold Bat* concerns the tarring and feathering by a sixth-form Celt of the statue of the comically pumped-up local Conservative member, Sir Eustace Briggs, 'mayor of Wrykyn, a keen politician and a hater of the Irish nation'. A fragment of future autobiography crops up when we are told that 'the boy who smokes at school is bound to come to a bad end. He will degenerate gradually into a person that plays dominoes in the smoking-rooms of ABC shops with friends who wear bowler hats and frock coats.'[10]

In *The Head of Kay's*, the autobiographical overtones are even stronger. The story concerns the troubles of one Robert Fenn, a prominent pupil at Eckleton School who has, much against his inclinations, been placed in charge of a house notorious for its habits of indolence and indiscipline. One day, at a climax in his affairs, Fenn receives a letter from his older brother, an Old Eckletonian who had, in the natural order of things, gone on to a university:

> Cambridge had not taught him a great deal, possibly because he did not meet the well-meant efforts of his tutor half-way. The net result of his three years at King's was – imprimus, a cricket-blue, including a rather lucky 83 at Lord's; secondly, a very poor degree; thirdly and lastly, a taste for literature and the drama – he had been a prominent member of the Footlights Club. When he came down he looked about him for some occupation which should combine in happy proportions a small amount of work and a large amount of salary, and finding none, drifted into journalism, at which calling he had been doing very fairly ever since.[11]

In this episode, which is perfectly typical of Wodehouse the purveyor of schoolboy fiction, heresy jostles heresy. The elder Fenn is not only no scholar, but has clearly made no effort to take advantage of the privilege bestowed upon him by one of the world's most august cultural conspiracies. And though his time at Cambridge has been wasted, he remains cheerfully unrepentant. He has slacked, not because he is a moral leper, but because slacking is exactly what any other ordinary young man would have done in his position, and he makes no secret of the fact that the most desirable possession in all the world for him would be the kind of sinecure which made it possible to enjoy a life of happy parasitism. He has discovered that the next best thing to not working is to be a free-lance journalist, and is now living in a style which suggests that the wages of sin is tolerable comfort. But by far the most original aspect of the paragraph is its assumption of the reader's interest in and knowledge of the world beyond the school gates. With the example of the older Fenn before them, schoolboy readers could hardly help realizing that no matter what their instructors might tell them to the contrary, the circumscribed life of a public school is not after all the very heartland of human experience. Fenn has been a modest educational failure. Finding himself at Cambridge, he has contributed so little to the cultural good name of Eckleton that Thomas Arnold, had he been acquainted with the facts of the case, would have snorted in disgust.[12] Yet Fenn has won through. The mildness of the narrative style cannot altogether conceal that it is enunciating a violent heresy.

With *The White Feather*, Wodehouse returns to Wrykyn, where he becomes more outspoken than ever against the old Farrar–Reed convention, although perhaps his derision is tempered by an uneasy feeling that he is himself indulging in the cardboard heroics of the bad old days. The story concerns the scarlet sin committed against the unwritten code by Sheen, a keen scholar and a diffident mixer who runs away when his schoolmates become involved in a fracas with the townees. Sent to Coventry by a disgusted and frankly faintly disgusting school, Sheen wins back his good name by taking boxing lessons from the great Joe Bevan, one-time World Lightweight Champion and a prodigious Shakespearean scholar bearing himself like the true descendant of Shaw's Cashel Byron that he undoubtedly is.[13] Under this benign tutelage, Sheen carries all before him and wins the silver medal at the Public Schools Championships at Aldershot. Once again the derivations from the popular literature of the period are too glaring to be overlooked, only this time instead of Anstey and Reed it is A. E. W. Mason, author of *The Four Feathers*, with Sheen playing Harry Feversham to the dervishes of the Wrykyn townees, and the boxing ring at Aldershot serving as the Stone House at Khartoum. Mason was the best-known writer to come out of Dulwich College before Wodehouse himself, who, with *The White Feather*, must have sensed that he was approaching the end of his career as a writer of school stories.

His effective demolition of the genre comes when Drummond, the boy whose regard Sheen covets most of all, considers the latter's attempt to re-establish himself:

> It seemed to him that Sheen was trying to 'do the boy hero'. In the school library which had been stocked in the dark ages, when that type of story was popular, there were numerous school stories in which the hero retrieved a rocky reputation by thrashing the bully, displaying in the encounter an intuitive but overwhelming skill with his fists. Drummond could not help feeling that Sheen must have been reading one of these stories. It was all very fine and noble of him to want to show that he was No Coward After All, like Leo Cholmondeley or whatever his beastly name was, in *The Lads of St Ethelberta's*, or some such piffling book. . . . If he wanted to do the Cholmondeley business, let him go and chuck a kid in the river and jump in and save him.

A few pages later Wodehouse defends his platform by invoking the ghost of his hero Anstey; Sheen, having been deprived for the moment of the chance to perform his deed of gallant redemption, is ruminating on the gulf between life and literature:

> The Fates were against him. In stories, as Mr Anstey has pointed out, the hero is never long without his chance of retrieving his reputation. A mad bull comes into the school grounds, and he alone (the hero, not the bull) is calm. Or there is a fire, and whose is that pale and gesticulating form at

21

the upper window? The bully's, of course. And who is that climbing up the Virginia Creeper? Why, the hero, who else? Three cheers for the plucky hero.

Not that Wodehouse was declaring total war on a narrative convention. In spite of their persistent blasphemies, the school novels are scattered with observations on school life which the ecclesiastical policemen of *The Boy's Own Paper* would have applauded heartily. We are told that 'headmasters are usually good judges of character', a bromide worthy of Farrar at his most obsequious. There are other taboos which Wodehouse cannot bring himself to defy, then or later. When in a subsequent volume Mike Jackson, pride of Wrykyn and one of the most brilliant young cricketers in England, finds himself unemployed, he weighs the chances of staving off genteel destitution by becoming a professional, knowing that such a resort will constitute a social outrage compared to which the crime of a Sheen would seem a mere playful peccadillo. But even in his extremity, Mike realizes that if he were to embrace the serpent of professionalism, he must be careful not to compromise those innocent parties, his cricketing brothers. He tells himself that 'it is impossible that he should play for his own county on his residential qualification. He could not appear as a professional in the same team in which his brothers were playing as amateurs'. As a nonagenarian, by which time the distinction between cricketing patricians and hired hands had disappeared, at least in the legal sense, Wodehouse remained unable to liberate himself from the code of his youth:

> I say, what's happened to English cricket? I understand there aren't any amateurs any more. They pay people like Cowdrey?[14] I wonder how that's arranged, and how much they get. In my day the Fosters[15] . . . I never understood how all of those brothers played first-class cricket all summer, every summer.[16]

Wodehouse is surely being excessively naïve, and must have known that the old Gentleman–Player distinction of his boyhood was a social rather than a financial one, and that many amateurs, that is, public school men, who lacked the financial wherewithal to buttress their pretensions, managed to continue playing as amateurs by adopting one of three tactics: either they found the kind of blessed sinecure which eventually fell into Mike Jackson's lap, or they took unacknowledged fees for their services in the style of England captains like W. G. Grace and A. C. Maclaren, or they were appointed to paid but technically non-cricketing posts such as county club treasurer or secretary. It is no coincidence that Wodehouse should have singled out as his example of the amateur-paragon the Fosters, for it was that remarkable brotherhood which gave him the idea of the Jacksons, a transmutation of reality which led, apparently by accident, to his liberation forever from the constraints of the quadrangle.

Early in 1907, roughly concurrent with *The White Feather*, Wodehouse began work on the serial which later became known as *Mike*. At first glance the book appears to belong with the rest of the school tales. The setting of Wrykyn had already been made familiar in *The Gold Bat* and *The White Feather*, in which an unspecified Jackson had flitted intermittently across the landscape. The criterion of character was still a purely sporting one; like Fenn in *The Head of Kay's*, young Jackson is already at full professional standard while still a schoolboy cricketer, and he eventually proves his primacy before the world by transforming single-handed an obscure school into a cricketing force to be reckoned with. But *Mike* went benignly wrong. The plot concerns a congenitally unintellectual hero who is removed from Wrykyn by an irate father, and transferred to Sedleigh, a minor public school run on such eccentric lines that sport is sacrificed to the pursuit of knowledge. At first Mike, bitterly disappointed at having been removed from a great cricketing school, retires to sulk in his tent, but gradually he conceives the daring idea of building Sedleigh into a side so powerful that it can take on Wrykyn itself. There is nothing in any of this which would seem out of place in the earlier books; but in the second section of the saga of Mike Jackson, there suddenly emerges from the text the novelist of the future, Wodehouse the artist, Wodehouse the adult comedian, Wodehouse the linguistic contortionist. On his arrival at Sedleigh, Mike is confronted by a stranger. The moment is the most dramatic of Wodehouse's long literary career, for up to now he has been exclusively a spinner of school tales whose nuances were never intended for an adult readership at all, in which regard he was being more original than perhaps he knew. Kipling's *Stalky and Co* had been written for parents, Farrar's ecumenical extravaganzas for divines and pedagogues. Wodehouse tried to entertain pupils of the very type of schools featured in the text. The transition from this kind of juvenilia to the maturer moonshine of vintage Wodehouse, although an unconscious process, may be seen happening, quite clearly, in the saga of Mike Jackson, in that moment when our hero meets the stranger:

> A very long, thin youth, with a solemn face and immaculate clothes, was leaning against the mantelpiece. As Mike entered, he fumbled in his top left waistcoat pocket, produced an eyeglass attached to a cord, and fixed it in his right eye. With the help of this aid to vision he inspected Mike in silence for a while, then having flicked an invisible speck of dust from the left sleeve of his coat, he spoke. 'Hullo,' he said.
> He spoke in a tired voice.
> 'Hullo,' said Mike.
> 'Take a seat,' said the immaculate one. 'If you don't mind dirtying your bags, that's to say. Personally I don't see any prospect of ever sitting down in this place. It looks to me as if they meant to use these chairs as mustard-and-cress beds. A Nursery Garden in the Home. That sort of idea. My name,' he added pensively, 'is Smith. What's yours?'
> 'Jackson,' said Mike.

'Are you the Bully, the Pride of the School, or the Boy who is Led Astray and takes to Drink in Chapter Sixteen?'

'The last, for choice,' said Mike, 'but I've only just arrived, so I don't know.'

'The boy – what will he become? Are you new here too, then?'

'Yes. Why, are you new?'

'Do I look as if I belonged here? I'm the latest import. Sit down on yonder settee, and I will tell you the painful story of my life. By the way, before I start there's just one thing. If ever you have occasion to write to me, would you mind sticking a P at the beginning of my name? P-s-m-i-t-h. See? There are too many Smiths, and I don't care for Smythe. My father's content to worry along in the old-fashioned way, but I've decided to strike out a fresh line. I shall found a new dynasty. The resolve came to me unexpectedly this morning. I jotted it down on the back of an envelope. In conversation you may address me as Rupert (though I hope you won't), or simply Smith, the P not being sounded. Cp the name Zbysco, in which the Z is given a similar miss-in-baulk. See?'

Mike said he saw. Psmith thanked him with a certain stately old-world courtesy.

'Let us start at the beginning,' he resumed. 'My infancy. When I was but a babe, my eldest sister was bribed with a shilling an hour by my nurse to keep an eye on me, and see that I did not raise Cain. At the end of the first day she struck for one-and-six, and got it. We now pass to my boyhood. At an early age, I was sent to Eton, everybody predicting a bright career for me. But,' said Psmith solemnly, fixing an owl-like gaze on Mike through the eyeglass, 'it was not to be.'

Here, for the very first time Wodehouse is indulging freely in his gifts for pastiche and persiflage. For once the plot is forgotten as the words begin to dance. Psmith, who has hardly drawn breath before launching a final annihilating attack on the old pietistic attitudes of public-school fiction, starts to describe his past in terms of literary convention. It is a habit he will sustain for as long as Wodehouse can keep up with him as he flits through the shires. When discussing his future as a member of the school Archaeological Society, he suggests to Mike that they 'will snare the elusive fossil'; when planning to attack the local wild-life, he says: 'We'll nose about for a gun at the earliest opp.' Not even the adult world has any defence against the dazzling legerdemain of his vocal resources; in defying instructions from a member of the school staff, he routs his adversary by bewildering him with the sheer frenzied eloquence of his technique, much as a professional conjuror might deploy the arts of prestidigitation to confound the sceptics in the house:

'One cannot, to take a parallel case, imagine the colonel commanding the garrison at a naval station going on board a battleship and ordering the crew to splice the jibboom spanker. It might be an admirable thing for the Empire that the jibboom spanker *should* be spliced at that particular juncture, but the crew would naturally decline to move in the matter until the order came from the commander of the ship.'

In retrospect is is easy enough to understand what has happened. Into this world of half-developed humans, Wodehouse has unwittingly flung a giant. For all his old school tie and his comprehensive mastery of quadrangular politics, Psmith is a fully-grown adult obliged by circumstances to splash about for a while in the backwaters of school life – which is a perfectly accurate description of Wodehouse himself at the time he began writing the saga of Mike Jackson. Instinctively he had been threshing around in an attempt to escape the limitations of a genre which was no longer able to contain the repertoire of his comic effects. And now, with this bizarre boy-man, he had stumbled on the device he so desperately required. It is instructive to watch how, once Psmith springs on stage, Wodehouse transfers his own persona from the games-playing, uncomplicated, unintellectual Mike Jackson to the insolent idler Psmith, armoured against fate, just as Wodehouse was, by a panoply of literary allusion. From the moment that Mike steps into that senior day-room, his days as hero are numbered, as surely as the days of boyhood itself are numbered; soon Psmith will begin to push Mike further and further towards the wings, until at last the time will come when the pride of the Jacksons will be relegated to an off-stage effect while Psmith comes into his rightful inheritance as one of the great comic creations of popular literature.

Psmith has been rightly defined by Richard Usborne as Wodehouse's first adult hero.[17] He makes the vital point that although Psmith does not despise his schooldays, 'he is unsentimental about them', as indeed he had to be, for Psmith the schoolboy has outgrown the study and the classroom just as Wodehouse the novelist had outgrown tales about house matches and breaking bounds. The two of them, the character and his creator, are superbly equipped to do battle in the outside world, and deploy the frame of *Mike* to effect their escape. But perhaps even the status of adult is not justice enough for the great Psmith:

> Psmith has the characteristics, not of a superannuated schoolboy, but of a god forced for a time to walk among mortals. He makes his single friend, as Apollo made him in Admetus. He acquires his most noticeable moral qualities – his name, his form of address – immediately at the commencement of his servitude. He retains throughout his adventures a curious invulnerability.[18]

But even a god must be seen to have sprung from somebody's loins. Where do Psmith's origins lie? Certainly in the early school stories there are broad hints that the linguistic versatility of which Psmith is the first finely-tuned instrument is beginning to stir itself. As early as *A Prefect's Uncle*, there had been signs that Wodehouse was beginning to consider the possibility of turning the English language on its head, as for instance in the description of Farnie's friend Pringle, whose surpassing sin was a sense of superiority:

> At an early period of his life – he was still unable to speak at the time – his grandmother had died. This is probably the sole reason why he had never taught that relative to suck eggs.

Later, when Farnie, who after all has Psmith's precocious insolence if not his sense of style, is the object of someone's sarcasm, he retaliates to devastating effect:

> Farnie, in a series of three remarks, reduced him, figuratively speaking, to a small and palpitating spot of grease.

Several of the boys at Wrykyn and St Austin's have a gift for prestissimo verbal improvisation, but it is in Psmith that the qualities of studied insolence, intellectual maturity and a whimsical savouring of the ridiculous are brought together for the first time. Psmith becomes possible through Wodehouse's emerging mastery of a style of comic expression depending for its effect on the contrast between the solemn correctitude of the form and the hysterical daftness of the content. Just as a limerick amuses by counterpointing the inscrutable logical rumpty-dump of its metre with the scatty senselessness of its message, so Wodehousean metaphor becomes effective because of its apparent gravity concealing an adamant refusal to be serious about anything; only a pedant could have added the adjective 'palpitating' to Farnie's phrase about the grease, and only a knockabout comedian could have seen the need for the pedantry. As a devotee of W. S. Gilbert, Wodehouse, by the time he created Psmith, would have been familiar with the dictum which Oscar Wilde had already appropriated; in the stage directions for his comedy *Engaged* (1881), Wodehouse's father-figure had written, 'It is absolutely essential to the success of this piece that it should be played with the most perfect earnestness and gravity throughout.'

Psmith is the first Wodehouse character to raise the vexed question of the degree to which his inventions were inspired by reality. In his ninety-third year, Wodehouse had something of considerable interest to say about this:

> The character of Psmith . . . is the only thing in my literary career which was handed to me on a plate with watercress round it, thus enabling me to avoid the blood, sweat and tears inseparable from an author's life. Lord Emsworth, Jeeves and the rest of my dramatis personae had to be built up from their foundations, but Psmith came to me ready-made.[19]

In invoking Emsworth and Jeeves as examples of pure moonshine, Wodehouse was being comically disingenuous, as we shall see, but in disclosing the origins of Psmith even as he denies the origins of all the rest of his characters, he is perhaps practising a disingenuousness of a subtly different kind:

> A cousin of mine, who had been at Winchester, happened to tell me one night of Rupert D'Oyly Carte, the son of the Savoy opera's D'Oyly Carte, a schoolmate of his. Rupert . . . was long, slender, always beautifully dressed and very dignified. His speech was what is known as orotund, and he wore a monocle. He habitually addressed his fellow Wykehamists as 'Comrade', and if one of the masters chanced to inquire as to his health, would reply, 'Sir, I grow thinnah and thinnah'.[20]

Young D'Oyly Carte's mannerism of addressing the world as though it was standing at the barricades is whimsical enough for a Wykehamist of the period, but where does such precocious political posturing come from? Wodehouse offers no explanation of the forces which transformed his cousin's friend into so improbable a receptacle of revolutionary passion. It will be remembered that in the Mike Jackson stories, Psmith has embraced Socialism in a fit of pique after his father's action in whisking him out of Eton and into Sedleigh has deprived him of the otherwise certain honour of representing Eton against Harrow at Lord's. One of the most eccentric demagogues of Victorian England, and a man whose reputation would certainly have been known to Wodehouse, was Henry Mayers Hyndman (1842–1921), founder of the Socialist Democratic Federation, the first Marxist organization in English political life, and a man so fastidious in his dress that Bernard Shaw said of him that 'he seemed to have been born in a frock-coat and top hat. He was a leading figure in any assembly, and took that view of himself with perfect confidence'. More to the point, in his youth Hyndman was a considerable cricketer who scored two half-centuries for the Sussex county side and who went to his grave still smarting from the injustice of having been passed over for his cricket blue. It was this grievous disappointment which altered Hyndman's whole attitude to society:

> He complained of the peculiarly British technique by which the ruling class absorbed rising labour leaders who proved only too willing to sell out to the dominant minority after they had 'obtained their education from well-to-do Socialists who have been sacrificing themselves for their sake'. The tone suggests some justification for the friends who said that Hyndman, a cricketer, had adopted Socialism out of spite against the world because he was not included in the Cambridge eleven.[21]

Whatever the ingredients of the D'Oyly Carte–Hyndman cocktail which created Psmith, there can be no question that it is he who marks the emergence of classic Wodehousean Man, the character who springs the lock on the wider world waiting outside school bounds. Psmith is the one who takes credit for having smuggled Wodehouse across the frontiers of adult fiction, in the course of which delicate operation he understandably runs away with the saga of Mike Jackson, obliterating that equable fellow and usurping his role as hero, insinuating himself into the comic consciousness so adamantly that his creator had no choice but to allow Psmith several more books in which to dissipate his effervescence; by the time the process was complete, Psmith had become one of the great stars of Wodehouse's extra-ordinary repertory company. In the closing paragraph of *Mike and Psmith*, the two friends, having carried Sedleigh to a predictably sensational victory over Wrykyn, decide to celebrate by going in search of a little harmless fun:

> 'Let us now sally out and see if we can't promote a rag of some sort in this abode of wrath. Comrade Outwood has gone over to dinner at the School House, and it would be a pity to waste a somewhat golden opportunity. Shall we stagger?'
> They staggered.

Or rather Psmith staggers and Mike meekly follows, relegated to the rank of a supernumerary in Psmith's essentially grown-up affairs. There were to be no more school stories, or at least none seen through the eyes of a schoolboy. Any future involvements with the education system would be from the viewpoint either of a palsied old boy like Bertie Wooster, or of the schoolmasters who feature in *The Little Nugget*. Wodehouse's schooldays were over at last.

By a freakish collusion between temperament and experience, those schooldays left Wodehouse with a commitment to the schoolboy sensibility to which he remained forever steadfast, and which had the unexpected effect of making his work unique. For although Psmith insisted on breaking out, he took with him the intellectual and emotional luggage of a schoolboy. He and his followers may have been at large in the world of great affairs, but they arrived there still acting and reacting like the fifth-formers they would always remain. That is why there can be no sex in Wodehouse's world, only romance, no morality, only posture, no dogma, only laughter. Writers like J. M. Barrie, Kenneth Grahame and E. Nesbit have enshrined the world of the small child; a few have even attempted to penetrate the secret of infancy, Lewis Carroll triumphantly, A. A. Milne disastrously. Hundreds of writers became exclusively purveyors of public-school life, but only Wodehouse pursued the odd idea of disguising his fifth-formers as responsible citizens and letting them loose among grown men and women. The point is well made by J. B. Priestley, the very last person to be accused of Wodehouse-boosting:

> I believe this man, who lived so long, wrote so much, earned several fortunes, was really a schoolboy. He was of course no ordinary schoolboy, but a brilliant super-de-luxe schoolboy. This explains what he wrote, why he succeeded, how he behaved. His 'eggs, beans and

crumpets' give us a schoolboy's notion of Edwardian young men-
about-town. His sexless young women, running round breaking off
their engagements, and his formidable bullying aunts, all belong to a
schoolboy's world. So do his eccentric or quite dotty dukes and earls.
His behaviour was mostly that of an elderly schoolboy: those letters
anxiously inquiring about the School Second Eleven; his helpless
dependence on his womenfolk to decide for him where he lived; his
idiotic capture by the Nazis in the Second World War; there is no sign
of a mature man here. Together with his talent for the absurd, this
explains his success. Most of us who enjoy him still have a schoolboy
somewhere in us, and to reach that schoolboy (aged about fifteen or
sixteen), to let him enjoy himself, is a perfect escape from our adult
problems and trials.[22]

Even the most casual examination of the school novels raises the ghost of
that body of work with which they have often been compared. Wodehouse's
most famous rival in the field is Charles Hamilton (1876–1961), the mild-
mannered eccentric who published under pseudonyms whose best-known
variants are Frank Richards and Martin Clifford, and whose most famous
inventions, Greyfriars and St Jim's, have lit the dreams of millions of
Englishmen who never saw the inside of a real public school. At first sight
the parallels are striking. Both men pitched their fictions in a timeless
Edwardian never-never land; both described an essentially celibate society;
both stressed the unbridgeable abyss sundering their heroes from the
townees; both steeped their prose in quotations from the classics and the
Savoy operas; both were preoccupied with sport but indulged in diversions
of mystery and detection. And, most vital to their method, both presented
life at a boarding school as a life hermetically sealed off from the expediencies
of ordinary existence. Because of these striking resemblances, Wrykyn and
St Austin's are often assumed to be companions to Greyfriars and St Jim's,
with the wide fame of Psmith complemented by the even wider fame of Billy
Bunter. And probably because nothing of Hamilton's has survived apart
from his school stories, there has been a tendency to credit him with the
invention of a genre which Wodehouse freely borrowed and adapted only
very slightly.

But Hamilton/Richards, for all his stupefying industry, producing the
equivalent of a full-length novel every week for nearly thirty years, never
entirely liberated himself from the sanctimony of his predecessors.
Whenever the doggish Loder lights a cigarette or backs a horse, the tutting
of pietists hangs heavy on the Greyfriars air. Herbert Vernon-Smith has
only to pick up a cue down at the local pothouse to become known as The
Bounder; no such stigma would ever have attached to him for the same
misdemeanour at Wrykyn, where idiocies like Herbert Spencer's 'A proficiency at billiards is a sign of a misspent youth' were received with the
derision they so richly deserved. This perversion of moral fervour is dominant in Hamilton for the excellent reason that he strove to achieve it, seeing

himself as a potential power arraigned with the angels, claiming that his creation of Huree Jamset Ram Singh, 'a coloured boy on equal terms with the other boys', had had 'a good effect'. Wodehouse in contrast never dreamed of having any effect at all on readers except to divert them into laughter but, in spite of this fundamental difference between the two men, most annotators of school fiction have seen Wodehouse as one of the earliest beneficiaries of Hamilton's perfecting of the public school as a fictional frame, with its inter-house, inter-form, inter-group rivalries. And yet the two men represent moral opposites. Here is the uncle of Hamilton's Harry Wharton in full mealy-mouthed flow:

> 'I have come home from India to find that you have run completely wild under the charge of my sister, and I should not be doing my duty to my dead brother if I did not take you in hand and make at least an attempt to put you on a better road.'

One has only to savour Colonel Wharton's diocesan pomposity in the context of Farnie's palpitating spot of grease to perceive that their respective creators had much less in common than at first meets the eye. Hamilton is celebrating avuncular authority, Wodehouse lampooning it. But in spite of the fact that while the fictions of Greyfriars and St Jim's are morality plays, those of Wrykyn and St Austin's are anti-authoritarian comedies, even the most vociferous Wodehouseans tend to give precedence to Hamilton, which is curious because, even had the two men been identical in their attitudes, there would still be the question of dates. It was Wodehouse and not Hamilton who pioneered the Edwardian public-school story.

The Pothunters was written during 1902; by 1905, when Hamilton published his first St Jim's story, five Wodehouse school books had appeared. The first Greyfriars tale was written a year later, by which time Wodehouse was already embarked on the last of his. Considering that both men were ploughing the same furrow, it seems surprising that neither should have mentioned the other in his memoirs; the omission calls to mind the case of Carroll and Lear, another occasion when the deafening mutual silence was perhaps more revealing than anything which either party might have said. Hamilton was an avid researcher in his own field, and certainly knew all about Wodehouse. Whether or not the monocle of Arthur Augustus D'Arcy was passed down from young D'Oyly Carte is uncertain, but one biography reveals that Hamilton's bookshelves carried 'reference and travel books, dictionaries and the works of Latin scholars. Novels of Walpole, Wodehouse and Talbot Baines Reed rubbed covers with the complete set of post-war Billy Bunter books'.[23]

But the most profound difference between the two writers, the one which places Wodehouse in a different category altogether, is that, having plumbed the depths of the schoolboy sensibility, he then shifted it into the adult world. This is the contradiction lying at the heart of all his work, that the lunatic excesses of his characters are seen to be logical, or at least predictable, once we recognize the protagonists as adolescents let loose, as though by some cosmic practical joke, into the adult world. This is the essence of the entire œuvre, the rich earth in which all the thistledown felicities are rooted, and it is something as far beyond the range of Hamilton as the square-jawed heroics' of Wharton in adversity would be for Wodehouse. With *Mike* he set out to write a conventional school yarn, only to find himself propelled by Psmith's insouciance out on to the high seas of the great world, with Priestley's super-de-luxe schoolboy at the helm. This explains why Wodehouse's boys are intellectually and culturally aware in a way that Richards' are not. Wharton, Tom Merry and company are confined to a cerebral territory which extends no further than the occasional fragment of dog Latin and perhaps an oblique reference now and then to Greeks and Romans. For all the evidence they offer of intellectual curiosity they may as well be living in a bucket. This is not at all the case with the boys of Wrykyn and St Austin's, who are constantly exchanging sub-literary quips and quoting popular contemporary sources without feeling the need to give chapter and verse; in *The Gold Bat* there are references to Jerome's plaster-of-Paris trout – destined to play a part in Psmith's subsequent adventures – Micawber, Lord Todmoddy, Edna May, Robert Louis Stevenson, *San Toy*, Rider Haggard, *Rodney Stone*, Carrie Nation, Bob Fitzsimmonds and Mrs Fezziwig. It is not that Wodehouse is being self-consciously culturally aware, simply that he is a realist. His own experience had taught him how real-life public schoolboys behaved. Hamilton only described how he thought they might behave.

His infancy and childhood evidently having left him with no burning desire to retrieve them, Wodehouse virtually ignored both those phases, seeing them as little more than devices for comic relief, usually through the expression of a fastidious distaste. Not until his males have graduated to inky fingers and mistranslations of the Peloponnesian War can he contrive to make them move and talk and dance. Hamilton remained circumscribed physically by the quadrangle, morally by Mr Quelch's thunder; Wodehouse liberated his schoolboys, spilling them out into the streets and clubs and country houses of the outside world, with spectacular results. And it committed him to his future as a comedian, because to the schoolboy everything is a joke, in which assumption he is sometimes wiser than his elders. It may be that the reason for the contrast between the two men is at least partly to do with the fact that Hamilton knew he was writing for a different market from any of his predecessors in the genre. Farrar, Reed and Wodehouse worked in the knowledge that their tales would fall into the hands of those intimately connected in one capacity or another with public school life. Hamilton was labouring on behalf of an altogether more plebeian readership, those elementary and secondary school boys who patronized the tuppenny bloods of the comic world, readers whose ignorance of the procedures at the great public schools was so comprehensive that it could only be compared with Hamilton's own. For this champion of the ivy-bearded ramparts of The Old School appears never to have attended one. Perhaps there lies the most profound difference of all between the respective begetters of Bunter and Farnie. Hamilton had never lived at a great public school. Wodehouse certainly had.

Wodehouse passed through Dulwich under the impression that he was treading the Elysian Fields. For the rest of his life he looked back to his time there as though to a walk through the paradise gardens, retaining his strong allegiance to the place, and standing obstinately across the path of those who propounded the fashionable view that public-school life was brutalizing, decadent, philistine, corrupting and utterly pointless. Throughout his lifelong correspondence with Townend, he marks this allegiance with references to his visits. Although he was hardly any longer an Englishman in the geographical sense, having committed himself to that tribe of wandering scribes who go where the work is, he snatched every chance to go down to Dulwich to watch an important game. In 1928 he writes to Townend that 'Dulwich have got a red-hot team this year'; in 1929 he goes to the old school to watch the Mill Hill game; in 1932 he writes from the Dorchester Hotel: 'I never in my life experienced such suspense as during that second half in the Sherborne match, culminating in Billy Griffith scoring that superb try.[24] Isn't it strange that one can still be absorbed by Dulwich footer? I never saw such splendid defensive work as we put up. It was easily the best school match I have seen.' In 1934 he writes from Le Touquet, reviewing the puzzling inconsistencies in current form which causes Dulwich to win some and lose some; two years later, marooned in Hollywood, he contemplates the stern injustices of life with: 'Isn't it extraordinary how we never seem to get the breaks against Haileybury? I remember one very wet day when we scored four tries and they also scored four and converted one from the touchline, a thing that wouldn't have happened again in a hundred times. I call it a very good performance beating St Paul's. If they could take fifteen points off Bedford, they must be a good side. Incidentally, isn't it amazing that you and I, old buffers of 55, with Civilization shortly about to crash, can worry about school football? It is really almost the only thing I do worry about.' He was still worrying five years later, when, trying to grasp the fact that Oxford University had awarded him the degree of Doctor of Letters, he went down to his school to watch a cricket match against St Paul's. It was to be the last time he ever set foot on the plains of paradise, but he remained steadfast to their memory; in 1945 he writes to Townend in Paris: 'I was thrilled by what you told me about Dulwich winning all its school matches last cricket season, including Harrow and Malvern. It's odd, but I don't find that world cataclysms and my own troubles make any difference to my feelings about Dulwich.' Nothing ever would affect those feelings; in that same year he asks: 'Was 1944 a very wet summer in England? I ask because that was the year we won all our seven school cricket matches and the lad at the head of the averages had an average of 25.' A year later, still in France, he is heartened by the school's flying start to the rugby season and wonders 'if it is going to turn out one of the big sides, like 1909?' Three weeks later, by which time it seems as though even the 1909 record will be broken, he writes: 'Isn't it odd, when one ought to be worrying about the state of the world and one's troubles generally, that the only thing I can think of nowadays is that Dulwich looks like winning all its school matches?' It was not odd at all, not for a man who was, like all his characters, a spry young sixth-former cunningly disguised as a sober citizen.

There were moments when there intruded into the idyll of his Old Alleynian equanimity the shadows of self-doubt. He was well aware that the received psychological truth of his era regarding literary composition was that an artist must have endured excruciating adolescent agonies of mind and body if he hoped to produce masterpieces, and was almost apologetic for not having endured them himself. In 1945 he writes to Townend that he has just read a review of a new book which is 'apparently the same old anti-public-school stuff. I often wonder if you and I were unusually fortunate in our schooldays. To me the years between 1896 and 1900 seem like Heaven. Was the average man really unhappy at school? Or was Dulwich in our time an exceptionally good school?' Was he fortunate in his schooldays? In attempting to discover how far Wodehouse was indulging in retrospective sentimentality, it is as well to remember that his combination of sporting ability, academic curiosity and a congenitally eupeptic disposition probably made him the perfect Edwardian schoolboy. One might be inclined to leave it at that, except that by a most convenient and congenial coincidence, there was during Wodehouse's time another boy at Dulwich just as dedicated to the art of writing, destined to be just as successful in his own very different way, and even to be able to claim the creation of a character as notorious as Jeeves.

In 1900, at about the time that Wodehouse was pottering in the sixth form waiting to be moved on by circumstances beyond his control, an American divorcee called Florence Chandler arrived at Alleyn Park, Dulwich, so as to be near her son Raymond, about to be enrolled at the college as a first-former studying Latin, French, Divinity, History and Geography. In his second year Chandler moved over to the Modern side, and subsequently moved back again, reading Caesar, Ovid, Livy, Virgil, Plato and Aristophanes. He played rugby and cricket with the same enthusiasm but with less success than Wodehouse and, like him, found the pronouncements of Gilkes unforgettable ('Cicero had a large plant of conceit growing in his heart, and he watered it every day'; even more relevant to the issue of Philip Marlowe administering rough justice in mean streets, 'A man of honour is one who is capable of understanding that which is good; capable of subordinating the poorer part of his nature to the higher part').[25] Chandler remembered Gilkes as a stickler for clear prose who contrived to drive home the need for linguistic control by instructing boys to translate Cicero and then, days later, inviting them to translate it back again. When asked if he detected any Gilkesian influence either on his own style or on Chandler's, Wodehouse doubted it. But in his own way Chandler was as dogged an apologist as Wodehouse for what he found at Dulwich, saying that 'a classical education saves you from being fooled by pretentiousness, which is what most current fiction is too full of'. When J. B. Priestley, in praising Chandler, remarked, 'They don't write like that at Dulwich', Chandler commented: 'That may be, but if I hadn't grown up on Latin and Greek, I doubt if I would know so well how to draw the line between what I call a vernacular style and what I should call an illiterate or faux naïf style. That's a hell of a lot of difference to my mind.'[26]

For the rest of his life Chandler retained a respect and affection for Dulwich College, which he considered had provided him with just enough literary self-confidence to survive the trials of his own apprenticeship. But the parallels with Wodehouse are very much closer than a mere sentimental attachment to an old school tie. Both men were academically sufficiently talented to have gone on to Oxbridge. Both were deprived of the opportunity through straitened financial circumstances. Both were at the mercy of avuncular whim. Both were put to work in uncongenial clerkly jobs, Wodehouse in a bank, Chandler in the Civil Service. Both were indifferent to their temporary fate, knowing it to be temporary because of the iron resolve they shared to become writers. Both expressed their indifference to employment in the same unconcerned terms, Wodehouse remarking: 'I didn't know what it was all about', Chandler saying: 'I was a bit passive about the whole thing'.[27] And both retained connections with Townend; in 1952, when Wodehouse was settling into his last home at Remsenburg, Long Island, Chandler lunched with Townend, although there is no reference to the meeting in Townend's letters to Wodehouse. It is perfectly clear from the common attitude of all three men long after they had left their schooldays behind them that they regarded the years at Dulwich as one of the most pleasurable as well as one of the most beneficial episodes of their lives. Between them, Bertie Wooster and Philip Marlowe comprise a formidable if faintly incongruous Old Alleynian lobby.

But while for Chandler his schooldays were no more than a brief interlude before a confrontation with America, for Wodehouse Dulwich remained for all time the Eden of his recollections, not just as a school but as a particularly blessed spot on the earth, a location to be used time and again as the setting for high jinks and skullduggery. In his books Dulwich, SE 21 becomes transmuted into Valley Fields, SE 21: an enchanted place where romantic adventures accrue to a personable young man as inevitably as they do to Marlowe in Bay City. Whenever Wodehouse wishes to reward a character for being a good egg, he plants him in the fertile soil of Valley Fields, although in the early fictions he is still referring to it by its fictitious name of Dulwich. When his favourite son Mike Jackson ventures out into the harsh world of economic expediency in search of his first lodgings, he selects Acacia Road, Dulwich. The lady who opens the door to him is so glum-looking a prototype of the music-hall landlady that Wodehouse actually takes the trouble to designate her as a member of the Wilkie Bard rather than the George Robey school.[28] Jackson is unutterably depressed the moment he steps into his room: 'It was a sort of Sargasso Sea among bedrooms.' Without realizing it, he has stumbled into an alien world of worn lino, two-shilling alarm clocks, 'The Monarch of the Glen' slightly flyblown, Cassell's *Home Educator* copiously thumb-marked, and runner beans clinging limply to swaying poles in lilliputian back gardens. 'Seven and six a week and coals at sixpence a scuttle,' his landlady briskly informs him before abandoning him to his fate, from which he is rescued only a few days later by the godlike Psmith.

But if Wodehouse is so resolved on idealizing the area, why Mike's divine discontent? The explanation is that there were at least four quite distinct Dulwiches and three of them represented the classes. When Jackson falls into the hands of his pantomime dame, he is sinking into the lowest stratum of all, where terraced houses are rented at thirty pounds a year and young men are taken in and done for in defiance of the ban on lodgers instituted by landlords fearful that their properties might slide even further down the social scale. This is the underside of Dulwich life, far removed from the spacious, tree-lined avenues of the prosperous middle classes, with their coach-houses and capacious gardens; it is not even to be mentioned in the same breath as the world of the in-betweens, the clerks and counterhands who conduct a stately processional each morning to the railway station, top-hatted, frock-coated, gladstone-bagged, with the *Daily Mail* under their arms and their hearts set on the 8.16 to the City. Between these groups there smouldered the mutual distaste which, during the election in *The Head of Kay's*, threatens to burst into the flames of physical confrontation. But the Wilkie Bard brigade, though it shunned the toffs, might still aspire to their grandeur. A few years after Wodehouse moved on from Dulwich into the wide world, the family of ten-year-old V. S. Pritchett moved in. The embryonic critic and short-story writer saw no reason why he should not join the ranks of 'the college boys who strolled the streets in their blue striped caps'[29]; he would picture himself and his friends 'swaggering arm-in-arm like the college prefects',[30] and may well have achieved his ambition had not the expectations of the examiners incorporated rather more Latin than was customary among the sons of the Dulwich lower orders. It is a tribute to the pervading figure of Charles Hamilton that in recounting his failure to win a Dulwich scholarship, Pritchett shrugs his shoulders and, like a million other sons of the proletariat, equates the fiction with the reality by remarking, 'Farewell Greyfriars'.[31]

In his maturity the self-confident Wodehouse grew into the habit of simply announcing the desirability of Valley Fields and leaving it at that, but in the early novels he evidently felt the obligation to provide his characters with convincing motives for happening so consistently to light on the district. And so he discloses that Valley Fields is paradisal, not just because nectar flows from its taps but because there is a public school, *the* public school, at its heart, and, as every civilized gentleman knows, where there is a public school there is cricket and where there is cricket there is balm for a bruised soul. When Jackson reconciles himself to those awful lodgings there is a wild dream in his heart:

> He had settled on Dulwich, partly because, knowing nothing about London, he was under the impression that rooms anywhere inside the

four-mile radius were very expensive, but principally because there was a school at Dulwich, and it would be a comfort being near a school. He might get a game of Fives there sometimes, he thought, on a Saturday afternoon, and in the summer, occasionally cricket.

In such a mood did Wodehouse kiss his schooldays goodbye, unwillingly, apprehensively, glancing back lovingly over his shoulder while stumbling on towards an unknown fate. In another context Pritchett talks of the suburban young man of the period who 'catches the train and sits under the green lamp in the stony daylight of Lombard Street, working on documents from Hong Kong or Sydney'.[32] When he wrote those lines, Pritchett may well have had Wodehouse in mind. The green lamps of Lombard Street, shining grimly down on oriental credits and debits, awaited the arrival of their latest sacrificial offering.

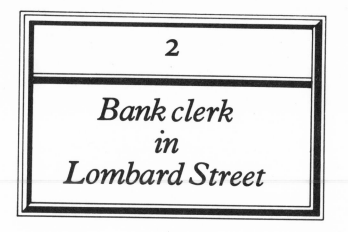

2

Bank clerk in Lombard Street

'PSMITH IN THE CITY' IS THE MOST OVERTLY autobiographical of all the Wodehouse novels. Other, later books may tell us more about a specialized milieu, for instance professional musical comedy in *Jill the Reckless*, or the non-musical theatre in *Barmy in Wonderland*, or preparatory schools in *The Little Nugget*, but none tells us so much about Wodehouse himself. For this reason the book is doubly revelatory, for not only does it disclose a great deal about its author in that crepuscular interlude between his leaving Dulwich and entering Fleet Street, but it also demonstrates the extent to which, even at this early stage, he had mastered the subtle art of refining the humdrum material of ordinary life into pure moonshine. Although it was his fourteenth published novel, written long after the more pressing anxieties of the free-lance existence had been left behind for ever, in spirit it belongs to that uneasy moment when he had been obliged to go out into the world without enough money to protect himself from its more tiresome obligations.

It is therefore not surprising that *Psmith in the City* is based cheerfully on the irrefutable argument that most work is a distasteful necessity which nobody in his right mind would ever dream of performing unless he needed the money desperately. This elementary fact of life, which often appears to have been beyond the comprehension of politicians, economists, tycoons, headmasters, social historians, bishops and sundry other groups so genially flayed alive by Wodehouse, is well-enough known to the working class itself, most of whose members, being of sound mind, would much rather go to the races, or breed pigeons, or just loaf around, if they possibly could. For most people, there is always something better to do than go to work, the only exceptions being men like Wodehouse himself, whose first, abiding love proved also to be his hobby, his profession and his lifelong obsession. But for a brief moment, as the new century opened, there was a problem. Wodehouse, like a great many worthy young blades before him, found himself with his education completed a shade prematurely, before he had quite perfected the arrangements for following his profession. He knew perfectly well what he intended doing; it was simply a matter of persuading the rest of the world to encourage him to do it. *Psmith in the City* is a graphic account, comparatively speaking, of what happened to Wodehouse during his brief residence in limbo.

The problem facing Mike Jackson and his friend Psmith in *Psmith in the City* is simply – what to do? Having recently left Sedleigh School in precisely the same condition that their creator had once left Dulwich, over-educated and under-capitalized, the two of them are shoved into employment in the Lombard Street branch of a financial conspiracy called the New Asiatic Bank. Although the wages are a perfect disgrace and the duties tedious, the two young men are given to understand that they can consider themselves lucky to have been given this golden opportunity to improve themselves. It is apparently not just anybody who is worthy of employment at the New Asiatic, and it is only because of the fluke of Psmith's father's acquaintance with its manager that the arrangement has been possible. This manager, Mr John Bickersdyke, is a distinguished exhibit in that gallery of red-necked apoplectic pills who snort their way through the canon; he has taken on Mike as a grudging favour, but it is his motive for hiring Psmith which provides the fuel for comedy. While staying at the country house of the Psmiths, Bickersdyke is soon given to understand by the son and heir that he, Bickersdyke, only moves through this world at all because of some grievous breach in the arrangements pertaining to human evolution. Smarting from the dialectical indignities heaped upon him by a mere schoolboy, Bickersdyke decides to take advantage of the opportunity to employ Psmith, in order to persecute him as only a boss can persecute his underlings. The reader knows that this ambition of Bickersdyke is doomed to founder on the rock of Psmith's considerable style. Psmith knows it. But Bickersdyke does not, and it is the account of his annihilation at his young enemy's hands that provides the narrative spine on which Wodehouse is able to drape the details of his own private story.

The opening chapter is devoted almost entirely to the exposition of the theory that the modern banking executive is by definition a creature in whom the common courtesies of social intercourse have been ruthlessly expunged, a philistine whose sensibilities have been so blunted by long years at his nefarious trade that he no longer realizes quite how monstrous he must appear to others. To resort to the argot of the quadrangle, Bickersdyke is a tick. He has 'hard thin lips' and is a prey to 'strong prejudices'. Psmith assumes that Bickersdyke's fortune has been acquired dishonourably, while Mike regards him as 'a blighter', which is literally true in the sense that Bickersdyke is one of those men who casts a deadly blight on the lives of all his employees, a collection of unfortunate young public-school men and chalky old scriveners, who are obliged to sign on at Lombard Street every morning or forfeit their bonuses for punctuality. But this is the least of their troubles. There is something else about life in Lombard Street which has the interesting effect of making all its young men miserable no matter how optimistically inclined they might tend to be.

For the New Asiatic is a sort of way-station on the Great Imperial Trunk Road, an embarkation point from which 'men are always leaving for the East'. After three years' training, in which conscripts enjoy a brief acquaintance with each department, starting with the infantile simplicity of Postage and graduating to the terrifying complexities of Fixed Deposits, the trainees are then shipped out to the Far East, where 'you're the dickens of a big pot straight away, with a big screw and dozens of native johnnies under you'. That this kind of autocratic life is not good for a man's soul is borne out by the unfortunate example of the veteran Mr Gregory, whose inhumanity has achieved so advanced a stage of degeneration that he is able to preside over Fixed Deposits with no visible sign of cerebral distress. Gregory has already done his turn in the East, 'where he had acquired a liver and a habit of addressing those under him in a way that suggested the mate of a tramp steamer'; Psmith feels that Gregory shouts all the time, 'as if he were competing against a high wind', and soon reaches the conclusion that if this is the condition to which a man is reduced by missionary work in the outposts of empire on behalf of the shareholders of the New Asiatic, then there is very little to be said for a career in banking unless you happen to own the bank.

But at least Psmith has no burning ambition which is being frustrated by his incarceration in Lombard Street. He is one of those fortunate men who, in the course of a dazzling Wodehousean career, will never be stalked by the incubus of restless ambition, and he rejects life at the bank simply because, of all the things he has ever experienced in his brief career, fooling around with ledgers and accounts is by far the most ridiculous. For his friend, however, the situation is very different. To Mike Jackson, plunged into the stultifying negation of the Post Room routine, nothing could seem more remote from green fields and boundary ropes. He has no sooner stepped across the threshold of Bickersdyke's ignoble domain than shades of the prison house begin to loom. While Psmith exults in the defiance of an amused condescension, it is Mike who suffers the pangs of misery and frustration. Where has all the bright promise of the pavilion and the tea-tent fled? What has Bickersdyke, that contemptible blister on the face of existence, to do with life as a young man ought to be living it? Looking about him, Mike feels much compassion for the poor wretches frittering away a threadbare lifetime in the service of the bank, and very much more for himself, for although he is so simple and uncomplicated a soul that, before *Psmith in the City* is told, Wodehouse will have phased him out of the reckoning once and for all, Mike is no fool, and senses in his own modest way that he is some sort of sporting genius even less suited than the rest of them to a deskbound existence. And each time he is tempted to reconcile himself to his lot, finding some hint of a redeeming virtue in the life at Lombard Street, he is sustained in his bitterness by a cherished nebulosity called the public school spirit, which he defines as 'pride in the school and its achievements'. On the other hand, 'nobody can be proud of the achievements of a bank'. After all, think what a good public school may do to transmute the male animal from an odious midget to a truly civilized being. Mike decides that 'a boy should not be exhibited publicly until he reached an age when he might be in the running for some sort of colours at a public school'. Indeed, it is only the presence of other athletes alongside him at the New Asiatic which makes life there bearable for him. Some of the other trainees are familiar to him as honoured adversaries on the Big Sides of his sporting past, a fact which stirs up in his mind a thought which he can never quite manage to articulate but which is to do with his dawning realization that sometimes life can be rather more earnest than it has any right to be. Somewhere along the stony road to Lombard Street, Mike begins to feel, there has been some terrible betrayal.

But he is ready to admit that there are moments when daily existence among this unwilling company of clerks and book-keepers takes on a kind of lugubrious charm of its own. Because none of them expect to be there for very long before being shipped out east, Bickersdyke's young men succeed in smuggling across the frontier of life in Lombard Street a hint of that rugged insouciance nurtured in the more indulgent world of study fires and muddy changing rooms, a world which evidently constitutes the last refuge of English eccentricity:

> There was West, who had been requested to leave Haileybury owing to his habit of borrowing horses and attending meets in the neighbourhood, the same being always out of bounds and necessitating a complete disregard of the rules regarding evening chapel and lock-up. He was a small, dried-up youth, with black hair plastered down on his head. He went about his duties in a costume which suggested the sportsman of the comic papers. There was also Hignett, who added to the meagre salary allowed him by the bank by singing comic songs at the minor music halls. He confided to Mike his intention of leaving the bank as soon as he had made a name. He told him that he had knocked them at the Bedford the week before, and in support of the statement showed him a cutting from the *Era*, in which the writer said that 'Other acceptable turns were the Bounding Zouaves, Steingruber's Dogs and Arthur Hignett'. Mike wished him luck.

Clearly life in the company of such engaging fellows cannot be miserable all the time, and as Mike gets to know his contemporaries at the bank, and as he comes to assert his primacy among them in the one field where he is completely at ease, the cricket field, running up a string of big scores in lesser club cricket, he comes to see that not even a City bank is completely lacking in charm:

> Life at a bank is at its pleasantest in the winter. When all the world outside is dark and damp and cold, the light and warmth of the place are comforting. There is a pleasant air of solidity about the interior of a bank. The green shaded lamps look cosy. And the outside world offering so few attractions, the worker, perched on his stool, feels that he is not so badly off after all.

The reference to a time when 'all the world outside is dark and damp and cold' is an excellent example of what Henry Higgins would have described as native woodnotes wild, and might almost have been dragged verbatim out of one of those contemplative romantic song verses for which Wodehouse was later to become famous. Nor is this by any means the only example in the novel of the blandishments of the clerkly life evoking the quaint aroma of song and dance:

> A bank's day ends gradually, reluctantly, as it were. At about five there is a sort of stir, not unlike the stir in a theatre when the curtain is on the point of falling. Ledgers are closed with a bang. Men stand about and talk for a moment or two before going to the basement for their hats and coats. Then, at irregular intervals, forms pass down the central aisle and out through the swing doors. There is an air of relaxation over the place, though some departments are still working as hard as ever under a blaze of electric light. Somebody begins to sing, and an instant chorus of protests and maledictions rises from all sides. Gradually, however, the electric lights go out. The procession down the centre aisle becomes more regular; and eventually the place is left to darkness and the night-watchman.

The echoes of Thomas Gray in Wodehouse's carefully orchestrated dying fall are perhaps misplaced in a passage which has been staged like the opening tableau in a musical comedy, but whatever the prevailing mood, poetic or terpsichorean, there is no question that, of the story's twin heroes, it is Mike who senses the sadness of dispersal at the day's end, an introspective device which Psmith would probably regard as a betrayal of his belief that those with only one life to live might as well try to enjoy as much of it as possible.

Psmith's superior worldly knowledge tells him that outside every dullard is a larky schoolboy trying to get in, and disposes his forces accordingly. In order to nullify the disapproval of one of the senior clerks, he investigates the possibilities of the said clerk's secret passion, and, after raking the barren ground of philately, dried seaweed, Hall Caine,[1] brass rubbings and the Near Eastern Question, discovers that the breach in the castle walls consists of an idolatrous allegiance to the fortunes of Manchester United. He then saturates himself so completely in the prosodic conventions indulged in by the sporting prints that he is able to murmur to Mike before retiring for the night that 'the Mancunians pushed the bulb into the meshes beyond the uprights no fewer than four times', a feat which so impresses him that he adds with a wink of his monocle, 'Bless the dear boys, what spirits they do enjoy', an observation which illustrates Psmith's true function in the story, which is to unleash the linguistic sprites forever bubbling underneath the surface of the narrative. Psmith is one of the great rococo lords of language, an embellisher of genius with an unlimited repertoire at his disposal; in asserting his willingness to work, he defines himself as 'a bee, not a drone, a Lusitania, not a limpet'; subsequently in stating the identical case to a different witness, he discloses a new set of epithets: 'I am a toiler, not a flatfish. A sizzler, not a squab.' His adversaries, unable to follow his gist but uneasily aware that the echo of derisory laughter floats on the air, tend to retire deep in thought.

To Psmith, one style of pastiche is as beguiling a challenge as another, and so, having triumphantly deployed the terminology of rusting stanchions to extract the sting of one potential enemy, he turns to coterie politics to perform the same trick with another, and it is through his delighted immersion in the private fortunes of old Mr Waller that he and Mike get their first sight of the proletariat in full seditious cry. By the time Psmith arrives at the New Asiatic, the rampant parlour socialism of his Sedleigh days has dwindled to little more than an instrument of conversational irony, if indeed it was ever very much more. He now snatches gleefully at the chance to embroil himself in the altogether more earnest brand of revolutionary fervour of Waller, an elderly fellow-clerk who, for all his political attitudes, possesses a geniality of disposition which draws from Wodehouse the lofty accolade of a comparison with the White Knight. Waller lives in a district of south-east London thinly disguised as 'Kenningford', where the local pastimes include 'smashing shop windows and kicking policemen'. Waller's socialism is very different from Psmith's, having sprung from the roots of the old puritan conscience. He crusades for Temperance, attends church regularly, and presides over the family hymns every Sunday, none of which tenets is easily found in Psmith's eccentric interpretation of Marxism. In order to keep the plot moving, Psmith attends a political meeting in a locale so unfamiliar to him as to present unexpected problems. Mr Waller lives at Clapham Common, which is not a district of which Psmith has much experience, although one would have thought that in view of its proximity to the Surrey county ground at the Oval, he need only have asked Mike. Where, speculates Psmith, might this mysterious place be? 'One has heard of it, of course, but has its existence ever been proved? I think not. Having accomplished that, we must then try to find out how to get to it. I should say at a venture that it would necessitate a sea voyage.'

Unabashed by the paradox of arriving at a socialist meeting in that defiant symbol of the bourgeoisie, a taxi, Psmith learns that the revolution which all right-minded men so fervently desire is being impeded by the fact that of the two demagogic champions in Mr Waller's life, one scatters aitches 'as a fountain its sprays in a strong wind', and the other is 'handicapped to some extent by not having a palate', a pair of impediments which both Psmith and Wodehouse seem to find a great deal more amusing than posterity does. It would be unwise, however, to interpret the joke as a statement of the case for conservatism. Waller's politics have only been drawn into the story at all in order to expose the flank of his political opponents, and Bickersdyke in particular. For the very nastiest thing about Bickersdyke, worse by far than his bullying nature, his pomposity, his conceit, even his gross ignorance of cricket, is his ambition to win Kenningford in the Unionist interest. At his first campaign meeting he expresses hearty contempt for Free Trade, Alien Immigration and any attempt to victimize the Royal Navy with Budget cuts, although when he says with reference to this latter problem that 'we must burn our boats', Psmith, lurking at the back of the hall, enquires with lethal innocence how Bickersdyke proposes helping the Navy by burning boats.

But there are more serious weaknesses in Bickersdyke's moral position than a few mixed metaphors, and the course of his political career is worth close examination for the light it sheds on Wodehouse's view of conventional politics. When Bickersdyke opens the Kenningford campaign, we are told that he awaits his first public meeting 'with mixed feelings':

> He had stood for Parliament once before, several years back, in the North. He had been defeated by a couple of thousand votes, and he hoped that the episode had been forgotten. Not merely because his defeat had been heavy. There was another reason. On that occasion he had stood as a Liberal.

Naturally a man is permitted to change his mind, but the process, Wodehouse reminds us, does tend to make him painfully vulnerable later on.[2] It may be that Bickersdyke, as he marches into Kenningford, has seen the error of his ways and sincerely believes that the cause he is espousing is the only one that can save his country. He may even be right to do so, just as Mr Waller and his comrades also believe that theirs is the true way. But Bickersdyke is not just a Tory, not just a Tory apostate, but something much nastier, a Tory apostate who has arrived at his position through worldly advancement. As the theme of the election is developed, the air becomes aromatic with the delicate scent of humbug, and Psmith's deadly weapon in his running battle with the forces of reaction is the Minute Book of an ancient institution called the Tulse Hill Parliament, whose long-demolished walls once rang with the seditious indiscretions of the same Bickersdyke who now offers himself as a pillar of patriotic rectitude calling for more guns and less foreigners to turn them on. It is through Waller that Psmith learns about the Tulse Hill Parliament, and is able, at a delicate stage in his war against entrenched authority, to read aloud to Bickersdyke a few choice extracts from its Minutes:

> Psmith looked across at him with a bright smile. 'They report you

verbatim,' he said. 'And rightly. A more able speech I have seldom read. I like the bit where you call the Royal Family bloodsuckers. . . . Your political views have changed a great deal since those days, have they not? It is extremely interesting. A most fascinating study for political students.'

All men, it seems, cut their political cloth to suit their pockets, and perhaps the only reason that Waller has remained true to his youthful ideals while Bickersdyke has welshed on his, has less to do with honour than with the fact that Bickersdyke has become a manager and Waller has not. Even Psmith the schoolboy Marxist cares so little for the Class War that he does not bother to break Bickersdyke. The only practical use to which he is willing to put the Tulse Hill time bomb is to threaten his boss with exposure on the eve of the poll unless Mike Jackson is reprieved from dismissal. A few half-formulated suspicions continue to linger. If Psmith can so easily destroy Bickersdyke's pretensions by waving the evidence of Tulse Hill before him, why has Waller, who has been holding the same evidence all those years, never deployed them to the same end? One of the most astute of all Wodehouse commentators has suggested that what Wodehouse is implying is that the opportunist political scoundrels of this world will always take cynical advantage of the inability of its idealists to play what the Little Nugget would have defined as dirty pool.[3] The very impulses of altruism and fundamental decency which have led Waller along the stony road to utopian Socialism are those which prevent him from pushing home his case forcefully enough to win the war. The argument goes that within a single paragraph Wodehouse is defining his own political detachment by dismissing both the placeman Bickersdyke for having no morality, and the idealist Waller for having too much of it. It is just possible, however, that Waller has withheld the Tulse Hill Minutes not through excessive scrupulosity but because it was a good idea which had simply never occurred to him.

Bickersdyke in the meantime wins the seat, but only by a slender majority, and only because of one utterly irrelevant but deadly factor. Psmith, who knows his Eatanswill and his Tankerville,[4] reports that the electors 'seemed to be in just that state of happy intoxication which might make them vote for Bickersdyke by mistake'. But the vital factor is of a rather different nature:

> It had been discovered, on the eve of the poll, that the bank manager's opponent, in his youth, had been educated at a school in Germany, and had subsequently spent two years at Heidelberg University. These damaging revelations were having a marked effect on the warm-hearted patriots of Kenningford, who were now referring to the candidate in thick but earnest tones as 'the German Spy'.[5]

By the time he published *Psmith in the City*, Wodehouse was already established as the leader of a one-man conspiracy to explode the myth of an imminent German invasion threat, a flourishing industry in the lower foot-hills of Edwardian cultural life which had brought to the faces of a great many publishers and impresarios that roseate glow which comes when a public display of patriotism is subsidized by handsome financial dividends. In strict literary terms, infinitely the best of the German spy-invasion-scare books is Erskine Childers' *The Riddle of the Sands*, a curious work which almost loses its way through its author's mistaken impression that he is compiling a guide to yachtsmanship. Childers was genuinely concerned at the degree of military unpreparedness to which the British seemed reconciled, although it must be accounted one of the crueller ironies of the period that his enemies were at least capable of mustering enough ammunition to dispose of poor Childers before a firing squad some years later. His imitators in the German-scare line were rather less in earnest, except perhaps for the central figure in this lucrative corner of the entertainment business, Field Marshal Roberts. Roberts had been fulminating for years against the regrettable lack of bel-licosity in the British, had contributed introductions to at least thirty books on the subject, including one by Childers, and in 1905 had resigned from active duty to assume the presidency of the National Service League, an organization dedicated to the panacea of universal military training. When in that very year Mr Balfour assured the House of Commons that invasion 'was not an eventuality which we need seriously consider', Roberts, overlooking the chance to point out that there were hardly any eventualities of any kind which Mr Balfour felt he need seriously consider, instead counter-attacked on the wrong front in the House of Lords: 'I have no hesitation in stating that our armed forces are absolutely unfitted and unprepared for war.'

Posterity, faced with a choice between Roberts and Balfour, may well be inclined not to choose at all, while noting that in 1905 Britain was indeed as safe as houses even though Mr Balfour said so. However, concurrent with his public activities, Roberts was engaged on other, more clandestine opera-tions, in partnership with a pot-boiling author of the period called William Le Queux, whose popularity is explained by his style, which has been defined as 'crude even for a hack'.[6] This incongruous pair were at work on a new scare-novel to be entitled *The Invasion of 1910*, in which Britain is overrun by the Kaiser's forces, succeeds in throwing them out but only at the expense of a compromise peace in which Germany is fobbed off with Denmark and Holland. In view of the fact that back in 1894 Le Queux had published *The Great War in England in 1897* and that this great war had never remotely threatened to materialize, it might be supposed that his credibility in this department had been somewhat eroded by the tide of events. On the contrary, his new version of the old old story became his most popular work, thanks in no small measure to the support of that other distinguished political thinker, Lord Northcliffe. It was Northcliffe, proprietor of the *Daily Mail*, who financed to the tune of £3,000 a reconnais-sance trip by Roberts and Le Queux along the east coast of England, although Roberts, who planned the invasion with respect to prevailing mili-tary principles, was dismayed to discover that those principles were not quite in accordance with others, connected with matters of newspaper circulation, with which his lordship seemed so preoccupied. The route of Roberts' invaders took in no towns which read the *Daily Mail*, a fact which casts a revealing light on the Field Marshal's strategic flair. In the end tactics had to be sacrificed to circulation, and the invasion route amended in accordance with the nation's newsreading habits. Bloody but evidently unbowed, Roberts wrote in the introduction to Le Queux's book:

> The catastrophe that may happen if we still remain in our present state of unpreparedness is vividly and forcibly illustrated in Mr Le Queux's new book which I recommend to the perusal of everyone who has the welfare of the British Empire at heart.

Presumably it was only the innate humility of an old soldier which prevented Roberts from adding that Le Queux's indispensable new work was also his own, and humility again which caused him to countenance such excessively modest passages as:

> 'Well, if what you say is the actual truth, today is surely the blackest day that England has ever known.'
> 'Yes, thanks to the pro-German policy of the Government and the false assurances of the Blue Water School. They should have listened to Lord Roberts,' snapped his lordship.

Roberts and Le Queux in the course of their researches had picked up some outlandish ideas about the hymn-singing, tea-drinking, self-denying Mr Wallers of their world, claiming that the degeneration of a once-great nation was due to the undermining of religious faith by 'Socialism, with its creed of "Thou shalt have no other God but thyself" and its doctrine "Let us eat and drink, for tomorrow we die" '. Under the circumstances it is perhaps understandable that our two patriots should have preferred the fierce puritanism of Northcliffe, who expressed his sense of the deep seriousness of the occasion by hiring sandwich-men to march along Piccadilly in German uniforms on the first day of serialization in the *Daily Mail*.

A far deeper irony is that of all those who were imperilling the security of the Empire, it was Roberts himself who imperilled it the most, for while the Socialists and the Little Englanders tended generally to abide by the law, Roberts sailed as close to the winds of treason as he was able without actually blowing up Buckingham Palace. For he was the leader among those men who contributed to the danger of defeat in a war with Germany by buttressing the general European impression that Britain, riven by the sectarian crises of Ireland and the resulting disaffection among the officers of its armies, was unable to defend itself. It was Roberts who announced to the world that 'any attempt to coerce Ulster would result in the utter ruin of the Army', Roberts who called on Sir Edward Carson in order to congratulate him on committing the treasonable act of gun-running, Roberts again who arranged for the Ulster Volunteers to find a commanding officer. That such a man should be so anxious about England's state of unpreparedness in a hypothetical German war is a rich joke, but not rich enough to prevent the runaway success of *The Invasion of 1910* and its translation into twenty-seven languages, including, naturally, German.

It might be wondered what all this has to do with P. G. Wodehouse. The answer is that of all the professional writers of the period, it was Wodehouse alone who published an *anti*-war-scare novel in which the weapons of the farceur are used to murderous effect on the school of Le Queux. *The Swoop or, How Clarence Saved England* has been described as 'the only comic contribution to Edwardian invasion literature'.[7] More to the point, it is also the only contribution to that literature which blows a raspberry at Lord Roberts; other targets include General Baden-Powell, Herbert Gladstone, the commercial theatre, and, most pointedly, the prosodists of the *Daily Mail*. *The Swoop* is brief but deadly, recounting in only 20,000 words the events following on one of the most remarkable coincidences in world history, the simultaneous converging on British soil of nine foreign armies, each operating in abysmal ignorance of the other eight. While the Germans are establishing a foothold in Essex, the Russians under Vodkakoff are in Yarmouth, the Mad Mullah has captured Portsmouth, China is at the gates of the picturesque Welsh watering place of Lllgxplll, the army of Monaco is advancing through Auchtermuchty, a band of Young Turks is occupying Scarborough, Brighton has fallen to Moroccan brigands, Margate is under siege from Bollygollan natives, and the Swiss Navy, not content with shelling Lyme Regis, is preparing to land troops west of the bathing machines. Lord Roberts, it would appear, has most mischievously misled the nation regarding the magnitude of the peril threatening it.

Amid the shrieking chaos, the lone voice of heroism belongs to one Clarence Chugwater, who, when we first meet him, is most sensibly dressed in the modest camouflage so dear to the heart of General Baden-Powell, 'a flat-brimmed hat, a coloured handkerchief, a flannel shirt, a bunch of ribbons, a haversack, football shorts, brown boots, a whistle and a hockey stick'. The stern practicality of this attire does not bode well for the invaders, who prove in the end to be pitifully ill-equipped to cope with Clarence's ability to imitate frogs, moles and owls. When not blowing his whistle or impersonating assorted wildlife, Clarence is given to sapient observations like 'England, my England!' and 'England has need of such as you', and is especially chagrined to see that the notorious middle-class preoccupation with profit has extended into the very heart of his own family: when two German emissaries arrive at the front door, Clarence's father tries to let the house to them, his elder brother attempts to interest them in an insurance policy, his younger brother tries to persuade them to give him a fair price for his motor-bike, while his two sisters hector them into purchasing tickets for a charity show in aid of hungry old-age pensioners. Frankly, this is the least of Clarence's patriotic problems, the most acute of which is the difficulty of making his countrymen see the extent of their unpreparedness. When he tries to press home his arguments, he is denied:

'Do you ever read the papers? Don't you know that we've got the Ashes and the Gold championship and the Wibbley-wob championship and the Spiropole, Spillikins, Puff-Feather and Animal Grab championships? Has it come to your notice that our croquet pair beat America last Thursday by eight hoops? Did you happen to hear that we won the Hop, Skip and Jump at the last Olympic Games?'

This complacency is shared by the popular press; on the day of the German invasion, the stop press column of Clarence's halfpenny newspaper reads:

Fry, not out 104; Surrey 147 for 8. A German Army landed in Essex this afternoon. Loamshire Handicap: Spring Chicken 1; Salome 2; Yip-i-addy 3. Seven Ran.

Only when the enemy hordes are smashing through the soft underbelly of sporting England does the gravity of their predicament strike the English, who take note of the atrocities and realize at last that they have a fight on their hands:

The troops of Prince Otto had done grievous damage. Cricket pitches had been trampled down, and in many cases even golf-greens dented by the iron heel of the invader, who rarely, if ever, replaced the divot. Fishing was at a standstill. Croquet had been given up in despair. Near Epping the Russians shot a fox. . . .

This is only the beginning. Soon the Russians, on a route-march, 'had walked across the bowling screen at Kennington Oval during the Surrey v. Lancashire match, causing Hayward to be bowled for a duck's egg. A band of German sappers had dug a trench right across the turf at Queen's Club'.[8] And later, when the great battle to fling the invaders into the sea is due to start, the locals realize that matters have been exceedingly ill-timed, for once the battle begins

it would mean a heavy loss to those who supplied London with its Saturday afternoon amusements. The matinees would suffer. The battle might not affect the stalls and dress circle perhaps, but there could be no doubt that the pit and gallery receipts would fall off terribly. To the public which supports the pit and gallery of a theatre there is an irresistible attraction about a fight on anything like a large scale. When one considers that a quite ordinary street fight will attract hundreds of spectators, it will be plainly seen that no theatrical entertainment could hope to compete against so strong a counter-attraction as a battle between the German and Russian armies. The various football grounds would be heavily hit too. And there was to be a monster roller-skating carnival at Olympia. That also would be spoiled.

A deputation of amusement-caterers hurried to the two camps within an hour of the appearance of the first evening paper. They put their case plainly and well. The Generals were obviously impressed. Messages passed and repassed between the two armies, and in the end it was decided to put off the outbreak of hostilities till Monday morning.

Clarence has most cunningly brought about this neutral match between two of the enemies of England by encouraging them to argue about the relative size of the fees their commanders are getting for appearances in West End music halls, a development which had originally burgeoned thanks to the commercial initiative of the impresario Solly Quhayne and his brothers Kern, Colquhoun, Coyne and Cowan.[9] At last Clarence with his Boy Scout force clears all the invaders out of England, being rewarded for his gallantry with – a booking in a music hall, where he is announced as follows:

This 'ero will perform a few of those exercises which have made our Scouts what they are, such as deep breathing, twisting the right leg firmly round the neck, and hopping on one foot across the stage. He will then give an exhibition of the various calls and cries of the Boy Scouts – skilful imitations of real living animals. In this connection, I 'ave to assure you that 'e 'as nothing whatsoever in 'is mouth.

Ghosts from the Wodehousean pantheon flit across the scene. The suggestion that armies function more effectively when comprised entirely of generals is a nod in the direction of W. S. Gilbert;[10] the remark that 'the German shells had had one excellent result, they had demolished nearly all the London statues' harks back to the reaction of Dickens to the suggestion that a monument be erected to him, to which he had replied that if people really wished to please him, then instead of erecting another statue, they should knock down one of the old ones. The text follows a long and honourable tradition in ridiculing the rapacity of popular entertainment by observing that 'if an impulsive gentleman slew his grandmother with a coalhammer, only a small portion of the public could gaze on his pleasing features at the Old Bailey. To enable the rest to enjoy the intellectual treat, it was necessary to engage him, at enormous cost, to appear at a music hall'. When inquiring as to Boy Scout readiness, Clarence is assured: 'Some of them are acting a Scout's play, sir; some are doing Cone exercises; one or two are practising deep breathing; and the rest are dancing an Old English Morris Dance.' The prose style of Lord Northcliffe's hirelings is marginally improved upon with:

In the stalls I noticed a solid body of Russian officers. These soldiers from the Steppes. These bearded men. These Russians. That sit silent and watchful. They applauded little. The programme left them cold.

The Trick Cyclist. The Dashing Soubrette and the Idol of Belgravia. The Argumentative College Chums. The Swell Comedian. The Man with the Performing Canaries. None of these could rouse them. They were waiting. Waiting. Waiting tensely. Every muscle taut. Husbanding their strength. Waiting. For what?

Mr Herbert Gladstone points out that as he had 'let so many undesirable aliens into the country already, he did not see that a few more made much difference'. A well-known judge asks 'What is an invasion?', and Mr Seymour Hicks expresses the pious hope that nobody hurts Mr George Edwardes. Most pointed of all is Wodehouse's jibe, on behalf of himself and his publisher, Alston Rivers, at the expense of the Roberts–Le Queux lobby:

> It may be thought by some that in the pages which follow I have painted in too lurid colours the horrors of a foreign invasion of England. Realism in art, it may be argued, can be carried too far. I prefer to think that the majority of my readers will acquit me of a desire to be unduly sensational. It is necessary that England should be roused to a sense of her peril, and only by setting down without flinching the probable results of an invasion can this be done. This story, I may mention, has been written and published purely from a feeling of patriotism and duty. Mr Alston Rivers' sensitive soul will be jarred to its foundations if it is a financial success. So will mine. But in a time of national danger we feel that the risk must be taken. After all, at the worst, it is a small sacrifice to make for our country.

It might be said of this badinage that at least the sensitive soul of Lord Roberts was immune to it through being unaware of its existence. The assumption is unwise. It appears that both the invasion-scare literature of the period and its comic antidote were causing grave concern in the airier reaches of English public life. Indeed, with Le Queux's text being translated into the languages of every potential enemy of the Empire, Mr Asquith had little choice but to decide, in the very year which saw the publication of *The Swoop*, to do something about the Condition of England. And so he appointed a sub-committee to the Committee of Imperial Defence, chaired by Richard Haldane, whose task was to examine the Official Secrets Act of 1889 with a view to discovering if there was any substance in the claims of Lord Roberts among others that the population of the old country consisted entirely of foreign espionage agents. In their book, Le Queux and the Field Marshal had suggested that this army consisted of disguised waiters, clerks, bakers, barbers and servants, representing a working-class monopoly of perfidy which might have appeared more disquieting still to Mr Asquith had it only included a few vintners. But it has since been suggested that what Haldane and his fellow-patriots on the sub-committee found even harder to take than the highly lucrative patriotism of Roberts and Le Queux was Wodehouse's derisory reaction to it. It was at the suggestion of the sub-committee that MI5 was created, after which Haldane, having made the world safe from a German threat, was hounded by Northcliffe's newspapers for being pro-German, a wonderfully profound conclusion at which his lordship had arrived on learning that Haldane had been dastardly enough to learn the language and to visit the place. In 1915 Haldane was kicked out of the Cabinet, an event which so disorientated the train of his political thought that it eventually caused him to join the Labour Party. Perhaps before being dismissed he was first investigated by the same anti-espionage agency which he had originally called into being. At any rate, the episode was much more comical than anything Wodehouse had contrived to put into *The Swoop*. After all, at the time of his dumping of Mr Haldane's political body, Mr Asquith had most sedulously been treading grapes for a great many years, and yet it occurred to nobody to accuse him of being a Frenchman.

Psmith in the City appeared only eighteen months after *The Swoop*, and clearly, when Wodehouse addressed himself to the not altogether unpleasant task of flinging mud at Bickersdyke, the recollection of those who contrived to cash in on the anti-German scare was still vivid. Having shown the man to be a liar, a bully, a turncoat, a fool and a coward, Wodehouse also makes him one of those counterfeit patriots who cry wolf in order to create a diversion while they steal a sheep. The fact is that if he had managed to think of any plausible way of making Bickersdyke also a rapist, a child molester, a body-snatcher or a dramatic critic, he would have done so. The satire in the book is gentle, perhaps even genteel, but it is none the less implacable, and the reader is surprised to realize that for all its air of good-natured persiflage, the book's effect has all the severity of a polemic, in the sense that no young man exposed to its contents could ever take seriously again the suggestion that he become a bank employee. All the young recruits at the New Asiatic wish passionately they were somewhere else, and all its old stagers are either embittered, bullying or half-dead. Waller is a cipher, Gregory a ranting noodle, Rossiter a ghost whose real life is lived out vicariously on the terraces at Old Trafford and in the gossip columns of *The Athletic News*. There is not one occupant of that bank who feels the faintest affinity with its destinies, a spark of affection for its personality. The bank is a moloch swallowing up young men like Bannister at one end of the process, and disgorging them ruined and unrecognizable like Gregory at the other. And the more obnoxious a man is, the better he may expect to flourish within the bank's limits. Its manager is therefore by definition its most odious employee of all, a philistine and a poseur who cannot even win an election without resorting to the contemptible device of a xenophobia which is not only crudely conceived but also quite insincere.

Psmith in the City is in effect a terrible warning against the perils which lie in wait for a young man, threatening to place him at the mercy of the Gradgrinds of the Post Room and the Bounderbys of Fixed Deposits. One of Wodehouse's most famous predecessors in the cavalcade of the English comic novel had made one of his heroes an employee in just such a bank as Mike Jackson and Psmith came to know. But evidently Jerome K. Jerome had no strong opinions regarding the Financial Question which bedevils *Psmith in the City*, saying only that the banjo-strumming George 'goes to sleep at a bank from ten to four each day, except Saturdays, when they wake him up and put him outside at two'. Nevertheless, Jerome provides Psmith with a deadly weapon in his guerilla war against Bickersdyke. When the prospective Unionist member for Kenningford attempts to lull the audience at a political meeting by passing off as his own the famous Jerome joke about the plaster-of-Paris trout in the glass case, Psmith seizes the chance to reduce the assembly to chaos by exposing this dreadful man as someone so felonious by nature that he cannot even discuss politics without stealing someone else's laughs. It is this xenophobe, this purloiner, this braggart, this man who struts in front of the bowling screen, on whom fortune has smiled at the New Asiatic, and who is now at the heart of the demoniac conspiracy to crush the hope out of the young men who fall into his orbit. Wodehouse shows him to be without a shred of decency, until at last the reader is tempted to wonder at the source of all this hatred. What have the real-life Bickersdykes of this world ever done to Wodehouse that so mild-mannered and benign a man should exact such terrible revenge?

During the summer term of 1900, Wodehouse's career as a schoolboy, having reached a climax of some magnificence in the previous year, now modulated imperceptibly into an adult key. In the student republic of Dulwich he was an eminent figure, a star athlete who had distinguished himself both on Big Side and at the Public Schools Boxing Championships, an accomplished scholar for whom the composition of rhymed couplets in Latin and Greek had become second nature, an editor of the school magazine, and one of those members of the sixth form who appeared to be sailing as if in the natural order of things to a brilliant university career. His finest hour as a schoolboy had come in the previous summer, when, on 3 June 1899, he had enjoyed an afternoon such as adolescents dream about: in the home match against Tonbridge, Wodehouse had skittled the enemy, taking seven wickets including that of the great Kenneth Hutchings. While it is difficult to take the measure of such a performance in absolute terms, it should be remembered that public schools cricket of the period was congested with young players destined to achieve success at international level. Hutchings, for instance, went on to become one of the great international batting stars of the Edwardian era, whose century for England against Australia at Melbourne in the tour of 1907–8 has won a permanent place in cricket history. As for Wodehouse's team-mate, N. A. Knox, no less an authority than Sir Jack Hobbs once described Knox as the most fearsome bowler he had ever faced. The diffident Wodehouse, though he was never to forget his triumph against Tonbridge, was inclined to pooh-pooh his own distinction in the matter: when asked, many years later, if he did not consider it the ultimate sporting accolade to have shared the school bowling duties with no less a record-breaker than Knox, Wodehouse replied, 'Oh, but he was frightfully young. I've always been proud that I used to go on to bowl before him, but he was a child then'.[11]

Although Wodehouse was never again to scale the heights of 3 June 1899, he continued to play a leading part in the melodrama of the school, and was, in the words of his study-mate Townend, 'someone of importance in the life of Dulwich'. And all the time he was stepping out the closing measures of his Dulwich career, the prospect of the university loomed invitingly. In those days pupils at the great public schools moved on to Oxbridge as naturally as many of them later graduated to the Consular Service, the Indian Civil or the Stock Exchange. Wodehouse's elder brother Armine, less of an athlete but a gifted amateur pianist endowed with all the social graces, had won a scholarship to Oxford, where he was now in residence, and where, it was assumed, Plum would soon follow him. His father Ernest, however, having travelled home for the last time on the floating social clubs of the P and O, was beginning to realize that a return to the old country would be something in the nature of a mixed blessing. Having served out his time and returned home in anticipation of a modest but sufficient pension, Ernest was only jumping to the same conclusions as thousands of his countrymen. After all, he had performed dutifully in the service of Queen and Empire. He had upheld those impeccable standards of rectitude instilled at Repton. He had shown the flag. He had placed a thousand tiny sacrificial offerings on the altar of imperial devotion, and could surely now sit back in the reasonable expectation of reward from a suitably grateful motherland. However, it seems that Ernest had reckoned without that mischievous streak which the motherland was known to disclose from time to time regarding its more abject devotees. The whole Wodehouse economy hung by a thread from that pension. But what he had forgotten to reckon with on that day in 1867 when he sailed into Hong Kong harbour was that when the time came for him to collect his reward, he would learn that the British, when they kept insisting on their sincere desire to adopt as many native customs as seemed compatible with the dignity of a conqueror, were being not altogether dishonest. Ernest's retirement pension was paid to him in rupees.

The rupee, not surprisingly, was one of the more volatile of imperial currencies and, in recalling the affair, Wodehouse seems to adhere to the Conspiracy theory of history rather than to Ernest's understanding that he had simply been the victim of bad luck:

> My father had retired and was living on a pension and it was paid to him in rupees. And of all the dirty tricks, being paid in rupees is the worst, because it was always jumping up and down and throwing fits. Just about the time when I was leaving Dulwich I was going to try for a scholarship at Oxford. I think I'd probably have got one. Suddenly the rupee started going down. It was decided there wasn't enough cash to send me to Oxford even if I got a scholarship.

Throughout that last summer term Wodehouse had been immersing himself in Homer and Thucydides, but just when he was, in his own words, 'full to the brim with classic lore and spoiling for a good whack at the examiners, down came the rupee'. As he was later to put it, 'Learning drew the loser's end and Commerce got me.'

How it got him was a predictable enough story. When the cavorting rupee started to rip holes in the family purse, Ernest attempted to plug the leak by the accepted methods of his class and era. He might not possess the funds to complete his second son's education, but the possibilities of the System were not quite exhausted yet. In his years of dispensing justice on the Peak, Ernest had been a considerable figure, and it was not now too difficult for him to pull the strings which would bring salvation to young Plum. He remembered that one of the weightiest of all Hong Kong's institutions had an outpost in London, and he played his hand accordingly, acquiring for Plum a coveted post in the City branch of the Hong Kong and Shanghai Bank in Lombard Street, at which hitherto undistinguished premises there was now played out one of the greatest comedies of British financial history:

> I have always thought it illustrative of the haphazard methods of education in the nineties of the last century that I should have been put on the Classical side at Dulwich and taught to write Greek and Latin verse and so on when I was going to wind up in a bank. I had had absolutely no training for commerce, and right through my two years in the bank I never had the slightest inkling of what banking was. I simply could not understand what was going on.

Whether the son, in being expected to apply his views on Horace to the intricacies of debit and credit, was in a more ridiculous predicament than his father, in bringing to the support of the opium racket a grasp of Virgil, is a point which neither of the two victims ever explored, but it was soon clear that the son had nothing like the same stern devotion to duty that his father had, having been endowed with a far more sensible grasp of the relative importance of things:

> Life in the bank – after the first month or two – was quite pleasant. My fellow clerks were all public school men – from Bedford, Merchant Taylor's, Dulwich and other schools where parents could not afford a university career – and the atmosphere was on the informal side. We ran a football and a cricket team, of both of which I was a member, and there was a general idea of not taking banking very seriously. I suppose the other fellows had more of a grip on things than I did, but there was none of that grim atmosphere which prevails in the usual London bank, where a clerk in the London office knows that he is going to be in the London office for the rest of his life. Everybody except me was counting the days till he would be able to 'give a Langdon', which was the term for the party you gave at the Langdon public house when you 'got your orders' and were sent East.

The financial nature of the salvation which Ernest had arranged was not spectacular. For his labours in Lombard Street, the new apprentice was paid £80 a year, 'just like finding it in the street', to which munificent sum Ernest added another £80 of his own:

> There were only two things connected with Higher Finance that I really understood. One was that from now on all I would be able to afford in the way of lunch would be a roll and butter and a cup of coffee, a discovery which, after the lavish midday meals of school, shook me to my foundations. The other was that if I got to the office late three mornings in a month, I would lose my Christmas bonus. One of the great sights in the City in the years 1901–2 was me rounding into the straight with my coat-tails flying and just making it across the threshold while thousands cheered. It kept me in superb condition, and gave me a rare appetite for the daily roll and butter.

It may be that Wodehouse, in stressing the hardships of living in London on three pounds a week, was taking a leaf out of the book of one of his great journalistic heroes, J. M. Barrie, whose fierce resolve to romanticize the circumstances of life in the Big City sometimes led him to gild the lily beyond all reason. Throughout the year of 1885, Barrie, so he later claimed, survived on a daily dinner of 'four provocative halfpenny buns from a paper bag'.[12] Even so, it seems doubtful that either he or Wodehouse ever actually went hungry, which suggests that both men were guilty of a little affectation. But if the hunger legend may be discounted, there was something of infinitely greater value which Barrie was to pass on to the apprentice bank clerk, as we shall see. For the moment, Wodehouse struggled along on his £3 a week, necessarily forgoing the pleasures of the town. In his nineties, when asked by an interviewer to describe a typical night out in the West End at the turn of the century, Wodehouse had this to say:

> As I remember it, they used to turn out the lights at a place like the Savoy pretty early, about twelve o'clock or something. I think night life was very mild in those days. And of course I had no money, I couldn't go in for it much.[13]

In underlining his comprehensive failure as a bank clerk, Wodehouse went to great pains to explain that what undid him was sheer cerebral insufficiency, and that those who assumed that his soul must have been above the sordid machinery of huckstering were sadly misled:

> I was just a plain dumb brick. I proved to be the most inefficient clerk whose trouser seat ever polished the surface of a high stool. I was all right as long as they kept me in the postal department, where I had nothing to do but stamp and post letters, a task for which my abilities well fitted me, but when they took me out of there and put me into Fixed Deposits, the whisper went round Lombard Street, 'Wodehouse

is at a loss. He cannot cope.' If there was a moment in the course of my banking career when I had the foggiest notion of what it was all about, I am unable to recall it. From Fixed Deposits I drifted to Inward Bills – no use asking me what Inward Bills are, I never found out – and then to Outward Bills and to Cash, always with a weak, apologetic smile on my face and hoping that suavity of manner would see me through when, as I knew must happen ere long, I fell short in the performance of my mystic duties.

When Psmith bludgeons Bickersdyke into submission by brandishing the cudgel of the minutes of the Tulse Hill Parliament, it is with the intention of saving Mike Jackson from dismissal for cashing a forged cheque. Wodehouse's crime was less serious and for that very reason more derisory of the principles on which the bank had been constructed. One day while labouring in the Cash Department, Wodehouse was handed a new ledger, whose blank pages so tempted him that he decided to enter upon them his comic description of the Formal Opening of the New Ledger:

> It was the most terrific piece. Though fifty-five years have passed since that day, it is still green in my memory. It had everything. There was a bit about my being presented to his Gracious Majesty the King which would have had you gasping with mirth. ('From his tie he took a diamond tie-pin, and smiled at me, and then he put it back.') And that was just one passing incident. The whole thing was a knock-out. I can't give the details. You will have to take my word for it that it was one of the most screamingly funny things ever written. I sat back on my stool and felt like Dickens when he had finished *Pickwick*.

Soon the euphoria of creation began to die down, and Wodehouse removed the soiled page from the ledger. The Head Cashier, after wrongly accusing the stationers of supplying faulty materials, was then confronted with the Head Stationer, who, according to Wodehouse, began the following exchange with the cashier:

> 'Somebody must have cut out the page.'
> 'Absurd,' said the Head Cashier. 'Nobody but an imbecile would cut out the front page of a ledger.'
> 'Then you must have an imbecile in your department. Have you?'
> The Head Cashier started. This opened up a new line of thought. 'Why, yes,' he admitted, for he was a fair-minded man, 'there is P. G. Wodehouse.'

With no Psmith to save him, Wodehouse was questioned, made his confession, and adds, 'It was immediately after this that I found myself at liberty'. So ended his association with the Hong Kong and Shanghai Bank. He had been in Lombard Street for two years, long enough for him to have enlivened the mythology of that otherwise austere conspiracy:

> My total inability to grasp what was going on made me something of a legend in the place. Years afterwards, when the ineptness of a new clerk was under discussion in the manager's inner sanctum and the disposition of those present at the conference was to condemn him as the worst bungler who had ever entered the Hong Kong and Shanghai Bank's portals, some white-haired veteran in charge of one of the departments would shake his head and murmur, 'No, no, you're wrong. Young Robinson is, I agree, an almost total loss and ought to have been chloroformed at birth, but you should have seen P. G. Wodehouse. Ah, they don't make them like that nowadays. They've lost the pattern.'

Nor is *Psmith in the City* by any means his last word on the subject; for some years after the publication of that novel, he continued to fling out characters whose lives have gone seriously wrong through the sad inability to sidestep Fixed Deposits or Inward Bills. In 'The Tuppenny Millionaire' we are introduced to one George Balmer:

> In London at the present moment there exist some thousands of respectable, neatly dressed, mechanical, unenterprising young men, employed at modest salaries by various banks, corporations, stores, shops, and business firms. They are put to work when young, and they stay put. They are mussels. Each has his special place on the rock, and remains glued to it all his life.

Even closer to home is Rutherford Maxwell, hero of 'In Alcala'. Rutherford is an even more exact replica of Wodehouse in the City than either Mike Jackson or Psmith:

> He was an Englishman, and the younger son of an Englishman; and his lot was the lot of the younger sons all the world over. He was by profession one of the numerous employees of the New Asiatic Bank, which has its branches all over the world. It is a sound, trustworthy institution, and steady-going relatives would assure Rutherford that he was lucky to have got a berth in it. Rutherford did not agree with them. However sound and trustworthy, it was not exactly romantic. Nor did it err on the side of over-lavishness to those who served it. Rutherford's salary was small. So were his prospects.

From Wodehouse's unwillingness to take his place on the rock, from the terrible revenge he exacts from Bickersdyke and company, from the care with which he instructs us that the only reason for Psmith's dangerous flirtation with Marxist dogma is the frustrating of his expectation of a career at Eton, we might be excused for assuming that at the back of Wodehouse's rigorous rejection of the clerkly life lay the glittering prizes of a lost university career. The truth of the matter is rather different, its retrospective irony being that if Ernest had only had the faintest inkling of the kind of exotic creature he had fathered, the entire episode of the Hong Kong and Shanghai Bank need never have happened. Because £80 a year was all he could afford out of his meagre harvest of rupees, he was convinced that even with a scholarship, Oxford was out of the question. So he hit on the bank as the source of a further £80. By this compromise Plum would be saved from both the shabby-genteel predicaments of the downstart son and the disgrace of soiling his hands with anything more demeaning than ink. Ernest did his duty according to his lights and in any case there was no alternative he could see.

In fact there was an obvious alternative and Plum had suggested it the moment crisis loomed. The deprivation of a university career he could take in his stride; what he could not stomach was the peremptory rejection of his own dearest wish. By the time the rupee began its calamitous descent, Wodehouse was perfectly capable of making his own way without the assistance of either Ernest or the bank, and, in view of the fact that he made no secret of this commercial potential, Ernest seems to have reacted with an obtuseness excessive even for a Victorian paterfamilias. The clue is contained in the passage in *Psmith in the City* where Wodehouse is describing the extra-mural diversions of the New Asiatic's young men. In addition to West's horse-stealing adventures, Hignett's modest successes before the footlights, and Wragge's exercise of his talents in demogogy in the cause of Flat Earth theories in Hyde Park on Sunday afternoons, there is Raymond, 'who dabbled in journalism and was the author of "Straight Talks to House-wives" in *Trifles* under the pseudonym of Lady Gussie'. Even before entering the bank, Raymond, that is Wodehouse, had already succeeded in crashing Fleet Street; in pure mathematical terms, Plum's earned income during his last year at Dulwich actually exceeded his father's. There is no question that had he reached Oxford, he would there have followed the precedent of John Buchan, who had gone up six years before and published several works while in residence, won a place in *Who's Who* while still an undergraduate, and had, in the words of his biographer, 'paid his way at Oxford entirely by his scholarships and literary earnings'.[14] Wodehouse's feats were almost as precocious. In February 1900, when still preoccupied with his duties as a high-tackling forward in the Dulwich First xv, he sold a story to *The Public School Magazine* for half a guinea. In the summer term, he followed up with articles on 'Football at Dulwich' and 'School Cricket in 1900', by which time he had started a diary in which he entered all his literary earnings, and could see that he had stumbled on his own salvation. When Ernest announced contingency plans for coping with the fluctuating rupee, Wodehouse suggested he be allowed to live the life of a free-lance writer. Ernest, however, belonged to a class and a generation which took honest labour to mean anything unpleasant to perform, and reacted predictably:

Putting this project to my parents, I found them cold towards it. The cross all young writers have to bear is that, while they know that they are going to be spectacularly successful some day, they find it impossible to convince their nearest and dearest that they will ever amount to a row of beans. Write in your spare time, if you really must write, parents say, and they pull that old one about literature being a good something but a bad crutch. I do not blame my parents for feeling that a son in a bank making his £80 a year, just like finding it in the street, was a sounder commercial proposition than one living at home and spending a fortune on stamps.

So Wodehouse dutifully entered on his Lombard Street servitude and wrote in what little spare time remained. He knew he had only a limited amount of time in which to succeed. Throughout his banking days he was pursued by the threat of his eventual transfer to the East, for he knew that if he was to become a writer, 'this could only be done by remaining in London'. In his Markham Square bedsitter, which he defined as 'horrible lodgings in the Chelsea neighbourhood off the King's Road', he wrote, with desperate speed, stories, articles, essays, verses, and soon digested one of the prime facts of the literary life: 'What I always feel about rejection slips is that their glamour soon wears off. When you have seen one, you have seen them all.' His attitude towards his apprenticeship is confused. At one moment he is insisting that 'worse bilge than mine may have been submitted to the editors of 1901–2, but I should think it very unlikely', and the next he is confessing:

> The curious thing about those early days is that in spite of the blizzard of rejection slips, I had the most complete confidence in myself. I knew I was good. It was only later that doubts on this point began to creep in.

In any case, whether or not the editors regarded him as a producer of bilge, there were so many of them that their sheer proliferation was encouraging. In those days a starving writer could hardly throw himself out of a window without landing on a magazine editor, a paradisal state of affairs which Wodehouse recalled with sad affection in 1949 when writing to Townend about the death of *The Strand*:

> As practically everything I have written since July 1905 appeared in the Strand, I drop a silent tear, but I can't say I'm much surprised, for anything sicker-looking than the little midget it had shrunk to I never saw. Inevitable, I suppose, because of paper shortage. And in my opinion never anything worth reading in it, either, the last year or two.
>
> How on earth does a young writer of light fiction get going these days? Where can he sell his stories? When you and I were breaking in, we might get turned down by the Strand and Pearson's, but there was always the hope of landing with Nash's, the Storyteller, the London, the Royal, the Red, the Yellow, Cassell's, the New, the Novel, the

Grand, the Pall Mall, and the Windsor, not to mention Blackwood, Cornhill, Chamber's and probably about a dozen more I've forgotten. I was looking at the book of acceptances and payments which I kept for the first five years of my literary career, and I note that in July 1901 I sold a story to something called the Universal and Ludgate Magazine and got a guinea for it. Where nowadays can the eager beginner pick up one pound one like that?

In his two years in Lombard Street Wodehouse sold eighty stories and articles, and would no doubt have trebled that figure had he been able to devote all his time to the work instead of only two or three hours a night. In sizing up the journalistic market in relation to his own style and range of subject matter, he had been extremely astute, reducing to a bare minimum the false starts with which the literary apprentice invariably squanders his energy. But in referring to this precocious beginning, Wodehouse later suggested that it might have been more precocious still had it not been for the baleful influence on his impressionable young mind of one of the most fascinating curiosities of later Victorian literature, a novel which is almost forgotten today but which at the time of its vogue had a profound effect on the quantity as well as the quality of English fiction. This book had first appeared in 1892 and, by the time Wodehouse was beginning to peep over the palisades of adolescence, had become something of a vade-mecum for the aspiring free-lance, having been written by someone as well qualified as any man ever was to describe the journalistic life.

In March 1885 there had arrived in London, from Kirremuir via Nottingham, an obscure journalist called James Matthew Barrie, intent on making himself indispensable to those battalions of editors whose eventual passing Wodehouse so deeply lamented. In his determination to succeed, Barrie romanticized everything with a cold-blooded relentlessness which he later apotheosized in the remark of one of his characters: 'There are few more impressive sights in the world than a Scotsman on the make.' No incident was too trifling, no person too insignificant, to be transmuted into an acceptance cheque. He even romanticized his own arrival, making out of it a chapter of autobiography; on stepping down on to the platform of St Pancras Station on the morning of 29 March 1885, he had not reached the ticket-collector before noticing that the newspaper placards were proclaiming an essay he had sent off only a few days before. Encouraged, he says, by the thought that he had earned a guinea after being in London for one minute, Barrie went about his self-appointed task with implacable efficiency, writing about everything from the nesting habits of rooks to the pleasures of bad cricket, from London club life, of which he knew nothing, to the thoughts of a six-year-old, about which he had forgotten everything. The most significant of all these squibs is 'A Rag of Paper', written in response to the challenge of friends who one day noticed a scrap of paper dancing in the gutter and defied Barrie to turn it into a banknote. Barrie produced from it what he defined as a journalistic soap bubble which soon found its way into the pages of the *St James's Gazette*, an experience which brought home to him the vital truth that because he was writing about his attitude to things rather than about the things themselves, the subject matter was of no importance – or rather, the subject matter was always the same, himself. The literary improvisor should strive to make a theme appear not like itself but like himself. Barrie acted upon this discovery with spectacular results until, at last, having made a living from writing about anything, he carried the process to its logical conclusion and made a rather better living by writing a novel about people who make a living from writing about nothing. It was this book which came to Wodehouse's notice in his last year at Dulwich and which pointed in the opposite direction to the counters of the Hong Kong and Shanghai Bank.

When a Man's Single is a dated, whimsical romance hopelessly crippled by those evasions regarding the realities of love which were to make such a sorry mess of Barrie's private life, although not even its reticences can quench the considerable vitality which Barrie poured into the book. The story opens with the gratuitous sadism of the killing off of a small child, and closes with the excruciating archness of the hero discussing possible arrangements for his own funeral. But buried in the agglutinate mess of the novel is one of the most influential passages in English fiction of the period. It was to become notorious as a manual for thousands of young men aspiring to the halfpenny-bun liberty which Barrie so fulsomely describes. The narrative concerns one Rob Angus, a young citizen of the village of Thrums, who arrives in London in search of the literary life:

> During his first month in London, Rob wrote thirty articles, and took them to the different offices in order to save the postage. There were many other men in the streets doing the same thing. He got fifteen articles back by return of post and never saw the others again.

He reports on his progress to an old hand called Rorrison, who hears of the thirty rejects and says:

> 'Yes, and you will have another thirty rejected if they are of the same kind. You beginners seem able to write nothing but your views on politics, and your reflections on art, and your theories of life, which you sometimes even think original. Editors won't have that, because their readers don't want it. Every paper has its regular staff of leader-writers, and what is wanted from the outside is freshness. An editor tosses aside your column-and-a-half on evolution, but is glad to have a paragraph saying that you saw Herbert Spencer the day before yesterday gazing solemnly for ten minutes in a milliner's window.'

Having delivered this lecture, Rorrison then takes Angus for an audience with the man who has made a legendary success by observing its precepts. Mr Noble Simms is a free-lance scribbler with a reputation for being able to squeeze an article out of anything or anybody he happens to encounter, but Angus, defiantly on his guard, leaves at the end of the evening convinced that at any rate Simms has failed to extract any copy from him. Next day on glancing in a newspaper he is amazed to find himself and his walking stick the subject of a thousand words by Simms. The truth embodied by the episode is simple enough, and being simple, often escapes the perceptions of the literary tyro, who threshes around in search of significant themes instead of embracing the ruthlessness of Simms, who says at one point, 'My God, I would write an article, I think, on my mother's coffin'. Barrie, the two-guinea trifler *par excellence*, wrote, figuratively speaking, about his mother's coffin a thousand times, having invented Simms only in order to make his own statement on the nebulous relationships between Art and Fleet Street. His journalistic apprenticeship was a brilliant affair and, as it receded into the past, Barrie fell deeper and deeper in love with it, at last saying to his own young self, 'We had some good old miserable times together, didn't we? Do you remember how we followed the postman from door to door, under the moon, in rain, in fog, to see him drop our fate in the letter-box or go heartlessly by?'[15] The tone was seductive enough to be picked up by Barrie's biographer Denis Mackail, who spoke of 'a forgotten kind of bachelor life, with peace and stability stretching out from it in all directions with its simple and innocent pleasures, its evenings by firesides, its holidays on houseboats, its ninepenny cigars, and its tobacco at nine shillings a pound'.[16]

Mackail was not the only fellow-writer to be seduced by the vision of Grub Street invented by Barrie. In *Experiment with Autobiography*, H. G. Wells describes how, as a young literary hopeful, he composed an essay called 'The Universe Rigid' whose theme was so inscrutable as to reduce Frank Harris, the editor confronted by it, to raging bewilderment. Waving the proofs of the offending treatise before Wells' face, Harris shouted, 'Dear Gahd! I can't understand six words of it. What do you *mean* by it? For Gahd's sake tell me what it is all *about*. What's the sense of it? What are you trying to say?' At which desperate juncture of his career Wells finds the all-important clue:

> I hit quite by accident upon the true path to successful free-lance journalism. I found the hidden secret in a book by J. M. Barrie called *When a Man's Single*. Why had I never thought in that way before? For years I had been seeking rare and precious topics. 'Rediscovery of the Unique'! 'Universe Rigid'! The more I was rejected the higher my flights had flown. All the time I had been shooting over the target. All I had to do was lower my aim – and hit. . . . I lay in the kindly sunshine beneath the white headland of Beachy Head and read my Barrie. Reading him in the nick of time. How easy he made it seem! I fell into a pleasant meditation. I reflected that directly one forgot how confoundedly serious life could be, it did become confoundedly amusing. For instance, those other people on the beach. . . .[17]

Two days later the *Pall Mall Gazette* had accepted Wells' 'On Staying at the Seaside'; before it appeared in print Wells had sold a second article called 'The Man of the Year Million'. He was on his way at last, in furious pursuit of the gilded hypothetical Noble Simms. And Wodehouse's experience was identical – except that it worked in reverse:

> H. G. Wells in his autobiography says that he was much influenced at the outset of his career by a book by J. M. Barrie called *When a Man's Single*. So was I. It was all about authors and journalists and it urged young writers to write not what they liked but what editors liked, and it seemed to me that I had discovered the prime grand secret. The result was that I avoided the humorous story, which was where my inclinations lay, and went in exclusively for the mushy sentiment which, judging from the magazines, was the thing most likely to bring a sparkle into an editor's eyes. It never worked.

Perhaps for the sake of a whimsical paradox Wodehouse is magnifying the malign effect upon his fortunes of Barrie's advice. In July 1901 he was published in *The Public School Magazine*. In August he appeared in *Answers*. Soon he was accepted by *Tit Bits, Fun*, the *Weekly Telegraph, St James's Gazette, Today* and *Sandow's Physical Culture Magazine*. From January to March 1902 *The Public School Magazine* serialized his first novel, *The Pothunters*. On 9 September 1902, the entry in his diary reads, 'This month starts my journalistic career.' No sooner had he parted company with the Hong Kong and Shanghai than he had appeared in *The Globe* and the *Daily Chronicle*, besides receiving his author's copies from A. & C. Black of *The Pothunters*. He sold work to *Scraps*, made his début in *Punch*, received cheques from *The Sportsman*, the *Evening News, Vanity Fair, Royal, Echo* and the *Windsor Magazine*. At the end of December 1902, after less than four months away from Lombard Street, his journalistic earnings amounted to £65.6s.7d, or pro rata more than his earnings at the bank and his father's allowance put together. Plum had been right and Ernest had been wrong. On leaving Dulwich he should either have been allowed to fend for himself in the open market, as he had requested, or he should have been encouraged to follow his brother Armine to Oxford and subsidize his scholarship as John Buchan had done, with earnings from journalism and authorship. The bank had been a horrible mistake, an unnecessary mistake. Wodehouse had simply been obliged, against his inclinations, to waste two priceless years, jumping to the commands of the Bickersdykes of the industry. Years later, with *Psmith in the City*, he took his revenge.

3

Free-lance in New York

A PUBLIC-SCHOOL FAST BOWLER
adept at the composition of Greek iambics does not seem quite the most
likely candidate for the role of trail-blazer of a transatlantic narrative style
and, in scouring the meagre environmental details of young Wodehouse's
daily round, it might be too easy to overlook the one small portent of so
improbable a development. Idle curiosity and a vague journalistic optimism
must have had something to do with it and, in the light of his subsequent
spectacular triumphs as a songwriter, the lure of Broadway might also have
been a factor, although no hint of this influence is suggested in anything that
Wodehouse ever said. The most powerful attraction of all which New York
held for the disconsolate and baffled bank clerk was probably the most
incongruous one ever to alter the course of a successful writer's life. At
Dulwich he had been a promising heavyweight boxer who might have
pursued trophies in the amateur ranks had not poor eyesight caused him to
hang up his gloves, although he retained his keen interest. Boxing held for
him the same fascination as cricket and rugby, with the important difference
that all its virtuosi were three thousand miles away. In apologizing for the
sad lack of intellectual content in his motivation, he explains away his first
American visit as follows:

> Why America? I have often wondered about that. Why, I mean, from my
> earliest years, was it America that was always to me the land of ro-
> mance? It is not as though I had been intoxicated by visions of cowboys
> and Red Indians. Even as a child I never became really cowboy-

Above Plum Wodehouse, aged seventeen (standing, second from right), in the side that, with the exception of Gullick (far left), deputising for the absent child prodigy, N. A. Knox, went down to Tonbridge on 3 June 1899 in spite of Wodehouse's brilliant bowling.

Right There is much of PGW in the hero of *Mike*, the novel which signals the drift away from school life towards the outside world.

"ONE, TWO, THREE—GO!"

What followed was distinctly a miscarriage of justice. When Rigby had picked up—in the following order—himself, his table, his chair, his books, his pen, and his ink-pot, and mopped up the last drop of ink on his waistcoat with his last sheet of blotting-paper, he proceeded to fall upon the much-enduring Reginald with the stick which he took with him to church on Sundays. Long before the interview concluded, Reginald had reason to regret that it had not been left behind in the pew on the previous Sabbath.

In the case of another hero in similar circumstances we read that "Corporal punishment produced the worst effect upon Eric. He burned, not with grief and remorse, but with rage and passion." Or words to that effect. Just so with our Reginald. His symptoms were identical. In his diary for that day the following entry appears :—

"Got up. Washed. Said my prayers. After school two cads, Linton and Menzies, heaved me over the partition wall ... Rigby's table,

"Let go, you cads!" shrilled Reginald.

"Stop that beastly row there!" shouted Rigby from the other study. "Is that you, Rankin? Come here. I want you."

"I told you so," whispered Menzies. "Come along. Better go by the short cut."

He grabbed Rankin by the knees.

"Saves time," agreed Linton, attaching himself to Rankin's shoulders. "One, two, three—go!"

"Do you hear, Rankin?" said Rigby. "Come here."

And Reginald came.

and Rigb
fault at
prayers.
After
Menzies
clusion
a conf
with R
Wryky
into tr
was g
So Li
study
whicl

"THE SWOOP" OR, HOW CLARENCE SAVED ENGLAND

BY P. G. WODEHOUSE

ILLUSTRATED BY C. HARRISON

ONE SHILLING NETT

ALSTON RIVERS

Above Readers of *The Captain* would have picked up with derisory delight the facetious reference to the odious Eric. *Right* Clarence Chugwater, lonely hero of Wodehouse's anti-war-scare novel, whose reward for saving England from massed invasion is a booking at a music hall where he performs 'a few of those exercises which have made our Scouts what they are, such as deep breathing, twisting the right leg firmly round the neck, and hopping on one foot across the stage'.

Opposite The face that would have looked into the eyes of Kid McCoy in 1904.

'The fact is, I cannot tear myself away from Blandings Castle. The place exercises a sort of spell over me.' Wodehouse in 1928 at Hunstanton Hall, the setting for *Money for Nothing*.

Right The London production of the Broadway hit *Oh Boy!* opened at the Kingsway Theatre on 27 January 1919 with a slightly amended title.

Far right The 1927 Bolton–Wodehouse libretto for *Oh Kay!* had Gertrude Lawrence playing the part of a duke's sister who conspires with him to smuggle bootleg liquor into America.

Below The novelist–musical comedy writer during the 1928 run of *A Damsel in Distress*, a play adapted from his novel about a musical comedy writer. Production costs were divided between Wodehouse himself, the producer–cricketer Basil Foster, A. A. Milne and the owner of the automobile, Wodehouse's co-adaptor Ian Hay.

GEORGE GROSSMITH & EDWARD LAVRILLARD
PRESENT
THE NEW MUSICAL COMEDY

OH JOY!

BOOK & LYRICS BY
GUY BOLTON AND
P. G. WODEHOUSE

MUSIC BY
JEROME KERN

NESTING TIME
AN OLD FASHIONED WIFE
A PACKET OF SEEDS
A PAL LIKE YOU
ROLLED INTO ONE
TILL THE CLOUDS ROLL BY
WORDS ARE NOT NEEDED
YOU NEVER KNEW ABOUT
THE FIRST DAY OF MAY

Price 2/- Each Net.
SELECTION - - 2/6 Net

LONDON
FRANCIS, DAY & HUNTER

Mr and Mrs Wodehouse with daughter Leonora. The dedication to *The Heart of a Goof* reads: 'To my daughter Leonora, without whose never-failing sympathy and encouragement this book would have been finished in half the time.' When told of Leonora's death, Wodehouse remarked: 'I always thought she was immortal.'

conscious, and to Red Indians I was definitely allergic. I wanted no piece of them. And I had no affiliations with the country. My father had spent most of his life in Hong Kong. So had my Uncle Hugh. And two other uncles had been for years in Calcutta and Singapore. You would have expected it to be the Orient that would have called to me. 'Put me somewheres east of Suez', you would have pictured me saying to myself.

On 16 April 1904, when the *St Louis* set sail for New York, Wodehouse was on board travelling second-class, inspired by dreams very different from those which had tempted his relatives to sail off in the opposite direction:

> This yearning I had to visit America, rather similar to that of a Tin Pan Alley songwriter longing to get back, back, back to his old Kentucky shack, was due principally, I think, to the fact that I was an enthusiastic boxer in those days and had a boyish reverence for America's pugilists – James J. Corbett,[1] James J. Jeffries,[2] Tom Sharkey,[3] Kid McCoy[4] and the rest of them. I particularly wanted to meet Corbett and shake the hand that had kay-oed Sullivan. I had a letter of introduction to him, but he was in San Francisco when I landed, and I did not get to know him till a good many years later, when he was a charming old gentleman and one of Broadway's leading actors.[5]

Is Wodehouse being merely facetious in an attempt to distract our attention from any suspicion of an artistic odyssey undertaken in deep earnestness? His behaviour on arrival suggests that his description of himself as a reasonably athletic young man besotted with the great princes of the prize ring is genuine enough. Although he failed to meet his hero Corbett, he did succeed in striking up an acquaintance of sorts with two of the most remarkable pugilistic cards of all time, although neither of these introductions led to a very lasting friendship. Young Griffo, the Australian lightweight, should have been a mine of Runyonesque revelation, but proved to lack the priceless gift of knowing what it was about himself that might be interesting to other people. Griffo, whose short neck and wide shoulders rendered him one of the most freakish lightweights ever seen, used to display his skill with a series of notorious parlour tricks. At least four of his professional contemporaries testified that they had come across Griffo one day seated outside an open-air café plucking flies from the air between finger and thumb. When confronted by sceptical challengers, Griffo did not always wait until a contest had been arranged to settle the debate. His favourite tactic was to stand on a spread handkerchief and defy his opponent to land a blow upon him. Not even his frequent intoxicated condition in the ring had any effect on either his technical skill or his gift for derisory epigrams at the expense of his opponent. And yet when he described to Wodehouse how he had first met the World Lightweight Champion Joe Gans, he displayed a deficiency in the power of dramatic irony amounting more or less to imbecility:

'Somebody asks me would I like to meet Joe Gans, he's over at that table. Would I like to meet Joe Gans, he says, he's over at that table, he says, and I say I would. So he takes me to the table and says, "Here's Young Griffo, Joe," he says, "he wants to meet you," he says. And sure enough it was Joe all right. He gets up from the table and comes right at me.'

I was leaning forward by this time and clutching the arms of my chair. How cleverly, I thought, just as if he had been a professional author, this rather untutored man had led up to the big moment. 'Yes,' I gasped, 'and then?'

'Huh?'

'What happened then?'

'He shakes hands with me. "Hello, Griff," he says. And I say, "Hello, Joe." '

That was all. You might have thought more was coming, but no. He had met Gans, Gans had met him. It was the end of the story.

The encounter with Kid McCoy was much more animated but no less distressing in its way. Wodehouse's dream of shaking the hand that had knocked out John L. Sullivan took a more practical turn when he went out to White Plains to watch the Kid training for a title fight with a rival professor called Philadelphia Jack O'Brien.[6] After whiling away a richly educational afternoon watching the Kid go through his paces, Wodehouse was suddenly visited by a suicidal urge to win undying glory. He later confessed that, even at the time, he experienced a vague sensation of behaving in a manner likely to get him certified. Having witnessed the Kid's formidable technique at close range, this short-sighted retired heavyweight from Dulwich College expressed the desire to step into the ring with McCoy, who assured Wodehouse he would be delighted to box him,

and as we were preparing ourselves for the journey he suddenly chuckled. He had been reminded, he said, of an entertaining incident in his professional career, when he was fighting a contender who had the misfortune to be stone deaf. It was not immediately that he became aware of the other's affliction, but when he did he acted promptly and shrewdly. As the third round entered its concluding stages he stepped back a pace and pointed to his adversary's corner, to indicate to him that the bell had rung, which of course was not the case but far from it.

'Oh, thank you so much,' said the adversary, 'very civil of you.'

He dropped his hands and turned away, whereupon Kid McCoy immediately knocked him out.

It was at this stage in the proceedings that Wodehouse, beginning to be afflicted with mild self-doubt, later said that he developed a yellow streak 'plainly visible through my clothing'. Even as he prepared for his ordeal, he began to interrogate himself:

'Is this wise, Wodehouse?' I asked myself. 'Is it prudent to go getting yourself mixed up with a middleweight champion of the world whose sense of humour is so strongly marked and so what you might almost describe as warped? Is it not probable that a man with a mind like that will think it droll to knock your fat head off at the roots?'

The thought that the most gifted comic novelist of the century was now about to expose himself to so practical a man of affairs remains as frightful now as it suddenly seemed to Wodehouse then, who only elected against the tactic of legging it for the railway station because of his family pride. He was, as he later wrote, at a young man's crossroads. The Kid would probably have preferred to say double-crossroads:

At this moment, as I stood there this way and that dividing the swift mind, like Sir Bedivere, there was a clatter of horse's hooves and a girl came riding up. This was the Kid's wife – he had six of them in an interesting career which ended in a life sentence for murder in Sing Sing prison[7] – and she caused a welcome diversion. We all became very social, and the McCoy–Wodehouse bout was adjourned sine die. I remember that girl as the prettiest girl I ever saw in my life. Or maybe she just looked good to me at the moment.

At which point Kid McCoy passes out of the annals of English literature, leaving Wodehouse to sublimate the incident in the figure of the far more affable Kid Brady, lightweight contender out of New York City whose failure to get a shot at the title is very soon rectified by that consummate pugilistic entrepreneur Psmith. But the affair of Brady and the New York periodical *Cosy Moments* was still far into the future on the day that Wodehouse so nearly had his head removed at the roots. How had the penniless bank clerk risen to the dizzy apex of second-class Atlantic travel on the ss *St Louis*?

After he had been incarcerated in Lombard Street for a few months, it occurred to Wodehouse to test the strength of his old school ties. A London newspaper called *The Globe* ran a daily feature, 'By The Way', a ragbag of jokes, verses and topical allusions, whose assistant editor was one William Beach Thomas, an ex-schoolmaster from Dulwich College. Using their common background as a letter of introduction, Wodehouse received from Thomas the assurance that on those occasions when he, Thomas, felt like taking the day off, Wodehouse might deputize for a remuneration of ten shillings and sixpence. He made his début under this arrangement on 16 August 1901, and was so elated by the editor's acceptance of seven of his items that he began to hope for an offer of permanent employment. There followed from *The Globe* a silence as of the tomb, which was suddenly broken in the following March with an offer to deputize for a week while Thomas went off somewhere. While his employers at Lombard Street grieved over the bout of neuralgia said to have laid their protégé low, Wodehouse further acquainted himself with life in Fleet Street, being so delighted by what he found there that any lingering doubts about the wisdom of adopting a journalistic career vanished for ever. In September, Thomas was due for his annual five-week holiday, and Wodehouse, unable to manufacture a neuralgic fiction of so protracted a length, resigned from the bank and went to work for *The Globe*, even though aware that the engagement was to last only five weeks. No doubt he was consoled by the hope that his past achievements on 'By The Way' had elevated him to the post of unofficial heir designate; sure enough, when Thomas resigned in August 1903, his protégé was appointed assistant editor of 'By The Way' at three guineas a week. In April 1904 he went to America on the Kid McCoy holiday; soon after his return the editor of the column resigned and Wodehouse took over at a salary of five guineas a week. It was in December of that same year that his first song lyric was performed in a professional theatre, and although in the next few years he published all his school novels, initiated a song-writing partnership with Jerome Kern and wrote hundreds of short stories, it was his work on 'By The Way' which occupied much of his thought if not much of his time:

> There was an evening paper called *The Globe*. It was 105 years old and was printed on – so help me – pink paper. It carried on its front page a humorous column entitled 'By The Way'. There was quite a bit of prestige attached to doing it. The column itself was an extraordinary affair. You would quote something from the morning paper and then you'd make some little comment on it. It was always the same type of joke.[8]

The duties attached to 'By The Way' were intense but hardly arduous. Wodehouse says that his presence at the office was required only from ten o'clock until noon, after which he was free to dash back to his rooms in Chelsea and continue writing the squibs, essays, reviews, stories and novels which he sensed would one day liberate him from the drudgery of newspaper deadlines. In the meantime, it was not so degrading a drudgery, and the versifying duties in particular which *The Globe* expected of him must have given him intense delight. Even at Dulwich he had been able to express himself in rhyme with no discernible effort, and all his subsequent work is scattered with proof of an affection for verse so ingrained that he cannot resist making his heroes and heroines recite their own modest poetic effusions to each other with that steely shyness which is the hallmark of the amateur. More to the point regarding the 'By The Way' column, he never quite relinquished his command of the curious journalistic convention of the period of describing trivial events in rhymed couplets. In *The Indiscretions of Archie*, published in 1921, one of the characters reads in a newspaper an account of the previous night's New York West Side Pie-eating Championships. Because the passage is printed in prose, the eye is duped for a moment into thinking this is mere journalistic pastiche; only gradually does the Wodehousean laughter begin to echo, and the sentences to reform themselves in fours:

For yesterday we took a trip
to see the great Pie Championship,
where men with bulging cheeks and eyes
consume vast quantities of pies.
A fashionable West Side crowd
beheld the champion, Spike O'Dowd,
endeavoured to defend his throne
against an upstart, Blake's Unknown.
He wasn't an Unknown at all,
he was young Washington McCall.

There follows a parenthetical apology from the versifier, who is far too modest to claim for himself a place among the giants of antiquity:

We freely own we'd give a leg
if we could borrow, steal or beg
the skill old Homer used to show.
(He wrote 'The Iliad', you know.)
Old Homer swung a wicked pen,
but we are ordinary men,
and cannot even start to dream
of doing justice to our theme.
The subject of that great repast
is too magnificent and vast.
We can't describe (or even try)
the way those rivals wolfed their pie.

Wodehouse remained as editor of 'By The Way' for several years, and was eventually prised out of that cosy journalistic corner through the activities of a New York peculator called A. E. Baerman, who masked a successful career in genteel burglary by posing as a literary agent. In June 1906 Newnes published a new Wodehouse novel called *Love Among the Chickens*, based on an idea contributed by Townend; in the course of telling the story, the author digresses on the technical problems encountered by the farceur who stumbles on the responsibilities of more solemn narrative:

It would be interesting to know to what extent the work of authors is influenced by their private affairs. If life is flowing smoothly, are the novels they write in that period of content coloured with optimism? And if things are running crosswise, do they work off the resultant gloom on their faithful public? If, for instance, Mr W. W. Jacobs had toothache, would he write like Hugh Walpole? If Maxim Gorky were invited to lunch by Lenin, would he sit down and dash off a trifle in the vein of Stephen Leacock?

That passage, which speaks volumes concerning its author's opinion of Walpole and Lenin, occurs in the very book which caused Wodehouse's affairs to go so crosswise as to alter the whole course of his career. With *Love Among the Chickens* Wodehouse was convinced that for the first time he had composed a book likely to appeal to American readers. He accordingly sent the book west, where, after residing briefly at one or two New York addresses, it fell into the acquisitive hands of Baerman, who soon wrote informing the author that he had arranged for a fee of one thousand dollars for the American serial rights. To Wodehouse, whose highest payment to date for a serial had been £60, this sum seemed like 'great gravy'. The money was to be dispatched in October. By Christmas Wodehouse was beginning to get nervous. In March he sent Baerman a cable, which elicited the response of a letter bearing Baerman's signature but not his cheque. In mid-May there arrived Baerman's cheque but not his signature. As Wodehouse later wrote, 'My association with Baerman was the making of me. Critics say my work would be improved by being less morbid, but nobody has ever questioned its depth. That depth I owe to A. E. Baerman. (He owes me about two hundred dollars.)'

At last Wodehouse decided that the only hope of getting anything out of Baerman would be to confront him and, as the agent had no immediate plans for coming to England, it seemed clear that Wodehouse must go to America, which he did in May 1909. On arrival he went to see Baerman, who gave him, not the money, but an address where a writer short of funds might live cheaply. Within a week he had found a more honest agent than Baerman, which admittedly is not saying much, and been the stupefied recipient of $500, for 'The Good Angels', a story purchased by *Cosmopolitan*, and 'Deep Waters' which appeared in *Collier's Weekly*. He now did some rapid arithmetical calculations. The profit from those stories, raised in six days, equalled about five months' labours on 'By The Way'. The implications were too obvious to ignore. He cabled his resignation to *The Globe*, bought himself a second-hand typewriter and a copy of Bartlett's *Familiar Quotations*, and began operations as a New York free-lance, the beauty of the strategy being that he could maintain concurrently all his links with those English magazines trained in the art of paying him for his work.

But the flying start in New York proved to be cruelly misleading. In less than a year he was in full retreat, back at his desk at *The Globe*, chastened by his failure to find American editors willing to pay him for his work on a regular basis. On the credit side there was the considerable consolation of the American publication of his new novel *The Intrusion of Jimmy*, published in London a few months later as *A Gentleman of Leisure*. Under the circumstances it is hardly surprising that *A Gentleman of Leisure* should represent its author's first serious attempt to come to grips with the problem of dual literary nationality. The action of the story begins in New York before switching to Wales. The hero Jimmy Pitt is a Londoner well-known along Broadway. The heroine is the American daughter of an English immigrant; in the final chapter father and daughter are both delighted to resettle in the Old Country while, for those American readers who might otherwise have felt lonely at the prospect of kissing all the principals goodbye, there is the solace of the fade-out, in which the dese-an-dems-an-doze cat-burglar Spike Mullins embarks at Southampton on the SS *St Louis*, hungry for the fleshpots of the Bowery. The mixture seems not to have bemused New Yorkers; within a year a dramatized version was running at the Playhouse Theatre, a development marked by Wodehouse's subsequent dedication of the book 'To Douglas Fairbanks, who many years ago played "Jimmy" in the dramatized version of this novel'.

In his few months in Greenwich Village, Wodehouse had quickly learned that between Dulwich and Manhattan there are certain vital differences not mentioned in any of the guide books, and that, of these differences, the most striking is to do with attitudes towards law and order. When, in *The Pothunters*, the boys of St Austin's are confronted by the police, it occurs to none of them to question the integrity of their inquisitors. Their grasp of diplomacy, perhaps; their powers of ratiocination very likely; but never their honesty. Although the constabulary of old England is not always quite innocent, it at least subscribes to the theory that people assume it to be so and that, in a marginally better world than this one, it might really be so. However crooked an English policeman might happen to be, he never fails to pay lip-service to the pretty fiction of his own unbending rectitude. In New York this is not so, or at least not in the days of Kid McCoy and Spike Mullins. In that open-hearted community there devolved upon the constabulary no such obligation to pretend to stand above the capitalist system which had proved such a benison to everybody except Red Indians.

When Jimmy Pitt takes on a wager to commit a burglary without getting caught, he finds himself embroiled in the coils of lawlessness. Not the professional, scrivener's lawlessness exemplified by a Baerman, but corruption of a much more fundamental kind, flourishing in a society which has become so thoroughly attuned to its discordant overtures as to mistake it for ordinary life. Pitt soon discovers that the father of the girl he loves is a Captain of Police called McEachern, who had entered the force 'with the single idea of becoming rich':

> Some policemen are born grafters, some achieve graft, and some have graft thrust upon them. McEachern had begun by being the first, had risen to the second, and for some years now had been a prominent member of the small and hugely prosperous third class, the class which does not go out seeking graft but sits at home and lets graft come to them.

McEachern is a disgraced ex-Etonian who has been banished to the west and has adopted a surname with Celtic overtones through the advice of three empirical thinkers called O'Flaherty, O'Rourke and Muldoon, who explain to him that a profitable career in the New York police is rendered much more possible by an assumption of Irishness. Encouraged by the thought that even Captain Kidd had had to start in a small way, McEachern had slowly amassed 'the $3,000 which was the price of his promotion to detective-sergeant'. As

Wodehouse explains, McEachern 'did not like paying $3,000 for promotion' but, like all good capitalists, he acknowledges that 'there must be sinking of capital if an investment is to prosper'. As a sergeant, McEachern had managed to step up the rate of his profitability, until at last he found 'that he had $15,000 to spare for any small flutter that might take his fancy. Singularly enough, this was the precise sum necessary to make him a captain'. By the time Jimmy Pitt meets him, McEachern stands 'like Moses on the mountain, looking down into the Promised Land', which in this case happens to be the Old Country; having been banished for his crimes, McEachern has flourished in a less particular society where he has compounded those crimes so profitably as to have arrived at last in a position to buy back his old place in society.

But it is not until Pitt attempts to burgle McEachern's house that the reader begins to be fully educated in the extent of police graft in the city. The policeman catches Pitt in the act, and the latter is puzzled to see that his captor, instead of threatening arrest, or showing rage, is actually delighted to make his acquaintance under such unfortunate circumstances. The moment is an example in action of the methods of the better type of grafter who 'sits at home and lets graft come to them'. With that brisk efficiency which has brought him to his present eminence, McEachern instructs Pitt to come to his office the next day for a business discussion, so that the pair of them can resolve the question of the percentage McEachern will collect from now on from the proceeds of what he takes to be Pitt's lucrative career; it is only because the thief is more honest than the policeman that he is able to outface the crook who is destined in the end to be his own father-in-law.

In all this exposition there is no trace of surprise on Wodehouse's part, or disgust, or moral outrage. He is simply reporting the tribal customs of a remote society, almost as though to question the precepts of that society would be tantamount to insulting his hostess. But why does public outrage not topple the McEacherns of the city? Are they not answerable to the civic panjandrums who control their destiny? The answers to these questions are provided in a book published five years later, *Psmith, Journalist*, in which Psmith, having followed Mike Jackson to the New World, finds himself with so little to do while Mike goes off to educate the savages into the rudiments of cricket that he becomes involved in a slightly different aspect of metropolitan chicanery. This time, as though troubled by the thought that his English readers might mistake his reportage for facetiousness, Wodehouse appends a brief explanatory note to his romance:

> The conditions of life in New York are so different from those in London that a story of this kind calls for a little explanation. There are several million inhabitants of New York. Not all of them eke out a precarious livelihood by murdering one another, but there is a definite section of the population which murders – not casually, on the spur of the moment, but on definitely commercial lines at so many dollars per murder. The 'gangs' of New York exist in fact. I have not invented

them. Most of the incidents in this story are based on actual happenings. The Rosenthal case, where four men, headed by a genial individual calling himself 'Gyp the Blood', shot a fellow-citizen in cold blood in a spot as public and fashionable as Piccadilly Circus and escaped in a motor car, made such a stir a few years ago that the noise of it was heard all over the world and not, as is generally the case with the doings of the gangs, in New York only. Rosenthal cases on a smaller and less sensational scale are frequent occurrences on Manhattan Island. It was the prominence of the victim rather than the unusual nature of the occurrence that excited the New York press. Most gang victims get a quarter of a column in small type.

The journalistic evaluation of eminence with which the note closes is appropriate enough, for it introduces the story of Psmith as the owner–editor of a periodical called *Cosy Moments* which, under his tutelage, alters overnight from a hearts-and-flowers bromide to a crusading enemy of slum landlordism. The crookedness of the town, so far from outraging Psmith, merely comes up to his expectations; indeed, at first, before he has learned the art of turning over stones, he is bitterly disappointed at the glum legality of what he sees:

> We find a town very like London. A quiet, self-respecting town, admirable to the apostle of social reform, but disappointing to one, whom, like myself, arrives with a brush and a little bucket of red paint, all eager for a treat. I have been here a week, and I have not seen a single citizen clubbed by a policeman. No negroes dance cake-walks in the streets. No cowboy has let off his revolver at random in Broadway. The cables flash the message across the ocean: 'Psmith is losing his illusions.'

He retrieves them soon enough when he starts publishing attacks on slum landlords. He is threatened with physical violence, shot at, and finally obliged to recruit the professional expertise of Kid Brady in order to protect himself. He calls up Brady because the police are less than useless to him, being composed of a rank and file of O'Flahertys and O'Rourkes commanded by a higher echelon of McEacherns. In any case the gang warfare of which Psmith soon finds himself a part is only one manifestation of a widespread civic corruption. Fortunately for Psmith, one of the most powerful of all the gang-leaders, the sentimental cat-lover Bat Jarvis, takes a shine to him. And Bat Jarvis is comfortably beyond the law:

> The New York gangs, and especially the Groome Street gang, have brought to a fine art the gentle practice of 'repeating', which, broadly speaking, is the art of voting a number of different times at different polling stations on election days. A man who can vote, say, ten times in a single day for you, and who controls a great number of followers who are also prepared, if they like you, to vote ten times in a single day for

you, is worth cultivating. So the politicians passed the word to the police, and the police left the Groome Street gang unmolested and they waxed fat and flourished.

The same problems which beset Psmith in his campaign to disclose the identity of the slum landlords have been afflicting Kid Brady in his attempts to get a shot at the lightweight title. As Psmith's fellow-journalist Billy Windsor tells the Englishman, 'It's all graft here. You've got to let half a dozen brutes dip into every dollar you earn, or you don't get a chance. If the Kid had a manager, he'd get all the fights he wanted. And the manager would get nearly all the money.' The same hard truths apply to the dispensation of justice; when Psmith helps to haul into the courts a plug-ugly called Repetto, the outcome is a foregone conclusion. Repetto is acquitted on the testimony of his fellow-thugs, by which time it begins to dawn on Psmith that the reason why the administrators of the city are giving him so little help in his campaign to hound the slum landlords is that the administrators are themselves the villains of the piece. When Psmith asks Billy Windsor about a politician called Waring, he is told that Waring used to be Commissioner for Buildings:

> 'What exactly did that let him in for?'
> 'It let him in for a lot of graft.'
> 'How was that?'
> 'Oh, he took it off the contractors. Shut his eyes and held out his hands when they ran up rotten buildings that a strong breeze would have knocked down, and places like that Pleasant Street hole without any ventilation.'
> 'Why did he throw up the job?'
> 'His trouble was that he stood in with a contractor who was putting up a music hall, and the contractor put it up with material about as strong as a heap of meringues, and it collapsed on the third night and killed half the audience.'

At the end of it all, Psmith has finally completed his New York education, and has passed with such honours that he can now instruct Mike Jackson in the same sad lessons which Billy Windsor has been imparting to him. Jackson, whose experience of America has been limited to the cricketing last-ditchers of Philadelphia, cannot understand why Psmith has resorted to the unorthodoxy of the Kid Brady ploy. Patiently Psmith explains why it is useless to run to the law for protection:

> 'We have mentioned the matter to certain of the force. They appeared tolerably interested, but showed no tendency to leap excitedly to our assistance. The New York policeman, Comrade Jackson, like all great men, is somewhat peculiar. If you go to a New York policeman and exhibit a black eye, he will examine it and express some admiration for

the abilities of the citizen responsible for the same. If you press the matter, he becomes bored, and says, "Ain't youse satisfied with what youse got? G'wan!" His advice in such cases is good, and should be followed.'

The best that Wodehouse can bring himself to say about the city is delivered through the agency of Windsor, whose experience as a newspaper reporter has

> given him the knowledge that is only given in its entirety to police and newspapermen: that there are two New Yorks. One is a modern, well-policed city, through which one may walk from end to end without encountering adventure. The other is a city as full of sinister intrigue, of whisperings and conspiracies, of battle, murder and sudden death in dark by-ways, as any town of medieval Italy. Given certain conditions, anything may happen to anyone in New York.

By the time he completed *Psmith Journalist*, Wodehouse was a battle-hardened veteran of the city. Just as *A Gentleman of Leisure* is the work of an unknown free-lance writer existing in Greenwich Village, so *Psmith Journalist* springs out of the experience and sophistication of the maid-of-all-work at the offices of a magazine called *Vanity Fair*, which, although its editorial policy was very far removed from that of *Cosy Moments*, afforded its staff writers the same wide opportunities to further their civic education. As Wodehouse rose rapidly in his several professions, the New York of McEachern and Bat Jarvis recedes from the New York of his reveries, to be superseded by an altogether more glamorous and apparently more respectable town where tycoons incur the inevitable dyspepsia which is the price of their opulence, and impresarios can bring themselves to believe six impossible libretti before breakfast. The Spike Mullins prototype survives, but only as slapstick relief, a transposition into mannered prose of the cartoon burglar with mask, hooped jersey and knapsack with 'Swag' printed in bold lettering. But it is revealing that even as early as the escapade of Jimmy Pitt and the adventures of Psmith down among the landlords, Wodehouse is already meshing disparate fictions together by introducing the leading characters of one as supporting players in others. The most impressive of all the sureties regarding Jimmy Pitt's fitness as a hero is the fact that he once boxed an exhibition bout with Kid Brady. And when Mullins asks him for details of his big London jobs, Pitt replies, 'Did you hear of the cracking of the New Asiatic Bank in Lombard Street?' McEachern too is an honorary citizen of the world which his creator is already beginning to reveal, for he owes his early career at Eton to the charity of an uncle who was at the time 'a man of substance in Lombard Street'.

By now Wodehouse is moving swiftly towards the resolution of his problem, the perfecting of a transatlantic fictional approach to draw readers in equal numbers from both cultures. Gradually his plots begin to be governed by characters who, like their creator, have made the discovery that crossing

the ocean is very much easier than finding your way about once you have
arrived. In order to stabilize the myth of this English-speaking conspiracy,
he established certain tenets to do with money, virility and a sense of
humour, but mainly with money. For example, it may safely be taken as a
general rule that, heroes like Lord Emsworth apart, wherever two or more
members of the landed gentry are gathered together, they are found to be
trembling with eagerness to get their hooks into the nearest gaggle of rich
Americans. For the English by now are sadly impoverished, reduced by the
sting of death duties and the inroads of inbreeding to the unfortunate
predicament of men raised in the expectancy of an unearned income which
no longer exists, and which they are debarred from replacing by the very
congenital dottiness which is the hallmark of their breeding.

Balanced against this race of gibbering bankrupts are their American
counterparts, either hard-necked tycoons tempered in the fires of canning
factories and cattle empires, or meek tycoons chained by matrimony to
demented social climbers animated by a passion to show the folks back in
Duluth or Omaha or Pasadena that they possess that attribute which none of
them can define but which, in the long reaches of sleepless nights in five-star
hotels, they tend to define as class, it being one of the golden rules of this
world that when, say, Jeeves and some Long Island heiress refer to class,
they are thinking of subtly differing concepts. It follows that when Americans come thundering into Wodehousean England, it is usually to buy
something; when English aristocrats come pattering out on to the terrace to
receive American interlopers with civility, it is usually to sell them something, whether a castle, a painting or a younger son. Wodehouse's mid-
Atlantic convention is essentially a mercantile one, run on strict profit-and-
loss lines. Each half of the equation has something which the other half
covets desperately, and if as a rule it is the Americans who come off second-
best, that is due less to any chauvinistic bias on the part of their creator than
to the fact that very often what the invading Yankee hordes are trying to buy
is so intangible that it can hardly be described, let alone wrapped up and
carried away. Although a baronial hall occupied by American tycoons remains a baronial hall, they certainly remain American tycoons.

What emerges from this confrontation between the breeding of the old
world and the dividends of the new is an Athens–Rome axis, in which rich
Americans, anxious to acquire what Mrs Howard Steptoe in *Quick Service*
refers to as 'a much-needed spot of polish', hope to come by that indefinable
and elusive property by doing exactly what Mrs Steptoe does, recruiting the
services of a penniless scion of the aristocracy to instruct them in the social
graces, the irony being that, no matter what benisons the beleaguered
English peerage may be induced to shower on the Mrs Steptoes of this world,
she will remain what nature has made her. As to exactly what that is, even her
nearest and dearest remain unsure, just as, in *Hot Water*, J. Wellington
Gedge of Glendale, California, could not tell you for the life of him exactly
what his wife did before he married her. That she was the widow of an oil
multi-millionaire he is perfectly well aware; that the deceased oilman left

her his multi-millions he is never allowed to forget. But what of the distant days of her spinsterhood? Gedge, ruminating from the sanctuary of the French coast, cannot help considering the possibility that she may once have been a contender for the light-heavyweight title, but soon abandons this theory in favour of something more realistic – 'He sometimes thought she might have been a lion tamer.' But whatever she was then, Mrs Gedge knows with unshakeable conviction what she desires to be now. She desires to be the wife of the United States Ambassador to France, a prospect which fills Mr Gedge with such terrified loathing at the thought of tricorn hats and silken knickerbockers that he consorts with a pair of New York confidence tricksters called Soup Slattery and Oily Carlisle in the conviction that their harmless chicaneries can hardly be less edifying than the life of a tricorned, silken-knickerbockered pantaloon.

But not all Americans are consumed with snobbery or reduced to the texture of blancmange by conjugal poltroonery. When young, Americans are often acceptable creatures, sometimes even desirable. One of Gedge's connections is Packy Franklin, an ex-All-American footballer who comes all the way to London only to fall for the beautiful daughter of a down-home windbag called Senator Ambrose Opal, a solemn rhetorician with 'the massive forehead which seems to go with seats in the American Senate'. Until the power of true love amends his judgment, Franklin finds Europe too small, and is consumed with self-pity at the thought of being 'tied to this one-horse town, this London, miles away from all the tense human drama; it made him feel like a caged skylark'. Perhaps he should have taken as his model a man bringing qualities of stoic acceptance to the ordeal of exile, Freddie Threepwood, who has been whisked away by conjugal nepotism from the cobwebbed columns of Debrett to an altogether more vital and meaningful way of life selling dog biscuits in Long Island.

One of the most useful habits of American travelling tycoons is their consistent success in shaking off or outliving their spouses and moving on with a pathetic optimism curiously American, to what they fervently believe will be more judicious liaisons. Consequently their family trees are forever being garlanded with the poison ivy of a past which, although perhaps unfortunate for its principals, is food and drink to the comic novelist, who cannot have too many ex-relations for the deployment of his forces. Mr Chinnery in *Summer Moonshine*, one of the great fish-glue impresarios of the modern epoch, has always believed that variety is the spice of matrimony and, believing it, has acted upon it with a boldness positively Jeffersonian in its fearless integrity:

> Like so many substantial citizens of his native country, he had married young and kept on marrying, springing from blonde to blonde like the chamois of the Alps leaping from crag to crag.

Perhaps the error which the Chinnerys of this world make is not to travel east and win the hearts of pure, tomboyish girls with names like Kay and

Jane, although their failure to see the wisdom of this course often has benign results; Lord Emsworth is finally relieved of the presence of his sister Constance, 'the Führer of Blandings Castle', by her marriage to a simpletonian New Yorker called James Schoonmaker. His lordship finds such names peculiar, although he is willing to take a balanced view of the problem of transatlantic nomenclature. While marvelling that his son Freddie can not only bring himself to sell dog biscuits in Long Island but sell them in company with a man called Bream Rockmuteller, he admits that, for sheer exoticism, a name like that of his acquaintance, Lord Cork and Orrery, succeeds admirably in maintaining the ascendancy of the Empire.

While Emsworth is suitably impressed by the vast range of holdings possessed by J. B. Polk, it has to be remembered that not all American millionaires have sought their happy lot; a few, like Wilbur Trout in *Summer Moonshine*, have their tycoonery thrust upon them:

> Wilbur Trout was a young man of great amiability whose initial mistake in life had been to have a father who enjoyed making money and counted that day lost which had gone by without increasing his bank balance. Had he been the son of someone humble in the lower income tax brackets, he would have gone through the years as a blameless and contented filing clerk or something of that order, his only form of dissipation an occasional visit to Palisades Park or Coney Island. Inheriting some fifty million dollars in blue chip securities somewhat unsettled him, and he had become New York's most prominent playboy.

Trout, however, is not quite so shallow as his flamboyant social record suggests; in a curiously perceptive moment, when he encounters an ex-fiancée at of all places Market Blandings Station, his thoughts are coloured by overtones of Damon Runyon and F. Scott Fitzgerald:

> They spoke for awhile of the old days, of parties he had given at Great Neck and Westhampton Beach, of guys and dolls who had been her fellow guests at those parties, and of the night when he had dived into the Plaza fountain in correct evening dress.

If Trout's wealth is inherited, there are many American plutocrats who owe their comforts to their own initiative, none less than the enemy of the crag-leaping Chinnery, Sam Bulpitt, a man who navigates the stormy passages in his own life by whistling the choicer items of Tin Pan Alley history. Bulpitt is an American archetype, the energetic go-getter moving to eminence through the inviting chaos of a classless society, beginning in true Irving Berlin fashion as a singing waiter, sinking to the degradation of a travelling salesman in vacuum cleaners before winning through to the purple of the nation's foremost process server. Chinnery, whose own beginnings were modest enough to have embraced an apprenticeship in the retail end of the hot-dog market, recognizes Bulpitt as a worthy adversary, as well he might, for Bulpitt has been around in rather more than the merely geographical sense:

> 'One time I slapped a plaster on Young Kelly, the middleweight challenger, in his own home. He was having supper with his brother Mike, the all-in wrestler, his cousin Cyril, who killed rats with his teeth, and his sister Genevieve, who was a strong woman in vaudeville. What crossed my mind was the time I handed the papers to that snake charmer. Sixteen snakes of all sizes, and he sicked 'em all on to me.'

Bulpitt's only professional defeat had been at the hands of yet another tycoon, one Elmer Z. Zagorin, the Night Club King, whose possession of fifty million dollars had not prejudiced him in his refusal to pay a forty-dollar bill for hair restorer on the undeniably logical grounds that it had failed to restore his hair. Zagorin had foiled Bulpitt by dying on him, expiring from a heart attack brought on by the sheer excitement of being tailed by so resourceful a man – 'Like all these well-to-do millionaires, he hadn't been able to get a kick out of anything till I came along.' And yet Bulpitt, formidable as he might be, recognizes true class when he sees it, making an observation of some relevance to the constant transatlantic debate conducted in Wodehouse's world. In analysing the behaviour of Lord Abbot, who is being difficult about a marriage, Bulpitt remarks, 'Those haughty English aristocrats are like that. Comes of treading the peasantry underfoot with an iron heel, I guess.' In *Uneasy Money*, Lord Dawlish, who has been led to believe that 'there's a lot of money to be made out there', makes some the easy way when Ira J. Nutcombe of Chicago leaves him a million pounds for curing his tendency to slice his approach shots. Eustace in *The Girl on the Boat*, poetry-writing son of a theosophist screwball called Mrs Horace Hignett, is engaged for a while to the daughter of the New York millionaire Rufus Bennett. Not that Mrs Hignett is altogether complacent in the matter of the financial balance of power between our two great nations. As befits the authoress of such daunting works as *The Spreading Light* and *What of the Morrow?*, she has taken steps to spread the light today, by conducting a one-woman invasion of the west:

> About this time there was a good deal of suffering in the United States, for nearly every boat that arrived from England was bringing a fresh swarm of British lecturers to the country. Novelists, poets, scientists, philosophers and plain, ordinary bores. Mrs Hignett had come over with the first batch of immigrants; for, spiritual as her writings were, there was a solid streak of business sense in this woman, and she meant to get hers while the getting was good. She was halfway across the Atlantic with a complete itinerary booked, before ninety per cent of the poets and philosophers had finished sorting out their clean collars.

The great turning point in Wodehouse's mid-Atlantic development is *Piccadilly Jim* (1917), in which we meet the playboy Jimmy Crocker and the meek-mannered tycoon Peter Pett, whose marriage to the deadly carnivore Nesta Ford Pett, society hostess and sloppy novelist, has endowed him with the unfortunate inheritance of a stepson called Ogden, star of an earlier novel set in England, *The Little Nugget*. Ogden, being a ward of the well-heeled, is a fair mark for kidnappers, who have made the sport of snatching the little wretch 'as popular as football', especially with Mr Pett, who earnestly believes that the only educational institution equipped to cope with his stepson is Sing Sing. Indeed, Ogden Ford is so odious a character that he casts a pall over the novel in which he makes his début, a pall which not even the levity of his creator is altogether able to disperse. With *The Little Nugget*, Wodehouse appears to have started out with the intention of composing a lightly parodic version of a conventional Victorian work in the style of a Wilkie Collins novel; both in its introductory chapter summaries – 'In which the Little Nugget is introduced to the reader, and plans are made for his future by several interested parties' – and in the device of switching the focal point by changing narrators, the book nods deferentially in the direction of *The Moonstone*, but not for long. As if impatient to get on with the story, Wodehouse soon abandons his plan and proceeds in more conventional style without quite succeeding in dispersing the gloom conjured by Ogden's ugly nature. In fact, *The Little Nugget* does not read like a comic novel at all; the tone is altogether too sombre for the propagation of the straight-faced joke it embodies. Ogden is the hopelessly spoiled son of the rich who chews tobacco in the dormitory and responds to a mild caning by smashing every window in the building.

What is the effect of this monstrous boy on the gentle Mr Pett? Perhaps no more calamitous than that of Nesta's sister Eugenia on Jimmy Crocker's father, an ex-actor called Bingley Crocker, who has been dragged to London in the wake of his wife's demented social snobbery. Exile is always painful, but especially so in the summer months for a baseball fanatic, and, once the baseball season starts, Bingley tends to lapse into a state of narcolepsy reminiscent of the miner's dream of home. His wife, one of those visigoths to whom the subtle distinctions of life are non-existent, sends him to cricket matches under the impression that that game is identical to baseball. On the day before we meet him, Crocker has been packed off to the Oval to watch Surrey play Kent in the County Championship, and has returned home in that condition of numbed imbecility to which American tourists invariably succumb in such circumstances. The aftermath comprises one of the great set pieces of transatlantic comedy, making one of the most affecting moments throughout the entire Wodehousean oeuvre; when the baffled Bingley Crocker reads his morning paper in a forlorn attempt to discover exactly what it is that he is supposed to have seen at Kennington, we may observe the chronicler of Mike Jackson introducing the earnest subject of cricket into a fictional context for the last time. In a few subsequent novels and short stories, particularly 'How's That, Umpire?', cricket features prominently, but it is in *Piccadilly Jim* that for the last time the game is presented as a symbol of the Higher Life.

Crocker's problem is that by attending the match and then reading the newspaper report he is only compounding bored confusion with anguished bewilderment. If the actions of the players were clouded in mystery, the description of their movements seems positively demented. In a despairing last effort to maintain a hold on his own sanity, Crocker summons Bayliss the butler, and is astonished to discover that Bayliss too was present at the Oval, purely from choice, and considers that what he saw there was highly exciting. Crocker questions this, at which Bayliss patiently explains that it was 'a sticky wicket'. This is news to Crocker, who until now has not suspected the remote possibility of the existence of such a phenomenon. Again Bayliss attempts to clarify his employer's cluttered mind, telling him that the reason why, to the uninitiated, the action might have appeared quiet was that the wicket, that is, the turf, was sticky, that is, wet, which caused the batsmen to bat slowly, that is, cautiously, because 'the stickiness of the wicket enables the bowlers to make the ball turn more sharply in either direction as it strikes the turf'. By now Crocker, reduced to intellectual disarray by all this arcane instruction in a game where the pitcher actually desires the ball to hit the ground before reaching the enemy, begins to experience pains in the head, and in resignation abandons the semantic approach in favour of the purely statistical, turning to what, with the touching innocence of a savage, he calls 'the boxscore'. Here he reads that Hayward[9] has been 'c Woolley[10] b Carr[11] 67'. Bayliss tells him that this means that after scoring 67 runs Hayward has been caught off a delivery by the slow bowler Carr. On hearing that Hayward, or indeed anybody, is capable of scoring 67 runs in a single innings, Crocker is reduced to abject wonder, informing Bayliss that not even Home-Run Baker is capable of such feats. Bayliss, imperturbable as befits his station, replies, 'I am not familiar with Mr Baker, sir.'

In this touching scene, as Athens politely agrees to educate Rome in the finer points, we see the Dulwich College fast bowler heading unobtrusively for the pavilion for the last time, aware that his hope of commanding mid-Atlantic support demands the jettison of a game which, for all its loveliness, has failed to take root in a land which prefers the regrettable excesses of baseball. Very soon after this painful exchange between Crocker and Bayliss, there is another, more joyous conversation between Crocker and the newly-arrived Mr Pett. Never having succeeded in curbing his unfortunate democratic tendency to open his own front door to visitors instead of leaving such lowly duties to the likes of Bayliss, Crocker has been mistaken for the butler by Pett, just as, in identical circumstances a generation earlier, Ann Pornick had so forgotten her new station as Mrs Arthur Kipps as to open her front door to the knock of the Reverend G. Porrett Smith and family, and allowed them to assume she was her own housemaid. But Crocker's indiscretion has happier results. Recognizing Pett as an emissary from the civilized side of the world, he cannot resist the temptation to ask him for the latest news of his beloved New York Giants, and can hardly contain his happiness when Pett tells him they are leading in the pennant race:

> 'Matty's in shape.'
> 'He is? The old arm working well?'
> 'Like a machine. He shut out the Cubs the day before I sailed.'[12]

Wodehouse stands alone among the novelists of his time in his ability to integrate within the limits of a single character on a single day an awareness of two committed ball-throwers so violently contrasted in style and attitude as Donald Ward Carr and Christopher Mathewson but, at the time he wrote *Piccadilly Jim*, there was no doubt that his allegiances lay so strongly with Carr that it would have seemed ridiculous to everybody, Wodehouse included, to suggest that one day his position might change. But the passage of time brings in the wildest wonders, as we shall see.

In studying the plight of those two hapless henpecked exiles, Pett and Crocker, it is hard to decide which of them was in the more unfortunate position. Admittedly Mrs Crocker had dragged her victim to England while Pett had been allowed to stay home for most of the time. But then Pett had to endure the double torment of marriage to a wife who was not only rampant with snobbery but was also a follower of that basest of all human occupations, the writing of romantic novels. Crocker, in pleading the desperation of his case, would no doubt nominate as evidence the terrible precision of his wife's aspirations. For it is a long time now since her vague reveries began to congeal into practicality; at one point we find Bingley glumly making lists of his coming transmogrification:

> Lord Crocker
> Lord Bingley Crocker
> Lord Crocker of Crocker
> The Marquis of Crocker
> Baron Crocker
> Bingley, first Viscount Crocker.

It may not quite approach the gaseous wonder of Lord Cork and Orrery, but it is serious enough to reduce poor Bingley to the status of something that has just crawled out of an apple. He knows that Mrs Crocker is serious enough, and has, so to speak, cased out the joint with a thoroughness which has left no last corner of that joint uncased. She is well aware, for example, that if young Jimmy Crocker persists in dining with professional pugilists and being ejected from the best restaurants only after a struggle, then her plans for smothering Bingley in an ermine shroud will never come to fruition. She has already heard of the case of a deserving man who, after contributing lavishly to party funds, was fobbed off with a lousy knighthood simply because his son had a habit of indulging low tastes. Bingley therefore has a vested interest in Jimmy's misdemeanours, which may yet save him from the disgrace of ennoblement.

Pett, meanwhile, does little more than Bingley to please Mrs Crocker. When they meet, she sizes him up like a vivisectionist on the prowl:

> She was thinking how hopelessly American Mr Pett was; how baggy his clothes looked; what absurdly shaped shoes he wore; how appalling his hat was; how little hair he had; and how deplorably he lacked all those graces of repose, culture, physical beauty, refinement, dignity and mental alertness whch raise men above the level of the common cockroach.

By common cockroach she presumably means other men, and in this regard Jimmy would seem to agree with her. While he likes old Pett, he has scant regard for those business abilities which have led him into his present impasse; it takes Jimmy the wastrel to see through the pretence of Big Business that it has to work hard and show intelligence in order to gratify its lust for gold. Jimmy believes that it is 'quite easy to make a large fortune. I watched Uncle Pete in his office this morning, and all he does is sit at a mahogany table and tell the office boy to tell callers that he has gone away for the day'. Having divined the innermost secret of the capitalist system, Jimmy Crocker dances off the last page into the arms of the heroine, leaving the rest of the characters torn between an obstinate conviction that America is 'a land of adventure, it's a place where anything may happen', and an ambition to muscle in on the ancient European tradition. When Wodehouse suggests that anything may happen, he is thinking particularly of petty larceny and a cheerful, indiscriminate violence:

> Candy-selling aliens jostled newsboys, and huge drayhorses endeavoured to the best of their ability not to grind the citizenry beneath their hoofs. Eastward, pressing on to the City Hall, surged the usual dense army of happy lovers on their way to buy marriage licences.

Patriots from both sides of the ocean might be inclined to wonder why, if Mrs Bingley Crocker so fervently desired to practise the art of snobbery, she did not practise it on her native ground. The answer is that while, like Bernard Shaw's aunt, she would have refused an earl because he was not a duke, any old earl, even a bogus one, was more acceptable to her than the genuine imitations to be found in New York society. That is why she is so scornful of the social activities of her sister Mrs Pett, who is content to splash about in the backwaters of the larger life:

> Mrs Pett prided herself on the Bohemian elements in her parties, and had become during the past two years a human dragon, scooping genius from its hiding places and bringing it into the open. At different spots in the room stood the six resident geniuses to whose presence in

the home Mr Pett had such strong objections, and in addition to these she had collected so many more of a like breed from the environs of Washington Square that the air was clamorous with the hoarse cries of futurist painters, esoteric Buddhists, vers libre poets, interior decorators and stage reformers. . . . Men with new religions drank tea with women with new hats. Apostles of free love expounded their doctrines to persons who had been practising them for years without realising it. All over the room throats were being strained and minds broadened.

Like Wodehouse himself, Pett cannot abide any kind of poet, but especially the kind that cheats by not bothering to rhyme. To Pett the lowliest Tin Pan Alley hack is a nobler creature than the charlatans who roam about his house – 'She's literary, you know. She's filled the house with poets and that sort of thing.' At the last, the two worms turn. Pett and Crocker assert their manhood, although the latter soon unasserts his when he is filled with compassion at the sight of his wife, shorn of her dreams. Crocker junior, who thinks that tycoonery is child's play and is perhaps right, melts into the sunset with nothing more to sustain him in his newfound maturity than a beautiful bride and a certain limited experience in newspaper offices, precisely the assets which Wodehouse himself had possessed not so many years before writing the book.

Piccadilly Jim is built on symbols which were soon to become familiar to all Wodehouse readers, the twin pillars of a plot located in Piccadilly and Park Avenue, the interim ocean voyage linking one with the other by furthering the cause of romance, the interplay between innocent malingering regenerated by true love, and worldly greed so insatiable that it has moved on from money to titles, with all its creatures flung into constantly shifting deployments through the licence of assumed and mistaken identity. It is a novel written by a man who has seen his lyrics sung at the Aldwych Theatre as well as at the Princess, who has learned the conventions of musical comedy plotmaking, who has come to be accepted as readily by the editor of *Vanity Fair* as by his counterpart at the offices of *The Strand*, who has known the limited pleasures of life in Greenwich Village as intimately as those in Dulwich Village. His constant crossing to and from New York, his partnership with Jerome Kern, his courting of the future Mrs Wodehouse at Long Beach, above all his rejection for service in the Great War by both the British and American authorities, who disqualified him for the poor eyesight which years before had put paid to his pugilistic ambitions, all these factors contributed to the gradual process by which he became a dual citizen, a kind of literary Herbert Marshall ploughing not one lonely furrow but two at the same time.

But cleverly as he amended his imaginative flights to suit two disparate audiences, Wodehouse was unable to cope with one aspect of the problem. When Crocker looks to Bayliss for enlightenment regarding the previous day's events at the Oval, he is speaking for all America, and there are not always Baylisses on hand to be so obliging. There was nothing for it but to banish cricket from the fictional Eden of his imaginary world. But cricket had been a priceless asset to him in the past, and had indeed, through the agency of Psmith and Mike Jackson, helped to transport him from the Big Side of mere schoolboy yarnspinning into the world of adult fiction. All his past experience told him that, no matter what the purveyors of *vers libre* might insist to the contrary, a world without sport-besotted men is not a world which bears much resemblance to the real thing. And so if cricket had to be abandoned in the cause of mid-Atlanticism, what could he put in its place? Not Association football, which he had used successfully enough in *Psmith in the City* and in an early short story called 'The Goalkeeper and the Plutocrat'; although his knowledge of the game was surprisingly wide for a graduate of a rugby-playing institution like Dulwich, it was clearly of no practical value in a land whose footballers wrapped themselves up in bolsters with the firm intention of stamping each other to death. And yet he was better equipped than any other writer of his time to write about team games, combining as he did unique technical resource, unflagging literary industry, and experience as a player at a fairly high level.

It should be stressed that in kissing cricket goodbye, he did so only in fiction, not in life. His letters to Townend refer constantly to the triumphs and disasters of the Dulwich players and, on a more exalted plane, to the failure of the England bowlers to curb the genius of Bradman. But passionately though he loved the game, he knew it must be expelled from his work. Cricket was like some rare wine: it would not travel. Tours like the one which had taken Mike Jackson to Philadelphia had fallen on barren ground after all. That cause was dead. But there was one other game which most assuredly would travel, had already travelled, a game whose highland origins had not prevented it from being annexed by the athletes of the New World. This game was golf, which had the added inestimable advantage of being curiously prone to the excesses of corpulent millionaires who came on to the links in search of a youth they had lost and perhaps never possessed. Wodehouse himself was never much of a player but, in confessing his inadequacies, he insisted on his love of the game and wondered whether 'we of the canaille don't get more pleasure out of it than the top-notchers'. In that remark lies the germ of at least half his golf stories, which concern men like the late Ira J. Nutcombe, who was willing to give away a fortune in return for the reduction of his handicap.

The great golf campaign opened in 1922 with *The Clicking of Cuthbert* and, by the time it closed more than fifty years later with the publication of *The Golf Omnibus*, the technical terms of the game had changed rather more than the antics of the players who used them. In 1973 Wodehouse sadly asked himself what had happened to the armoury of the old days, the mashie, the cleek, the spoon and baffy. But those had been the happy times before the marauding hordes descended from the west to snatch the laurels from the hands of the gallant pioneers. In his youth, Wodehouse recalled that to be a golfing virtuoso you had to have been born in Scotland, 'preferably with a name like Sandy McHoots or Jock Auchermuchty'. These men were not as other men for, apart from having unpronounceable names, they were demi-gods:

> And how we reverenced them. 'These', we said, 'are the men whose drives fly far, like bullets from a rifle, who when they do a hole in par regard it as a trifle.' Of such as these the bard has said 'Hech thrawfu' raltie rorkie, wi' thect ta' croonie clapperhead and fash wi' unco' pawkie.' And where are they now? How long is it since a native Scot won an Open? All Americans these days, except for an occasional Mexican. . . . I wonder what Tommy Morris, winner of the British Open four years in succession, would have had to say to all this number six iron, number twelve iron, number twenty-eight iron stuff. Probably he wouldn't have said anything, but made one of those strange Scottish noises at the back of his throat like someone gargling.[13]

In turning to golf as a source of material, Wodehouse soon found himself committed to an approach radically contrasted to his earlier cricket writing. The most striking single truth about the Mike Jackson–Psmith cricket tales is that they are romances without a heroine, in which the accounts of cricket matches are presented with all the punctilio of a *Morning Post* report. These accounts are seriously intended, technically highly informed, and very nearly reach the point where they become running commentaries. In the golf stories, although sometimes the climax consists of a hole-by-hole description of some vital challenge match, the *raison d'être* of the story is never the game itself but the misuse to which the protagonists are putting it in the hope of determining the future direction of their lives. In story after story, stern-faced young men battle it out on the links, not for the glory or a silver cup, but for the love of some sylph in brown brogues awaiting the outcome in the clubhouse, having been raised to believe that a proficiency at golf is the sign of a well-spent youth. People challenge each other to golf matches for every imaginable reason except that golf itself is an important part of life. Destinies are resolved on the Wodehousean links, trysts are plotted, hashes settled, marriages arranged, fortunes won and lost. The clubhouse is the scene of ecstatic betrothals and tearful returnings of the ring. Strong silent men are forever being purged in the banked fires which lie smouldering beneath the bunker at the short thirteenth, and a mate can prove her sterling worth by understanding that the cardinal rule in life is never to throw your head up. Although much of the humour of the narrative derives from the purblind fanaticism of some golfers, the underlying assumption is always that in the last reckoning, the game matters far less than the personal issues it might be made to resolve. When Mike Jackson strives so mightily to transform Sedleigh School from a cricketing plague spot to a worthy opponent for the great cricketing public schools, he strives in the awareness that if he succeeds, then Sedleigh will continue to be awarded coveted fixtures, and to enjoy a vastly improved sporting status long after he has left and been swallowed up in the maelstrom of adult life. By excelling at cricket he believes he can alter the physical circumstances of pupils of the school currently still in swaddling clothes. And it will all have been worth while because it is a truism that the better the quality of cricket in a young man's environment, the better the quality of his life. In contrast, Wodehouse's golfers yearn for virtuosity, not for the sake of the game itself, nor in the mere pursuit of excellence, but in order to win a lady's hand, or ingratiate some tycoon, or further their own fortunes in some way. They play golf for extra-golfing reasons whereas, for a Mike Jackson, life and cricket have become very nearly the same thing. It is revealing that while all the cricket stories are without heroines, there is not one among Wodehouse's golf fictions which does not have a beautiful damsel ready to step out on to the first tee. In other words, the golfing stories are essentially frivolous, while the cricket tales are not.

One obvious explanation for this contrast is that while he was writing cricket fiction Wodehouse, little more than a schoolboy himself, knew he was writing for other schoolboys who took the game in deadly earnest, whereas the golf stories were composed for an adult readership which had been advised to regard their author as a master-comedian. There is another contributory factor. Although he was an accomplished cricketer, Wodehouse never rose in the golfing world much higher than a clubhouse mutt whose prowess never remotely approached his enthusiasm. When he was writing the Mike Jackson stories, he loved cricket far too much, and perceived its subtleties far too well, to poke fun at it. But as a golfer he was slightly farcical and so determined to make a farce out of the game generally. There is not one player among his golfing heroes and heroines who is not either making jokes about the game or embodying the most facetious joke of all, an inability to get the game into focus.

As to the mentality which is so blinkered as to regard the deity as the Great Scorer in the Sky, there is the cautionary example of Mortimer Sturgis in 'A Mixed Threesome', who, when accused of aspiring to too large a family, innocently asks, 'What's bogey?'. By the time he published *The Heart of a Goof* (1926), Wodehouse had refined his method to imply that the true meaning of pantheism is that God and Golf are one:

> It was a morning when all nature shouted 'Fore!'. The breeze, as it blew gently up from the valley, seemed to bring a message of hope and cheer, whispering of chip-shots holed and brassies landing squarely on the meat. The fairway, as yet unscarred by the irons of a hundred dubs, smiled greenly up at the azure sky; and the sun, peeping above the trees, looked like a giant golf ball perfectly lofted by the mashie of some unseen god and about to drop dead by the pin of the eighteenth. . . . Plus fours gleamed in the sunshine, and the air was charged with happy anticipation.

His *Golf Omnibus*, which should perhaps have been titled *The Mashie of an*

Unseen God, reveals one other very curious fact about Wodehouse's golfing stories, which is their involvement with culture generally and literature in particular. Time and again the negation of golfing virtue is defined as a taste for the composition of execrable novels or unreadable poetry, or even, as in the case of hideous Rodney Spelvin, both. McCay, the club secretary in 'Archibald's Benefit', is so impenitent a sentimentalist that he can 'take Browning without anaesthetics'. Archibald, in contrast, extends his love of poetry no further than the works of George M. Cohan, and cannot take Browning at all. But it is his misfortune to fall in love with Margaret, who is notorious for her habit of quoting Tennyson at people whether she dislikes them or not. In the end all is well, because Margaret turns out to be a poetic fake who learns to love Archibald the moment he wins a tournament. In *The Clicking of Cuthbert*, the confrontation between Culture and Golf becomes tangible when the meetings of the Wood Hills Literary and Debating Society are punctuated by the sudden intrusion of golf balls mishit from the nearby fourth tee; when the young novelist Raymond Parsloe Devine was reading from his works, a sliced ball had very nearly decapitated him; 'two inches to the right, and Raymond must inevitably have handed in his dinner-pail.' Devine is a rising young novelist, and at this crisis in his affairs, Wodehouse tells us, he rose a clear foot and a half. When Cuthbert, the culprit, falls for Adeline, he is horrified to learn that while she is unimpressed by his feat of winning the French Open, she is idolatrous towards Devine because 'he is more Russian than any other young English writer'. At which point Cuthbert makes one of the most pointed remarks which Wodehouse ever published: 'I should have thought the wheeze would be to be more English than any other young English writer.'

The battle is now joined between the healthy philistine slicer of golf balls and the author of impressively unreadable works of fiction. Cuthbert, instead of trying to play the game on tom tiddler's ground, makes a disastrous attempt to carry the battle to the enemy by attending lectures on *vers libre* poetry, the Seventeeth-century Essayists, the Neo-Scandinavian Movement in Portuguese Literature, and something which Wodehouse mysteriously defines as 'other subjects of a similar nature'. There is no telling what damage Cuthbert might have inflicted on his game had it not been for the sudden development by which the abstraction of Russian literary realism is made flesh in the arrival at the local clubhouse of the great Vladimir Brusiloff:

> Vladimir specialized in grey studies of hopeless misery, where nothing happened till page three hundred and eighty, when the moujik decided to commit suicide.

As Wodehouse observes, 'it was tough going for a man whose deepest reading hitherto had been Vardon on the Push-Shot'. When Cuthbert feels obliged by his love of Adeline to attend one of Brusiloff's lectures, he is not at first encouraged:

> Doubtless with the best motives, Brusiloff had permitted his face to become almost entirely concealed behind a dense zariba of hair, but his eyes were visible through the undergrowth, and it seemed to Cuthbert that there was an expression in them not unlike that of a cat in a strange backyard surrounded by small boys.

At first, as Cuthbert notices the cloud of deep depression surrounding Brusiloff, he wonders if the Russian realist has not had bad news from home. On the contrary, the latest Russian bulletins have cheered up Brusiloff no end:

> Three of his principal creditors had perished in the last massacre of the bourgeoisie, and a man whom he owed for five years for a samovar and a pair of overshoes had fled the country, and had not been heard of since.

The source of the man's wretchedness is not the thought of home, but the suspicion that everybody attending the lecture conceals about his or her person the manuscript of a realist novel, which makes him wish 'he had stayed at his quiet home in Nijni-Novgorod, where the worst thing that could happen to a fellow was a brace of bombs coming in through the window'. His audience hardly suspected any of this because, when he spoke, Brusiloff 'gave the impression that each word was excavated from his interior by some up-to-date process of mining'. Wodehouse now plays his trump card. This paragon of morbidity, this lion of literary salons all over suburbia, this dedicated creative artist, thinks much less of the heroes of Russian fiction than he does of the creator of Psmith, whom he reveres so highly that he is willing to extend to him the accolade of parity:

> 'No novelists any good except me. Sovietski – yah! Nastikoff – bah! I spit me of dem all. No novelists anywhere any good except me. P. G. Wodehouse and Tolstoi not bad. Not good, but not bad. No novelists any good except me.'

A man whose creative faculties are in such perfect working order cannot very well fail to see the transcendental beauty of golf, and Brusiloff soon announces that his true gods are not Gogol or Dostoevsky but Abe Mitchell and Harry Vardon. It is not long before Cuthbert and Adeline are married, while Devine drifts off to California, where he occupies his time in the composition of scenarios for the Flicker Film Company, which may be a fate worse than death, but no less than a pretentious novelist deserves.[14]

Wodehouse uses the same plot in 'Chester Forgets Himself', in which Chester Meredith falls for Felicia Blakeney. He thinks she is a highbrow, but secretly she yearns for a lover so ignorant that he does not know 'whether Artbashiekeff was a suburb of Moscow or a new kind of Russian drink'.

Chester is saved from the true depth of self-abasement only by his past experience:

> Those who have not had the benefit of a sound training in golf are too apt to go wrong. Goaded by sudden anguish, they take to drink, plunge into dissipation, and write vers libre.

Chester's difficulty resides in the fact that Felicia's mother is a slushy novelist who publishes works with titles like *The Stench of Life*, which is itself a sequel to *Grey Mildew*. Fortunately for him, Felicia has had more than enough of all this and flings herself into his arms the moment she realizes that this man, who regards the links as 'Nature's cathedral', tends to swear like a sailor when things do not go smoothly on the greens.

But the most obnoxious manifestation in all Wodehouse's works of the Anti-Golf is Rodney Spelvin, who modestly describes himself as 'a maker of verbal harmonies'. Spelvin, when we first meet him in 'Rodney Fails to Qualify', adheres to the Obscurantist school of poetic composition; when an editor innocently inquires after the precise meaning of a morceau entitled 'Wine of Desire', the poet responds by volunteering the information that the said morceau is a sonnet, not a mining prospectus. Clearly, a man of such presumption is up to no good, and it is no time at all before he is upstaging the golf-playing William Bates in the struggle for the soul of Jane Packard, although the love-poetry which Rodney flings at her foolishly impressionable head, so far from being an authentic Spelvinesque effusion, has a distinctly Gilbertian ring about it:

> You are the tree on which the fruit of my life hangs.

Spelvin's undoing comes when he rashly expresses a preference for the landscape to Jane's driving; instead of complimenting her on having belted one straight down the middle, he observes of the scene that 'that calm wooded hollow, bathed in the golden sunshine reminds me of the island-valley of Avilion'. Five years later he is back again, having managed to transmogrify himself by the power of pure egomania into a novelist of 'the neodecadent style'. His latest success, *The Purple Fan*, very nearly unhinges Jane's reason, and it is only when she becomes distracted by her infant son's failure to hold a mashie in the correct way that she realizes that Spelvin can never be to her what William is. But men who write novels like *The Purple Fan* are not easily put off, and two years later Spelvin is back again, threatening the heart of William's maiden sister Anastasia. She, however, being a dedicated golfer, proves more than equal to the challenge, and ends by converting him away from the fleshpots of the aesthetic life on to the straight and narrow path which leads to the first tee. Rodney forsakes literature and becomes an apprentice golfer tremulous with ambition, and can hardly believe his luck when Anastasia agrees to take him in hand, saying, 'I may be a vers libre poet but I have some sense of what is fitting'.

The time was not distant when Rodney Spelvin, who in these stories is little more than a literary archetype, would become the receptacle of a much more specific disgust, as we shall see.

Many of these tales of passion on the links are acted out in a locale so vague as very nearly to qualify as limbo; British and American readers could identify with them in equal parts, although the latter often had the satisfaction of knowing that Wodehouse was pitching the ball in the middle of their territory. In 'High Stakes', a pair of unscrupulous tycoons, Bradbury Fisher and J. Gladstone Bott, vie for the services of an admirable Crichton called Blizzard. When Bott acquires a baffy used by the great Bobby Jones in his first Infants' Tournament, Fisher goes insane with jealousy, and offers his rival four million dollars for it. Bott refuses to bite. What he wants is Blizzard, the greatest butlerine virtuoso on Long Island. The only slight hitch comes when the two men try to agree on the stakes:

> 'Very well. I'll play you for Blizzard.'
> 'Against what?'
> 'Oh, anything you please. How about a couple of railroads?'
> 'Make it three.'
> 'Very well.'

The plot of 'High Stakes', which owes much to that ancient American classic *Ruggles of Red Gap*, reveals the interesting theory that when it comes to golf there is such a thing as honour among thieves. When Blizzard changes hands as a result of the great golf match, neither player dreams of welshing on the bet. And yet who are Fisher and Bott? Nothing more than a couple of hornswogglers whose rivalry had first flowered in somewhat less auspicious circumstances than those in which the reader finds them:

> At Sing Sing, where each had spent several happy years of early manhood, they had run neck and neck for the prizes which that institution has to offer. Fisher secured the position of catcher on the baseball nine in preference to Bott, but Bott just nosed Fisher out when it came to the choice of a tenor for the glee club. Bott was selected for the debating contest against Auburn, but Fisher got the last place on the crossword puzzle team, with Bott merely first reserve.

In such ways did Wodehouse change sports as well as locales in mid-career, remaining forever true to his precept of mixing up the two English-speaking nations so inextricably that some of his novels can hardly be defined as to their spiritual location at all. One of his last novels, *Company for Henry*, is also one of his most underrated, as well as being revelatory in its full display of the mid-Atlantic technique. Published in 1967, it is set in a vaguely modern England in which the impoverishment of the gentry has reached so crucial a stage that any American is bound to appear in the glowing lineaments of a saviour. To Henry Paradene, owner of Ashby Hall in Sussex, the fact that a rich New Yorker called J. Wendell Stickney believes himself to be a distant family connection sounds providential and the clanging of the merchandise of Stickney's Dairy Products very much like the arrival of the marines. For Paradene is penniless, desiring nothing more than to dump his ancient pile on the first sucker he can find, and return to the simple life he once enjoyed as a member of the chorus in second-string musical comedy companies. Indeed, he loathes Ashby Hall so vehemently that in distracted moments he 'thought nostalgically of theatrical lodgings in Middlesbrough and Huddersfield'.

The story of how Henry wins through constitutes a riot of Wodehousean themes. Just as the English hero has known life in the arcadia of musical comedy, so has Stickney's Aunt Kelly metamorphosed into 'a Ziegfeld Follies girl who had been left out in the rain and had swollen a little'. The hero Bill Hardy aspires to write the kind of murder thrillers to which Wodehouse himself was addicted, and is such a good egg that his creator has endowed upon him the ultimate blessing of residency in Valley Fields. Hardy has something else in common with his creator, his failure to reach those ancient halls of learning for which all his early training had prepared him. When the heroine asks him if he ever went to Oxbridge, Hardy, carefully prompted by the son of Ernest Wodehouse, replies, 'Neither, worse luck. My uncle didn't approve of universities. He was one of those men who go into business at the age of sixteen and think anything else is a waste of time.'

But the man who demands most of our sympathies is Henry Paradene himself, for not only has he inherited, through a most unexpected succession of deaths in the family, a house he does not want, but he is also borne down by the assumption of every likely buyer that he, one of the Sussex Paradenes, would die rather than part with this architectural symbol of his lineage. When Aunt Kelly lets slip that Stickney is in love with Ashby Hall, Henry bluntly replies, 'Then I wish he'd buy it':

> Kelly was astonished. 'You wouldn't sell?'
> 'Wouldn't I!'
> 'But I thought you landed proprietors, if that's what you call them, would die rather than part with the old home.'
> 'Not this landed proprietor. What I want is money.'
> 'Don't we all?'

Of course Kelly loves Paradene as utterly as Stickney loves Ashby Hall, but the differences of vocabulary make it difficult for either party to realize it for a while. When, as a first solicitous gesture, Kelly asks Henry how he is fixed for lettuce, he replies, 'You want to make a salad?'. In the end the various knots are tied with customary Wodehousean neatness, but not before Wodehouse has achieved the perfect mid-Atlantic simile. Henry is considering a plan which has been suggested to him by the rest of them, and he finds it odd that they believe it to be foolproof when 'all the time there was a flaw in it which should have stood out as plainly as a Palm Beach suit at the Eton and Harrow match'.

One wonders if Wodehouse quite realized when he coined that memorable phrase that the Eton–Harrow match, once a social occasion to stand with Henley and Royal Ascot, no longer attracted much attention. The brakes parked at the boundary's edge, the festive detonation of champagne corks, the promenade across the sacred turf during the luncheon interval, were no more. The game was not even played at Lord's any more, and had become relegated so far into the cricketing background that most of the newspapers never even bothered to report it. Did Wodehouse care? Perhaps not. By the time he wrote *Company for Henry* a most extraordinary metamorphosis had taken place within him. Because it had proceeded at such a tortuous rate, because his outward appearance underwent no change, because his style remained blessedly unpolluted by any literary vanities except his own, Wodehouse until the day he died appeared to be an archetype of a certain type of Englishman whose aim had always been, in life as in literature, to remain more English than any other English writer. But appearances are sometimes more deceptive than we suspect. For the last third of his life Wodehouse remained in the United States, exposed to its art and its commerce, its television, its diet, its climate, its dress – and its sports. In an interview conducted with a BBC producer in 1975, he made the following responses:

> PGW: Don't do much in the way of writing about cricket, because I've been writing for America too, and they don't know anything about it here. My game now is baseball. Are you interested in baseball. Oh, I'm crazy about it.
>
> INT: Do you find it as interesting as cricket?
>
> PGW: Oh yes, I think so. I'd much rather watch a baseball game than a cricket match. I think what's wrong with cricket, that is, if you're keen on one team – I was very keen on Surrey – well, I'd go to see Surrey play, say, Lancashire, and I'd find that Lancashire had won the toss, and they'd bat all day, whereas with baseball, the other side only bats about ten minutes at the most.
>
> INT: Do you have a team you support here?
>
> PGW: The Mets are my team. They're doing sort of wobbly. They aren't doing frightfully well, but they aren't doing frightfully badly. But the awful thing is that Tom Seymour, a great pitcher, they relied on him to win half their games. He sort of lost his form and they can't win anything now.
>
> INT: Do you think living in a faster country attracted you to baseball?
>
> PGW: I don't know why I suddenly got interested in it. Isn't it funny? For years I hadn't paid any attention to the game and now I'm frightfully keen on it.
>
> INT: My recollection of village cricket is that it's a very pleasant way of spending an afternoon sitting in the sun.

PGW: Yes, you really want to have a book or paper or something to read, and just look at the game every now and then.

We consider those words and recall that when Henry Paradene was passing the time of day with a few friends, Wodehouse had written, 'They were chatting amiably of the prospects of the Sussex team in the county cricket championship.' In the long long ago it would simply never have occurred to him that the word 'cricket' in that phrase was anything but a tautological outrage. Then we consider once again the famous tableau in *Piccadilly Jim* and realize with a start of sad astonishment what has happened. Bayliss the butler has turned into his master, Bingley Crocker.

4

*Lyricist
on
Broadway*

ON A SUNDAY MORNING IN JUNE 1903, a party of people travelled due north out of London in that mood of eager expectation tempered by slight apprehension which usually accompanies an invitation from a famous man. The destination of the travellers was Grim's Dyke, a huge mock-Tudor pile standing in a hundred acres of Harrow Weald, and whose elongated chimneys pointed inexorably to the hand of Norman Shaw. The original name of the estate had been Graeme's Dyke, which the present owner, one of the most relentless punsters of the nineteenth century, had corrupted to its more forbidding aspect in deference to his own curmudgeonly status. The punster was William Schwenck Gilbert, the greatest purveyor of comic light verse of the age, the mastermind behind those archetypal Victorian masterpieces the Savoy Operas, and a blunt Englishman with a fearsome reputation for not suffering fools gladly if indeed at all; even his fellow-magistrates on the Uxbridge bench went in awe of him, and one of the celebrities who frequented Grim's Dyke had likened the experience to 'living in a literary fireworks factory'.

Among the guests travelling out to Grim's Dyke that Sunday morning was an obscure and diffident employee of the Lombard Street branch of an imperial bank, a twenty-one-year-old nobody with an excessively modest conception of himself which he later defined as 'shrinking floweret'. Being a bank clerk, this matter-of-fact young man was in a condition of chronic penury, and had contrived to dress for the occasion only with a little help from his friends. 'There was I,' he reminisced half a century later, 'tucked

95

away inside my brother Armine's frock-coat and my cousin George's trousers', relieved to discover that as there were fourteen invited to lunch, it ought to be possible for him to sit unobtrusively enough through the proceedings. The reason for his invitation has long since been lost, but it may well have been Gilbert's wariness about being one of thirteen diners. If that was so, then he need not have bothered, because bad luck was about to descend upon his head and upon the bank clerk's in equal proportions.

And yet, had he been less diffidently inclined, the bank clerk might easily have ingratiated himself with his distinguished host through his intimate knowledge of and deep passion for Gilbert's verse. Even as he sat down to lunch under the butler's gelid eye, the bank clerk was himself already a published author with a habit of interpolating Gilbertian references into his work at the slightest opportunity. In the previous year he had published *The Pothunters*, in which Charteris, presiding over a school magazine supper, plays 'extracts from the works of Messrs Gilbert and Sullivan' on the banjo, a recital improbably described as 'an intellectual treat'. Even as Wodehouse entered the portals of Grim's Dyke, it was in the knowledge that the printers were preparing for publication a work entitled *A Prefect's Uncle*, in which the eponymous hero Farnie, attempting to borrow from several friends simultaneously, 'rather liked the notion of being turned into a sort of limited liability company, like the Duke of Plaza Toro'.[1] Nor is Farnie alone in his familiarity with the canon; when Marriott improvises a limerick, he follows its rendition with the defence: '"Little thing of my own", he added, quoting England's greatest librettist. "I call it 'Heart Foam'. I shall not publish it." '[2] England's greatest librettist, however, was unaware of these tributes, and the bank clerk was far too paralyzed with shyness and hero-worship to offer his credentials; instead, squirming with painful rapture at the awareness that he was in the presence of history, he sat there among the gilded napery, saying nothing and wanting desperately to behave according to the lights of his host, an aspiration rendered problematic by the fact that he had not the faintest idea what those lights might happen to be.

Midway through the meal the bank clerk became vaguely aware through the haze of his own confusion that the great man was telling a story, a favourite story, told many times before at this very table, polished to the point where it now shone with the dull lustre of ancient myth. The bank clerk could tell this from the faintest intimations of resignation which flattened still further the expression of glazed inhumanity on the butler's face. This was the life for a penniless free-lance spare-time writer. One of the supreme comedians of English literature was recounting a humorous anecdote. The bank clerk settled down in anticipation of this wonderful intellectual treat:

> It was one of those long, deceptively dull stories where you make the build-up as tedious as you can, knowing that the punch-line is going to pay for everything, and pause before you reach the point so as to stun the audience with the unexpected snaperoo. In other words, a story

which is pretty awful till the last line, when you have them rolling in the aisles.

As Gilbert proceeded on his ponderous way, the bank clerk's bliss began to seep away, to be replaced by a bafflement which quietly modulated into disenchantment and at last into a deep sadness. The story, which concerned the Drury Lane impresario Sir Augustus Harris, did not seem to be very amusing after all. And yet it must be, because it was being told by the immortal W. S. Gilbert. If the author of *The Bab Ballads* thought something was funny, then it *was* funny, by definition. The bank clerk began to ache with a desire to find the story amusing. He longed to achieve that explosion of hysterical joy which only the very best stories induce. He prayed for the inspiration to scream with amusement, to shake with mirth, to giggle, even to snigger. But how? He began to try to will the raconteur to sublime heights of comic genius and himself to a suitably abject response, till at last, as the story arrived at the aposiopesis which signals the coming punch-line, the clerk, tense with vicarious ambition for his hero, and mistaking the pause which heralds the climax for the climax itself, suddenly let out a great scream of idolatrous laughter:

> I had rather an individual laugh in those days, something like the explosion of one of those gas mains that slays six, and it lasts for above five minutes, by which time the company had begun to talk of other things, and Gilbert never got the point of it in at all. And it was at this juncture that I caught my host's eye.
>
> I shall always remember that glare of pure hatred which I saw in it. If you have seen photographs of Gilbert, you will be aware that even when in repose his face was inclined to be formidable and his eye not the sort of eye you would willingly catch. And now his face was far from being in repose. His eyes beneath their beetling brows seared my very soul. In order to get away from them, I averted my gaze and found myself encountering that of the butler. His eyes were shining with a doglike devotion. For some reason which I was unable to understand, I appeared to have made his day. I know now what the reason was. I suppose he had heard that story build up like a glacier and ramble to its conclusion at least fifty times, probably more, and I had killed it.

So ended the first and last recorded encounter between William Schwenck Gilbert, master of the art of versifying to music, and his successor in that department, Pelham Grenville Wodehouse.

Two months after that calamitous lunch, Wodehouse became a permanent member of the staff of 'By The Way', which meant that he was now composing light verse to order six days a week, than which there was no finer apprenticeship for anyone aspiring to Gilbert's mantle. In October 1903 there came further obeisance at the Savoy shrine in the form of a third school novel called *The Gold Bat*, in which a schoolmaster, suspecting the presence of burglars, is likened to General Stanley in *The Pirates of Penzance*:

The man who finds his conscience ache
No peace at all enjoys;
And, as I lay in bed awake,
I thought I heard a noise.

By December 1904, by which time he had published his fourth and fifth books, Wodehouse had also penetrated at last the cardboard battlements of musical comedy; an actor called Owen Hall commissioned him to write a lyric to be included in a show called *Sergeant Brue* at the Strand Theatre. Wodehouse obliged with an item called 'Put Me in My Little Cell', and was so enraptured by what he had done that, after attending a performance on 12 October, he confided to his diary: 'Encored both times. Audience laughed several times during each verse. This is fame.'³ It was not quite fame, but Wodehouse inched closer to that dubious target in the spring of 1906 when the actor-manager Seymour Hicks, having noted the neat professionalism of the words of 'Put Me in My Little Cell', hired Wodehouse on a part-time basis at a salary of £2 a week, as a writer of additional lyrics for the Aldwych shows, which meant that Wodehouse was now to acquaint himself with a new working partner, an American songwriter called Jerome Kern, another of Hicks' semi-permanent minions. There are two contradictory versions of the first meeting between the new partners. The Kern account suggests that, with Hicks looking on, Kern played several melodies to Wodehouse, who then took them and composed lyrics for them to everybody's great advantage. Wodehouse's version is more picturesque, and is for that reason highly revealing of his attitude towards Kern, which hardly changed in a lifetime, a tendency to regard the composer as the fount of musical wisdom, a Broadway genius wise in the ways of both backstage and front-office fraternities; Wodehouse remembered meeting Kern for the first time inside the Aldwych, where Kern was sitting in his shirtsleeves playing poker with a bunch of actors:

When I finally managed to free him from the card table and was able to talk to him, I became impressed. Here, I thought, was a young man supremely confident of himself – the kind of person who inspires people to seek him out when a job must be done.

Although Wodehouse may be gilding the lily just a little here, his view is corroborated by many subsequent Kern collaborators for, although by all accounts not quite the most lovable of men, Kern was indeed one of the great songwriting wiseacres, gifted with a cunning brain, a questing intelligence,⁴ an eye for the profitable investment, and, what was absolutely vital to associates like Wodehouse, the resilience and self-confidence to hold his own with even the toughest eggs among the impresarios.⁵ None of these attributes would have been of much relevance, however, had not Kern also possessed a degree of professional ability which has hardly ever been matched in popular music. Indeed, so rare an artist was he that without some understanding of the nature of his achievements, Wodehouse's exalted status as an innovative lyricist inside the American theatre, if nowhere else, remains incomprehensible.

Kern is rightly acknowledged as the bridge between the hothouse heroics of Hapsburgian melodrama and the emergence of an authentically American school of theatre composition, the bridge across which George Gershwin, on his own admission, so blithely skipped during the 1920s.[6] Before Kern, Broadway musical thinking was dominated either by Viennese imports, successes shipped over from London, or the jolly coarsenesses of the vaudeville tradition exemplified by the chauvinistic excesses of George M. Cohan. For several years Kern received no encouragement to write a complete musical comedy score at all,[7] having to content himself with the occasional interpolated melody in Broadway adaptations of European imports. Although these additional songs of his were invariably singled out for praise from reviewers numbed by Hapsburgian plot and subplot, there was a time when Kern decided that his talents would be more regularly rewarded if he brought them to London, then the heartland of musical comedy and operetta. Hicks was already acquainted with his work through Kern's additional numbers in 1903 for the New York production of a Hicks confection called *An English Daisy*, and took him on at the Aldwych.

Comparatively little is known of the arrangements agreed upon between Hicks and his two young protégés, but a glimpse of Wodehouse's mentor in action may be caught in a most unexpected place. When last seen, the deposed house captain Fenn, leading light of Kay's House at Eckleton School, was en route to the local theatre to see a production of his elder brother's first musical comedy. When he arrives at the stage door, Fenn is ushered into the dressing-room of Higgs, the actor-manager responsible for Fenn major's sudden spectacular eminence:

> Fenn found himself in a small room, a third of which was filled by a huge iron-bound chest, another third by a very stout man and a dressing-table, while the rest of the space was comparatively empty, being occupied by a wooden chair with three legs. On this seat his brother was trying to balance himself.

Higgs, expressing his disenchantment with the barnstorming life, exclaims, 'These provincial dressing-rooms. No room! Never any room! No chairs! Nothing!' We are told that he spoke 'in short, quick sentences, and gasped between each'. But his petulance evaporates once he makes his entrance:

> Mr Higgs' performance sealed the success of the piece. The house laughed at everything he said. He sang a song in his gasping way, and they laughed still more.

The real-life Hicks seems to have been slimmer than Higgs, and with a nose which one Kern biographer has described as 'conspicuously pointed',[8] but certainly in the suave confidence of his vocal delivery he carried shows in precisely the way that Fenn's Mr Higgs does at Eckleton.

While the Kern partnership represents very nearly the sum total of Wodehouse's commitment to the musical stage, so far as Kern was concerned it was no more than the prelude to a subsequent career of startling brilliance and worldly success;[9] while Kern achieved many masterpieces without Wodehouse, Wodehouse achieved none without Kern, a fact partly explained by Kern's unusually slow rate of development as a songwriter. He came to maturity very much later than is customary for composers, and never really perfected the style which produced so many ballad masterpieces until the late 1920s, by which time the alliance with Wodehouse was already dissolved. Today Kern is recognized as the master romanticist of American popular music, whose score for *Show Boat*, outstanding though it remains, was little more than an overture to the work to come, those ballads whose sumptuous harmonic rhetoric and brilliant flirtations with modulation within the melodic structure remain unmatched to this day. A short list of Kern's great achievements in this line would include none of the work he did with Wodehouse. There is an excellent reason for this which has nothing to do with any shortcomings on Wodehouse's part. Through some quirk of musical temperament, Kern, for all his originality and erudition, was never quite comfortable with the type of faster, brighter song which creates the illusion of proceeding of its own volition. Throughout his life he remained preoccupied with the kind of song he could compose best, the romantic ballad which sweeps through two or more tonalities to achieve an almost operatic grandeur. But the bouncing, animated pieces like Gershwin's 'Soon' or Porter's 'Always True to You in My Fashion' or even Donaldson's 'My Baby Just Cares for Me' seem to have been beyond him. And it was precisely these buoyant trifles to which Wodehouse's breezy rhyming mannerisms were best suited. Had Kern not been serving his own apprenticeship in the years of his Wodehouse shows, an apprenticeship in which the profundities of 'All The Things You Are' and 'The Song Is You' were still far into the future, it seems doubtful if he and Wodehouse would have made an effective partnership at all.

That they did match each other to perfection there can be no doubt. For Hicks they began with a political lampoon called 'Mr Chamberlain', whose references to Tariff Reform so diverted the town that the song became the best-known feature of *The Beauty of Bath*, which opened at the Aldwych on 19 March 1906. Later in life Wodehouse was inclined to give the credit to Kern, saying that the lyric was 'a pretty poor effort all round, but Jerry's melody was so terrific that the number used to get six or seven encores every night and I spent most of the next year writing encore verses'. And yet 'Mr Chamberlain', with its topical allusions and tendency to pasquinade, was clearly the kind of item which succeeds through the wit of its jokes rather than the grace of its melody. Certainly Kern must have been deeply impressed by the dexterity of its versifying techniques for, although once the show had opened he returned to New York and for several years lost touch with his partner, he never forgot him; for the next few seasons, while Kern advanced steadily through the ranks of local musicians hired to concoct additional material for Ruritanian musical melodrama, Wodehouse was shuttling between New York and London as a free-lance journalist of prolific tendencies. It was not until 1915 that he encountered Kern again.

By this time the status of both men had changed prodigiously, Wodehouse being the well-regarded author of fifteen light novels, the progenitor of Psmith and the author of a Broadway play, *A Gentleman of Leisure*. As for Kern, he had already passed the great watershed of his career, 'They Didn't Believe Me', a 1914 song which not only established his reputation once and for all, but is often said to have signalled the emergence of a whole new school of American songwriting.[10] And yet Kern, for all his hard-won eminence, had apparently only to catch a glimpse of Wodehouse to ditch his current lyricists and offer the Englishman a resumption of the old partnership. The circumstances were ironic, and arose out of the fact that while Kern was a composer to the exclusion of all else, Wodehouse had already become a past-master in the free-lance's salvation, diversification. Having published novels, staged a play, written songs, won a reputation as a readable feature writer, become a well-known producer of short-stories and a part-time editor, he was now engaged in operations at the offices of *Vanity Fair* which Kern would certainly have regarded as nefarious. Wodehouse had become a theatre critic.

In the previous year he had married Ethel Newton Rowley, and now required some regular source of income, which he managed to arrange by adopting a repertoire of journalistic disguises soon to become familiar to readers of the magazine as J. Plum, Pelham Grenville, C. P. West, P. Brooke-Haven and several others. It was this ghostly gallimaufry which was responsible for roughly half the monthly contents of the magazine, leaving to one P. G. Wodehouse the duty of covering events on Broadway. On the evening of 23 December 1915, Wodehouse bade farewell for the moment to Plum, Grenville, West and Brooke-Haven and set out for the Princess Theatre to review a new musical comedy, and by so doing changed the course of his life. It would be interesting to know how much freedom he enjoyed to say exactly what he felt about the plays he saw; a few years later his successor as dramatic critic at *Vanity Fair*, Dorothy Parker, caused a crisis in the magazine's affairs when her review of Billie Burke, alias Mrs Florenz Ziegfeld, caused offence which reached the ears of Condé Nast, owner of the magazine, who promptly insisted on Miss Parker's removal from the post.[11] Whatever constraints may have been imposed on Wodehouse, it is doubtful if he received much moral support from his editor, Frank Crowninshield, 'in whose unclouded countenance', Edmund Wilson once wrote, 'I caught the image of those who never ask a real question or are racked by a real passion'.

The Princess Theatre on 39th Street was a kind of midget white elephant whose frontage was hardly more generous than, and whose takings were hardly in excess of, the kosher restaurant next door. It was administered by the resourceful Elizabeth Marberry and had only 299 seats, a numerical whimsicality explained by the fact that the theatre had been built by the Shubert brothers, compared to whose entrepreneurial shenanigans the excesses of all previous managements in theatrical history are seen to be the harmless gambolling of spring lambs; the fire regulations of the period applied only to theatres with 300 or more seats, and so the Shuberts, not particularly anguished by the notion that circumstances might conceivably set fire to audience and performers, had thoughtfully installed 299.[12] The aesthetic consequences were profound, and today the Princess musicals are remembered as being revolutionary in an era when so many big Broadway shows still displayed so much merchandise from the junkyards of the Austro-Hungarian Empire. Miss Marberry's policy might be called indigenous lilliputianism, the presentation of a series of small-scale shows featuring tiny orchestras and which jettisoned the chorus line in favour of characters moving through a plot which exchanged the inanities of Ruritania for those of Main Street. To someone like Wodehouse, all this must have been a revelation, because every fibre of his modest being had always reacted against the comically grandiloquent garbage of the archetypal Hapsburg plot, with its bogus barons and its milkmaid duchesses mouthing trite impossibilities with all the histrionic assurance of people eating goulash under water.[13] There is little doubt that when he turned up on 39th Street for the New York opening of *Very Good Eddie*, Wodehouse was anticipating an enjoyable evening, especially as the composer was Kern.

Wodehouse now takes up the story, investing it with several of the stock jokes of the back-stage musical. When the performance gets under way Kern is found standing anxiously at the back of the stalls with his librettist, an Englishman called Guy Bolton, who tells Kern with some surprise that there is at least one man in the tenth row who appears to be enjoying it. Kern peers into the stalls and says 'Wodehouse', which Bolton mishears as 'Good house'. The lyrics come wafting across the footlights: —

> Any old night is a wonderful night
> If you're there with a wonderful girl.

This information has a depressing effect on Kern, who mutters, 'Lousy lyric', at which one of the customers turns in his seat and says, 'Look, if you don't like the show, why don't you get out?' Kern and Bolton then retreat through a door and continue watching through a crack. Bolton decides there is something wrong with the heroine's face, but the doorman corrects him. 'She's walking on her hands. Saving her face for the last act.' When Bolton wonders aloud why they never thought of asking the doorman to write the jokes, he replies, 'I'd have been glad to help out if I'd known the show was supposed to be funny.' More lyrics drift out:

Give me your hand,
You'll understand,
We're off to slumberland.

This is altogether too much for Kern, who turns to his partner and says, 'Why don't you get Plum to do your lyrics?' Later that night, at a party in Kern's apartment, the proposition is put to Wodehouse. Bolton's journal reads:

> Eddie opened. Excellent reception. All say hit. To Kern for supper. Talked with P. G. Wodehouse, apparently known as Plum. Never heard of him, but Jerry says he writes lyrics, so, being slightly tight, suggested we team up. W so overcome he couldn't answer for a minute, then grabbed my hand and stammered out his thanks.

Bolton, it appears, had misread Wodehouse's hesitancy. Having become the first drama critic in history to be nobbled by an invitation to join the writers whose work he had been sent to judge, Wodehouse confided to his diary:

> To opening of Very Good Eddie. Enjoyed it in spite of lamentable lyrics. Bolton, evidently conscious of this weakness, offered partnership. Tried to hold back and weigh the suggestion, but his eagerness so pathetic that consented. Mem: Am I too impulsive? Fight against this tendency.

Fortunately he never fought against it. Miss Marberry's new triumvirate began writing musical comedies tailored to the lilliputian vanities of the building in which they were to be presented. Not more than two sets, not more than twelve girls, not more than eleven musicians. No more crown princes masquerading as butlers, no more milkmaids who turn out at the final curtain to be heir to several thrones, no more cast-lists reading like extracts from the *Almanach de Gotha*. Most interesting of all, no more love lyrics striving through blowsy euphemism to elevate sexual attraction to some kind of metaphysical abstraction. What Wodehouse undertook the moment he began working at the Princess was the removal west of the axis of American musical comedy, as Kern must have suspected he would. In terms of technique, of vocabulary, of production values, the effect was so extraordinary that the great lyricists to come, men like Ira Gershwin, Oscar Hammerstein, Howard Dietz and Lorenz Hart, all of them a few years younger than Wodehouse, were to be lavish in their acknowledgment of the debt they owed him. It was all fortuitous to say the least; at the very moment when Kern, Irving Berlin and George Gershwin were beginning to create colloquial American song, Wodehouse turned up with the flair for writing its lyric counterpart.

The Wodehouse–Bolton scenario of the first offer of partnership is, it appears, no more and no less than that, a scenario, shaped and polished by the most accomplished literary comedian of the century. At least one of Kern's biographers has examined the events of the opening night of *Very Good Eddie* in the identical spirit of those earlier spoilsports who investigated the Reverend Dodgson's claim that the story of *Alice in Wonderland* was first narrated in 'the golden afternoon' and found that the weather that day was 'cool and rather wet'. Several months before *Very Good Eddie* opened, Kern had presented another New York show called *Ninety in the Shade*, with libretto by the ubiquitous Harry Smith. In this show was a song called 'A Packet of Seeds', with words by Wodehouse, proving that he and Kern must have made contact and entered on some sort of professional arrangement long before the facetiousness in the foyer of *Very Good Eddie*. It is just possible that 'A Packet of Seeds' was a relic from the early London partnership, remembered by Kern and dragged into a musical sorely in need of comic relief; certainly the whole demeanour of the song is less typical of Broadway than of the English music-hall genre-item sung by some top-hatted and slightly tipsy Clarence de Clare of a noble house:

> If I'd a garden where girlies would grow,
> You'd find me there with my spade and my hoe.
> My little garden I never would leave,
> I'd work from daybreak until the eve.
> Daytime and night I would cheerfully toil,
> I'd kill the blight and encourage the soil,
> And when at last I had cleared it of weeds,
> I'd go and buy me a packet of seeds.
>
> All through the winter they'd lie there below,
> Snugly tucked under a mantle of snow.
> April at last rain and sunshine would bring,
> Then all my flowers would bloom in the spring.
> Primrose and Myrtle and Lily I'd see,
> They'd be there growing for no-one but me.
> Delightful creatures, a garden of girls,
> With fairest features and lovely curls.
> All round my garden in rapture I'd roam,
> I'd stay all day there, I'd never go home.
> I can't imagine what more a man needs
> Than lots of ground and a packet of seeds.

The comicality has been rendered quaint by the vast changes to the face of the popular song during Wodehouse's lifetime, but it remains interesting for its illustration of the sheer range of his comic effects; just as in the novels he can flit from Pooter to Harry the Horse, with a passing nod at Leacock, Anstey and Jerome, so in his song lyrics he appears to have assimilated several successive styles of rhyming in the course of developing his own. In 'A Packet of Seeds', an item reeking of the slapstick of the old Oxford Music

Hall, he still insists on the sly quotation from the Savoy Operas in the fourth line of the second verse and, although once he was embarked on the Bessie Marberry episode he left this kind of facetiousness far behind, we suspect that like Galahad Threepwood, who carried into old age the beatific vision of Dolly Henderson pink-tighted at the Tivoli, he never quite lost his affection for it.

To the Princess Theatre shows he brought this range of comic effects but, what was much more important, he brought also an ability to express without mawkishness the innocent romantic tendernesses required by the libretti; his best efforts in this regard have weathered the years far better than their obscurity might suggest:

> I was often kissed 'neath the mistletoe
> By small boys excited with tea.
> If I'd known that you existed
> I'd have scratched them and resisted, dear,
> But I never knew about you, oh, the pain of it,
> And you never knew about me.

The thought of the Merry Widow singing those endearingly infantile lines at the Prince of Pilsen is enough to demonstrate the extent to which Wodehouse, in contributing his rhymes to the Princess shows, was amending the expression on the face of the Broadway lyric. 'You Never Knew About Me', written in 1917, is an item especially pertinent to the neglected issue of how far his Broadway career affected his style as a novelist, as we shall see. For the moment, he was devoting to the requirements of Kern and Bolton almost all of his prodigious creative energy. In 1917 he was involved in the freakish number of six New York opening nights, having completed all the lyrics of *Kitty Darlin'* and *The Riviera Girl*, written all the lyrics and part of the book of *Have a Heart, Oh, Boy!* and *Leave It to Jane*, and contributed sketches to *Miss 1917*. Apart from the notorious Harry B. Smith, who was guilty of 123 Broadway shows, no musical writer had ever committed himself to so many assignments in one season, and yet in that same year Wodehouse published two novels, *Piccadilly Jim* and *Uneasy Money*, and also contributed short stories to *The Strand* and *Saturday Evening Post*. He was, in effect, a part-time lyricist, a status which did not inhibit his renowned successors from naming themselves proudly amongst his disciples. Howard Dietz defined Wodehouse as 'the lyric writer I most admire'. Hart is said by his biographer to have been 'inspired by Wodehouse'; Johnny Mercer included Wodehouse in his short-list of six lyricists whose work would be discussed by the students of the twenty-first century. Richard Rodgers wrote of the Princess shows:

> They were intimate and uncluttered and tried to deal in a humorous way with modern, everyday characters. They were certainly different – and far more appealing to me – from the overblown operettas, mostly

imported, that dominated the Broadway scene in the wake of *The Merry Widow* and *The Chocolate Soldier*.[14]

The most vociferous of all Wodehouse's admirers has been his friend and sometime collaborator Ira Gershwin, whose testimony can stand for all the rest:

> Wodehouse's talent in this field has never been fully recognized. As far as I'm concerned, no-one wrote more charming lyrics than he in the period from just before World War I to the Twenties. Certainly I admired him greatly, and in a letter to me (Nov 10, 1961) he wrote that Richard Rodgers had sent him a telegram not only congratulating him on his 80th birthday but telling him how much Larry Hart, Oscar Hammerstein and Dick himself had been taught by Plum through the years.[15]

Exactly what qualities were they which Wodehouse brought to the theatre that he should so completely have bowled over his peers? First, his technical resource and his perfectionism in applying it, a legacy no doubt of the endless light verse demanded by the old 'By The Way' column. He once confided to Ira Gershwin that the greatest challenge and the biggest worry to him in writing a lyric was to come across a section of song requiring three double rhymes. But there is no evidence of technical difficulties of any kind in his Broadway verses. The rhythmic stresses fall with that neat inevitability which is the hallmark of the vintage comic lyric, and their content shows how skilfully Wodehouse acquired the art indispensable to the songwriter, economy. His convict sings:

> Oh, I wish I was back
> With a rock or two to crack,
> With my pals of the class of Ninety Nine.
> How I miss the peace and quiet
> And the simple, wholesome diet
> Of that dear old-fashioned prison of mine.

In his review of ancient history he reflects on the curious habits of royalty:

> When out with Cleopatterer, men always made their wills.
> They knew there was no time to waste
> When the gumbo had that funny taste.
> They'd take her hand and squeeze it, they'd murmur, 'Oh, you kid!',
> But they never liked to start to feed till Cleopatterer did.

It was in the Cleopatra song that Wodehouse, displaying his happy knack of digesting the broader effects of American vernacular, created the imperishable couplet:

She gave those poor Egyptian ginks
Something else to watch besides the sphinx.

No wonder that Kern, his world awash with the sticky tides of Ruritania, grasped at this refreshing levity as at a lifeline. Recalling the blissful collaboration on the Joe Chamberlain song ten years before, and perceiving both the equanimity of the Englishman's temperament and the efficiency of his creative engines, Kern now entered on a second and much more exhaustive partnership which was to last eight years and create the songs for eleven productions.

The student of Wodehouse's affairs, as he contemplates the spectacle of his subject entering the maelstrom of the New York theatre, cannot help exulting in the unique creative process which was now about to begin even though there was nobody, Wodehouse included, who suspected it. As the dramatic critic of *Vanity Fair* went home to bed after attending the opening night party of *Very Good Eddie*, the germs of several novels and short stories, of countless characters and phrases and incidents, were about to enter his bloodstream. He was in the unique position of a man already gainfully employed in an occupation requiring for its maintenance a constant supply of whimsical experience, entering on a new job which, apart from being attractive in itself, is certain to provide him with a whole world of fresh ideas and people. For it was now that Wodehouse found himself plunged into the society of professional colleagues so comically outrageous as to leave an indelible stain on his imagination. The first of these was the semi-mythical beast Abraham Erlanger, 'who eats broken bottles and conducts human sacrifices at the time of the full moon'. Erlanger, who looked like an uneasy compromise between an inflated Peter Lorre and a punctured Sydney Greenstreet, had grown into the habit of beguiling the *longueurs* between productions by convincing himself that he was Napoleon Bonaparte. In a poor man this harmless vanity often leads to the limited pleasures of a padded cell; in a rich impresario it tends merely to contribute to his reputation as an interesting character, and this was what happened to Erlanger, who would audition applicants for the post of his personal barber by having them read Napoleon's letters in the original. He was also known to keep a loaded revolver in his desk, 'no doubt', explained the kindly Wodehouse, always seeking the extenuating circumstance, 'in case he ever met the Duke of Wellington'. The first meeting with Erlanger was dispiriting, not just because there were rumours to the effect that the revolver was rather more than a stage prop, but also because the great man kept at his side a twelve-year-old boy of unusually repellant aspect whose appointment as advisor was due to the striking proximity of the level of his intelligence with that of the average Broadway audience. But in the end the association proved so profitable for Wodehouse that he ended by observing, 'Why shouldn't a fellow shoot a chap from time to time if the situation seemed to called for it? What's the sense of having a loaded revolver if you never use it?'

The man best qualified to answer that question may well have been

Colonel Henry Savage, a theatrical producer of inclinations so crooked that, according to one of his victims, the actor Donald Brian, 'he could hide at will behind a spiral staircase'; Wodehouse later explained the Colonel's limp by surmising that 'probably in the course of his career he had been bitten in the leg by some indignant author'. There was Ray Comstock, producer of the Princess Theatre shows, who insured against the kicks of Prohibition by stashing two dozen cases of whisky in his office loft, where it was boiled by the steam pipes until it exploded, lending an ambience of frivolous indulgence to the lower floors for some years afterwards. There was Charles Dillingham who, much to his own delight, had made the discovery that 'women aren't gentlemen'. There was the actress Justine Johnstone, whose gold-prospecting explorations along Broadway had proved so fruitful that by the time Wodehouse encountered her in the 1919 production *Oh, Boy!*, she was able to dismiss a $7,500 pearl necklace with the remark, 'It's just something to wear while slumming'. There was Irving Berlin, displaying anxiety that one of his two pet toucans might indulge in a fit of pique and take one of his fingers off, 'the one I play piano with'. And most spectacular of all, there was the designer Joe Urban, an exile who brought with him the authentic Hapsburgian aura in the form of malapropisms so adamantly Viennese in spirit that conversational exchange took on the stimulating properties of a lottery. Urban, surrounded by the alcoholic over-indulgence of those who exploded whisky in lofts, would have drunk milk, except that it tended to cuddle in his stomach. It was his practice to take a hotel room only a stone's jump from the theatre, so that his work might be delivered at the drop of a bucket. Urban hated it whenever jokers tried to push his leg, or nuisances dodged his footsteps, and would vow revenge by muttering darkly, 'Just you mock my words'. The only reason he endured the life of the musical theatre at all was, he said, because that environment seemed to draw him 'like a maggot'.

There were also certain precepts regarding work in the musical theatre which Wodehouse began to acquire the moment he resumed the Kern partnership, for instance that 'during the reading of a play, a manager has to have something to do that will keep him usefully employed', also the following guide-lines for all those would-be dramatists callow enough to make a foray into the mysterious East, as Wodehouse had done with a turkey called *The Rose of China*:

> Have nothing to do with anything with a title like *The Rose of China* or *The Willow Pattern Plate* or *The Siren of Shanghai* or *Me Velly Solly*. . . . soon your heroine goes cute on you, saying, 'Me Plum Blossom. Me good girl. Me love Chlistian god velly much'. Bolton and I cannot say after this length of time whether or not the heroine of *The Rose of China* turned out in the end to be the daughter of an American missionary, kidnapped by Chinese bandits in her infancy, but it would seem virtually certain that she did. All heroines of Chinese plays turn out in the end to be daughters of American missionaries, kidnapped by

bandits in their infancy. This is known as Shipman's Law.[16] There is no reason to suppose that in this instance there would have been any deviation from the straight party line.

But Wodehouse rejoiced even in the flops, for a reason which rendered him unique in the musical theatre of his, or indeed of any day. His situation embodied a paradox: while a long run might be more lucrative in the short run, undoubtedly a short run, or even no run at all, would prove the more productive in the long run, if not to the librettist, then certainly to the comic novelist standing in the wings. The man capable of concocting a Psmith or a Threepwood will hardly bother to lick his wounds when being victimized by a Savage or an Erlanger. On those occasions when he was faced with the challenge of manufacturing a libretto which should not only be meaningful, romantic and witty but should also incorporate the talents of a troupe of performing dogs or seals; when he could overhear a chorus boy demanding shoes that were larger 'but only on the inside'; when he could listen to his dialogue filtered through the dubious muse of Miss Johnstone as she played two roles simultaneously, answering her own questions with her own answers; when he could savour the antics of a fellow-librettist like Bill McGuire, of whom he once wrote to Townend, 'You would love him. He's exactly like Ukridge';[17] when reality was bombarding him in this way, what need was there for fantasy? Circumstances were conspiring to thrust plot, character, situation and dialogue at him almost too generously for him to get it all down on paper, so arduous were his journalistic duties and so multifarious his creative commitments in the period of the Princess Theatre shows. Not only was he producing lyrics and libretto for several productions a year, and simultaneously publishing novels and short stories, but for a while he also retained his position as the many-headed correspondent of *Vanity Fair*, actually being reduced at one point to the freakish extremity of reviewing his own work because there was nobody else on Crowninshield's skeletal staff capable of taking its measure:

> I feel a slight diffidence about growing enthusiastic about *Miss Spring-time*, for the fact is that, having contributed a few little lyrical bijoux to the above (just a few trifles, you know, dashed off in the intervals of more serious work), I am drawing a royalty from it which has already caused the wolf to move up a few parasangs from the Wodehouse doorstep. Far be it from me to boost – from sordid and commercial motives – a theatrical entertainment whose success means the increase of my meat-meals per week from one to two, but candour compels me to say that *Miss Springtime* is a corker. It is the best musical play in years.

Wodehouse was being excessively modest, as usual. When confronted by the Princess Theatre entertainments, even the most hardened cynics among the New York Press seemed to lose their heads. Dorothy Parker, sent to assess a production in February 1918 called *Oh, Lady! Lady!*, reacted in *Vanity Fair* as follows:

Well, Bolton and Wodehouse and Kern have done it again. Every time these three gather together, the Princess Theatre is sold out for months in advance. You can get a seat for *Oh, Lady! Lady!* somewhere around the middle of August for just about the price of one on the stock exchange. If you ask me, I will look you fearlessly in the eye and tell you in low, throbbing tones that it has it over any other musical comedy in town. But then Bolton and Wodehouse and Kern are my favourite indoor sport. I like the way they go about a musical comedy. I like the way the action slides casually into the songs. I like the deft rhyming of the song that is always sung in the last act by two comedians and a comedienne. And oh, how I do like Jerome Kern's music. And all these things are even more so in *Oh, Lady! Lady!* than they were in *Oh, Boy!*.

One newspaper critic defined the small scale of the Princess Theatre shows as 'kitchenette productions', and another, confronted by *Oh, Boy!*, suggested that 'pleasing parlour entertainment has found its way to the stage'. The anonymous reviewer of *The New York Times*, unable to control his enthusiasm, broke into verse:

> This is the trio of music fame,
> Bolton and Wodehouse and Kern.
> Better than anyone else you can name,
> Bolton and Wodehouse and Kern.
> Nobody knows what on earth they've been bitten by,
> All I can say is I mean to get lit and buy
> Orchestra seats for the next one that's written by
> Bolton and Wodehouse and Kern.

Of a later show, *Leave It to Jane*, the critic Gilbert Seldes wrote, regarding the lyrics which Wodehouse pretended to have knocked off while resting from more significant labours:

> They had the great virtue which Gilbert's lyrics have, and which,I am told, the comic verses of Molière and Aristophanes also have: they say things as simply as you would say them in common speech, yet they sing perfectly. There was nothing Plum wanted to say that he couldn't say to music.

Possibly what Wodehouse found more difficult than writing the lyrics was finding the collaborators who were supposed to supply the tunes. The obsessively industrious Wodehouse, than whom no professional writer was ever more meticulous in the matter of sitting down each morning and producing his daily output, was distracted as well as amused by the vortex of default which swirled about him in the New York musical theatre. A contract, it seemed, was no more than a faint rumour of an obligation; as for an assignation, it was usually honoured only in the breach, as he soon discovered on being paired off with Irving Berlin for a show called *Sitting Pretty*. In December 1922 he writes to Townend that he and Bolton are to share the duties of book and lyrics to be performed to Berlin's music by the Duncan Sisters. Six days later he is complaining:

> We are having the devil of a time over the Duncan Sisters show. All attempts to get hold of Irving Berlin about the music have failed. We went into New York last Monday to keep an appointment with him and found that he had had to rush off to the dentist. He then made a date with me over the phone to lunch with him on Thursday and work all the afternoon. I went in and called at his flat and he was out and had left no message. Heaven knows when the thing will ever be finished.

Sitting Pretty was scheduled to open in October 1923 and the Duncan Sisters, in an effort to find something to do in the meantime, asked the management to allow them to fill in the first few months of the time by staging their own comic version of *Uncle Tom's Cabin*. Permission was granted, and the Duncan Sisters' squib, *Topsy and Eva*, became such a big hit in Chicago that the two girls backed out of the hypothetical *Sitting Pretty*, which gave Berlin a legitimate excuse to resign from a commitment he had never really entered into. Jerome Kern was then called in and two other actresses engaged as stars, in a show which had by now drifted so far from its original premise as to bear no resemblance to it at all. It is not surprising that *Sitting Pretty* proved to be the only Bolton–Wodehouse–Kern show not to survive a New York season.

Confusion of a different kind surrounded the staging of *Rosalie*, a 1928 production whose backstage politics rank as the most byzantine of any show of the period. The muddle began with receipt by Ziegfeld of a forty-two-page telegram from bibulous Bill McGuire outlining a plot based loosely on the visit to New York of Queen Marie of Rumania. The precise extent of McGuire's inebriation at the time was not recorded, but he was at least sober enough to have named the show after Ziegfeld's mother, a Mrs Rosalie de Gez. Overcome by a paroxysm of filial devotion, Ziegfeld asked one of his sisters, married to a rich businessman, to back the show as a gesture of respect for their dear old mother. Having expressed his loyalty to the family by guaranteeing himself if not his sister against possible loss, Ziegfeld saw that he was obliged to hire McGuire as librettist, if only because nobody else would be able to understand the contents of the marathon telegram. But Ziegfeld knew perfectly well that McGuire would never deliver the finished work in time, so after engaging McGuire he then hired Bolton to pick up McGuire's pieces. But hiring Bolton meant hiring Wodehouse also, so Ziegfeld now found himself with three writers for a non-existent property. The situation became further complicated with his recruitment as leading lady of his ex-mistress Marilyn Miller, for whom he still trembled with desire. But hiring Miss Miller meant hiring also her current lover, the dancer

Jack Donahue, which Ziegfeld did. He now began to look around for a composer and lyricist, but chose so badly that according to Wodehouse the two unnamed men turned up on the first day of rehearsals and 'announced that they had finished one number and hoped to have another one done shortly, though they couldn't guarantee this'. At last Ziegfeld sacked both men and began at the beginning once more by approaching Sigmund Romberg, who was, however, just about to begin rehearsing his *The New Moon* and could not spare the time. Ziegfeld then approached George Gershwin, who was, however, just about to begin rehearsing his *Funny Face* and could not spare the time. Ziegfeld then called both composers together and modestly requested that they produce a score between them in three weeks, even though hiring George meant hiring also his lyricist brother Ira. This Ziegfeld did. He now had two librettists, McGuire and Bolton, two composers, George Gershwin and Romberg, and two lyricists, Wodehouse and Ira Gershwin, to say nothing of a leading lady who kept resisting his advances while enjoying an affair with the leading man.

The two composers did what they could in the little time available, George Gershwin in particular cramming the score with so many discarded items from previous productions that when the producer Vincent Freedley attended the first night he sat there bewildered by his suspicion that he had seen the show somewhere before. And so he had; four of Gershwin's songs had come from *Funny Face, Primrose, Strike Up the Band* and *Oh, Kay!*. Here is Wodehouse's mild-mannered account of the madness of his predicament:

> I came here with George Grossmith to do *The Three Musketeers* for Ziegfeld, and we finished a rough version on the boat. But like all work that is done quickly, it needed a terrible lot of fixing, which was left to me as George went home. I was working gaily on it when a fuse blew out in Ziegfeld's Marilyn Miller show-book by Bolton and McGuire. Ziegfeld called in two new composers, Rombert and Gershwin, and asked me to do the lyrics with Ira. I wrote nine in a week and ever since have been sweating away at the rest. Meanwhile Gilbert Miller wanted a show in a hurry for Irene Bordoni, so I started on that too – fixing the Musketeers with my left hand the while. By writing the entire second act in one day I have managed to deliver the Bordoni show in time, and have now finished the lyrics of the Flo show and the revised version of the Musketeers, and all is well – or will be till Flo wants all the lyrics rewritten, as he is sure to do. We open the Bolton–McGuire–Ira Gershwin–Wodehouse–George Gershwin–Romberg show in Boston next week. It's called *Rosalie* and I don't like it much, though it's bound to be a success with Marilyn and Donahue in it.

There were still further complications. Harassed by the regiments of people who claimed to be working on the Ziegfeld and Miller productions, Wodehouse moved out of his New York apartment and took a room at the

The innocent abroad. PGW in Hollywood, filling in time between non-existent assignments by staring into the mind of Jacob Z. Schnellenhamer.

Top PGW (right) with Herbert Grierson on 21 June 1939 at Oxford University, where he received an honorary degree.

Above The most disastrous interview in PGW's life: Associated Press correspondent Angus Thuermer finds Wodehouse in an internment camp on Christmas Eve, 1940.

Opposite The most catastrophic day in PGW's life: at large with an acquaintance in Berlin, 26 June 1941, the day on which he agreed to deliver the notorious broadcasts.

Keep in mind that Gussie thinks Bertie loves Madeline — she will be trying all through to get M. to chuck Gussie & marry Bertie.

Feb 9. 1948

JEEVES NOVEL

Tentative outline:- Bertie's old Oxford friend, Beefy Anstruther, on being told by the Gudgeon that she has met Bertie, gets in touch with him and asks him to be his best man. Wedding is imminent at Beefy's ancestral seat. There is a big house party for the wedding and Madeline and Gussie are there.
Beefy tells Bertie that all is not well between Gussie and Madeline, as Gussie is flirting with vamp. This decides Bertie to go down.
No, I think Madeline must not be there yet, only Gussie.
The story works along to point where Madeline finds Gussie with vamp and breaks off engagement. Bertie hears of this and fears for his own safety. Gudgeon has row with Beefy and breaks off engt. As lesser of two evils Bertie gets engaged to Gudgeon. This of course makes Beefy want to slosh him.
Now work in the theft of the necklace and we have something.

Try it with Honoria Glossop instead of Gudgeon. Bertie gets hurry call from Sir Roderick Glossop. He goes to his place and Sir Roderick tells him that Honoria has just got engaged to a man who knows all about jewels and that he, Sir R., has pinched the necklace which has to be given to her on her wedding day in order to put on a play he has written.

Or shall it be that Honoria is not actually engaged but is being courted by man. Sir Roderick got down vamp to distract man and vamp did the Antony stuff to Sir R. and Sir R. is now engaged to her. Bertie suggests getting Barrymore down to distract vamp. (Sir R. has written letters to vamp).

No, I think it works better with Gudgeon.

Jeeves's solution cd be to get the two couples playing golf in rain as in Feet of Clay.

I could make Beefy in insurance business and start with him coming to Bertie and getting him to take out insurance. Then when Beefy wants to slosh Bertie, Jeeves points out to him that his company will be annoyed.

Surely I can get something out of Bertie being pursued by Beefy. Bertie could take refuge in girl's room and so get engaged to her.
In that case, Bertie could not actually be engaged to Gudgeon. She might come to him with sad story about Beefy and Bertie kiss her., and be seen by Beefy.
Or would that work better for Gussie?

~~Suppose Gussie kisses Gud~~

Above Wodehouse was the most painstaking of plot-makers and boiler-downers, calculating that the published work represented less than half of the writing involved.
Opposite The world of Jeeves and Wooster made flesh in (top left) a *Strand* magazine illustration of Bertie and Tuppy Glossop at the beginning of 'Jeeves and the Song of Songs', (top right) a 1960 jacket featuring Bertie, the Rev. Aubrey Upjohn and Bobbie Wickham with the Brinkley Court butler and (bottom) a detail of the jacket for the 1930 novel, *Very Good, Jeeves*.

Jeeves, Reginald; valet; b. *c.* 15 October 1881, Brixton; *s.* of Basil Jeeves (philologist) and Daisy Wiggins (barmaid of the 'The Cow and Crescent')
Previous employers: Esmond Haddock, JP; Dame Daphne Winkworth; the Earl of Worplesdon; Digby Thistleton
Clubs: Junior Ganymede
Hobbies: shrimping at Herne Bay
Address: c/o Bertram Wilberforce Wooster, Berkeley Mansions, W1

Above A lifetime's addiction to mystery stories began with Sherlock Holmes and ended with Perry Mason. The thriller writer PGW admired most of all was Edgar Wallace, for his gesture of employing two butlers working a day and night shift.

Opposite In old age, when taking a census of his most faithful adherents, PGW tended to count the legs and divide by four. Here is the sponsor of the 'P.G. Wodehouse Shelter for Cats and Dogs' in conference with an emissary.

Overleaf A hundred books later, a man accompanied by a friend tramps the Long Island woodlands thinking of Valley Fields, Ukridge and company.

Great Neck Golf Club. Ziegfeld, whose mind was far too devious to be capable of following any uncomplicated event, immediately began to accuse him of playing golf all day instead of working, a charge which Wodehouse was pleased to refute by producing lyric after lyric. Miraculously, *Rosalie* was well-received, its Broadway opening being immeasurably enlivened by an address during the first act intermission by Mayor James Walker on the brilliance of his new fiscal policy.

But by the time Mayor Walker began his speech, with Freedley sitting in the stalls trying to work out how it was possible to attend a first night for the second time, the most revealing moment in the history of *Rosalie* had already taken place. The out-of-town tryout in Boston had been a chaotic affair, with the running time assuming the proportions of a nightmare for the writers who would have the job of cutting it down to size. And it was here, on this first night, that a small act of domestic virtue took place which tells us as much about Wodehouse in the musical theatre as we need to know. Historians of the genre have often wondered how the creative artist, trapped in a maelstrom of intrigue, chicanery and managerial incompetence, ever contrived to produce any work at all and still retain his sanity. Each writer found his own salvation, either like McGuire in the bottle, or like Romberg in cheerfully unashamed plagiarism ('On a Romberg first night, the audience goes *into* the theatre whistling Tchaikovsky'), or even like Gilbert, who adopted the practice of walking the Thames Embankment while a Savoy first night was proceeding. Wodehouse's method was the most normal of all, being indeed so normal as to strike awe and wonder into the hearts of even his most phlegmatic associates. Fifty years later, Ira Gershwin had still not reconciled himself to it:

> I must tell you about this wonderful, charming man Wodehouse. We collaborated on the lyrics to *Rosalie* for Ziegfeld. We opened in Boston in the big theatre there, I can't think of its name. Anyway, the place was very crowded with Harvard boys, there were a lot of standees, and we were overlong in the first act. I'm five feet six or seven and Wodehouse is very tall, and we were watching the show together at the back, but while he could see what was going on, I couldn't see anything at all. So he was giving me an account of the proceedings. As I say, we were running overlong, and the first act ended at twenty minutes to eleven and the second act was due to start about ten minutes later. And I felt a tap on my shoulder from Wodehouse. I said, 'What is it?' And he reached in his pocket for his Ingersoll watch and he said, 'Ira, it's eleven o'clock, I must toddle off to bed.' And he left. This is the opening night of his show. Plum was an avid reader, and naturally he wanted to get up early to go to the bookstalls along the Charles River. But I've never heard of anybody leaving his own show on opening night at the start of the second act because he wanted to toddle off to bed.[18]

The twin episodes of *Rosalie* and *The Three Musketeers*, both of which opened in the new year of 1928 and both of which ran for over 300 performances, marked very nearly the end of the road for Wodehouse in the musical theatre. The partnership with Kern had swiftly disintegrated through the early 1920s and, although no reason for the dissolution of so successful a partnership has ever been given, the history of American popular song has usually revealed that Kern was not quite the most accommodating of collaborators. Indeed, he must be conceded the dubious honour of being one of the very few men capable of bringing the sublimely equable Wodehouse close to losing his temper. Probably the days of the alliance were numbered from the moment in 1920 when the two of them found themselves on opposing sides of a contract. Yet again the culprit was Ziegfeld, who was guilty of playing his old game of assigning too many writers to too few productions. Bolton and Kern were working on a show called *Sally*, and Wodehouse, writing busily away in London, had been asked to supply the lyrics, from which point confusion, misunderstanding and contractual contradictions conspired to breach the peace.

In his customary methodical way, Wodehouse had posted the lyrics for *Sally* to Bolton and Kern, only to read in the trade press that someone else had already been commissioned to write them. To his beloved step-daughter Leonora, Wodehouse wrote on 28 November 1920:

> I forgot to tell you in my last letter the tale of the laughable imbroglio – or mix-up – which has occurred with Jerry Kern. You remember I sent my lyrics over, and then read in *Variety* that some other cove was doing the lyrics and wrote to everybody in New York to retrieve my lyrics. Then that cable came asking me if I would let them have 'Joan of Arc' and 'Church Around the Corner', which, after a family council, I answered in the affir. Well, just after I had cabled saying all right, I got a furious cable from Jerry – the sort of cable the Kaiser might have sent to an underling – saying my letter withdrawing the lyrics was 'extremely offensive', and ending, 'You have offended me for the last time!', upon which the manly spirit of the Wodehouses (descended from the sister of Anne Boleyn) boiled in my veins – when you get back I'll show you the very veins it boiled in – and I cabled over, 'Cancel permission to use lyrics'. I now hear that Jerry is bringing an action against me for royalties on *Miss Springtime* and *Riviera Girl*, to which he contributed tunes. The loony seems to think that a lyricist is responsible for the composer's royalties. Of course, he hasn't an earthly, and I don't suppose the action will ever come to anything, but doesn't it show how blighted some blighters can be when they decide to be blighters?

Peace was eventually declared, legal proceedings dropped, the two Wodehouse lyrics went into the show, and *Sally* triumphed. There was a third Wodehouse lyric in the show which contains strong Gilbertian overtones, complete with strictly British allusions which may have baffled Broad-

way audiences. These verses were apparently the joint work of Wodehouse
and another Englishman called Clifford Grey, the 'some other cove' to whom
Wodehouse refers in the letter to Leonora:

On the banks of the Schnitza Kommisski,
Lord Northcliffe's expected out there.
He will speak by the day or the week,
And at banquets preside in the chair.
He alone they will offer the throne,
So the country quite firm it will be,
He will make it, they say, just like England today,
Where the Schnitza flows down to the sea.

On the banks of the Schnitza Kommisski,
No animals act on the stage.
Little dogs do not hop over logs
And canaries aren't smashed in the cage.
Elephants dressed in comical pants
Are not goaded to climb up a tree,
And no flea ever will bite the top of the bill
Where the Schnitza flows down to the sea.

On the banks of the Schnitza Kommisski,
We're all simply hopeless at sports.
Every team thinks we're simply a scream,
Our results a succession of noughts.
All the world simply puts us to bed,
We are dubbed with a capital 'D'.
So the English, I hear, we will challenge next year,
Where the Schnitza flows down to the sea.

Ironically, the most enduring Kern–Wodehouse song of all did not register
until long after both men were committed to other enterprises. After the
dispute over *Sally*, the two men never worked together in New York by
premeditation, although they twice wrote shows for London and at least
once, on the occasion of *Sitting Pretty*, were flung into each other's arms by
the defaulting Irving Berlin. But those who labour in the vineyards of the
musical theatre soon learn that loose ends will always dangle, and that no
property, or piece of a property, is ever dead. What now occurred to confirm
once and for all Wodehouse's stature as a songwriter was unusual but hardly
extraordinary. In order to understand how such a bizarre event came about, it
is necessary to return to the context of the Edwardian musical theatre, before
the outbreak of the Great War had cut off the supply of Austro-Hungarian
operettas, a period when, of all the composers vying for work, none was
regarded as more lowly than the native American. Wodehouse has even
claimed that Kern once told him that the American impresario Charles
Frohman actually employed Kern in the mistaken impression that he was

dealing with an Englishman. At any rate, Kern in those early days was certainly reconciled to writing songs and then leaving them in the bottom drawer until the day dawned when somebody influential might deign to listen to them.

At some time around 1906–7, Kern wrote just such a tune, which appears to have then gone to ground and remained there for several years, apparently unseen by anybody but Kern himself. At the end of 1917 the Princess Theatre team, having scored such a success with *Oh, Boy!*, began working on a successor, eventually to be called *Oh, Lady! Lady!*. Kern remembered his 1906 melody and showed it to Wodehouse, who promptly provided it with a lyric:

> I used to dream that I would discover,
> The perfect lover,
> Some day.
> I knew I'd recognize him if ever he came round my way.
> I always used to fancy then,
> He'd be one of the godlike kind of men,
> With a giant brain and a noble head,
> Like the heroes bold in the books I read.
>
> But along came Bill, who's quite the opposite of all the men
> In story books.
> In grace and looks,
> I know that Apollo
> Would beat him all hollow,
> And I can't explain,
> It's surely not his brain
> That makes me thrill.
> I love him because he's wonderful,
> Because he's just my Bill.
>
> He can't play golf or tennis or polo,
> Or sing a solo
> Or row.
> He isn't half as handsome as dozens of men that I know.
> He isn't tall and straight and slim
> And he dresses far worse than Ted or Jim.
> And I can't explain why he should be
> Just the one, one man in the world for me.
>
> He's just my Bill, he has no gifts at all, a motor car
> He cannot steer,
> And it seems clear
> Whenever he dances,
> His partner takes chances,
> Oh I can't explain,
> It's surely not his brain

That makes me thrill.
I love him because he's – I don't know,
Because he's just my Bill

The *Oh, Lady! Lady!* songs were generously received at the first night in February 1918. The old-new piece was not among them, having been dropped because it was felt that the modesty of its sentiments would show up the hero in a poor light. Some years later Wodehouse and Kern, invited aboard Ziegfeld's yacht, a floating palace appropriately christened *The Wench*, took care that one of the young ladies present was proficient in the art of singing 'Bill', the hope being that Ziegfeld would be so impressed by it as to purchase it for one of his productions. In the event, the plan worked too well, Ziegfeld being so taken by the song that he offered to have an entire musical comedy written around it, an expedient which did not quite seem the most suitable one for the song so far as Kern and Wodehouse were concerned. By 1926, with Wodehouse no longer committed to the Kern partnership and gradually drifting away from the musical theatre altogether, his ex-collaborator found himself wrestling with the amorphous mass of Edna Ferber's best-selling novel about Mississippi riverboat entertainers. On reading *Show Boat*, Kern had conceived the irrational ambition to convert it into a musical, even though well aware that its plot and characters, carrying implications regarding the forbidden theme of miscegenation, were hopelessly heretical in the context of the musical theatre of the period; indeed, it may well have been its very unsuitability which commended the novel to Kern, by now impatient with the idiotic conventions of the average Broadway musical libretto. At any rate, working with his new partner, Oscar Hammerstein, he somehow contrived to persuade Ziegfeld that a musical based on *Show Boat* was commercially viable.

Miss Ferber's novel would have defeated the efforts of the most gifted adapters in the world, and Hammerstein was not altogether to blame for the comically lopsided aspect of the finished article, comprising a first act embracing the events of three weeks, and a second covering twenty years. In this interminable second act, there is a moment when the character Julie, forsaken by all her old friends on the *Cotton Blossom*, auditions for a Chicago night-club engagement. It is one of those rare moments in any musical comedy where the literal sentiments of the song are not required to have relevance to either the plot or the characters, for a singer might choose any song in the world for an audition piece. Kern, never a man to spurn a short cut, capitalized on this fact by plucking 'Bill' from the limbo of lost causes and slipping it into the famous audition scene in *Show Boat*, where it became one of the sensations of the decade, transforming its singer, Helen Morgan, into an international star.

Not that the 'Bill' which Miss Morgan so memorably rendered perched on a grand piano was quite the 'Bill' which had been dropped from *Oh, Lady! Lady!*. While the two original verses had survived the years, the two choruses had not, and had undergone slight but subtle amendments:

Along came Bill, who's not the type at all,
You'd meet him on the street and never notice him.
His form and face,
His manly grace,
Are not the kind that you
Would find in a statue,
And I can't explain,
It's surely not his brain
That makes me thrill.
I love him because he's wonderful,
Because he's just old Bill.

He's just my Bill, an ordinary boy,
He hasn't got a thing that I can brag about.
And yet to be
Upon his knee
So comfy and roomy
Feels natural to me.
And I can't explain,
It's surely not his brain
That makes me thrill.
I love him because he's – I don't know –
Because he's just my Bill.

It seems likely that had 'Bill' not achieved its improbable apotheosis in a show for which it had never been intended, Wodehouse's work as a lyricist would be forgotten completely today by all except the later writers who imbibed his precepts of the colloquial lyric. 'Till the Clouds Roll By', a deceptively simple-sounding song from *Oh, Boy!*, has deservedly survived in a minor sort of way, but it is 'Bill', with its understated felicities, which justifies the lavish praise showered upon its author by the likes of Hart, Hammerstein, Rodgers, Dietz, Mercer and Ira Gershwin. It is therefore relevant to insist that 'Bill' is indeed Wodehouse's work, especially as at times there has been confusion on this point. At least one historian has assumed that because the 'Bill' of *Oh, Lady! Lady!* and the 'Bill' of *Show Boat* are two different works, then it must mean that they are the work of two different hands. Apart from the fact that this is deductive reasoning reduced to the level of gibberish, there are two impeccable proofs of the validity of the song as a Wodehouse work. The first is that in telling his story of the night on board *The Wench*, Wodehouse is specific regarding the state of the lyric to 'Bill' at that stage in its chequered career, which was the identical state to the one subsequently heard by audiences at *Show Boat*. And as the jaunt on the yacht took place before Kern had even contemplated working with Hammerstein, there can be no question of the latter having amended the original words to the form in which the world knows them. The other proof is Hammerstein's own declaration in 1946, when the show was successfully revived:

I am particularly anxious to point out that the lyric for the song 'Bill'
was written by P. G. Wodehouse. Although he has always been given
credit in the program, it has frequently been assumed that since I wrote
all the other lyrics for *Show Boat*, I also wrote this one, and I have had
praise for it which belongs to another man.[19]

Although he was no longer associated professionally with Kern, and although there had been some uncomfortable moments in their partnership,
Wodehouse never lost his deep affection for the composer, saying that 'his
well of melody was inexhaustible, and he loved work. You could not give
him too much of it'. Wodehouse continues:

It was this habit of always working and seldom sleeping that eventually
undermined his health. He hated to go to bed. His idea of a quiet home
evening was to sit at the piano composing till about five in the morning. Often in the Princess days my telephone would ring in the small
hours.
'Plum? Jerry.'
'Good heavens, Jerry, do you know what time it is?'
'Quite early, isn't it? Are you in bed?'
'I was.'
'Oh. Well, I've just got that first act duet we were worrying about. Get
a pencil and paper.'
His telephone was on the piano, and he would play me the melody
and I would take down a dummy[20] and totter back to bed. Jerry probably
stayed up and worked on the second act trio.
I remember spending the weekend at his house in Bronxville once,
and around midnight I happened to mention that I had taken a
bungalow at Bellport, Long Island, for the summer.
'Let's go and look at it,' said Jerry.
'Tomorrow, you mean?'
'No, now,' said Jerry, and he insisted on driving off there and then in
his car. Bronxville is about forty miles one side of New York and
Bellport about eighty on the other side. We got there at three in the
morning, inspected the bungalow and drove back, Jerry at the wheel,
sound asleep most of the time. I had to keep nudging him, and he
would wake up and say, 'Oh, did I doze off? Sorry'. It was not one of the
rides I look back to as among my most enjoyable.
We did ten shows together and I was devoted to him. I saw him very
rarely after the road tour of *Sitting Pretty* in 1924, and I am told that he
got very solemn and serious towards the end of his life. But in the
Princess days he was one of the most cheerful and amusing men I have
ever met, and an angel to work with, which many composers aren't.[21]

After the departure of Kern from Wodehouse's career, after the debris of

Rosalie and *The Three Musketeers* had been swept away, there remained only one final episode involving Wodehouse directly in the musical theatre. In 1934 the producer Vincent Freedley, having by now gathered the wits mislaid at the opening of *Rosalie*, began to plan a new Cole Porter musical based on the idea of a pleasure ship with several eccentrics aboard which is wrecked at sea. His first choice for the book was the old firm of Bolton and Wodehouse, who duly set to work, completing their script in August 1934 before returning to Europe. At this stage life began imitating art in a most embarrassing way; in September the pleasure ship *Morro Castle* burst into flames off the New Jersey coast and went down with the loss of over a hundred lives. Clearly Freedley would now need to get the book substantially rewritten and, as neither Bolton nor Wodehouse was any longer at his disposal, he turned for help to the show's director Howard Lindsay, who went in turn to dramatist Russell Crouse. The two new librettists completed a fresh libretto from which all mention of a shipwreck had been excised; despite the minimal effect their original work had on the finished article, Bolton and Wodehouse retained a shared credit with Lindsay and Crouse. In any event, the episode remained so vivid in Wodehouse's memory that nearly twenty years later he published an account in the *New York Herald Tribune* of what was in effect his last appearance on any musical comedy stage:

> I have many pleasant memories of the days when the show was being readied for production, but none I like to recall better than the episode of the drunk at Le Touquet. That was where we collaborators finally got together. At the outset we were rather a scattered bunch. I had a villa at Le Touquet on the Normandy coast of France. Guy was living in Sussex, England, and Cole Porter, as far as I can remember, was in Heidelberg. It was Howard Lindsay, who was to direct the show, who suggested that it would be a good thing if we saw something of each other and had a conference or two, and he finally got us assembled at Le Touquet, which seemed a good central meeting place.
>
> The first thing Guy and I wanted to do, of course, was to hear the music, and as my villa contained no piano we all trooped down to the Casino, where there was one in a corridor leading off the gambling rooms. There the clicking of chips and the croupiers' calls competed with Cole's piano, bringing to our delighted ears the title song, 'You're the Top', and 'Blow, Gabriel, Blow'. Not only to *our* ears. Once, I recall, the door was pushed open by a pleasantly intoxicated young American socialite, who in his befuddled state concluded that Cole was a hired performer.
>
> 'Don't play that stuff,' he said. 'Play something good. Do you know "I Wonder Where My Baby Is Tonight"?' Cole did know it and played it without protest. Our visitor began to cry. 'That song hits me right here,' he said, thumping the region of his heart. 'Just been divorced, so can you blame me for wondering?'

We made sympathetic noises, and Cole played 'You're the Top'. The intruder came weaving back through the door.

'Forget that stuff,' he said. 'Do you know a number called "The Horse with the Lavender Eyes"? It drove us down from the Plaza to the church. Dawn said the horse had lavender eyes,' he continued brokenly, 'so we sang the song all the way down the avenue. Dawn O'Day, that was her stage name. Pretty, isn't it?'

He rose and laid a small column of 100-franc chips on top of the piano.

'What's that for?' we asked.

'For him,' he said, indicating Cole. 'He plays okay, but he picks out rotten numbers.'

The thought that will probably occur to anyone reading the programme of *Anything Goes* is that the management did not stint the public in the matter of authors. There are four of them – count them, four – not including Porter, who wrote the lyrics. The explanation is ready to hand.

The thing started as a Bolton–Wodehouse show, my own share in the melange of mirth and melody being confined, as I remember, mostly to lending moral support. The rough work, the writing, was done by Guy, and I would look in on him from time to time and say, 'How are you getting on?' and he would say 'Fine', and I would go away and return a day or two later and say, 'How's it coming?' and he would say, 'Swell'.

So far, so good. But when it was shipped off to New York, we sustained a painful blow. Guy, with my help, had turned out an excellent book, but unfortunately it was all about an ocean liner in peril on the high seas and it was just then that the *Morro Castle* tragedy occurred, rendering such a theme out of the question, and as neither of us could go to New York, each having a play of his own coming on in London, Vincent Freedley, our manager, suggested that Lindsay should revamp the script. He called Crouse in as collaborator, and that was how your grandfather did his bit in founding the famous Lindsay–Crouse partnership which led to *Life With Father*.[22]

But if the quarter-credit of *Anything Goes* was Wodehouse's modest swansong, it was not the end of his connection with the nebulous art of songwriting, nor the end of his influence on fellow-writers. For the rest of his life he indulged in the occasional vanity of composing a lyric, usually for some non-existent tune in some fictitious setting. But the last of his efforts in this line was intended for production, in a still-born musical called *Jeeves* which was planned for his ninetieth year. In that year he revealed for the first time the lowly origins of his most famous character:

I view the future with concern,
On every side, at every turn
Disaster seems to stare one in the face.

For Mr Wooster is, it's plain,
In what he calls the soup again
And liable to sink without a trace.
At times like these when on the verge
Of cataclysms, I've an urge
To seek a spot where life runs calm and slow.
And find release and peace at last
In the quiet haven where I passed
My happy childhood days so long ago.

In Brixton,
In lovely Brixton
Which I long so to see.
Yearning
To be returning
To London S.E.
I feel my place is
In that oasis,
Home of all that's brave and free.
Where on each street
Are always found
Strong men with feet
Upon the ground,
Where in each breast
As all attest
There's a heart of gold beneath the rest.
In Brixton,
My heart is fixed on
And it's there I would be.

As to Wodehouse's continuing influence upon his contemporaries, there occurred in 1937 the first and last instance of one lyricist writing a lyric consisting of a stylistic tribute to another. In composing the words for his brother's tunes in the 1937 movie *A Damsel in Distress*, Ira Gershwin wrote a set of verses with a specific purpose above and beyond the call of duty:

> When I did this lyric I remembered 'muddle through' as a Briticism, sometimes of criticism, sometimes of resolution, much used at the time of World War I and almost as prevalent as World War II's term of approval, 'good show'. Then, from various characters in Wodehouse came phrases like 'pip-pip', 'toodle'oo' and 'stout fella'.[23]

Just to underline the depth of his affection for his old partner, Ira prefaced one of the secondary songs, 'Things Are Looking Up', as follows:

> Sung by Fred Astaire to Joan Fontaine on the downs of Totleigh Castle, located in Upper Pelham-Grenville, Wodehouse, England.

In a letter to Townend dated 18 April 1953, Wodehouse remarks, 'How few of the people I mention are still alive. Flo Ziegfeld, Marilyn Miller, George Gershwin, Jerry Kern, George Grossmith, Bill McGuire . . . dozens of them, all gone.'[24] The few survivors clung together, each using the rest as a prop against the advancing years. Bolton later claimed, 'I hang on because of Plum', while Plum himself, equally solicitous for old friendships, maintained them to the point where he tended to display unconscious humour regarding them. On being informed that Ira was in poor health, he expressed concern and was reminded that Ira was after all approaching his eightieth birthday. At which Wodehouse, genuinely shocked, exclaimed, 'Good lord, is Ira really as old as all that?' At the time of this exchange, Wodehouse was ninety-two years and six months old.

Until the end of his life he remained in postal touch with Ira, who treasured the cards and letters, not just because of the whimsicality of their contents, nor even because the two men loved and admired each other so much, but because the survival of each man was to the other a surety that their mutual past was not yet lost. They were like two ancient mandarins of a vanished age, sitting back and observing with amused wonder the drunken financial cavortings of the latterday American musical. When on that day so many years before he had stepped aboard *The Wench* hopeful for the future of 'Bill' and been rewarded with the offer of a production, Plum had written: 'That's how simple it was to get backing in those days when big musicals cost fifty thousand to put on, a well-staged party with a few pretty girls, Irving or Jerry, Lou Hirsch[25] or Rudy Friml at the piano . . . and one lady guest carefully chosen for her voice.' In the last days of his friendship with Ira, Wodehouse, the man who, in the words of Alan Lerner, 'inaugurated the American musical', heard news of two Broadway productions which had speedily foundered at a combined cost to their backers of over a million dollars. Picking up a pen, he wrote his annual Christmas card to his old friend. The inscription read, 'Ira, we are well out of it.'

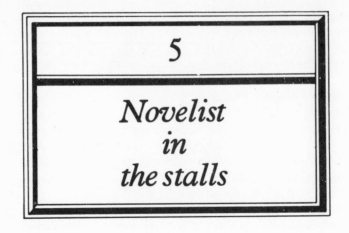

5

*Novelist
in
the stalls*

has displayed a more or less complete disregard for the revolutionary
work which Wodehouse performed in the musical theatre. Through either
lack of interest, or cultural snobbery, or sheer unawareness, it has not so
much rejected that work as ignored its very existence, preferring to simplify
its own critical duties by regarding him exclusively as a novelist and short-
story writer. In all those years when his boosters were honouring him so
lavishly either with hysterical praise or with its mirror-image, hysterical
abuse, they evidently never stopped to consider that in a field far removed
from literature and yet slyly related to it, Wodehouse's eminence was even
more spectacular than it was as a novelist. His life on Broadway has come
to be seen as a baffling aberration, an inexplicable folly, a frivolous departure from his real work and hardly to be included in the canon at all.
The British, very much offshore islanders so far as the twentieth-century
musical is concerned, have bypassed the whole episode, even though in so
doing they are turning their backs on the labour of half a lifetime, snubbing
work which was not only congenial to Wodehouse, but which also discloses
him in the unfamiliar guise of revolutionary stylist overthrowing an obso-
lescent tradition. This selective approach to his work has had the curious
effect of endowing him with two disconnected reputations. In America,
where *Show Boat* is frequently revived, his name alongside those of Kern
and Hammerstein is permanent proof of the long years he spent trying to find
a rhyme for 'moon' which was not 'June' but which might on a good day, as
he once suggested, be 'macaroon'. This explains why his sharepushers have

been Rodgers and Gershwin in America, Belloc and Waugh in Britain, where general readers continue to smile at the gentle felicities of their favourite comic novelist without noticing a preponderance of a certain specific and highly significant frame of reference.

The oversight is surprising, because the musical career, so far from being a hermetically sealed compartment of Wodehouse's art closed off at all points from the novels, had a profound effect on everything he wrote. After all, when a man has a hand in fifty-two dramatic works over a period of fifty years, the experience is bound to show in everything else he does. Wodehouse wrote more libretti than Gilbert, more plays than Lonsdale, and if there is something absurdly philistine about so baldly quantitative a comparison, it at least illustrates the extent to which for many years the man's art was subject to disciplines very far removed from the isolation of the writing desk and the galley proof. And yet the regiments of loyal readers who advanced so resolutely, decade after decade, on each new novel as it appeared, and who scoured the pre-war magazines in the hope of finding a new short story, apparently never noticed that very often what they were reading had been influenced at great depth by events on Broadway and in Tin Pan Alley. It was not just that the writing of the novels was being conducted concurrently with the composition of song lyrics – very often Wodehouse was enmeshed in the coils of both simultaneously – but that the technical demands of his stage work, style achieved at high speed, rigid formalism of metre, ruthless economy, the acquirement of a whole new creative system of knowledge unknown to his fellow-novelists, affected his fiction in four ways. It shaped his construction, enriched his vocabulary, expedited the problems of characterization, and, on some spectacular occasions, provided him with the perfect theme.

Of the effect on his construction at any rate there can be no dispute. As mentor to his old studymate Townend, Wodehouse revealed time and time again how his treatment of plot was constantly subject to the conventions of Broadway. Because Townend happened to be in need of frequent guidance regarding the working-out of his own plots, and because no more generous friend than Wodehouse ever existed, the latter became perhaps more explicit than any other author of the century about the way to go about shaping a story. And it so happens that these expositions, besides affording a fascinating glimpse inside the craftsman's workshop, confirm once and for all both the power and the value of the precepts picked up by the novelist in the course of his songwriting experiences. Here he is explaining to Townend how he goes about building a novel:

> The principle I always go on is to think of the characters in terms of actors in a play. I say to myself when I invent a good character for an early scene, 'If this were a musical comedy we should have to get somebody like Leslie Henson[1] to play this part, and if he found that all he had was a scene in act one, he would walk out. How, therefore, can I twist the story so as to give him more to do, and keep him alive till the fall of the curtain?'

Wodehouse repeated this lesson ceaselessly to Townend, drumming in to him the wisdom of the law which says that plot must be subjugated to the demands of a charming character:

> When you're doing a long story you have got to be most infernally careful of the values of your characters. I believe I told you once before that I classed all my characters as if they were living salaried actors, and I'm convinced that this is a rough but very good way of looking at them. The one thing actors, important actors, I mean, won't stand is being brought on to play a scene which is of no value to them in order that they may feed some less important character, and I believe this isn't vanity but is based on an instinctive knowledge of stagecraft. They kick because they know the balance isn't right.

And yet again:

> I believe there are two ways of writing novels. One is mine, making the thing a sort of musical comedy without music, and ignoring real life altogether; the other is going right deep down into life and not caring a damn. The ones that fail are the ones where the writer loses his nerve and says: 'My God! I can't write this, I must tone it down.'

And yet again:

> In writing a novel, I always imagine I am writing for a cast of actors. Some actors are natural minor actors and some are natural major ones. It is a matter of personality. Same in a book. Psmith, for instance, is a major character. If I am going to have Psmith in a story, he must be in the big situation.

Wodehouse was so faithful to this precept that, rather than cast his major characters in a minor role, he would abandon them altogether, which is precisely what happened to Psmith. Not long before his death, he offered an apologetic explanation for the sudden disappearance of Psmith from his work:

> The answer is simple. I can't think of a plot. A married Psmith, moreover, would not be quite the same. But obviously a man of his calibre is not going to be content to spend his life as Lord Emsworth's secretary. In what direction he branched out I cannot say.

And, being unable to say, rather than offer something unworthy of Psmith's eminence as a personality, Wodehouse simply let him go on his own way. It was a hard lesson, learned at the feet of characters like Justine Johnstone and her workmate Marion Davies, symbolic of the performer who assesses the profundity of a dramatic work not by the subtlety of its ethic or the depth of its poetic content but simply by counting up the number of lines contained in his role. One of the especial delights of Wodehouse's world is the major impact of his minor characters, a Rupert Baxter or a Percy Pilbeam, doomed never to play the leading role or get the girl, but rendered somehow unforgettable all the same; it appears that they owe their immortality to the creator's belief in the golden rule that before a performer can be expected to stir himself sufficiently to amuse an audience, he must be provided with a quantity of words and deeds commensurate with his own evaluation of himself.

But once having acknowledged his responsibility to flesh out even his lesser characters, Wodehouse then drew on the second of the assets provided by a life in the musical theatre. Most novelists have skated over the awkward truth that in everyday life people are forever humming, singing or whistling, and that such unselfconscious musical doodlings are perfectly natural. A few writers have allowed the reader to note the presence of this constant impromptu performance, but Wodehouse is very nearly the only considerable novelist in English literature who is able to hear *what* his characters are singing, in which regard he is able to display so encyclopaedic a knowledge of popular music that, even allowing for the cultural snobbery which has so ruthlessly excluded songwriting from even the anteroom of the arts, it seems extraordinary that his admirers in the literary world have never bothered to examine this facet of his work in any detail. One or two of his fellow-novelists have understood the usefulness of the song lyric as a device for pegging the action to a certain fleeting moment in the lives of their characters. In *The Great Gatsby*, Fitzgerald is very careful to let us know that when Nick Carraway and Jordan Baker are driving through Central Park, the song which they can hear drifting on the air is 'The Sheik of Araby', that when Gatsby coaxes the out-of-practice Mr Klipspringer to play the piano, the song he selects is one by Wodehouse's sometime partner Louis Hirsch called 'The Love Nest', and that in that fatal moment when Daisy leaves Gatsby's party, the 'neat sad little waltz' drifting out of the open door of the house is 'Three O'Clock in the Morning'. This precise, journalistic deployment of popular song in a narrative was later taken up by John O'Hara among others; in *Sermons and Soda Water*, his hero measures the intensity of his own spent emotions by the degree to which he can retain the songs of his youth, and finds that Gershwin's 'Do It Again' has finally emerged as the most Proustian symbol of all.

But in Wodehouse everybody aspires to musical paraphrase in this way. The very air the characters breathe is alive with the echo of half-remembered, never-forgotten melody. It is revealing enough that Freddie Threepwood should display a morbid attachment to the lyrics of 'April Showers', while Miss Peavey in *Leave It to Psmith* prefers 'The Beale Street Blues', that Orlo Vosper in *Pigs Have Wings* is partial to 'My Sweetie Went Away', that Mr Pickering in *Uneasy Money* places himself irrevocably out of court through his regrettable tendency to burst into 'I'll Sing Thee Songs of Araby', but there is the more acute case of Samuel Bulpitt in *Summer Moonshine*, who is a positive mine of information regarding the texts of 'Pennies From Heaven', 'Alice Blue Gown', 'What'll I Do?' and 'Happy Days Are Here Again'. Pugsy Maloney in *Psmith, Journalist* betrays his ethnic background by warbling 'My Little Irish Rose', while, in *The Mating Season*, the decrepitude of the church organ is indicated by the fact that 'for years it had been going round with holes in its socks, doing the brother can you spare a dime stuff, and now it was about due to hand in its dinner pail'. It is an infallible sign of Freddie Widgeon's hopeless lack of *savoir-faire* that in *Lord Emsworth and Others* he attempts a chorus of 'When the Silver of the Moonlight Meets the Lovelight in Your Eyes' while the pianist is playing 'Top Hat, White Tie and Tails'. Most spectacular of all, in the first chapter of *Thank You, Jeeves*, Bertie Wooster, inspired by recent exposure to Ben Bloom and his Sixteen Baltimore Buddies, picks up a newly-acquired banjolele and renders in quick succession 'Ole Man River', 'The Wedding of the Painted Doll', Singin' in the Rain', 'Three Little Words', 'Goodnight Sweetheart', 'My Love Parade', 'Spring is Here', 'Whose Baby Are You', and part of 'I Want an Automobile with a Horn that Goes Toot-Toot'.

Sometimes Wodehouse elaborates either by revealing further depths of musical character in these singing, playing, humming, strumming humans, or by paying oblique tribute to the writers responsible for the songs. Among the recipients of these slapstick garlands is the defaulting collaborator from *Sitting Pretty*, Irving Berlin, whose art is so potent as to have penetrated the very nearly impermeable consciousness of Clarence, ninth Earl of Emsworth, who, in *Galahad at Blandings*, begins singing, much to the narrator's surprise, 'something, if I remember, about there being a rainbow in the sky, so let's have another cup of coffee and let's have another piece of pie'. The habit is catching; before the end of the story Wilfred Alsop is echoing the identical sentiments, 'for he liked both words and music, the work, he had been given to understand, of the maestro Berlin, author and composer of "Alexander's Ragtime Band" and other morceaux'. He is at least more charitable than Jerry Nichols in *Bachelors Anonymous*, who boasts, 'I wouldn't knock off smoking for all the rice in China', without acknowledgments to the songwriter who popularized the phrase.[2] But behind all this professional camaraderie, was there just the faintest tincture of irritation in Berlin's elusiveness on the occasion of *Sitting Pretty*? Or was Berlin's unwillingness to collaborate with Wodehouse the upshot of some earlier breach of professional etiquette which the Englishman had committed? In a story called 'At Geisenheimer's', published in the *Saturday Evening Post* in 1921, the narrator describes the scene in a well-known restaurant:

All the tables were occupied, and there were several couples already on the dancing-floor in the centre. The band was playing 'Michigan':

I want to go back, I want to go back,
To the place where I was born.
Far away from harm
With a milk-pail on my arm.

I suppose the fellow who wrote that would have called for the police if anyone had ever really tried to get him on to a farm.[3]

The two opposing poles of reaction to the world of musical comedy, the Wodehousean and the conventional, are represented by Bill Dawlish in *Uneasy Money* and Ronnie Fish's Aunt Julia in *Heavy Weather*. Predictably it is the ogress-aunt who expresses the bigoted bourgeois view, remarking, 'I regard the entire personnel of the ensembles of our musical comedy theatre as, if you will forgive me for being Victorian for a moment, painted hussies'. Ronnie Fish, who wants to marry one, protests, 'But they've got to paint', at which Aunt Julia administers the *coup de grâce* with 'Well, they needn't huss'. Dawlish, on the other hand, is convinced that the world of song and dance is more effective than any politician as an emollient for the world's unease – 'He knew there had been some unpleasantness between England and the United States in seventeen something and again in eighteen something, but things had eventually been straightened out by Miss Edna May and her fellow-missionaries in *The Belle of New York*, since when there had been no more trouble.'[4] Fish eventually weds the chorus girl of his dreams, the desirable Sue Brown, establishing Wodehouse as one of the only two modern English novelists – the other is Sir Compton Mackenzie – to depict the ladies of the chorus as likely candidates for a happy domestic life.

Wodehouse's use of popular song in this way was by no means limited to the Broadway world of which he had been so distinguished a citizen. Esmond Haddock in *The Mating Season*, for example, renders 'The Yeoman's Hunting Song' so ineptly as to mislead Wooster altogether:

> He assumed the grave intent expression of a stuffed frog and let it rip. 'Hello, hello, hello. . . .'
> I raised a hand. 'Just a second. What are you supposed to be doing, telephoning?'
> 'No, it's a hunting song.'
> 'Oh, I see. I thought it might be one of those I'm going to telephone my baby things.'[5]

In *Summer Lightning*, Beach is caught in a moment of repose rendering 'There's a Light in Thy Bower', and in *Lord Emsworth and Others* we encounter 'a cove who looked like a plumber's mate' who sings 'Break the News to Mother'.[6] Even more abstruse, in *The Little Nugget* there is a drunk who renders that deathless couplet:

> I don't care if he wears a crown,
> He can't keep kicking my dawg aroun'.

Among those who are on the alert against this school of balladry is Psmith, who, when in New York, suggests to Mike Jackson that they sup at the Astor

Hotel Roof Garden in preference to anywhere else because 'to feed on such a night as this in some lowdown hostelry on the level of the street with German waiters breathing down the back of one's neck and two fiddles and a piano whacking out "Beautiful Eyes" about three feet from one's tympanum would be false economy'. Dangers of a different kind threaten the Mulliner dynasty in 'Best Seller':

> The night was very still. From far away in the distance came the faint strains of the town band as it picked its way through 'The Star of Evening' from *Tannhauser*, somewhat impeded by the second trombone, who had got his music mixed up and was playing 'The Wedding of the Painted Doll'.

As for the eccentrics of the older generation, they are naturally attached to the popular airs of a third category, the songs which had once echoed through the music halls of undergraduate days. Galahad Threepwood's imperishable love for the pink-tighted Dolly Henderson, for instance, had once caused him to take Lord Emsworth to the Tivoli to see for himself, an experience which had left his lordship with a memory which was at once undying and incomprehensible:

> 'Galahad took me to the Tivoli once when Dolly Henderson was singing there. A little bit of a thing in pink tights. Made you think of spring mornings. The gallery joined in the chorus, I recollect. How did it go? Tum tum tumpty tump? Or was it Umpty tiddly tiddly pom?'

Threepwood appears to have made a habit of dragging Emsworth into theatres and music halls; the problem was that his lordship, although he rather enjoyed these jaunts, and retained fragmentary impressions of the music, was never able to retain enough for anybody to identify the items. In the very last novel of Wodehouse's life, *Sunset at Blandings*, there occurs the following very touching passage:

> 'Bless my soul,' Emsworth said, 'that reminds me of a song in a musical comedy Galahad took me to when we were young men. About the Grenadier Guards guarding the Bank of England at night. How did it go? "If you've got money or plate in the bank",' sang Lord Emsworth in a reedy tenor like an escape of gas, ' "we're the principal parties to thank. Our regiment sends you a squad that defends you from anarchists greedy and lank. . . . In the cellars and over roof",' continued Lord Emsworth, who was not an easy man to stop, ' "we keep all intruders aloof, and no-one can go in to rob Mr Bowen of what he describes as the oof". Bowen must have been the manager of the Bank of England at that time, don't you think?

In editing the published edition of the uncompleted *Sunset at Blandings*, Richard Usborne, a wise and witty exegetist of Wodehouse's prose, made prolonged attempts to put a title and a date to this obscure musical comedy which so impressed Emsworth in his youth. However, appeals in the correspondence columns of a national newspaper drew nothing more substantial than the suggestion that perhaps after all the words were composed by Wodehouse himself, endeavouring to give one of his favourite characters something quaint to recall. Certainly, the choice of rhyme for 'aloof' has a Woosterian ring about it, especially as Wooster himself is prone to this kind of thing; at one stage he confesses that the sound of Gussie Mannering-Phipps attempting to sing 'reminded me of a night at Oxford when, but a lad of eighteen, he sang "Let's All Go Down the Strand" after a bump supper, standing up to his knees in the college fountain'.

Characters so thoroughly immersed in their own musical recollections are bound from time to time to confuse musical comedy with the real thing, to be so acutely aware of the conventions of one world as to be tempted to apply them to the other. In *Summer Lightning* there is an affecting moment when Pilbeam asks Beach when dinner is to be served, to which that marmoreal retainer and sometime performer of 'There's a Light in Thy Bower', replies, 'I put it back some little while, as gentlemen aren't punctual in the summertime':

> Pilbeam considered this statement. It sounded to him as if it would make a good song – Gentlemen aren't punctual in the summertime, I said in the summertime, so take me back, to that old Kentucky shack.

Pilbeam's descent into pastiche is followed by Wooster in *The Mating Season*, where a very famous phrase from a very famous popular song is used as a syntactical device. This time the writers being honoured are Richard Rodgers and Lorenz Hart. At a moment of crisis in his affairs, Bertie says, 'My heart stood still. I clutched at the windscreen for support and whatwhated.' When things deteriorate further, he adds, 'My heart stood stiller.' Finally panic sets it, and he remarks, 'My heart, ceasing to stand still, gave a leap and tried to get out through my front teeth.' The ballad 'My Heart Stood Still', introduced by Rodgers and Hart in their adaptation of Mark Twain's *A Yankee at the Court of King Arthur*, which opened in New York in 1927, is noted as the song around which has accrued one of the most famous of all Broadway legends; its authors described several times how the phrase had been blurted out by a lady-friend when all three of them narrowly avoided a serious accident one day in a Paris taxi-cab. Wodehouse must have quoted the phrase with mixed feelings, probably having savoured the anecdote of the Paris taxi with even mixeder ones. In 1918, working on the songs for *Oh, Lady! Lady!*, he had completed a lyric to a Kern melody called 'You Found Me and I Found You', in which there occurs the following passage:

SHE: I got a soaking,
   Now wasn't that provoking.
   One day when it began to rain.
HE: You simply made my heart stand still,
   Just think, you might have caught a chill,
   And if you'd caught the chill, you see,
   You'd not have caught the train.

On the wilder shores of Wodehousean scholarship, then, it remains a contentious issue whether, when Wooster described the antics of his heart, he was quoting Lorenz Hart or his own creator.

When the Englishman Archie Moffam attends a party in New York's Hotel Cosmopolis, it is to find the scene animated by the cast of what Wodehouse defines, with a wink at Ziegfeld, as 'The Frivolities', a bunch of star-spangled rowdies with taps on their shoes and nothing to speak of in their heads.[7] As the newspapers report the following morning:

> Thither, therefore, marched Mr O'Neill, his face full of cheese sandwich (for he had been indulging in an early breakfast or a late supper) and his heart of devotion to duty. He found there the Misses Pauline Preston and 'Bobbie' St Clair, of the personnel of the chorus of the Frivolities, entertaining a few friends of either sex. A pleasant time was being had by all, and at the moment of Mr O'Neill's entry the entire strength of the company was rendering with considerable emphasis that touching ballad 'There's a Place For Me in Heaven, For My Baby Boy is There'.
>
> The able and efficient officer at once suggested that there was a place for them in the street and the patrol-wagon was there; and, being a man of action as well as words, proceeded to gather up an armful of assorted guests as a preliminary to a personally-conducted tour into the cold night. It was at this point that Miss Preston stepped into the limelight. Mr O'Neill contends that she hit him with a brick, an iron casing and the Singer Building.

Although it seems likely that in saddling the formidable young ladies with so outlandish a song Wodehouse was indulging once more in his gift for parody, he was not so very far from the reality of Tin Pan Alley. A title like 'There's a Place For Me in Heaven' was a staple diet in the song-publishing business, in both the stress of its rhythm and the bathos of its sentiments. The archives reveal, among others, 'There's a Cabin in the Cotton', 'There's a Gold Star in her Window', 'There's a Little Street in Heaven', 'There's a Village in the Valley' and 'There's a Whistle in the Thistle'. Some years after the adventures of Archie Moffam, the industry surpassed itself with 'There's a New Star in Heaven Tonight – Rudolph Valentino', and still later, 'There's a Platinum Star in Heaven Tonight – Jean Harlow', both of which outrages have their roots in the title which would have been beyond even Wodehouse, 'They Needed a Songbird in Heaven so God Took Caruso Away'.

But the two songs of the time and place which affected Wodehouse most deeply were 'Sonny Boy' and 'Ole Man River', both of which were considered by him to be important enough to be the basis of a fable. In *Very Good, Jeeves* (1930), in an episode entitled 'Jeeves and the Song of Songs', Wooster is confronted by a Tuppy Glossop racked with adoration for an emergent opera singer called Cora Bellinger, who not only aspires to appearances at the Albert Hall but is built on the same lines. Her voice is so powerful that, five minutes after she has left a room, the plaster is still fluttering down from the ceiling, and in his stricken idolatry for this yodelling paragon Glossop plans to impress her by singing 'Sonny Boy' at an East End Lads' Club charity concert. Wooster receives this news with mixed feelings. His own considerable experience in rendering 'Sonny Boy' has left him with certain beliefs regarding it, for instance that 'that bit about the angels being lonely needs every ounce of concentration in order to make the spectacular finish', and that 'I considered it a song only to be attempted by a few of the elect in the privacy of the bathroom'. Jeeves then masterminds the wrecking of the Glossop–Bellinger alliance by persuading Wooster to appear in the same concert and sing the same song directly before Glossop, thus causing Glossop to get the bird and incur Cora's disapproval. In the event the song is rendered five times at the show, twice by outsiders, once by Wooster, once by Glossop, whose version causes the sudden arrival on his shirtfront of an overripe banana, and once by Miss Bellinger herself, whose rash decision to sing it to a doll and thereby mislead the audience into the expectation of acts of ventriloquial virtuosity causes a further outburst of criticism of the fruitarian school and brings the romance to a close.[8]

But it is in *Quick Service* that Wodehouse develops the theme of popular music to the point where song becomes a delineator of character. The heroine Sally Fairmile is besotted with one Lord Holbeton because of his habit of 'sitting down at the piano after dinner and singing such songs as "Trees" in a soft, quivery tenor voice'.[9] The dyspeptic tycoon J. Buchanan Duff is less impressed. Having been exposed to one of Holbeton's recitals, he has reached the conclusion that it 'sounds like gas escaping from a pipe. "But only God can make a tree." Bah! In a really civilized community crooners would be shot on sight'. Curiously enough, even Duff, who affects to despise the modern school of minstrelsy, is prone to the Wodehousean habit of conceiving his own existence in terms of verse and chorus. An American expatriate chafing under the restraints of social conventions in the village of Loose Chippings (pop. 4,916),

> Mr Duff's tastes had always been metropolitan. And now, although it was so brief a time ago that his arrival had made the pop. 4,197, it seemed to him that he had been here ever since he was a small boy, getting more bored every minute. Like some minstrel of Tin Pan

Alley, he was wishing that he could go back, back, back, to the place where he was born.

At this point enter Joss Weatherby, whose musical sensibilities are so superior to those of his rival Holbeton that he can say to Sally with perfect sincerity: 'Holbeton sings "Trees". It's sheer nonsense to say you love him.' At last the rivals lock horns, each marching into battle to the strains of his own vocal preference:

> When a man singing 'Trees' meets a man singing 'Old Man River', something has to give. They cannot both continue to function. Lord Holbeton generously decided to be the one to yield. It gave him a slight pang not to be able to do the high, wobbly note on the 'hair', but a man learns to take the rough with the smooth.

The symbolic significance of this moment, when the faded balladry of the old school is shouted down by the most famous song of Wodehouse's ex-partner Kern, written for a show in which Wodehouse's own name appeared as part-lyricist, is too pointed to miss, even though the book contains no hint that its author was connected professionally with the Weatherby contingent. Sally Fairmile remains the only modern heroine to resolve her romantic problems by the measurement of musical sensibility.

Archie Moffam, amused observer of the rendering by Ziegfeld's hirelings of 'There's a Place For Me in Heaven, For My Baby Boy is There', is yet another living proof of the way that, in Wodehouse's world, popular music reflects the changing moods and sometimes the very destinies of its inhabitants. Moffam is unique among Wodehouse heroes in being an ex-serviceman whose survival from years on the Western Front has left him with a relish for those minor pleasures of life which he had once feared he would never live long enough to savour. Moffam's conception of such un-Wodehousean abstractions as Patriotism, Duty and Bravery lie much closer to the surface of his temperament than his associates perceive. At first glance he is the conventional fop-fugitive from the Drones, the conventional silly ass utterly reliant on the resource, and the resources, of his lady-love. Having taken half-seriously the promise of a land fit for heroes to live in, he has at least been enterprising enough to discover that land, by marrying the daughter of a rich New York hotelier called Brewster who disapproves violently of his daughter's taste in heroes. So far as Brewster is concerned, Moffam is a parasitic simpleton, a foppish limey sponger who has fallen into the fortuitous romantic sinecure of son-in-law to the Brewster fortunes.

But Brewster has misread Moffam, whose indoctrination into the pleasures of civilization in Flanders has left him with one or two attributes so incongruous in a Wodehouse fable as to appear almost shocking. The first revelation comes when Moffam is confronted by an egomaniac musical comedy star called Vera Singleton, who gets a new husband every season and would stop at nothing to publicize the myth of her own genius. One night

Miss Singleton mistakes Moffam for a burglar and pulls a gun on him; his response is nonchalant:

> 'My dear old soul,' said Archie, 'in the recent unpleasantness in France I had chappies popping off things like that at me all day and every day for close on five years, and here I am, what! I mean to say, if I've got to choose between staying here and being pinched in your room by the local constabulary and having the dashed thing get into the papers and all sorts of trouble happening, and my wife getting the wind up, I'd much rather take a chance of getting a bullet in the old bean than that. So loose it off and the best of luck.'[10]

Soon afterwards, Moffam encounters a beggar whom he recognizes as a fellow-soldier who once showed him a kindness at St Mihiel and has now lost his memory. Moffam takes him back to Brewster's hotel, only to meet with a ruthless indifference from his father-in-law. Not completely unreasonable, Brewster does not demand the instantaneous removal of the tramp, but gives Moffam two seconds to complete the job, at which the worm turns:

> 'But you don't understand. This chappie has lost his memory because he was wounded in the war. Keep that fact firmly fixed in the old bean. He fought for you. Fought and bled for you. Bled profusely, by Jove. *And* he saved my life. . . . You can't sling a chappie out into the cold hard world who bled in gallons to make the world safe for the Hotel Cosmopolis.'

The immersion of this casual war hero into the trench warfare of Tin Pan Alley comes about through the renewal of his friendship with one Wilson Hymack, whom he had first met in the comparative sylvan peace of Armentières. Having survived the war, Hymack is now a clerk in the family business but wishes to write songs for a living. The news comes as no surprise to Moffam, who by this time is an experienced traveller in that world of the sporting and dramatic which so many heroes come to know. Already he has sat for his portrait, met a playwright, struck up a friendship with a star baseball player and been held up at gunpoint by a demented leading lady. So when Hymack sits at the piano and renders his latest masterpiece, 'It's a Long Way Back to Mother's Knee', Moffam is not only equipped to take the experience in his stride but is actually a shade blasé, asking his old comrade, 'Isn't it a little stale?', to which Hymack responds with one of the golden rules of his profession, 'Stale? What do you mean, stale? There's always room for another song boosting mother.' Hymack then proceeds with his recital, which presents the author with an acute technical problem, how to instruct the reader in the fact that this song about which Hymack is so proud and so protective, strikes precisely that elusive balance between saleability and imbecility which Tin Pan Alley is always looking for. There is only one way to convey the essence of Hymack's song, and that is to create it, which Wodehouse does, with transparent delight:

> One night a young man wandered through the glitter of Broadway.
> His money he had squandered, for a meal he couldn't pay.
> He thought about the village where his boyhood he had spent,
> And yearned for all the simple joys with which he'd been content.
> He looked upon the city, so frivolous and gay,
> And as he heaved a weary sigh, these words he then did say:
> It's a long way back to mother's knee, mother's knee, mother's knee,
> It's a long way back to mother's knee,
> Where I used to stand and prattle
> With my teddy bear and rattle
> Oh, those childhood days in Tennessee.
> They sure look good to me.
> It's a long way back, but I'm gonna start today.
> I'm going back, believe me, oh, I'm going back, I want to go,
> I'm going back, back, on the seven-three,
> To the dear old shack where I used to be,
> I'm going back to my mother's knee.

It might seem at first sight that in concocting the bathetic lunacy of his back-home parody, Wodehouse has gone too far, except that when measured against the straightfaced solemnity of successes of the period like 'Back Home in Tennessee' and 'My Mammy', to say nothing of the aforementioned execrable 'Sonny Boy', a piece like 'Mother's Knee' begins to take on the appearance of a really rather mild-mannered example of the genre.

When the recital is over, there follows a conversational exchange which reveals much about Wodehouse's feelings regarding Tin Pan Alley. Moffam's first reaction is to congratulate Hymack and ask him where he can buy a copy of the song. Hymack patiently explains that 'Mother's Knee' remains unpublished, and goes on:

> 'Writing music's the damndest job.' It was plain that the man was pouring out the pent-up emotion of many days. 'You write the biggest thing in years and you go round trying to get someone to sing it, and they say you're a genius and then shove the song away in a drawer and forget all about it.'

Here speaks the voice of Jerome Kern regarding 'Bill' and of the Gershwin brothers regarding 'The Man I Love', a song destined to be dropped from three successive Broadway productions and eventually find its way into the standard repertoire only through the back door of night-clubs and dance halls. Moffam, a self-confessed child in these affairs, then suggests that Hymack try the direct approach and play his song to a music publisher:

'No thanks. Much obliged, but I'm not going to play that melody in any publisher's office with his hired gang of Tin Pan Alley composers listening at the keyhole and taking notes.'

Eventually, Moffam gambles with Hymack's precious property and approaches a music publisher of his acquaintance called Blumenthal, who can recognize gold easily enough when confronted by it:

> It was sure-fire, he said. The words, stated Mr Blumenthal, were gooey enough to hurt, and the tune reminded him of every other song-hit he had ever heard. There was, in Mr Blumenthal's opinion, nothing to stop the thing selling a million copies.

Hymack lives as happily ever after as any songwriter can reasonably expect, while Brewster at last becomes reconciled to Moffam's permanent position in the family.

Wodehouse's picture of music publishers is more or less accurate, although Blumenthal is a composite portrait of Tin Pan Alley rather than a representation of any one of its leaders in particular. That in other cases the novelist was being more specific as a portraitist there can be no doubt at all. In *The Inimitable Jeeves*, written during the leisure hours of 1924 when everyone was trying to coerce Irving Berlin into writing the songs for *Sitting Pretty*, young Cyril Bassingham-Bassingham wangles a job in the cast of a Broadway revue called *Ask Dad*. A few days later, Wooster is invited by the producer, an old friend called George Caffyn, to go over to Schenectady to watch a preliminary dress rehearsal planned to commence at eight o'clock. Wooster, schooled by now in the wonderland time-scale of the musical theatre, turns up promptly at ten o'clock, to find Caffyn on stage talking to 'an absolutely round chappie with big spectacles and a practically hairless dome. I had seen George with the latter merchant once or twice at the club, and I knew that he was Blumenfield, the manager'. Young Bassingham-Bassingham has just finished his big song when there is an interruption:

> Old Blumenfield clapped his hands, and the hero, who had just been about to get the next line off his diaphragm, cheesed it. I peered into the shadows. Who should it be but Jeeves' little playmate with the freckles. He was now strolling down the aisle with his hands in his pockets as if the place belonged to him. An air of respectful attention seemed to pervade the building.
> 'Pop,' said the stripling, 'that number's no good.'
> Old Blumenfield beamed over his shoulder. 'Don't you like it, darling?'
> 'It gives me a pain.'
> 'You're dead right.'
> 'You want something zippy there. Something with a bit of jazz to it.'
> 'Quite right, my boy. I'll make a note of it.'

Wooster, stupefied at these goings-on, asks Caffyn why a hard case like Blumenfield should take advice from a mere juvenile delinquent:

> 'Nobody seems to know. It may be pure fatherly love, or he may regard him as a mascot. My own idea is that he thinks the kid has exactly the same amount of intelligence as the average member of the audience, and that what makes a hit with him will please the general public. While, conversely, what he doesn't like will be too rotten for anyone. The kid is a pest, a wart, and a pot of poison, and should be strangled.'

In a volume of autobiography called *Bring on the Girls*, giving an account of his life in the theatre, Wodehouse writes the following passage in an attempt to explain the presence of a child in the inner sanctum of that Bonaparte *manqué* Abraham Erlanger:

> It turned out that the stripling was some sort of a relation, a nephew or the son of a cousin or something, and he was a very valued and esteemed cog in the Erlanger organization. Aged twelve years, he had been selected by Erlanger as possessing exactly the intelligence of the average New York theatre audience. If he liked something, Erlanger reasoned, the public would like it, too. If he didn't, they wouldn't.

By the time he sketched that impression of his first Broadway impresario, Wodehouse was already approaching the end of his long flirtation with musical comedy, and Erlanger himself was very nearly at the end of a long and acquisitive career, eased into the St Helena of his last years by the three-headed apparition of the Shubert brothers. To see what Wodehouse felt about the New York stage at an earlier point in his lyric-writing, the stories in *The Man With Two Left Feet*, collected in 1917, and for the most part written in the previous two years, are highly revealing. The two stories about Geisenheimer's dance hall are saddled with an O. Henry sentimentality, but there are two other stories in the collection which remind us that there is a recurring fantasy in Wodehouse's fiction, concerning the layman who, for reasons usually to do with romantic love, suddenly finds himself in the nightmare situation of working as a performer in the song-and-dance business. Bassingham-Bassingham is only one example among several of the subsidiary characters who acquires an engagement and might just have been capable of carrying it off were it not for a cruel conjunction of events. The implication is that, with the lesser roles in the run-of-the-mill musical production, talent does not come into it at all. Anybody may conceal himself effectively enough in the back row of the average chorus, and in *The Man With Two Left Feet* there are two stories which make the point. Both are contemporaneous with that heady interlude in his life when Wodehouse, in his capacity as drama critic of *Vanity Fair*, was succumbing to the temptation of an offer of partnership so casually passed on by Kern and Bolton.

'Extricating Young Gussie' is constructed on the same idea that

Wodehouse was later to use in telling the tale of Tuppy Glossop's infatuation with Cora Bellinger except that, where Glossop aspired no further than an amateur charity concert, young Gussie, hoping to impress a young vaude-villienne called Ray Denison, changes his name to George Wilson and marches off to a New York office so sinister in its appearance that Wooster asks him what business he could possibly have there:

> 'Pros,' he said. 'Music-hall artists, you know, waiting to see old Abe Riesbitter. This is September the first, vaudeville's opening day. The early fall', said Gussie, who is a bit of a poet in his way, 'is vaudeville's springtime. All over the country, as August wanes, sparkling com-ediennes burst into bloom, the sap stirs in the veins of tramp cyclists, and last year's contortionists, waking from their summer sleep, tie themselves tentatively in knots. What I mean is, this is the beginning of the new season, and everybody's out hunting for bookings.'

Including Gussie, who soon lands a job in a tank town singing the kind of ballad that Wilson Hymack might have written for him:

> Gussie would clear his throat and begin, 'There's a great big choo-choo waiting at the deepo.'
> THE CHAPPIE (Playing chords): Is that so? What's it waiting for?
> GUSSIE (Rather rattled at the interruption): 'Waiting for me.'
> THE CHAPPIE: (Surprised): For you?
> GUSSIE (Sticking to it): 'Waiting for me-e-ee.'
> THE CHAPPIE (Sceptically): You don't say!
> GUSSIE: 'For I'm off to Tennessee.'
> THE CHAPPIE (Conceding a point): Now, I live at Yonkers.

It is extraordinary enough that Gussie should have reached this far in his new career, and even more so that Wooster should be so understanding about it. Wodehouse's explanation is interesting. It seems that there is in these affairs of the musical theatre such a thing as hereditary tendency. For Gussie's mother, Wooster's dreaded Aunt Julia, had once trod the boards herself:

> Nobody ever mentions it, and the family have been trying to forget it for twenty-five years, but it's a known fact that my Aunt Julia, Gussie's mother, was a vaudeville artist once, and a very good one too, I'm told. She was playing in pantomime at Drury Lane when Uncle Cuthbert saw her first. It was before my time, of course, and long before I was old enough to take notice the family had made the best of it, and Aunt Agatha had pulled up her socks and put in a lot of educative work, and with a microscope you couldn't tell Aunt Julia from a genuine dyed-in-the-wool aristocrat.

From which Wooster concludes that Gussie 'was reverting to type, or what-ever they call it'. So is Aunt Julia, who arrives to take Gussie out of the theatre only to meet her old partner Joe Danby, who still remembers with touching warmth her rendering of 'Rumpty-tiddley-umpty-ay', to which Julia, re-membering her manners, responds with, 'I always have said that you did the best back-fall in the profession. Do you remember how we put it across at the Canterbury, Joe? Think of it. The Canterbury's a moving picture house now, and the old Mogul runs French revues.' At this point Aunt Julia dares to wonder aloud if all those years ago Danby really loved her:

> 'Of course I was fond of you. Why did I let you have all the fat in 'Fun in a Tea-Shop'? Why did I hang about upstage while you sang 'Rumpty-tiddley-umpty-ay'? Do you remember my giving you a bag of buns when we were on the road at Bristol? Do you remember my giving you the ham sandwiches at Portsmouth? Do you remember my giving you a seed-cake at Birmingham? What did you think all that meant, if not that I loved you?

Gussie marries his vaudevillienne, Aunt Julia resumes her liaison with Danby, leaving Wooster with the impression that those who taste the joys of the professional life only to forsake it for more material splendours are likely to find their subsequent existence decidedly flat.

The theme of the outsider successfully invading the backstage world of pure and honest chanteuses is repeated in 'Bill the Bloodhound'. Both in its celebration of the irresistible attraction of the musical life, and its pastiche of the stage conventions of the Edwardian period, 'Bill the Bloodhound' is one of the most revealing stories Wodehouse ever published. Once again, it dates from the period in 1915 when the drama critic was about to metamor-phose into the professional lyricist, and may well have been written in Crowninshield's time. Its New York début was in *The Century* in February; four months later it was published in England in *The Strand*. 'Bill the Bloodhound' is the uplifting fable of Henry Pifield Rice, a young detective who falls in love with Alice Weston, a young musical comedy artist. Like the rest of her profession, Alice regards anybody who does any other sort of work as socially unacceptable and so, when Henry is instructed by his employers to shadow a member of the cast of a touring company to which Alice belongs, he is obliged to wear a succession of disguises so bizarre that at one juncture he is mistaken for a portion of Gorgonzola. In spite of the tantalizing proximity of Alice, Henry is happy enough, for 'the stage had always fascin-ated him. To meet even minor members of the profession off the boards gave him a thrill'. And so when the star of the company invites him to discard his disguises and become the company's mascot, he is delighted to accept, becoming in the process a world authority on the ramifications of a dramaturgic work entitled *The Girl from Brighton*, which is the archetype of a thousand shows like it:

The Girl from Brighton was one of those exotic productions specially designed for the Tired Business Man. It relied for a large measure of its success on the size and appearance of its chorus, and on their constant change of costume. Henry, as a consequence, was the centre of a kaleidoscopic whirl of feminine loveliness dressed to represent such varying flora and fauna as rabbits, Parisian students, colleens, Dutch peasants, and daffodils. Musical comedy is the Irish stew of drama. Anything may be put into it, with the certainty that it will improve the general effect.

Wodehouse is here faced with the identical problem which confronted him as Wilson Hymack began to sing 'Mother's Knee'. It is one thing to coin the aphorism of the Irish stew, quite another to bring home to the reader exactly what it is that audiences found when they took their seats for a performance of *The Girl from Brighton*. There is only one way to do this, and it is the same way as the one demanded by Hymack's little recital. The storyteller must provide the reader with tangible evidence. One night in mid-performance Henry is consumed by an uncontrollable urge to declare his love. He could not have picked a more delicate moment:

> The plot of *The Girl from Brighton* had by then reached a critical stage. The situation was as follows: the hero, having been disinherited by his wealthy and titled father for falling in love with the heroine, a poor shop-girl, has disguised himself (by wearing a different coloured neck-tie), and has come in pursuit of her to a well-known seaside resort, where, having disguised herself by changing her dress, she is serving as a waitress in the Rotunda, on the Esplanade. The family butler, disguised as a Bath-chair man, has followed the hero, and the wealthy and titled father, disguised as an Italian opera singer, has come to the place for a reason which, though extremely sound, for the moment eludes the memory. Anyhow, he is there, and they all meet on the Esplanade. Each recognizes the other, but thinks himself is unre-cognized. Exeunt all, hurriedly, leaving the heroine alone on the stage. It is a crisis in the heroine's life. She meets it bravely. She sings a song entitled 'My Honolulu Queen', with chorus of Japanese girls and Bulgarian officers.
>
> Alice was one of the Japanese girls.

How many soporific sessions in the Edwardian theatre of the West End, how many distressed Broadway nights in Crowinshield's service, how many imbecilic synopses of projected musicals that summary represents, remains unknown, but only a man intimately familiar with the insane conventions of the genre could have composed it. And only a farceur schooled in the fortunate accidents of theatre life could have his detective hero stumble on stage unintentionally to so great an effect that later the star of the show offers him a regular employment, brushing aside our hero's protestations:

'My boy, I can go down the Strand and pick up a hundred fellows who can sing and act. I don't want them. I turn them away. But a seventh son of a seventh son like you, a king of mascots like you – they don't make them nowadays. They've lost the pattern. If you like to come with me, I'll give you a contract for any number of years you suggest. I need you in my business. Think it over, laddie, and let me know tomorrow. Look here upon this picture, and on that. As a sleuth you are poor. You couldn't detect a bass-drum in a telephone booth. You have no future. You are merely among those present. But as a mascot -- my boy, you're the only thing in sight. You can't help succeeding on the stage. You don't have to know how to act. Look at the dozens of good actors who are out of jobs. Why? Unlucky. With your luck and a little experience you'll be a star before you know you've begun. Think it over, and let me know in the morning.'

The story ends with young Pifield having scaled such professional heights that he refuses even to see the managements offering him engagements; significantly, in that closing paragraph there is no mention of Alice.

In such diverse and diverting ways did Wodehouse's Broadway experiences illumine his fiction, enlivening the conversational exchanges, clarifying character outline, lending discipline to his structures, and occasionally providing the setting for a romantic denouement. It is perhaps not so great an influence after all – except that there is a fourth way in which his life as a songwriter–librettist enriched his work as a light novelist. On a few spectacular occasions, the world of song and dance provided him with a theme involving theatre politics, distinguishing Wodehouse from all his contemporaries once again with the exception of Sir Compton Mackenzie.[11] At least three times in the years of his partnership with Kern, in 1919, again in 1921 and yet again a year later, he wrote novels requiring for their successful execution a working knowledge of the professional stage in all its ramifications from front-of-house to backstage.

In the first of these novels, *A Damsel in Distress*, two dominant strands of his imagination, the English aristocracy and the Broadway meritocracy, mingle to produce a romance in which the blissful ignorance of Broadway regarding stately home protocol is more than matched by the gentry's abysmal unawareness of what goes on inside the twentieth-century theatre. George Bevan, a breezy young New Yorker, has been enjoying unqualified success as a composer of musical comedies, but on his arrival in London to supervise the transfer of his latest smash hit, *Follow the Girl*, soon lapses into a depression. Glutted with success and with no particular desire to remain in this colonial outpost of the musical theatre, he decides to return home as soon as he can, only to abandon all his plans on bumping into Lady Patricia Maud, only daughter of Lord Marshmoreton of Belpher Castle in Hampshire. Lady Maud, true to those plot conventions which govern Bevan's career, loves another, and it is not until she has been suitably disillusioned by the shortcomings of her fiancé that she realizes that George represents the very crown of manhood.

Once again, the musical theatre is represented as a kind of ragbag into which tumble the most incongruous people, very few of whom appear to have been intended by nature for their allotted roles. In *Follow the Girl*, for example, there is George's sisterly friend Billie Dore, who can contemplate her own predicament and reflect:

'It's funny about the show business. The way one drifts into it and sticks, I mean. Take me, for example. Nature had it all doped out for me to be the Belle of Hicks Corners. What I ought to have done was to buy a gingham bonnet and milk cows. But I would come to the great city and help brighten up the tired business man.'

And when George remarks that he did not know she was fond of the country, she answers, 'Me? I wrote the words and music.' Her discontent stems partly from the conviction that she is surrounded by lunatics. As she says to the theatre doorman:

'All composers are nuts, Mac. I was in a show once where the manager was panning the composer because there wasn't a number in the score that had a tune to it. The poor geek admitted they weren't very tuney, but said the thing about his music was that it had such a wonderful aroma. They all get that way.'

All except Bevan, who has kept his head despite his success and now desires only to convince Maud he is a worthy partner. Billie sympathizes, because she has known him for a long time, 'when he was just hanging around Broadway, looking out for a chance to be allowed to slip a couple of interpolated numbers into any old show that came along'.[12] One morning George awakes to find that he is so elated by this new sensation of love that he is no longer depressed; there follows a curious passage explaining why a young, presentable, rich man surrounded by young, presentable women as George is, should never have fallen in love before:

During the last five years women had found him more or less cold. It was the nature of his profession that had largely brought about this cooling of the emotions. To a man who, like George, has worked year in and year out at the composition of musical comedies, women come to lose many of those attractive qualities which ensnare the ordinary male. To George, of late years, it had come to seem that the salient feature of woman as a sex was her disposition to kick. For five years he had been wandering in a world of women, many of them beautiful, all of them superficially attractive, who had left no other impress on his memory except the vigour and frequency with which they had kicked. Some had kicked about their musical numbers, some about their love-scenes; some had grumbled about their exit lines, others about the lines of their second-act frocks. They had kicked in a myriad differing ways – wrathfully, sweetly, noisily, softly, smilingly, tearfully, pathetically and patronizingly; but they had all kicked; with the result that women had now become to George not so much a flaming inspiration or a tender goddess as something to be dodged – tactfully if possible; but, if not possible, by open flight. For years he had dreaded to be left alone with a woman, and had developed the habit of gliding swiftly away when he saw one bearing down on him.

One recalls Marion Davies, who, on being introduced to Bolton and Wodehouse, made her exit with 'Write me some funny stuff, boys, I want to be a comic'; and her friend Justine Johnstone who, on being invited to share Marion's eleven-room hotel suite, inquired dubiously, 'Where do I put my maid?'; and Marilyn Miller, who had not considered 'Bill' to be an item quite commensurate with her vocal talents.

The most revealing moment in the book occurs when Billie Dore, who has by now won that bizarre organ, Lord Marshmoreton's heart, explains to him that the man besieging Maud is no fly-by-night. His lordship has seen the show and is dimly aware, through the fog of horticultural ecstasy which surrounds him at all times, that Bevan wrote the music for it:

> 'Well, did he tell you that he draws 3% of the gross receipts? You saw the house we had last night. It was a fair average house. We are playing to over $14,000 a week. George's little bit of that is – I can't do it in my head, but it's a round four hundred dollars. That's eighty pounds of your money. And did he tell you that this same show ran over a year in New York to big business all the time, and that there are three companies on the road now? And did he mention that this is the ninth show he's done, and that seven of the others were just as big hits as this one? And did he remark in passing that he gets royalties on every copy of his music that's sold, and that at least ten of his things have sold over half a million? No he didn't, because he isn't the sort of fellow who stands around blowing about his income. But you know it now.'[13]

The trouble so far as George is concerned is that within the context of the cultural environment of Maud's life, he is totally unknown. When he finds himself sitting at Lord Marshmoreton's dinner table, half the guests have never heard of the musical comedy as an abstraction, let alone George's part in its history. Had he only been the author of a slim volume of vers libre selling in a limited edition of five hundred copies, they might at least have paid lip-service to his bank account; as things stand, they have no idea what he is or does. Even their praise is showered upon him for the wrong reasons; when one of the diners congratulates him on a second act lyric in *Follow the Girl* which goes:

Although poor poppa
Thinks it's improper,
Grannie's always doing it and nobody can stop her

George patiently explains, 'I'm not responsible for the words, you know. Those are wished on me by the lyricist.' At last Maud, who has after all merely risen from the ranks of the aristocracy, realizes that she is fortunate to be married to George, who belongs to the purple of musical commerce, and the Marshmoretons swiftly set about the task of absorbing the double shock of Marshmoreton's marriage to Billie Dore and Maud's to George Bevan.

A Damsel in Distress has attracted the interest of several Wodehouse commentators because of its obvious anticipations of later glories. As Richard Usborne reminds us, *A Damsel in Distress* is really a Blandings novel in thin disguise: 'Lord Marshmoreton is an echo of Lord Emsworth, Lord Belpher of Lord Bosham, Lady Caroline Byng of Lady Constance Keeble, Reggie Byng of Freddie Threepwood, Keggs the butler of Beach the butler, and Macpherson the gardener of McAllister the gardener.'[14] As Blandings had already been unveiled four years earlier in *Something Fresh*, it might seem surprising that Wodehouse, when he came to write *A Damsel in Distress*, did not either make Belpher Castle Blandings and have done with it, or reintroduce his new set of mirror-images in later works. Owen Edwards has suggested that in marrying off George and Maud, Wodehouse had left himself no further options, and that, unlike the Blandings novels, the story of Bevan was not open-ended.[15] More to the point, in flinging the archetypal Broadway composer against the ramparts of an ancient English pile, Wodehouse had found another way of reconciling the contradictory postures of his two careers, and, most satisfactory of all, had succeeded in bringing together the two locales which probably pleased him more than any other. With the nuptials of Lady Maud and George Bevan, the two halves of Wodehouse's artistic life are conjoined.

Two years later we get the briefest glimpse of Bevan for the last time as he flits tantalizingly across the landscape of *Jill the Reckless*. The hero Wally Mason is explaining to Jill Mariner how he first became a playwright:

'I found I had a knack of writing verses and things, and I wrote a few vaudeville songs. Then I came across a man named Bevan at a music publisher's. He was just starting to write music, and we got together and turned out some vaudeville sketches, and then a manager sent for us to fix up a show that was dying on the road and we had the good luck to turn it into a success, and after that it was pretty good going. George Bevan got married the other day. Lucky devil!'

Further links with *A Damsel in Distress* are provided by Nelly Bryant, a chorus girl stranded in London after her decision to stay on after the closure of *Follow the Girl*, and by a lyricist–librettist called Otis Pilkington, whose consecrated role in life it is to oust that particular type of entertainment from the theatres of America. It is this mission of Pilkington's which gives the book its pretext for, although there is the ostensible plot of romance between Jill and the debonair playwright Mason, *Jill the Reckless* is a novel whose leading character is not a person at all, but a comic opera entitled *The Rose of America*.[16] Everybody in the story is sucked into the jaws of this monstrous engine of musical destruction. Jill, suddenly rendered penniless by a speculating uncle, lands a job in its chorus; Mason, reeling from the effects of the crash of his latest solemn masterpiece, accepts a commission to rewrite it; Freddie Rooke, the archetypal Drone, manages to hold on for a little while to one of its leading roles. This time, instead of assigning the characters to their actions as though they were salaried actors, Wodehouse actually makes them salaried actors, so that he may conduct us, step by step, through the genesis of a musical comedy from reckless conception to New York reviews.

At the heart of this catastrophic episode in musical history is the impresario Isaac Goble, who combines a lust for box-office success with the kind of comically errant judgment which has led him to see promise of that success in *The Rose of America*. Nobody is able to explain this lapse of sanity, not even Wodehouse. After all, Mr Goble is not the kind of man to fall victim to the delusion of cultural profundity; when one of his actors pronounces the name of Omar Khayyam, he orders him to change it to 'Omar of Khayyam' in the belief that Omar was a poet who came from a town called Khayyam. So how had so innocent a flower committed himself to a turkey like *The Rose of America*?

> Because he was subject, like all other New York managers, to intermittent spasms of the idea that the time is ripe for a revival of comic opera. Sometimes, lunching in his favourite corner in the Cosmopolis grill-room, he would lean across the table and beg some other manager to take it from him that the time was ripe for a revival of comic opera – or, more cautiously, that pretty soon the time was going to be ripe for a revival of comic opera. And the other manager would nod his head and thoughtfully stroke his three chins and admit that, sure as God made little green apples, the time was darned sure going to be ripe for a revival of comic opera. And then they would stuff themselves with rich food and light big cigars and brood meditatively.

Usually the sickness wore off before Mr Goble could be got at, but this time the passionate Pilkington had caught him when the conviction that the time was ripe for comic opera was still whirling about in his head. What chance did he have of resisting the blandishments of this fiercely committed intellectual? After all, New York theatrical managers represent 'the lowest order of intelligence, with the possible exception of the limax maximus or garden slug, known to science'. Before he knows what has hit him, Goble is into *The Rose of America* up to his three chins and, in view of the extent of his commitment, it is revealing to take the measure of the man responsible for it.

Otis Pilkington is one of those Pateresque aesthetes who cannot bear to call a spade a spade, or even a chorus girl a chorus girl; when Jill asks him for a job in the chorus of *The Rose of America*, he reacts as Pater did when confronted by syringa, as though he is in great pain. Sternly he informs Jill that there is no chorus in *The Rose of America*, which is not, for her information, a musical comedy but a musical fantasy. The production will, however, have 'the service of twelve refined ladies of the ensemble', to which Jill responds with 'It does sound much better, doesn't it?'. According to Pilkington and his collaborator Roland Trevis, *The Rose of America* is as good as Gilbert and Sullivan, only better. 'The music', claims Pilkington, 'has all Sullivan's melody with a newness of rhythm peculiarly its own.' He then delivers the credo which animates his every waking hour and is destined to cause Goble so many sleepless ones:

> 'We feel that the time has come when the public is beginning to demand something better than what it has been accustomed to. People are getting tired of the brainless trash and jingly tunes which have been given them by men like Wallace Mason and George Bevan. They want a certain polish. . . . It was the same in Gilbert and Sullivan's day. They started writing at a time when the musical stage had reached a terrible depth of inanity. The theatre was given over to burlesques of the most idiotic description. The public was waiting eagerly to welcome something of a higher class. It is the same today. But the managers will not see it. *The Rose of America* went up and down Broadway for months, knocking at managers' doors.'

It had eventually arrived in Mr Goble's capacious lap, from which vantage point it now begins to leap into rehearsal. One by one Wodehouse brings on the stock company of the Broadway backstage world. There is the musical director Mr Saltzburg, who conducts operations with the sadness of a man convinced that his own unsung arias are far superior to the nonsense he is bringing into being. There is Johnson Miller, the famous dance director, whose deafness has proved to be no impediment, for he had 'an almost miraculous gift of picking up the melodies for which it was his business to design dances, without apparently hearing them'.[17] Miller is that *rara avis* along Broadway, the worker who means what he says: 'What Johnson Miller said to your face was official, not subject to revision as soon as your back was turned.' Then there is Goble himself, struggling to retain his sanity amid the madness of Pilkington's vision. When Goble walks into a rehearsal of *The Rose of America*, it takes only five minutes for his high spirits to descend to the point where he would cheerfully murder everybody in the building. Who can blame him?

He had been brought up in the lower-browed school of musical comedy, where you shelved the plot after the opening number and filled in the rest of the evening by bringing on the girls in a variety of exotic costumes, with some good vaudeville specialists to get the laughs. Mr Goble's idea of a musical piece was something embracing trained seals, acrobats, and two or three teams of skilled buck-and-wing dancers, with nothing on the stage, from a tree to a lamp-shade, which could not suddenly turn into a chorus girl. The austere legitimateness of *The Rose of America* gave him a pain in the neck. He loathed plot, and *The Rose of America* was all plot.

Into this maelstrom of solemnity walks the cheerfully commercial Mason, cured once and for all of his own pretensions regarding the serious drama, and announcing his instinctive opposition to the aspirations of the Pilkington school with a lyric positively bristling with precisely those qualities of philistinism which give to Pilkington the physical agonies that Goble receives from *The Rose of America*. Jill's heart, sorely tried by her professional obligations as a member of the chorus-which-is-not-a-chorus, gives a sudden leap as she hears:

> Just see them Pullman porters,
> Dolled up with scented waters
> Bought with their dimes and quarters.
> See here they come! Here they come!
> Oh see those starched-up collars,
> Hark how their captain hollers,
> 'Keep time, keep time'.
> It's worth a thousand dollars
> To see those tip-collectors,
> Those upper-berth inspectors,
> Those Pullman porters on parade.

This is the sort of stuff that Goble can understand. Desperate to extricate himself from the agglutinate mass of *The Rose of America*, he hires Mason to transform it from a plague spot to a moneymaker, even though Mason never bothers to hide his contempt for the impresario. But then,

> Mr Goble had the mental processes of a sheep. *Follow the Girl* was the last outstanding musical success in New York theatrical history: Wally had written it, therefore nobody but Wally was capable of rewriting *The Rose of America*. The thing had for Mr Goble the inevitability of Fate.

At the dress rehearsals in Atlantic City, Mason begins the task of converting Pilkington's catastrophe into something acceptable to Mr Goble's muse. A team of composers work in shifts to provide a new score, unmindful of the fact that Pilkington still owns seventy per cent of the rights. Jill then organizes a strike when one of the chorus girls is fired. Hastily Goble reinstates her and the production lurches on. Pilkington, his fine dreams of outGilberting Sullivan having fallen about his ears, is given such a reprimand by Goble that Wodehouse can bear to bring it to his public only at second hand, through the bowdlerizing of Mason:

> 'Goble told him in no uncertain words – I have never heard words less uncertain – that his damned rotten highbrow false alarm of a show – I am quoting Mr Goble – would have to be rewritten by alien hands.'

Even this experience does not acquaint Pilkington with any idea of the world he has taken on. It is not till the accountants deliver their lecture that he realizes what he has let himself in for. The news is that, up to the last dress rehearsal, he, Otis Pilkington, idealist and aesthete extraordinaire, the man who, after Goble has flayed him, recovers his equanimity by gazing at Japanese prints, he, paragon of all that is fine and pure in musical comedy, is liable for the sum of $32,859.68c. Costumes alone amounted to over ten thousand. And yet there is an item for $187.45c under the heading of 'Clothing'. Weren't costumes clothing? Then again, what did they mean by 'Academy.Rehl. $105.50c'. And what did they mean by 'Cut.$15'? And what did they mean by 'Frames $94.50c'? And what did they mean by inserting no fewer than seventeen separate items headed 'Props'?

Meanwhile, *The Rose of America* had staggered on to Baltimore and then Rochester. By the time it arrives in Syracuse, not even Jill has any hope left for its success. In fact, only Mason believes in its coming triumph, telling her:

> 'Take a look at it in another two weeks. I don't say musical comedy is a very lofty form of art, but still there's a certain amount of science about it. If you go in for it long enough, you learn the tricks, and take it from me, that if you have a good cast and some catchy numbers, it's almost impossible not to have a success.'

Inexorably *The Rose of America* moves into Connecticut, 'tacking to and fro like a storm-battered ship'. Not till it gets to Hartford do Mason's predictions start to come true. But Otis Pilkington never sees the show in Hartford. He has sold out in Syracuse. When *The Rose of America* is finally unveiled on Broadway, it creates so favourable an impression that professionals begin squabbling over its merits:

> A composer who had not got an interpolated number in the show was explaining to another composer who had not got an interpolated number in the show the exact source from which a third composer who had got an interpolated number in the show had stolen the number which he had got interpolated. And two musical comedy artists who were temporarily resting were agreeing that the prima donna was a dear

thing but that, contrary as it was to their life-long policy not to knock anybody, they must say that she was beginning to show the passage of years a trifle and ought to be warned by some friend that her career as an ingenue was a thing of the past.

There follow the customary Wodehousean convolutions of plot, ending with Jill's realization that Mason is the only man for her, just as Lady Maud had come to the identical conclusion regarding George Bevan two years earlier. *The Rose of America* sails on to favourable reviews and substantial dividends, leaving the reader wondering to what extent such moonshine has any relationship to the harsh realities of the real Broadway. After all, in Atlantic City *The Rose of America* is the greatest non-starter since the Confederacy. On Broadway, retaining its own name and nothing else, it is cheered to the echo. It is instructive that, a few years later, Ira Gershwin, on the road with *Funny Face*, was living through precisely the traumas that Wally Mason endures in *Jill the Reckless*:

> Practically half the score was thrown out and also most of the book, and it was almost completely rewritten by the time, six weeks later, it opened in New York.[18]

Undeterred by the chaotic working conditions of the musical theatre, Wodehouse had no sooner published *Jill the Reckless* than he began work on a new musical for London called *The Cabaret Girl*; concurrently he started to write another novel about life in the theatre. When the new novel appeared in 1922, it carried the following dedication:

TO GEORGE GROSSMITH.

Dear George,
The production of our mutual effort, *The Cabaret Girl*, is a week distant as I write this; and who shall say what the harvest will be?[19] But, whether a week from now we are slapping each other on the back or shivering in the frost, nothing can alter the fact that we had a lot of fun writing the thing together. Not a reproach or a nasty look from start to finish. Because of this, and because you and I were side by side through the Adventure of the Ship's Bore, the Episode of the Concert in Aid of the Seamen's Orphans and Widows, and the Sinister Affair of the Rose of Stamboul, I dedicate this book to you.

> P. G. Wodehouse,
> The Garrick Club.

The novel, *The Adventures of Sally*, is about an innocent young girl who invests a legacy in a straight play and in the course of her speculation meets a gallimaufry of theatrical scoundrels, a smattering of theatrical clowns, and the man intended by destiny and P. G. Wodehouse to be her husband. Thirty years later Wodehouse was to deploy the identical theme in *Barmy in Wonderland*, in which the exchanges are still being flavoured with textual allusions to the rehearsal rooms of the past. Dinty, the heroine, suggests that there's no business like show business, and Barmy Fotheringay-Phipps descends to the very ocean bed of humility by defining himself as 'a worthless cheque, a total wreck, a flop'. And one of Wodehouse's most ancient adversaries comes in for his last custard pie:

> How well I remember the day when I was wandering through the jungle on the Metro-Goldwyn lot and Louis B. Mayer suddenly sprang out at me from the undergrowth. He had somehow managed to escape from the office where they kept him, and I could see from his glaring eyes and slavering jaws that he had already tasted blood. Fortunately I had my elephant gun and my trusted native bearer with me.

After *Anything Goes* in 1934 Wodehouse had no further connection with the musical theatre, and although he continued to write for the stage both in London and in New York, his theatrical commitments gradually fell away as he became steadily more immersed in the topography of Blandings. After the episode with Cole Porter in Le Touquet, he still had more than forty years of steady writing before him, at an average of roughly a novel a year. To what extent did his own Broadway past become remote to him? In his last interview with Richard Usborne he could no longer remember if, on the famous occasions of 'Bill', he had written the words first or if Kern had handed him the tune, even though the genesis of that song, stretching from 1906 to 1927, remains one of the most fully documented legends of the profession. As he pottered on among the prize pigs of Shropshire and the chinless wonders of a timeless Mayfair, did he recall anything in the technical sense of his time as the gallant rescuer of the musical comedy lyric from Hapsburgian prolixity? It had all been so very long ago. By the time he moved into his nineties, the world of McGuire and Ziegfeld, Savage and Erlanger, was blurred by the patina of extreme antiquity. As his fellow-lyricist Sir Compton Mackenzie had written, 'dancers had gone, beauties had shrivelled . . . the silver-footed coryphees now kept lodging houses; the swanlike ballerinas wore elastic stockings; but their absence was filled by others; they were as little missed as the wave that has broken'.[20] In 1973, about to enter his ninety-third year, Wodehouse composed a short novel called *Bachelors Anonymous*, in which Mr Ephraim Trout, of Trout, Wapshott and Edelstein, Attorneys at Law, comes to a belated romantic awakening. And in seeking for the appropriate phrase to convey Mr Trout's erotic deprivations, Wodehouse suddenly dredged up from the depths of his own long experience a phrase which belonged back in that lost world when Kern and Bolton had enticed him into the palace of pure delights at the Princess Theatre. Mr Ephraim Trout had perhaps seen a performance of *Oh, Boy!* himself, back in 1917, and remembered a snatch or two of the songs. It would explain why, 'as a child of eight Mr Trout had once kissed a girl of six under the mistletoe at a Christmas party, but there his sex life had come to an abrupt halt'. The lyricist of 'You Never Knew About Me' is calling to the author of *Bachelors Anonymous* across primeval swamps of lost time.

6

Scriptwriter in Hollywood

JACOB Z. SCHNELLENHAMER, CAPTAIN of modern industry and self-acclaimed zillionaire, was a man poised uncertainly between two contradictory conditions of twentieth-century man. While even his professional enemies, and they were legion, would have hesitated before designating him a nincompoop, it was painfully obvious, even to the lowliest lickspittle lackey, that neither was he a compoop and that, no matter how passionately he might aspire to that exalted status, he would never achieve it. There were those apologists who condoned his cerebral shortcomings by categorizing him as one of history's victims, uprooted from his native soil and replanted in an alien land thousands of miles away, which would excuse, or at least explain, those eccentric syntactical deployments which were so disarming a feature of his English. But there were those who had known him way back when, who insisted that in the old days he had had just as much trouble with Russian. The sad truth was that, however varied his virtues, Jacob Z. Schnellenhamer was not equipped to be an intellectual. On the contrary, nature had taken infinite care to fashion him in a more prosaic mould, as one of those picaresque merchant-bandits endowed by circumstances with the oxymoronic status of Jewish philistine.

Had he attempted the conquest of any corner of the world requiring powers of aesthetic discrimination, or cerebral animation, or creative sympathy, Jacob Z. Schnellenhamer would have been a dead duck, none deader. His illiteracy, his lack of intellectual curiosity, would too soon have found him out. Indeed, nobody could conceivably have been less intellectu-

153

ally curious than Jacob Z. Schnellenhamer without actually being dead. And so, informed by some deep-seated instinct which told him where his destiny lay, he made a bee-line for a profession ideally suited to his considerable limitations. He had gone into motion pictures, gone into them with the same sigh of recognition with which a pig will slide into the mud. And there he had thrived, rising by the laws of levity to a position of such power, and the dispensation of such patronage, that strong men ran for cover when they saw him coming, and some of the most beautiful women in the world quailed before his frown; indeed, his physical aspect was so unfortunate that those beautiful women had just as often been known to quail before his smile.

But exotic a creature though he was, Jacob Z. Schnellenhamer was not quite *sui generis*. Although it is true that if this world was populated exclusively by his particular sub-species it would surely explode with a bang *and* a whimper, it so happened that inside the profession of which he was so bizarre an ornament, there was just sufficient territory available for megalomania of his type to flourish. There would always be a need for as many Jacob Z. Schnellenhamers as there were motion-picture studios for them to administer. For if the destinies of Jacob Z. had been shaped by his creation of Colossal-Exquisite, it was equally true that his coevals Isadore Fishbein and Benjamin Zizzbaum had been just as profoundly affected by their nurturing of Perfecto-Fishbein and Zizzbaum-Celluloid respectively. That Jacob Z. was truly *primus inter pares* is suggested by the fact that the great merger referred to in the histories as the Perfecto-Zizzbaum Corporation was the result of his inspiration. His power was virtually all-embracing, and of his competitors only Sigismund Glutz of Medulla-Oblongata had managed to retain his independence.

Whether or not Schnellenhamer and his peers were actually human had for many years been an issue of bitter acrimony among the world's distinguished zoologists. Among those who were in no doubt at all was that bright star in the motion picture firmament, Corky Potter-Pirbright, who, on returning home to England for a brief respite from the responsibility of being that celebrated two-dimensional goddess Cora Starr, nipped down to the Battersea Dogs' Home to purchase a mutt of indeterminate ancestry which she instantly christened Sam Goldwyn. The name proved to be peculiarly apt, for within minutes of his first important social engagement, as an extra in a stormy scene starring Corky and her errant brother Catsmeat, he had so disgraced himself as to require removal from the room. In subsequent episodes, Goldwyn had eaten a sofa cushion, been castigated by Dame Daphne Winkworth as 'a great, rough dog', been banished to the stables by a butlerine family connection of Jeeves called Silversmith, had struck back by taking a bite at his persecutor, who had reacted in turn by locking the dog in a cupboard. Such a career, packed with incident, called for definition, and it came at last from Bertie Wooster, who knew his movies well enough to spot vestigial resemblances to Wallace Beery in old ladies and to Edward G. Robinson in small boys. In defending the dog's reputation, Wooster insisted, 'Sam Goldwyn isn't dotty. I wouldn't say he was one of our great minds, but he's certainly compos.'

Corky Potter-Pirbright's cheerful contempt for the mogul mind might more easily have been dismissed as a mere outburst of personal pique had she been a failure in the dream factory. But, as Cora Starr, she had climbed to the dizziest heights of the star-girt mountain, which, in *The Mating Season*, are specified with meticulous precision. When Corky hears that her young cousin Thomas has been selling her autographs at a shilling a time, she reports with quiet satisfaction that, according to his information, 'a genuine Ida Lupino only fetches ninepence'. Nor is there any doubt that Thomas is well-informed in these matters. He knows what is what, and, according to Bertie, would willingly spend his last threepence on a stamp for a begging letter to Dorothy Lamour. Corky's high ranking is finally confirmed on the last page, when Thomas, broken-hearted at the news of Corky's impending nuptials with the heir to Haddock's Headache Hokies, is consoled by the thought that 'he may have lost Corky, but there's always Betty Grable and Dorothy Lamour and Jennifer Jones', to which Jeeves, yet another source of cinematic wisdom, replies, 'I understand those ladies are married, sir'. Corky's parity with Lamour and Grable marks her as a genuine star with little cause for complaint at the treatment she has received from the moguls. And yet she has only to catch a glimpse of an undisciplined hound for a vision of the unlovely Samuel Goldwyn to leap into her mind.

Somebody else who saw the Hollywood mogul as a regressive evolutionary step was Montrose Mulliner, who served for a time as assistant-director at Perfecto-Zizzbaum. Mulliner's consignment of the captains of Hollywood industry to the animal kingdom had occurred when he was put to work on an epic called *Black Africa*, starring a gorilla 'whose capture was said to have cost the lives of seven half-dozen members of the expedition, and was lodged in a stout cage on the Perfecto-Zizzbaum lot at a salary of seven hundred and fifty dollars a week'. Montrose, hardened by the demands of life at Perfecto-Zizzbaum, was prepared to take the gorilla in his stride, having been rendered so immune to sensation that until his fiancée urged him to the contrary, he had resolved to shun the creature altogether. But Rosalie Beamish, engaged as an extra in *Black Africa*, regarded everyone connected with that masterpiece as a fellow-artiste, including gorillas, and therefore required to be taken by Montrose to visit the animal's cage. Montrose obliged but considered the whole business ridiculous, saying to himself, 'If a man's duties brought him into personal contact with Mr Schnellenhamer, what was the sense of wasting time looking at gorillas?' Why bother with imitations when you can get the real thing?

In fact Montrose was much more frightened of Mr Schnellenhamer than he was of any run-of-the-mill primate, in which attitude he was at one with most of the employees at Perfecto-Zizzbaum, who ranged from Press Department workers like George Phybus 'whose brains resemble soup at a cheap restaurant. It is wise not to stir them', to underlings like Montrose himself, 'constantly addressed in the third person as "that fathead", and obliged to be so obsequious to so many people that it is little wonder that he comes in time to resemble one of the more shrinking and respectful breeds of rabbit'. Admittedly there were certain superficial resemblances between Mr Schnellenhamer and the gorilla, which turned out on examination to look like 'a stockbroker motoring to Brighton in a fur coat', but Montrose was under no illusion as to where the greater danger lay. For some time he had been attempting without success to muster the courage to ask Mr Schnellenhamer for a raise. Had it been the gorilla who held the studio purse-strings, then Montrose might have faced the ordeal readily enough. But Mr Schnellenhamer was no ordinary primate, and his minions knew from bitter experience that 'there was something about being asked to pay out money that always aroused the head of the firm's worst passions'.

This sad lack of good-will probably had something to do with the fact that Mr Schnellenhamer too had grave doubts as to the evolutionary status of those around him. Just as they considered him to be a disgrace to neolithic times, so he was convinced that they had only just crawled out of the primeval slime. The only difference was that while the disdain of the Montroses of this world could hardly wound him, Mr Schnellenhamer's indifference to his employees might easily put their very lives at risk. The acquisition of the gorilla and his subsequent reaction to its welfare was a perfect example. Mr Schnellenhamer was immensely proud of that gorilla, mainly because there were none at Medulla-Oblongata with the possible exception of Siggy Glutz himself. The loss of the lives of those seven half-dozen heroes in capturing the creature had been a severe blow which Mr Schnellenhamer had been able to bear with fortitude, especially as none of the lives lost had had any connection with his own. They never did. When Phybus, eager for publicity, arranged for the gorilla to escape from its cage, Montrose's horror at the thought of the lives which might be endangered seemed quite uncalled for. As Phybus told him:

> 'The stars have all been notified and are off the lot. Also the executives, all except Mr Schnellenhamer, who is cleaning up some work in his office. He will be quite safe there, of course. Nobody ever got into Mr Schnellenhamer's office without waiting four hours in the anteroom.'

However, Montrose's horror was not only tactless but unjustified, for the interesting reason that nothing at Perfecto-Zizzbaum was quite what it seemed. Mr Schnellenhamer's private secretary was a fugitive from vaudeville, where her bird-imitations had become legendary; Little Johnny Bingley, the 'Child with a Tear Behind the Smile', was really a forty-year-old midget from Connolly's Circus. As for the gorilla, it turned out to be an Oxonian, one Cyril Waddesley-Davenport, who had risen to the top of his profession only at the cost of financial sacrifice: 'The initial expenditure comes high. You don't get a skin like this for nothing, but there's virtually no overhead.' Emboldened by his conquest of a gorilla, even one whose savagery had been tempered in the fires of a Balliol education, Montrose went to Mr Schnellenhamer and got his raise, thus demonstrating the golden rule of the industry, which was that when dealing with wild animals, you had to be willing to grab any weapon to hand. All Mr Schnellenhamer's defeats were the consequence of some misdemeanour of his being discovered by a rival, the beauty of the system being that Jacob Z. and his associates embodied enough misdemeanours between them to stock a medium-sized penitentiary.

Johnny Bingley was a case in point. A strictly honourable man might have hesitated before attempting to pass off as a swaddling-clothed innocent a hard-boiled rye-drinker like Bingley, but Mr Schnellenhamer, thinking of the gross in Oshkosh and Kalamazoo, had hesitated not at all. That was all very well, but it exposed yet another of his flanks for, if ever Bingley should take it into his head to indulge in the luxury of a public confessional, the flags at Perfecto-Zizzbaum would surely be fluttering at half-mast. And sure enough, being rather more mature than Mr Schnellenhamer had led American Motherhood to believe, Bingley went out on a drinking spree one night with Wilmot, yet another of the Mulliner family connections who had found his way out to California. The very next morning, rumours reached Mr Schnellenhamer's sensitive ear that Bingley was on his way to the office with a demand for more money. Jacob Z., understandably dismayed by this threat to his hoard of nuts, instantly confided in Mr Levitsky, who grew so agitated that his cigar was seen to tremble. He was not, however, so distraught that he was lost for a stratagem: 'If he wants a raise of salary, talk about the Depression.' The conversation which followed reveals one of the most endearing aspects of the mogul mind: its uncorrupted illiteracy. When Schnellenhamer tried to express himself to Mr Levitsky and Mr Levitsky tried to express himself back to Mr Schnellenhamer, the English tongue began to buckle under the strain:

> 'Quiet. Respectful. . . . What's that word beginning with a "d"?'
> 'Damn?'
> 'Deferential. And what's the word beginning with an "o"?'
> 'Oyster?'
> 'Obsequious. That's what he is.'

A reasonably sane man might have assumed that the Schnellenhamers and the Levitskys, dimly perceiving through the gothic mists of their own thought processes their limitations in matters of literature, would willingly have delegated artistic responsibility to hired brains. On the contrary, if there was one aspect of the mogul mind more dominant than its ignorance, it was its bland self-confidence in matters of the fine arts, for it was the fatal flaw in the Schnellenhamer, Glutz and Fishbein personas that rampant egos forbade them to delegate anything to anybody. They were footing the bills, weren't they? Very well then, theirs was the right to dictate the shape of the product. The point is vital to any understanding of the nature of life in the industry and how it came to be that, no matter how many talented members of the literati Mr Schnellenhamer might lure out to the coast, the degree of idiocy in his pictures never wavered.

On the occasion of the Bingley crisis, the product in question concerned the trials of one Cabot Delancy, scion of an old Boston family, 'who has gone to the North Pole in a submarine, and he's on an iceberg, and the scenes of his youth are passing before his eyes'. Having penetrated this far, Mr Schnellenhamer's inward eye could see no further, and he turned for enlightenment to the serried ranks of writers sitting in at the story conference. What scenes might Cabot Delancy have seen as he sat there on the studio iceberg? Somebody suggested polo, at which Mr Schnellenhamer snorted with contempt and delivered one of the tablets of Hollywood law: 'Who cares anything about polo? When you're working on a picture you've got to bear in mind the small-town population of the Middle West.' But it was not till the story moved into its pastoral stage that Mr. Schnellenhamer, waxing lyrical, found himself tumbling over the trip-wire of his own inadequacies:

> 'It's got to be a lovely, peaceful, old-world exterior set, with bees humming and doves cooing and trees waving in the breeze. Listen, it's spring, see, and all around is the beauty of Nature in the first shy sun-glow. The grass that waves. The buds that . . . what's the word?'
>
> 'Bud?' suggested Mr Levitsky.
>
> 'No, it's two syllables,' said Mr Schnellenhamer, speaking a little self-consciously, for he was modestly proud of knowing words of two syllables.
>
> 'Burgeon?' hazarded an author who looked like a trained seal.
>
> 'I beg your pardon,' said Miss Mabel Potter, 'a burgeon's sort of fish.'
>
> 'You're thinking of sturgeon,' said the author.
>
> 'Excuse it please,' murmured Mabel, 'I'm not strong on fishes. Birds are what I'm best at.'

The point was that once having been appraised of the virtues of burgeoning, Mr Schnellenhamer was resolved to get only the best, informing the story conference, 'And when I say burgeoning, I mean burgeoning. That burgeoning's got to be done *right*, or somebody'll get fired.' When Wilmot Mulliner is finally promoted to executive status 'with brevet rank as brother-in-law', a fresh contract is required:

> At the desk, Mr Schnellenhamer had paused for a moment in his writing. He was trying to remember if the word he wanted was spelled 'clorse' or 'clorze'.

How could that kind of coyness in the face of the English language continue to flourish in a society so stuffed with literary sensibility that when the playwright Eustiss Vanderbilt signs a Perfecto-Zizzbaum contract, he arrives at the studio as 'one of a crate of twelve'? The explanation has something to do with the fact that a high percentage of the writers employed at the studio were not writers at all, but had simply been recruited by accident. As Mr Mulliner hastened to explain about yet another of his West Coast nephews, Bulstrode:

> 'My nephew was not an author. Nor was Miss Bottle. Very few of those employed in writing motion-picture dialogue are. The executives of the studios just haul in anyone they meet and make them sign contracts. Most of the mysterious disappearances you read about are due to this cause. Only the other day they found a plumber who had been missing for years. All the time he had been writing dialogue for the Mishkin Brothers. Once having reached Los Angeles, nobody is safe.'

This would explain the otherwise inscrutable moment in which Bulstrode Mulliner, encountering a young lady who had signed a writer's contract, asked her if she could write dialogue: 'A foolish question, for, if she could, the Perfecto-Zizzbaum Corporation would scarcely have engaged her.' Sure enough, the girl was just one more victim of Mr Schnellenhamer's Press Gang. Having arrived on the lot one day in the innocent hope of placing a few orders for her bootlegger-fiancé, she had been swept up in a sequence of misunderstandings which culminated, as most misunderstandings at Perfecto-Zizzbaum had a way of culminating, in her signing a contract disbarring her from leaving before the completion of a notorious turkey called *Scented Sinners*, thus evoking recollections of the weedy young man in spectacles who found himself attending Cabot Delancy story conferences: 'He had come to Hollywood to start a Gyffte Shoppe and had been scooped up in the studio's drag-net, and forced into the writing staff against his will.' Of the two victims, it was the young lady who was marginally deeper in the mire for, while the tale of Cabot Delancy would be resolved one day, *Scented Sinners* was doomed never to reach the final fade-out, and had long since become acknowledged as a kind of celluloid version of Penelope's knitting, doomed to be unravelled each night and started all over again next morning. One aged writer, a Mr Markey, had been working on treatments of *Scented Sinners* since he was a young man and had now reached the stage where he was convinced he saw spiders running up the walls. The predicament of his colleague Mr Doakes was even worse. One day, while working on a treatment of the picture, he started foaming at the mouth and screaming, 'No, no, it isn't possible'. But it was possible, thanks to Mr Schnellenhamer's faith in the team system, whereby a group of writers was put to work on a story without each of its individual members being told of the existence of any of the others. At the time of the mouth-foaming incident, the list of writers working on *Scented Sinners* included Mr Doakes, Mr Noakes, Miss Faversham, Miss Wilson, Mr Fotheringay, Mr Mendelsohn, Mr Markey, Mrs Cooper, Mr Lennox and Mr Dabney, although even this was hardly enough to satisfy Mr Schnellenhamer's restless soul. He reacted to the recital of the list with an abrupt 'That all?', and was hardly mollified when informed by his secretary that there had been one additional name, belonging to a missionary who had arrived at the studios in the hope of converting the extra girls to something or other. 'He started a treatment but he has escaped to Canada.' 'Tcha,' said Mr Schnellenhamer, 'we must have more vigilance, more vigilance.'

Whether it was the megalomania which fathered the idiocy or the idiocy which engendered the megalomania has remained enigmatic, but it may not be altogether irrelevant to the issue that over at Brinkmeyer-Magnifico, where the dictator was much more human, they ordered their affairs more rationally. Of course it was all relative, and nobody would deny that Brinkmeyer filled his sound stages with the same junk which so exercised the minds of Schnellenhamer and company. But the degree of the madness was marginally less hysterical. Brinkmeyer too had his fraudulent Fauntleroy in Joey Cooley, but at least Cooley's birth certificate confirmed his status as a minor. Brinkmeyer too conducted his lunatic story conferences, but at least on the Magnifico lot they had half-grasped the proposition which always eluded the tycoons of Perfecto-Zizzbaum. Brinkmeyer's men were beginning to realize that in the motion-picture business the stories over which they expended so many conference-hours, the plots to which they sacrificed so many sleepless afternoons, the dialogue they paid to have written and rewritten and rewritten again, none of it mattered, and that the vital factor in the box-office equation was star quality. Brinkmeyer could never quite bring himself to utter this blasphemy aloud, but the suspicion that it was true all the same was what distinguished the Magnifico story conferences from those of Schnellenhamer and his team:

> 'There's this gangster that's been made Public Enemy Number Thirteen, see, and he's superstitious, see, and he feels he won't never have any luck just so long as he's got this Thirteen hoodoo, see, so what does he do? He's too kind-hearted to go shooting up one of the Public Enemies that's higher on the list, though he knows that if he does that'll make him Public Enemy Number Twelve.'
> 'I see it as a Lionel Barrymore part,' said Eddie.
> 'Warner Baxter,' said Fred.
> 'Bill Powell,' said George curtly, putting them both in their places.

There was something else about Brinkmeyer which distinguished him from his fellow-moguls, and which must surely have counted for something when he finally handed in his dinner-pail. One of the things about which Schnellenhamer and his friends were sensitive to the brink of paranoia was the incongruity of their backgrounds in the context of the industry they controlled. They were hucksters, on a super-colossal scale it is true, but hucksters for all that. They were peddling a mass-produced artefact, and had arranged the factory conditions inside their studios accordingly. But the same vanity which impelled them to oversee artistic arrangements inspired them to insist on their onerous responsibilities as purveyors of creative work, for which reason their early training, as travelling salesmen, or middlemen, as small-time manufacturers of mundane domestic items, was something they preferred not to air too often. Brinkmeyer was the exception; not only did he admit to his humble beginnings, but he was actually frank enough to say that he preferred them:

> 'There I was, perfectly happy in the cloak and suit business, and I ought to have stuck to it. But no. Nothing would do but I had to go into the pictures. And look at me now. President of the organization, worth every cent of twenty million dollars. And what does it all amount to? Here I am, got to stand up there in spats with everybody staring at me, looking like a comic valentine. I might have known it would happen. It's always the way. You get on just the least little bit in this world, and the first thing you know they're putting up statues to you. The moment your back's turned. I ought to have stuck to the cloak and suit business.'

But not even Brinkmeyer, in whose breast there still beat something resembling a human heart, could mitigate the callous lunacy of his profession. The Magnifico lot was no freer than Schnellenhamer's from the deceits and treacheries and betrayals and double-crossings which made life so impossible. The outside visitor had hardly to set foot on Magnifico territory to sense that things could have been better:

> 'It occurred to me how little the outside world knew of the discontent that seethed in every bosom you met in Hollywood. The casual observer saw these bosoms going about the place and envied them, assuming that, being well provided with the stuff, they must be happy. And all the time discontent seethed. In my own little circle, April June wanted to be a wife and mother. Joey Cooley wanted to be back in Chillicothe, Ohio, eating fried chicken southern style. The butler wasn't any too pleased with things. And this Brinkmeyer sighed for the cloak and suit business. A bit poignant.'

Lying deep under the surface of this empire of the moguls, and never quite masked by its fundamental absurdity, was the faint but unmistakable rumble of corruption. While almost nobody in town was in any position to point the finger at anyone else without getting it bitten off, the motion-picture industry was populated almost entirely by those who, while ready to testify before the Supreme Court that they had never heard of murder, knew where the bodies were buried. When Sam Glutz, describing the experience of being mugged, confessed, 'I thought it was the end. My whole past life flashed before me', it was Schnellenhamer who replied solicitously, 'You can't have liked that' and Sam who responded, 'I didn't'. It was not that they were wicked men so much as moral defectives genuinely incapable of distinguishing right from might. When at some crisis point Schnellenhamer asked Fishbein how he, Fishbein, stood with Ben Zizzbaum, Fishbein had answered with disarming innocence, 'I stand fine with Ben. I heard something about him last week which I'll bet he wouldn't care to have known.' As for Schnellenhamer himself, he had only to overhear a disconsolate starlet muttering the vaguest of unspecified threats for him to fear that the game was finally up:

> For an instant Mr Schnellenhamer was conscious of a twinge of uneasiness. Like all motion-picture magnates, he had about forty-seven guilty secrets, many of them recorded on paper. Was it possible that . . . . Then he breathed again. All his private documents were secure in a safe-deposit box. It was absurd to imagine that this girl could have anything on him.

The curious thing was the way that the industry's corrupt heart spread its influence outward to consume the whole civilized world. Contemptible its ethics may have been, absurd its products ultimately were, but still there was no corner of the earth where the fame of Schnellenhamer's merchandise had not spread and, having spread, seduced the locals into compliance. Hungry wolves came from all over the world to prowl about Beverly Hills in the hope of picking up a few lambs, and there developed a positive stampede of deposed moguls from more venerable civilizations who arrived in town curious to see how these latterday robber barons managed their feudal affairs. When Schnellenhamer discovered that there was to be no champagne for his big dinner party, he was so mortified that he grabbed the nearest chesterfield for support. As his wife reminded him, 'Here we are, with a hundred and fifty people coming tonight, including the Duke.'

> Her allusion was to the Duke of Wigan, who, as so many British Dukes do, was at this time passing slowly through Hollywood.
> 'And you know how touchy dukes are,' proceeded Mrs Schnellenhamer. 'I'm told that the Lulubelle Mahaffys invited the Duke of Kircudbrightshire for the weekend last year, and after he had been there two months he suddenly left in a huff because there was no brown sherry.'

Nor was the Schnellenhamer crisis unusual. On that very night the Zizzbaums were in the identical plight, except that their guests included the Vice-President of Switzerland. Even that detached witness who perceived the discontent at Brinkmeyer-Magnifico was the third Earl of Havershot, who, at the risk of being labelled a patrician pot calling the plebeian kettle black, reported:

> 'Since the talkies came in, you can't heave a brick in Hollywood without beaning an English elocution teacher. The place is full of

Britons on the make, and if they can't get jobs on the screen, they work the elocution-teaching racket. References and qualifications are not asked for. So long as you're English, you are welcomed into the home. I am told that there are English elocution teachers making good money who haven't even got roofs to their mouths.'

But the conquest of the Old World was the least of Schnellenhamer's achievements. He had, for example, succeeded in putting maternal solicitude on a firm commercial basis. After Montrose Mulliner had rescued a baby-thespian from the simian clutches of Waddesley-Davenport, he found himself confronted by the child's grateful personal manager:

> The mother was kneeling before him, endeavouring to kiss his hand. It was not only maternal love that prompted the action. That morning she had signed up her child at seventy-five dollars a week for the forthcoming picture *Tiny Fingers*, and all through these long, anxious minutes it had seemed as though the contract must be a total loss.

But then what was a baby to Schnellenhamer, who made no distinctions between *Homo sapiens* and the lower primates? When he, Fishbein and Zizzbaum needed the help of Glutz, he suggested a deal to Zizzbaum:

> 'I've got it,' he said. 'We must go to Glutz of Medulla-Oblongata. He's never been a real friend of mine, but if you loan him Stella Svelte and I loan him Orlando Byng and Fishbein loans him Otto the Wonder-Poodle on his own terms. . . .'

A more devious villain never foreclosed on his own grandmother. And yet Schnellenhamer could give a passable imitation of a proper person when the need arose:

> His manner softened and became more appealing. This man knew well when to brandish the iron fist and when to display the velvet glove.
> 'And anyway,' he said, speaking now in almost a fatherly manner, 'you wouldn't want to quit till the picture was finished. . . .'
> He rose from his chair, and tears came into his eyes. It was as if he had been some emotional American football coach addressing a faint-hearted team.

This was the man whose features relaxed into a smile 'as he remembered that that morning he had put through a deal which would enable him to trim the stuffing out of two hundred and seventy-three exhibitors'. As to his sexual morality, nothing is known of it except that, at some point in the course of his Napoleonic chicaneries, he had paused long enough to woo the actress known to the trade as the Queen of Stormy Emotion. It seems that money was his fetish and power his aphrodisiac, which explained why he was a mogul and the rest of them were also-rans. It was Corky Potter-Pirbright who became maddened by Hollywood's unfortunate compulsion to trumpet its own romantic indiscretions. While on holiday back in England, she had been unfortunate enough to be trapped by an elderly lady whose brain had long since been reduced to mash through addiction to the movie fan magazines. At last she was rescued by Bertie Wooster:

'Thank God. I don't think I could have stood any more Hollywood chatter this afternoon. I wouldn't have believed that anybody except Luella Parsons and Hedda Hopper could be such an authority on the film world as is Mrs Clara Wellbeloved. She knows much more about it than I do, and I'll have been moving in celluloid circles two years come Lammas Eve. She knows exactly how many times everybody's been divorced and why, how much every picture for the last twenty years has grossed, and now many Warner Brothers there are. She even knows how many times Artie Shaw has been married, which I'll bet he couldn't tell you himself. She asked if I had ever married Artie Shaw, and when I said No, seemed to think I was pulling her leg or must have done it without noticing. I tried to explain that when a girl goes to Hollywood she doesn't *have* to marry Artie Shaw, it's optional, but I don't think I convinced her.'

It would seem that Schnellenhamer, who dismissed Montrose Mulliner as 'sardinic', had much to answer for, and that Levitsky, when he replied, 'Like a sardine, you mean?', had almost as much. The moguls had corrupted the literary and dramatic professions, had bent the law to suit themselves, had grabbed more power than any ten normal men would ever feel the need to possess. They had bullied their underlings and recruited everybody from the deformed to the infantile to the gigantic to the senile in their determination to make a fast buck. And at first glance it seemed that no impediment to their pleasure had ever confronted them.

But appearances were deceptive after all. Destiny had reserved for them the most terrible of all forms of retribution, which is to be punished by the fruits of one's own excess. The very fact that Schnellenhamer had the power to pick up a pen and transmogrify a provincial nobody into a world-famous millionaire may have gratified him at times, but it had the unforseen effect of exposing him to the mercy of every loony frustrated thespian in the world. For if Schnellenhamer had unlimited power, then his was the one fortress that needed to be conquered. Armies of bad actors, out-of-work actors, would-be actors, self-deluding actors, insane actors, beat a path to his door and, once there, drove him half-mad with their demands. For all his wealth, Schnellenhamer could not even buy a cup of coffee without submitting himself to the indignity of an impromptu audition. He could not drive down the street in the certitude that the pedestrians he passed were really pedestrians or just a bunch of extras striving to catch his eye. There was not a single member of any service industry in any district of California who might not be someone else in disguise. Schnellenhamer might spend a million dollars on building a nest, and another ten million on securing it from burglars, but, for all the comfort and protection it afforded him, he might as well have pitched a tent on the sidewalk. His very success had made him a marked man, and the subtlety of his predicament was that there was no escape from it except the dismantling of his empire and the consequent dispersal of his power to help all these screwballs. The question which so often exercised his brain was whether the power was worth the constant harassment, or whether peace might not be ample compensation for retirement into obscurity. He never found a satisfactory answer to that conundrum, but in the meantime the very industry he had built had become the monster which was devouring his whole existence.

For instance, on the night of the impending visit of the Duke of Wigan, he had telephoned his bootlegger, only to be told that that gentleman was out on other business:

> They were shooting a scene in *Sundered Hearts* on the Outstanding Screen-Favourites lot, and the bootlegger was hard at work there, playing the role of an Anglican bishop. His secretary said he could not be disturbed, as it got him all upset to be interrupted when he was working.

Then there was that business of the policeman and the parking ticket. Even as he handed Schnellenhamer the dreaded document, the cop had recited one of Hamlet's soliloquies 'to give him some idea of what he could do in a dramatic role'. But then, these days you could never trust the police. When caught red-handed with bootleg booze, he had entered on the customary financial negotiations only to discover that under certain circumstances there were still policemen prepared to be incorruptible:

> 'Only this morning I was saying to Mrs Schnellenhamer that I must really slip down to headquarters and give my old friend Donahue that ten dollars I owed him.'
>
> 'What ten dollars?'
>
> 'I didn't say ten. I said a hundred. One hundred dollars, Donny, old man, and I'm not saying there mightn't be a little over for these two gentlemen here. How about it?'
>
> The sergeant drew himself up. There was no sign of softening in his glance. 'Jacob Schnellenhamer,' he said coldly, 'you can't square me. When I tried for a job at the Colossal-Exquisite last spring I was turned down on account you said I had no sex-appeal.'
>
> The first patrolman, who had hitherto taken no part in the conversation, said, 'Well, can you tie that! When I tried to crash the Colossal-Exquisite, they said my voice wasn't right.'
>
> 'Me,' said the second patrolman, eyeing Mr Schnellenhamer sourly, 'they had the nerve to beef at my left profile.'

The sergeant had returned to his own grievance. 'No sex-appeal,' he said with a rasping laugh. 'And me that had specially taken sex-appeal in the College of Eastern Iowa course of Motion Picture acting.'

But difficult as things were out in the street, in the sanctity of the Schnellenhamer residence they were much worse. It was bad enough travelling to and from the studio, on which odyssey in the course of a single day he could recall being acted at by the studio watchman, a secretary, two book agents, the waitress who brought him his lunch, a life insurance man, a representative of a film weekly, the man with the benzedrine, a barber and the studio watchman once again. But even sitting at home Schnellenhamer was powerless to avoid this terrible tidal wave of frustrated melodramatics. That very morning he had been obliged to fire the butler for reciting 'Gunga Din' while serving the eggs and bacon. And later, when he had asked the new girl to bring him a drink, she had given him in quick succession Joy, Grief, Horror and Hate, ending with an impression of Cleopatra the warrior-queen at the Pasadena Gas-fitters' Ball. As someone had once said of him, 'He is not one of those men who are avid for entertainment. It is his aim in life to avoid it. He has told me that it is the motion-picture magnate's cross that everybody he meets starts acting on him in the hope of getting on the payroll.'

And so Jacob Z. Schnellenhamer, who was coarse, callous, ignorant, vain, greedy, treacherous and stupid, whose table manners were so atrocious that when he ate a sandwich it flew before him 'like a banner', whose literary sensibilities were so microscopic that he thought nothing of hiring once-sane men to write jokes into *Solomon and the Queen of Sheba*, got his retribution after all. So much for the simpletons who used to say that the motion-picture magnates shared with the Press barons the prerogative of the harlot through the ages, power without responsibility.

And there was something else to be said in mitigation of the super-colossal excesses of Jacob Z. Schnellenhamer, one last redeeming glint of a silver lining behind the vast cloud of avaricious semi-literacy for which he and his rivals had been responsible. It was this: however awful they may have been, however monstrous as men or disastrous as creators, at least they had never existed. Jacob Z. Schnellenhamer was, after all, not real.

In the late summer of 1929, having been summoned to New York to work on a non-existent Flo Ziegfeld production, Wodehouse found himself in the unaccustomed position of having no immediate deadlines to meet, and so decided to take a trip out to the West Coast. He was impelled more by curiosity than by any burning desire to work there. He was by now one of the world's most prosperous writers, and had more than enough work to occupy his time for years to come. But he had received overtures from the dream factory, and saw no harm in making a brief reconnaissance trip before drawing any conclusions. By the beginning of October he was back in New York, writing to Townend:

It seemed to me a good idea to take a few days off and go to Hollywood. I wanted to see what the place was like before committing myself to it for an extended period. I was there three days . . . I liked what little I saw and expect to return there in the summer. I have had three offers of a year's work, but I held out for only five months. The only person I knew really well out there was Marion Davies, who was in the show *Oh, Boy!*, which Bolton, Kern and I did for the Princess Theatre. She took me out to her house in Santa Monica and worked me into a big lunch at MGM, which they were giving for Winston Churchill. All very pleasant.

It was at this lunch that Wodehouse was able to catch his first glimpse of a motion-picture magnate in action. Louis B. Mayer, Vice-President and General Manager of the Metro-Goldwyn-Mayer Studios, had held both positions for five years and was to retain them for a further twenty-two. His apprenticeship for guiding the fortunes of Hollywood's largest studio had been at least as perverse as Ernest Wodehouse's for dispensing justice in Malaya, although there were those who thought they perceived analogies between Mayer's first job, in a junkyard, and his last, at MGM. He was soon to become Wodehouse's employer, so presumably Wodehouse must have been fascinated, and perhaps a shade perturbed, by Mayer's cheerfully tactless behaviour:

> Churchill made a speech at the lunch, and when he had finished Louis B. Mayer said, 'That was a very good speech. I think we would all like to hear it again', and it was played back from an apparatus concealed in the flowers on the table. Churchill seemed rather taken aback.

So was Wodehouse, who, having been introduced to Churchill for the seventh time in his life, noted Churchill's blank reaction and concluded that 'I must have one of those meaningless faces which make no impression whatever on the beholder'. No doubt at the time the incident of the hidden tape recorder must have struck him as a quaint and faintly comic example of the childlike pleasure which modern America derived from its new toys. But there was something ominous about it, too, as all MGM employees well knew, and which perhaps the percipient Churchill sensed when 'taken aback'. But it was to be some time yet before it began to dawn on Wodehouse precisely what type of men he was dealing with.

By November, while the New York financial community was generously providing Ira Gershwin with his favourite verbal image by arranging the Wall Street Crash, Wodehouse was living in Norfolk Street, London, writing busily while negotiations slowly developed on two fronts. Ethel was in California doing battle with MGM over terms, and it was while she was away that the second mogul materialized in Wodehouse's life. In December he wrote to Townend:

> I have just had a cable from Hollywood. They want me to do a picture
> for Evelyn Laye. This may mean a long trip out there pretty soon, but I
> don't expect to stay very long. I shall know more on December 21st
> when Samuel Goldwyn arrives in England.

Although his name took precedence over Mayer's on the MGM banner,
Goldwyn had always insisted on retaining a degree of autonomy which
qualified himself as an independent producer who financed all his own
pictures. By the time he arrived in London to parley with Wodehouse, he
was already legendary as the man who not only mangled the language of
Shakespeare but on occasion actually improved it. Some of his more notorious statements, for instance that a verbal contract wasn't worth the paper it
was written on, or that anyone who went to a psychiatrist wanted his head
examined, appear to have been manufactured for him by his writers, but it
was common knowledge in Hollywood that these Goldwynisms had their
origin in his genuine inability to say quite what he meant. Having committed a few malapropisms in good faith and perceived the humanizing
power of the laughter they engendered, Goldwyn had shrewdly made an
asset out of them, but if he never actually believed, like Schnellenhamer and
Levitsky, that when people were sardinic they went around imitating sardines, he certainly thought that *The Old Wives' Tale* was written by
Benedict Arnold and that these days every Tom, Dick and Harry was getting
christened Bill, and that William was a far more suitable name. But it was by
studying this theme of personal names that a student might be able to arrive
at a more accurate reading of his personality. Goldwyn's real name was
Goldfish, and the amended version had come about through his merger in
the early days with a man called Edgar Selwyn. The two partners, seeking a
compromise label for their product, finally arrived at a neologism comprising the first syllable of Goldfish and the last one of Selwyn; when one of
Goldwyn's confidantes was asked his opinion, he replied that a much more
honest arrangement would have been the first syllable of Selwyn followed by
the last one of Goldfish, 'because, as you well know, that is the way it is
certain to turn out to be'.

   That indeed was the way it turned out to be, and Wodehouse began to
realize it at the very first encounter. Goldwyn, for all his vaunted acumen,
appears to have displayed gross ineptitude in his grasp of prevailing market
prices, approaching one of the most successful commercial writers in the
world in the spirit of a medieval baron distributing largesse to the peasants:

> It looks as if Hollywood is off. I had some sessions with Goldwyn, but
> he wouldn't meet my price. The poor chump seemed to think he was
> doing me a favour offering about half what I get for a serial for doing a
> job which would be the most ghastly sweat. He said, when he sailed
> today, that he would think things over and let me know, but I'm hoping
> I have made the price too stiff for him. I don't want to go to Hollywood
> just now a bit.

How much money Wodehouse asked for remains unknown, but by May 1930 he was in Hollywood as a consequence of Ethel having extracted from MGM a contract for $2,000 per week for six months with an option for a further six.

The Hollywood that Wodehouse now stepped into was an industry still struggling to adapt to the new technology of talkies. The good old days of infantile sub-titles had gone forever, and producers committed to supplying so many cinemas with so many new pictures each year were desperate to acquire battalions of writers and, having acquired them, organize their labours on endless-belt lines. Many years later, indulging in retrospective facetiousness, Wodehouse said that when he arrived at MGM, it was to discover that writers were kept in little hutches: 'You could see their anxious little faces peering out through the bars and hear them whining piteously to be taken for a walk.' That, however, was the wisdom of hindsight. When he first took up his duties, he sensed none of this. For one thing he was granted special dispensation to work from the home which he and Ethel had rented from Norma Shearer, about five miles from the studio. His paymasters must have soon begun to suspect that they were harbouring a dangerous lunatic; whenever they telephoned instructions for him to attend a story conference, he would stride out the five miles to the studio, watched all along the route by gardeners, domestics and children scandalized by the spectacle of a Beverly Hills biped using the locomotive method of placing one foot before the other.

But if the moguls swiftly concluded that Wodehouse was a mad dog of an Englishman, he did not at first return the compliment, drawing instead the comically mistaken conclusion that Hollywood was a hard-working and super-efficient town dedicated to the sober pursuit of manufacture on a vast scale, a community which maintained such an hysterical industrial pace as to have flattened out all human idiosyncrasy into the rolling plains of conformity. In August he wrote to Townend:

> Oddly enough, Hollywood hasn't inspired me in the least. I feel as if everything that could be written about it has already been done. As a matter of fact I don't think there is much to be written about this place. What it was like in the early days I don't know, but nowadays the studio life is all perfectly normal, not a bit crazy. I haven't seen any swooning directors or temperamental stars. They seem just to do their job, and to be quite ordinary people, especially the directors, who are quiet, unemotional men who just work and don't throw any fits. Same with the stars. I don't believe I shall get a single story out of my stay here.

Of all the paragraphs that Wodehouse composed in nearly ninety years of unremitting literary labour, that one must surely rank as the most wrongheaded. It is dated 18 August 1930. The story of Cyril Waddesley-Davenport appeared in print before the end of 1932; by the summer of 1933 his cycle of Hollywood short stories was complete. What had caused him to perform such a brilliantly comic volte-face?

It must first be said that when he described Hollywood to Townend as a prosaic town, he had had, on his own admission, almost no experience of it. He had explained in an earlier letter that he saw very little of the movie world, hardly ever went to the studio, and for the most part mixed socially only 'with other exiles'. But gradually, as the encroachments of the moguls made themselves felt, Wodehouse began to see that he had become swept up in an amazing real-life extravaganza. One day he was summoned to Irving Thalberg's home to be instructed in how to adapt for the screen the musical comedy *Rosalie*, which Wodehouse had, of course, part-written for Broadway. He arrived at Thalberg's house accompanied by a stenographer whose job it would be to take down the great man's thoughts. After he had finished his recital, Thalberg asked Wodehouse if he would like the stenographer to read it back:

> I was about to say Yes (just to make the party go) when I suddenly caught the stenographer's eye and was startled to see a look of agonized entreaty in it. I couldn't imagine what was wrong, but I gathered that for some reason she wanted me to say No, so I said No. When we were driving home, she told me that she had had a latish night the night before and had fallen asleep at the outset of the proceedings and slept peacefully throughout, not having heard or taken down a word.

It was not altogether surprising that a recital by Thalberg of one of his own scenarios should have had such a soporific effect, for it was he who had invented the factory system of putting teams of men on to the same project in the belief that if one writer produced a good script, then it followed that eight writers could produce one eight times as good. He had then gone on to elaborate his idea with the kind of ingenuity which made his name a by-word for creative insight. Having dictated his *Rosalie* scenario to Wodehouse, he now required Wodehouse to write it up as a novelette, after which it would be turned back into another scenario: 'The prospect of this appals me, and I am hoping that the whole thing will eventually blow over, as things do out here.' Wodehouse was learning.

Thalberg's playful habit of assigning writers ten or twelve at a time affected Wodehouse from the beginning. His first project was a film called *Those Three French Girls* but, instead of being asked to write the story, he found himself given a script written by a number of other men. Having read it and decided that it was perfectly adequate and eminently shootable, he added a few lines of his own and awaited further instructions. In October he writes to Townend:

> Well laddy, it begins to look as if it would be some time before I return to England. The Metro people have taken up my option, and I am with them for another six months and Ethel has just taken a new house for a year. Which means that I shall probably stay that long.

By now it had dawned on him that, although showering his bank account with fairy gold, the moguls had not the remotest idea what it was they wanted him to do. After working for three months on the *Rosalie* project, he learned that as the moguls had decided that musicals were 'out', the film was to be scrapped. In February 1931 he tells Townend that the studio 'has just given me a job which will take up all my time for weeks'. Once again he was wrong, because the job they handed him had, like *Those Three French Girls*, already been done by divers hands. This time he inserted three lines of additional dialogue and earned his first screen credit. And that was the sum total of his contribution to the destinies of Metro-Goldwyn-Mayer. In March he sincerely believed he was writing *By Candlelight* for John Gilbert: 'This looks as if it might really come to something. Everything else I have done so far has been scrapped.' So was *By Candlelight* and, by the end of that month, the show-business periodical *Variety* was referring pointedly to the case of an 'English playwright and author who has been collecting $2,500 a week for eleven months without contributing anything really worth while to the screen'.

Perhaps not to the screen, but *Variety* was wrong to imply that Wodehouse had been idle during his year in California. He was the most prolific novelist and short-story writer of his epoch, and it would have been unthinkable for him to sit in his sunlit rented garden awaiting the brainstorms of Thalberg and company. Within a month of his arrival he had written three short stories and one act of a play. By the time MGM was ready to dispense with his services he had completed a novel, *Hot Water*, and must have been turning over in his mind the possibilities of this town which a few months before he had so summarily rejected as a source of inspiration. Later, when describing his Hollywood experiences, he wrote that 'destructive criticism is what kills an author . . . at that time there were authors who had been on salary for years in Hollywood without ever having had a line of their work used. All they did was attend story conferences'. It was Wodehouse's little vanity to discuss the Hollywood episode in terms of a prison sentence or a kidnapping:

> I got away from Hollywood at the end of the year because the gaoler's daughter smuggled me in a file in a meat pie . . . not every author accepted his fate so equably. The majority endeavoured to escape. But it was useless . . . capture was inevitable. . . . It was like the Bastille.

The question arises that if the work was so uncongenial to him, why did he allow himself to go west in the first place? Perhaps it was something to do with that diffidence in his nature which J. B. Priestley took to be a sign of immaturity, the passivity which followed where Ethel led. He had rejected Goldwyn's terms; she had accepted Mayer's on his behalf.

The first act curtain came down to a howl of outraged mogul virtue when, a few weeks after the expiry of his contract, Wodehouse was asked by MGM if he would give an interview to a lady from the *Los Angeles Times*. On 7 June 1931, the reporter, a Miss Alma Whitaker, quoted Wodehouse as follows:

They paid me $2,000 dollars a week – $104,000 – and I cannot see what they engaged me for. They were extremely nice to me, but I feel as if I have cheated them. You see, I understood I was engaged to write stories for the screen. After all, I have twenty novels, a score of success-ful plays, and countless magazine stories to my credit. Yet apparently they had the greatest difficulty in finding anything for me to do. Twice during the year they brought completed scenarios of other people's stories to me and asked me to do some dialogue. Fifteen or sixteen people had tinkered with those stories. The dialogue was really quite adequate. All I did was touch it up here and there.

Then they set me to work on a story called *Rosalie*, which was to have some musical numbers. It was a pleasant little thing, and I put in three months on it. When it was finished, they thanked me politely and remarked that as musicals didn't seem to be going so well they guessed they would not use it. That about sums up what I was called upon to do for my $104,000. Isn't it amazing? Personally, I received the most courteous treatment, but see what happened to my friend Roland Pertwee at Warner Brothers. He did a story for Marilyn Miller, and they slapped him on the back and said it was great. He returned to the studio as usual next morning, and was informed by the policeman at the gate that he could not be let in as he was fired. It's so unbelievable, isn't it?

But although unbelievable, it was also true, and the contradiction defines the difficulty lying at the heart of all Hollywood fiction. How does the satirist do justice to his theme without inducing in the reader the conviction that this may be entertaining stuff but it is clearly too mad to have any relationship to what actually went on? At first sight, Wodehouse's Hollywood stories are further-fetched than any other. Their characters are repeatedly tumbling over the rim of credulity into the pit of broadest slapstick. Their people are repeatedly behaving like animals and their animals like people. The reader is asked to suspend his disbelief when confronted by captains of industry who are not only sub-literate but clearly deranged, and by writers and performers who have been reduced by their own contracts to the status of chattels. What possible relationship could there be between the midgets and bird imitators of Wodehouse's extravaganza, and the sober-suited commanders who, by evolving the studio system and inventing the stratagem of type-casting, created the most potent mythology, and the only universal one, of the twentieth century? It was a problem which exercised Wodehouse much less than it did the moguls, who, on the occasion of the innocent interview with the lady from the newspaper, began to show themselves to him for the first time. According to Townend, the published interview made Wodehouse the most talked-about man in America; certainly it made him one of the least popular in Hollywood. The moguls swore undying enmity, and in New York, the ultimate source of all the fairy gold, the bankers took steps to prune studio expenses.

It so happened that on finding himself out of work in Beverly Hills,

Wodehouse was committed to six stories for the magazine *The American*, whose editor disconcerted him by asking for tales 'about American characters in an American setting'. Suddenly the solution seemed obvious. The Perfecto-Zizzbaum stories began to appear in quick succession. In assessing the degree of their accuracy as satire, it is instructive to remember what was said to the lady from the Los Angeles newspaper and to try to decide whether or not Wodehouse, in fulfilling the role of comic, had been gilding the lily. In this regard it is revealing to consider the testimony of a one-time matinée idol called Conrad Nagel, who, in addition to starring in countless Broadway and Hollywood productions, was a co-founder and one-time president of the Academy of Motion Picture Arts and Sciences. In spite of his intimate connections with this august body, Nagel had a considerable sense of humour, and much to say of relevance to the issues Wodehouse had raised. He recalled for example that at one stage Mayer 'was so mad at me that the worst punishment he could think of was to loan me out to Warner Brothers for a picture', adding pointedly that 'Mayer found he could make a lot of money loaning me out for far far more than I was receiving from MGM'.[1] The ghosts of Orlando Byng and Stella Svelte begin to loom. Nagel also had this to say:

> Hollywood was always a strange place. Whether you worked or not depended mostly on chance. For example, once they were going to do a picture with British dialogue. 'Nobody can write this except P. G. Wodehouse or a literary man of his calibre. That's it. Get P. G. Wodehouse.' So they started calling, looking all over for him. They couldn't find him. It turned out that he was right there in the studio. He had an office there for six months and was drawing a salary right along. This is a true story, and there were many other stories like it.[2]

A studio which mounts a search for a writer who is already on the payroll? Readers of *The Castaways* will recall that after years of investment in *Scented Sinners*, Mr Schnellenhamer decides to close down the project after discovering that the property belongs to someone else.

As for Mayer, who expressed his artistic tendencies by making a tidy profit out of renting actors to others, Wodehouse was gradually to acknowledge that there was no Schnellenhamerian excess, no Glutzian outrage, no Fishbeinal or Zizzbaumic crime, which could quite compare with the real thing. The concealed tape recorder at that first introductory lunch began to take on more sinister connotations when the performers on the various MGM sound stages discovered that microphones had been planted among them, so that Mayer could monitor all conversations and settle on his tactics accordingly. One day a child-star called Jackie Cooper arrived with his mother at Mayer's office with the object of procuring a more lucrative contract. In a gallant attempt to keep down studio overheads, Mayer prostrated himself on his own carpet and burst into floods of hysterical tears at the thought of man's ingratitude to Mayer. The Cooper delegation, however, having been forewarned, was forearmed and, by remaining unmoved, won a great victory – at which Mayer jumped up from the carpet, dashed his tears away and stood in a minatory pose over the child, issuing a grim warning that he must never, *ever*, ask for more money again. But even the Cooper sketch fades before the enormity of the Myrna Loy act. One day Miss Loy, having been issued with the ultimatum of a script even more bone-headed than usual, announced her adamant refusal to sign a renewal of contract. Mayer, who knew better than most men of Miss Loy's profitability at the box-office, asked her to discuss the matter. She duly arrived at Mayer's sanctum, at which the executive instantly collapsed on the same tear-stained carpet and had a severe heart attack. Miss Loy, horrified that by her intransigence she might have killed this old man, began to apologize. Once again tears splashed on to the carpet, Miss Loy's as well as Mayer's. At last, having walked into the room resolved that under no circumstances would she even consider signing a new contract, she found herself begging to be allowed to save his life by being vouchsafed the privilege of signing. She then departed, still sobbing, at which Mayer leapt up in his usual style and said brightly to his aide, 'Right. Who's next?' Clearly this was a man who 'knew well when to brandish the iron fist and when to display the velvet glove'. It was the iron fist he selected when paid a visit one day by the studio's hottest male property, Robert Taylor, who made the mistake of asking for more money. Without bothering to argue the point, Mayer ran round the table and, applying the ethics of the junkyard to the world of the arts, landed a right hook on Taylor's jaw which stretched out that unlucky idol on the carpet, which must by now have been showing signs of wear and tear. It was a scene which may well have been relished by an even more distinguished movie figure, Charlie Chaplin, who had entered this same office in an attempt to stop the genial father of the MGM family from using the Chaplin name without permission and had been laid out with a blow strikingly similar to the one which knocked out Taylor. All of these people had come to realize that 'there was something about being asked to pay out money that always aroused the head of the firm's worst passions'.

Mayer's behaviour was by no means untypical. Daryll F. Zanuck, head of Twentieth Century-Fox studios, a man who presented his cultural bona fides to posterity by complaining that a muff hung round someone's neck 'like a milestone' and then demonstrated his warm-hearted humanity by firing the man who corrected him, was once having trouble shooting a scene in which someone falls down a flight of stairs. He solved the problem by getting an old man in off the street, asking him to walk near the edge of the stairs and then giving him a shove. The old man broke both legs and Zanuck got his footage. James Cagney, starring in a gangster movie at Warner Brothers, was horrified to realize that real bullets were being used; when he complained he was advised that there was nothing to worry about because the danger was over now. When, in the story 'The Juice of an Orange', Schnellenhamer cuts down his overheads by reducing Wilmot Mulliner's salary from fifteen hundred dollars to four, he then relents, saying 'From now on we'll put you on the books as three. It's a more convenient sum than four. Makes less book-keeping'. But even Schnellenhamer could have picked up a few tips from David Selznick, who scoured the New York theatre reviews in order to find out which failed dramatists might be signed up on low salaries.

If, in the few remaining hours when he was neither hitting people, nor feigning death, nor having his carpet cleaned, Mayer ever read the short stories which Wodehouse began to publish soon after his departure from California, and whether, if he read them, he understood them, is doubtful; in one of the most arresting opening lines to any book about the motion-picture industry, Roland Flamini begins his exhaustive account of the making of *Gone with the Wind* as follows:

> Louis B. Mayer, the most powerful man in Hollywood, isn't completely illiterate, but reading is a struggle for him and making sense of what he reads a bigger one.[3]

In 1936 Wodehouse published *Laughing Gas*, an improbable saga about a child star who dreams of escaping from the studio and eating as much fried chicken southern style as he can lay his hands on. If Mayer did see the book, perhaps it would have been too much for his limited sensibilities to notice that the child star, Joey Cooley, shares the same initials as Jackie Cooper, and that the mogul in control of his destiny is one Brinkmeyer, which is at least close enough to B. Mayer to be interesting, certainly close enough to encourage the moguls to shun its author for evermore. The interview with the *Los Angeles Times* had been a crime against the unwritten laws of the film colony, which Wodehouse had then compounded by writing this cycle of Schnellenhamer stories, and then compounded again by publishing *Laughing Gas*. There seemed not the remotest likelihood that Hollywood would ever show any interest in him again. And yet in June 1934 Wodehouse is writing to Townend from Paris:

> I had an offer from Paramount the other day to go to Hollywood and had to refuse. But rather gratifying after the way Hollywood took a solemn oath three years ago never to mention my name again. Quite the olive branch.

Why should Wodehouse have considered accepting it? His market value, which had soared to $50,000 for American magazine rights in 1932, fell to $25,000 as the publishing world felt the grip of the slump, but even his reduced fees left him more than comfortably provided for, especially in view of his personal frugality as defined to Townend: 'Don't you find, as you get on in life, that the actual things you really want cost about £200 a year? I have examined my soul, and I find that my needs are a library subscription and tobacco money, plus an extra bit for holidays.' It is a pity that, in examining his soul, Wodehouse had not asked it to explain why he should ever have anything more to do with Hollywood, or it with him. At the end of 1936 he was back there, under contract once more to Mayer, and deploying the same old tactics of renting a house as far from the studio as was compatible with his obligations: 'A lovely place with a nice pool, but remote. Still, that's an advantage in a way, we don't get everybody dropping in on us.' It is difficult to decide whose behaviour was the more incomprehensible, MGM's in rehiring a man who had turned the industry into a public laughing stock, or Wodehouse's in agreeing to return.

Predictably the episode ended in fiasco. After being assigned in a vague sort of way to a musical picture in harness with the famous writer–drinker Bill McGuire, he could report by the following March that his option had not been picked up. After working for a while with McGuire, 'I gradually found myself being edged out. Eventually they came out into the open and said they had wanted McGuire to write the thing by himself all along.' By this time, however, Wodehouse was considering offers from several other studios, although there could have been no doubt in his own mind which one he would choose. For he was now about to become embroiled in the last act of a melodrama composed entirely of outrageous coincidences, a melodrama which he would never have thought of inventing himself because his professionalism would have warned him off its outrageous improbabilities.

One of the first people he met on his return to Hollywood was Fred Astaire, who told him that he was soon to start work on a musical version of Wodehouse's 1919 novel, *A Damsel in Distress*. It was natural enough that Astaire's studio, RKO, hearing that the author of the book was in town and available, should make overtures to him. On 27 March 1937, Wodehouse reported to Townend, 'It seems pretty certain that in about two weeks I shall be working on my *Damsel in Distress* which RKO bought for Fred Astaire.' On 6 May he is still waiting: 'There seems to be a probability that I shall do a four weeks job on *A Damsel in Distress*.' It was another month before he could report: 'I am sweating away at the Astaire picture.' But although he greatly admired Astaire and had considerable respect for the film's director, George Stevens, he soon came to realize that of all the ridiculous Hollywood episodes in which he had been involved over the years, this one promised to be the most absurd of all.

It will be remembered that *A Damsel in Distress* concerns the affairs of a musical comedy composer called George who comes from Brooklyn, is highly successful, and arrives in London to supervise the English production of one of his Broadway hits. It so happened that there existed in real life a musical comedy composer called George who came from Brooklyn, was highly successful, and had arrived in London more than once to supervise the English production of one of his Broadway hits. The realization that in living out his own life he appeared to be imitating Wodehouse's art struck George Gershwin so forcibly that, according to Wodehouse, he 'used his considerable influence to have it done on the screen'. By the time the RKO production was under way, the signs could hardly have been more auspicious so far as the author was concerned. This was the first and, as time has proved, the last time one of his novels would be filmed by a major studio; the composer and lyricist were two of his dearest friends from Broadway days; the star was his favourite among male performers; the director was one he is said to have respected above all others in the industry. And yet before the end of June, Wodehouse found himself battling to rescue the project from the RKO executives who, following the Thalbergian line, had evidently delegated the writing to several men simultaneously:

> When they bought it, they gave it to one of the RKO writers to adapt, and he turned out a script all about crooks – no resemblance to the novel. Then it struck them that it might be a good thing to stick to the story, so they chucked away the other script and called me in. I think it is going to make a good picture. But what uncongenial work picture-writing is. Somebody's got to do it, I suppose, but this is the last time they'll get me.

On 7 July George Gershwin died, having completed the score for the picture some time before; Wodehouse completed his part of the bargain in mid-August; the writer-credits for the picture include the names of Ernest Pagano and S. K. Lauren. By the time the picture was released, at the end of November, Wodehouse had left Hollywood for Le Touquet. He never went back.

By all logical processes, *A Damsel in Distress* should have been the good film that Wodehouse hoped it would be; but logic was never a distinguishing feature of the movies, and the RKO executives succeeded in making a mess so comprehensive that it is doubtful if Schnellenhamer at his most rampant could have done a more effective wrecking job. At the time of *A Damsel in Distress*, Astaire and Ginger Rogers were the most successful dance team in the history of the popular arts; in the industry's box-office returns for 1936 they had been placed third behind Shirley Temple and Clark Gable. But Miss Rogers had for some time been chafing at the restraints of the musical genre, and was now demanding the chance to display the great dramatic actress she suspected herself of being. Since 1933 she had made seven Astaire movies and was now resolved to show America that she could stand alone and at the same time find some easier way of making a living; after *Follow the Fleet* in 1936 she had told a reporter that she 'would like to take a vacation, digging mines'. Had she agreed to appear in *A Damsel in Distress*, then Wodehouse may well have been granted his 'good picture'. But while he was struggling on with his screenplay, Miss Rogers was busy with a 'dramatic' role in *Stage Door*, and RKO had to find a new partner for Astaire. With Schnellenhamerian inevitability, their choice fell on the worst-qualified actress in the whole of California, a non-singing, non-dancing English import called Joan Fontaine. The picture turned out to be the first flop of Astaire's Hollywood career; years later Miss Fontaine, who displayed a refreshing candour about her part in the fiasco, confided to Astaire that 'that damned picture put my career back four years'. So far as the movies were concerned, it finished Wodehouse's altogether.

He was understandably bitter about what had been done to a pleasant little property and was moved at the end of his life to come as close to a fit of spleen as his essentially benign temperament would permit. In 1975, *A Damsel in Distress* was republished as a paperback with the author's new preface:

> It was handed over to the hired assassins who at that time were such a feature of Dottyville-on-the-Pacific. The result was a Mess which for some reason is still shown occasionally on American television and causes sets to be switched off from the rockbound coasts of Maine to the Everglades of Florida. . . . The Manglers, as the official term was, proved worthy of the trust placed in them by the studio. The first thing they did was to eliminate the story and substitute for it one more suitable to retarded adults and children with water on the brain. Then they turned their attention to the hero. There was not much they could do here, but they did their best by engaging Fred Astaire and giving him nobody to dance with, so that he had nine solo numbers. . . .

There were a few redeeming features, all of them musical. At least two of the Gershwin songs, 'A Foggy Day' and 'Nice Work If You Can Get It', have survived the production, but Wodehouse was too modest ever to point out that one of the lesser songs in the score, 'Stiff Upper Lip', was Ira Gershwin's tribute to his old friend. Ira, who has described his lyric for the song as an attempt to incorporate as many Wodehouseanisms as possible, managed, among others, old fluff, chin up, old bean, dash it all and pip-pip.

The magnitude of the bungling of *A Damsel in Distress* defines the problem facing any would-be satirist of the movie industry. Would even Schnellenhamer and Glutz at their most simian have decided that the best way to get rich quick was to produce a musical starring an unmusical heroine? It is no wonder that the satirists of the industry could never quite rid themselves of the fear that no matter how outrageous their lampoons, reality was always likely to outflank them.

The most striking thing about Wodehouse's moguls is that throughout the stories there is not so much as a mention of a single person in the entire state of California who gives a fig whether they live or die. Schnellenhamer and company have everything except affection. Miss Fontaine, whose sense of humour remained miraculously unimpaired by her experiences in *A Damsel in Distress*, later reported that while attending the crowded funeral of the Columbia mogul Harry Cohn, she overheard one man say to another as they surveyed the huge throng at the graveside, 'It just shows you that people will still show up if you give them what they want'. When Goldwyn told the actor Dana Andrews, 'I love you like my own son', Andrews replied, 'Okay, Sam, what do you want now?'. When the actress Mae Marsh wrote a letter to a friend criticizing Goldwyn's judgment, she was soon eased out of the industry, discovering too late that all letters were opened and read; as

Edmund Wilson wrote, 'You couldn't send a telegram or a phone message from the studio.' In another context Wilson unwittingly evoked echoes of Brinkmeyer when he suggested that 'the great Goldwyn and the lamented Thalberg are the same megalomaniac cloak-and-suit dealers that their predecessors were',[4] men whose ordained role in life was to oversee 'great writers spelling "cat" for the unlettered', and who fondly imagined they were paraphrasing the 'toiling masses and their touching plight' in Paul Muni's false beard.[5]

If the truth be known, in writing his tales of life at Perfecto-Zizzbaum, Wodehouse was actually flattering the moguls fulsomely by omitting from the equation of their corporate soul the two factors which the reticence of a Dulwich College schoolboy forbade him from mentioning: their deplorable sexual etiquette and their fundamental loutishness. When Jack Warner bought the screen rights of *My Fair Lady*, he campaigned vociferously to do a Sol Hogwasch by casting Rock Hudson as Henry Higgins; this was the mogul who once enlivened a lunch given in honour of Madame Chiang Kai-shek by asking her who was looking after the laundry, and who is said to have categorized writers as 'schmucks with Underwoods'. Most of the moguls regarded *Porgy and Bess* as conclusive proof that George Gershwin had lost the art of melody, and it was Goldwyn who advised him to rediscover it by writing 'hits like Irving Berlin'. It was around the same time that David Selznick made his famous discovery that the constitutional crisis engendered by the romance between Edward VIII and Mrs Simpson enhanced the commerical possibilities of *The Prisoner of Zenda*. Cecil B. De Mille innocently endowed God with an American accent, while the head of MGM, always referred to by Michael Balcon as 'the unspeakable Mayer', was charged by the National Labor Board with 'making speeches to employees in which officers and leaders of the Screen Writers' Guild were referred to in opprobrious, vile and defamatory language. Soliciting employees to resign from the Guild and threatening those who refused with discharge. Threatening to close down the studio if certain organizational changes in the Guild occurred'; in 1939, 'with Poland overrun, Mayer still refused to produce movies that might give offence to Germany for fear of jeopardizing the market in central Europe, which was rapidly coming under German control. Metro stars were discouraged from making anti-Nazi statements'.[6] One wonders if even Schnellenhamer and Glutz would not have bridled at that – always provided that they were on horseback at the time.

Such were the daunting models confronting those writers who, having passed through the fires of studio life, attempted to describe what they knew. In Kaufman and Hart's anti-Hollywood farce *Once in a Lifetime*, the play ends with the destruction of the studio by a squadron of its own bombers; when someone questions the decision to raze the premises in this way, the reply comes back that if the head of the studio wishes the place to be bombed, then bombed it must be. For some years that denouement seemed too wildly fantastic to belong anywhere outside the realms of slapstick, until in the later 1930s Selznick, desperate to begin shooting *Gone with the Wind* even though still without a Scarlett O'Hara, set fire to his own back-lot in order to simulate the burning of Atlanta.[7] The same fate, of being outdone by events, lay in store for Wodehouse. It will be remembered that Schnellenhamer's gorilla was under contract at seven hundred and fifty dollars a week. Some years later Mayer's studio acquired the services of a collie called Lassie, an animal which became so popular that at one stage it was flown east to make personal appearances at Radio City Music Hall. During this engagement, Lassie stayed at the Plaza Hotel in a suite costing $2,500 a week.

Apart from their unwitting comicality, why should the moguls of Hollywood have proved so inviting to a writer like Wodehouse who had a thousand locales to choose from? The answer has much to do with his professionalism and his unflagging industry. He was a man who knew how to do only one thing, to write. He drove himself to become one of the most prolific stylists in the history of English literature, and he did so in the belief that one of the world's most useful precepts is an honest day's work for an honest day's pay. The one thing which never failed to baffle him was the spectacle of professional idleness. It affronted his sense of pride; to be idle and receive large sums of money for it seemed positively immoral. The most revealing remark in the interview with the lady from the Los Angeles newspaper was overlooked at the time but, had the moguls had the sense to savour it, they might then have been prepared for the appearance of the Schnellenhamer saga. Wodehouse said, 'They were extremely nice to me but I feel as if I have cheated them.' By shipping him west as one of a crate of twelve and thrusting a hundred thousand dollars in his hand in return for absolutely nothing, MGM had in effect made a dishonest man of him. It went against the grain. It breached the code of Valley Fields and Blandings Castle. The saga of Jacob Z. Schnellenhamer was the writer's revenge. Had its publication appeared in a scenario of the Bigger, Better and Brighter Motion Picture Company, then the head of that buoyant enterprise, Isadore Zinzinheimer, would surely have captioned it, with Wodehouse's full approval, 'Came the Dawn'.

7

Novelist in a padded cell

ON 15 MAY 1940, AN OBSCURE AND obscurantist German writer called Guderian broke through the French lines into open country and began a drive for the English Channel. Guderian, whose only previous connection with the fine arts had been a work entitled *Attention, Tanks!*, now began to make matters even worse by imperilling the cause of humorous literature. The eponymous heroes of his book rumbled into Amiens on the 19th, Abbeville on the 20th; two days later, *en route* to the glittering prizes of Calais and Dunkirk, his troops entered the pleasure resort of Le Touquet, a town which clearly had been doomed from the moment nine days before when Guderian, evidently not content with having crossed the muse, crossed the Meuse. By the time the Germans arrived in Le Touquet, the RAF squadron stationed there had decamped for home, after the pilot of its last remaining fighter plane had offered his one spare seat to the town's most famous English resident, Mr P. G. Wodehouse, who was living with his wife and dog at a house called Low Wood. But Mr Wodehouse, unwilling to be parted from wife and dog, declined the offer and instead gathered his brood into the car and pointed it at the nearby coast. After two miles the car broke down and the Wodehouses abandoned it in favour of a van belonging to a neighbour headed in the same direction with the same vague thoughts of flight in mind. The van covered another hundred yards before stopping, after which the Wodehouses decided to walk back to Low Wood and wait on events. On the 22nd Guderian's outriders turned up, and instructed Wodehouse to report each morning to their local functionary. On the 23rd the British began evacuating their Boulogne garrison, and by the

26th only Dunkirk remained as an escape route. By 14 June the Germans were in Paris; by the 17th the French had sued for peace; on the 23rd an armistice was signed. Wodehouse was cut off.

The sequence of events which now followed is simple enough to inscribe, difficult to understand and impossible to countenance. On 21 July he was interned and taken to a prison at Loos, armoured against fate by a volume of Tennyson and the complete works of Shakespeare. A few days later he was removed to an old barracks at Liège. In August he was removed to the Citadel at Huy, and by the beginning of September was installed in a lunatic asylum at Tost in Upper Silesia, where the routine was anything but rigorous and the only formal duties were to answer morning and evening roll call. So remote was Tost from the obscenities of concentration camp life that internees over the age of fifty were excused heavy labour, there were Sunday religious services, a social centre where inmates were able to amuse themselves and each other, and even, for those prisoners in specialized occupations, a degree of privacy, as Wodehouse discovered when he was endowed with his own padded cell in which to write *Money in the Bank*. It is just conceivable that to a political simpleton who all his life had been screened by the whimsicalities of his own temperament from the harsher realities, it might have seemed that a conqueror who provides his victims with facilities for the composition of light fiction was no conqueror at all, although it has to be said that to arrive at such a conclusion would require a lack of imagination bordering on a degree of asininity to which not even Ronnie Fish at his daftest would aspire. At any rate, Wodehouse laboured quietly away at Tost, beguiling the days of separation from Ethel and the comforts of home by compiling the improbable saga of Jeff Miller and George, Viscount Uffenham, in which style of life he may well have continued until his automatic release on achieving his sixtieth birthday, now little more than a year away, had not his friends innocently conspired to ruin him.

The powder trail was lit with the arrival at Tost in December of an Associated Press journalist called Thuermer, who, being American, could consider himself at peace with Mr Guderian's tanks. Thuermer met Wodehouse, discussed with him details of life in the camp, and then went away in the knowledge that, at least so far as the American public was concerned, he was in possession of something resembling a scoop. His interview with Wodehouse was published, at which there rose up from the United States a howl of excited dismay which in retrospect seems to have been rather more hysterical than the modest nature of Thuermer's achievement merited. After all, everyone knew that Wodehouse had been living at Le Touquet when the German army arrived. Nothing had been heard of him since, which would suggest that he was confined somewhere in Europe in conditions specially designed to prevent his hindrance of the German war effort. And yet the chorus of woe which greeted the news of Wodehouse's residence at Tost had something about it of deep shock as well as of sadness. Indeed, the reaction could hardly have been more animated had the subject of Thuermer's interview been an American, which raises a significant point.

It should not be forgotten that in the twenty years previous to his intern-ment, Wodehouse had enjoyed a career so mid-Atlantic in flavour that he might almost have been nominated as the archetypal mid-Atlantic man, a kind of literary Ronald Colman whose public accent was perfectly balanced between the intonations of Bunyan and Runyon, a professional with as many friends and colleagues on one side of the Atlantic as on the other; indeed, it may even be true to say that his earning capacity was greater in America where, quite apart from his reputation as a novelist, he was revered by the lyricists of Broadway as their founding father, than in Britain, where his revolutionary work for the colloquial song lyric had gone quite unregarded. In view of the fact that much of the mischief surrounding Wodehouse's catastrophic war was committed, in good faith or otherwise, by Americans, it is as well to remember that by the time he was captured he had attained a sort of unofficial honorary American citizenship. Had the engines of American publicity reacted to Wodehouse's capture as to that of other Englishmen, that is, if they had ignored it, then it seems unlikely that the powder trail would ever have been lit at all.

Thuermer's disclosure of Wodehouse's whereabouts inspired a campaign by well-meaning but tactless colleagues to engineer his release. The German Embassy in Washington was bombarded with appeals, and Guy Bolton worked on a petition signed by as many influential Americans as he could find. They could not, however, have been all that influential, because Wodehouse, oblivious of the efforts being made on his behalf, worked on in the padded cell at Tost, and was not released until 21 June 1941, only four months before his birthday. He was then brought to Berlin, where he told the ubiquitous American correspondents that it was 'a curious experience, being completely shut off from the outer world, as one is in an internment camp'. Ethel, who had been living at Pas de Calais, now borrowed money and joined her husband in Berlin, where she was reunited with him, under German surveillance, at the Hotel Adlon. On 26 June there arrived yet another American correspondent, one Harry Flannery of the Columbia Broadcasting System, who persuaded Wodehouse to broadcast to America, reading a script which Flannery had written. Wodehouse agreed, sensing that here was a way of reassuring his American friends of his survival. According to Flannery, the German Foreign Office, observing this solemn farce with increasing wonder, then asked Wodehouse if he would like to do a series of short-wave broadcasts to America, reading his own scripts. Again Wodehouse agreed, delivering five humorous talks on his experiences as an internee. The motives of his jailors appear to have been as confused as Wodehouse's. Had they intended to use the occasion as a propaganda triumph, either in Britain or America, then it seems unlikely that they would have allowed the scripts, which were by no means flattering to German cerebral performance, to go undoctored; perhaps they felt that the mere presence of Wodehouse's voice on the air, regardless of what it was saying, would constitute victory enough; perhaps they were too crass to detect the underlying current of raillery at their expense with which the five scripts were suffused. But whatever impelled their behaviour, it appears to have been sheer madness which impelled Wodehouse's. His delivery of the five broadcasts represented stupidity of a magnitude so overwhelming as to remain the despair of his admirers for ever after, to say nothing of Wodehouse, who continued to kick himself over the affair for the rest of his life.

The inevitable explosion at home occurred on 15 July 1941, when a *Daily Mirror* columnist called William Connor, who published under the pseudonym of Cassandra, delivered one of the most scurrilous personal attacks in the history of English journalism. The attack was not published, but took the form of a broadcast, following the nine o'clock news bulletin on the BBC Home Service. It began as follows:

> 'I have come to tell you tonight of the story of a rich man trying to make his last and greatest sale – that of his own country. It is a sombre story of honour pawned by the Nazis for the price of a soft bed.'

Quite apart from the regrettable shortcomings of its literary style, Connor's opening is a sloppy piece of journalism, incompetently researched and badly organized. Worse is to come. Adhering in all solemnity to the lines laid down in harmless facetiousness by Frank Sullivan's cliché expert, Mr Arbuthnot, Connor describes the two abortive attempts to leave Le Touquet as 'throwing a cocktail party', to Wodehouse himself as 'an elderly playboy', to the German soldiery as 'storm troopers', to the price of freedom as 'thirty pieces of silver'.[1] The broadcast ends with a description of an air raid at Dulwich: 'You should have been there, Mr Wodehouse, you, with your impartiality, your reasonableness, and perhaps even one of your famous little jokes.' For good measure, before the broadcast was done, Connor included accusations that Wodehouse was a quisling and that he 'worshipped the Führer'.

The battle lines were swiftly drawn. On one side the outraged patriots who, having swallowed Connor's stew at a single gulp, began choking in disgust at the spectacle of the most English of all English writers defecting to the enemy; on the other a small group of Wodehouse's fellow-professionals who, weighing the contents of the broadcast against their personal experience of the traitor, decided to follow their instincts and refute the charges on his behalf. What followed was one of the most extraordinary farces which has ever enriched the literary history of the British, a farce by turn richly comic as well as deeply tragic, and one so hysterical in tone, so passionate in intensity, so cynical in execution and so dubious in morality, that, as the decades slip by, posterity may well find it increasingly difficult to understand how it ever became a *cause célèbre* at all, and how so many prominent politicians so busy at the time mouthing imperatives like freedom and justice ever managed subsequently to slink away without the improving experience of anybody ever laying a glove on them.

The extravaganza first began to get under way with the appearance, in the wake of Connor's overture, of Outraged Reader fulminating with righteous indignation without first having bothered to confirm that the crime had been committed. The situation was best described by the first of Wodehouse's champions, Sir Compton Mackenzie:

> The *Daily Telegraph*, scenting from the vulgar reaction to Cassandra's pretentious drivel that denouncing Plummy Wodehouse as a traitor to his country was giving the wretched public what it wanted, started a correspondence for self-righteous nitwits to show off their patriotism.[2]

Some of them showed off their literary sensibilities too; in 1953 Wodehouse was still able to quote verbatim from one of the *Telegraph* letters to the effect that his books are 'peopled by men who have never worked and are moneyed and bored'. The infantalism of the argument, which would, if its logic existed, condemn Agatha Christie for murder, Zane Grey for rustling cattle and Damon Runyon for having no past, gives a fair idea of the intellectual level at which the debate raged. Mackenzie thought he detected even baser depths of cerebral dishonesty: 'I was disgusted to see how my fellow-authors were working off their jealousy when Wodehouse was given a DCL by Oxford University.'[3] The kind of thing which Mackenzie must have had in mind was the wonderful display by E. C. Bentley, who thought that Wodehouse's doctorate had been awarded under false pretences because 'he has never written a serious line in his life', by which of course Bentley meant that he had never detected one, which was not quite the same thing. Wodehouse turned this and other attacks with mild-mannered ease, pleading guilty to Bentley's half-witted charge and offering as consolation to his exasperated accuser the fact that 'never in a career greatly devoted to feeling like thirty cents have I felt more like thirty cents than when in a borrowed cap and gown (with scarlet facings) I stood in the Senate House, taking the treatment'. He used the same tactics in defusing the bomb so recklessly flung at him by Sean O'Casey, who, after struggling to coin a phrase insulting enough to apply to a mere clown, dismissed Wodehouse as 'English Literature's performing flea'. Wodehouse seems to have been genuinely flattered, perhaps because, while O'Casey had flung the epithet in apparent ignorance of the spectacular achievements of which a flea may be capable, Wodehouse, connoisseur of that vaudevillian life whose denizens sometimes elevated themselves through the sweat of their performing animals' brows to the rarified intellectual atmosphere of revue, recognized a compliment when he saw one:

> With that statement I scarcely know how to deal. Thinking it over, I believe he meant it to be complimentary, for all the performing fleas I have ever met have impressed me with their sterling artistry and that indefinable something which makes the good trouper.

Even Connor's accusations were scoured by their victim for some mitigating accuracy, and predictably enough he found one, confessing cheerfully to the charge of having the christian names of Pelham Grenville. Meanwhile, Mackenzie, monitoring the *Daily Telegraph* correspondence columns, was finally moved to enter the lists himself, on the occasion of an especially low blow delivered by one of Wodehouse's oldest friends:

> Finally I could stand no more when a letter was printed from A. A. Milne to say that people must realize how irresponsible P. G. Wodehouse was. Milne recalled hearing Wodehouse say that he should like to have a son but that he should not want to have him until he was old enough to have got his house colours. On July 11 I wrote to the Editor of the *Daily Telegraph*:

> > Sir,
> > There is a curious infelicity in Mr A. A. Milne's sneer at Mr P. G. Wodehouse for shirking the responsibility of fatherhood. Such a rebuke would have come more decorously from a father who had abstained from the profitable exhibitionism in which the creator of Christopher Robin has indulged.
> > I gather that Mr Wodehouse is in disgrace for telling the American public over the radio about his comfortable existence at the Hotel Adlon. Not being convinced that I am morally entitled to throw stones at a fellow-author, and retaining as I do an old-fashioned prejudice against condemning a man unheard, I do not propose to inflict my opinion upon the public, beyond affirming that at the moment I feel more disgusted by Mr Milne's morality than by Mr Wodehouse's irresponsibility.[4]

But in time of national peril, even Winnie the Pooh and Eeyore may be flung into the breach, and the editor of the *Daily Telegraph*, being a fellow of infinite jest, had his own methods of assessing journalistic priorities, and was suddenly surprised to discover that he had too little space at his disposal to accommodate Mackenzie's letter. As for the public rebuke to Milne's cant, it was to be left to its victim to deliver it, some years later, in rather different terms from those attempted by Mackenzie. But Milne's implication that Wodehouse deserved to be treated lightly for his misdemeanours because he was hardly responsible for his own conduct, was a curious way for one friend to defend another; the plea of guilty but insane may in extreme circumstances prove efficacious but it is rarely likely to sustain the friendship between accused and advocate. Milne was not to be the only writer to proceed along this thorny path.

Another very revealing defence of Wodehouse was that mounted by Howard Spring, than whom no living author could have been less likely to truckle to the whims of the monied classes. Spring was a pipe-smoking, no-nonsense ex-*Manchester Guardian* journalist who had graduated in middle age to the comforts of the best-seller lists, but still liked to see himself as the hard-headed investigative reporter not to be taken in by glib tongues; he gave the impression, both in his prose and through the camera lens, of a man whose eyes have been specially constructed for not having the wool pulled over them. He had consolidated his reputation as a novelist with two bulky middle-brow romances, *Fame is the Spur*, a political cautionary tale loosely based on the career of Ramsay MacDonald,[5] and *My Son, My Son*, a melodrama played out against a background of Irish nationalism in the Great War. The reader may beguile many hours browsing through these and several other innocuous Spring novels without ever coming across anything remotely resembling a joke. He published about twenty books and there is not a ghost of a smile in one of them. Even his lovers and his children have about them a depressing gravity of demeanour, while most of his adults seem to be rehearsing, unconsciously or not, for the death that is surely imminent. Almost the only light relief is provided by interludes of exfloriation, in which the narrative grinds to a halt to allow Spring to indulge his fancy for horticulture, festooning the text with lists of flowers which his botanist-heroes presumably find more interesting than does the reader. Being one of those earnest, humourless writers who confuse the true steel of seriousness with the cardboard imitation of solemnity, Spring regarded Wodehouse much as a dutiful schoolmaster might look on the class buffoon, as a disruptive influence not to be admitted to the councils of responsible adults.

But this did not mean that retribution was called for. A frown of disapproval was one thing, a public hanging quite another, and Spring, observing the literary morality of 1941, did not much like what he saw. In his years as a mildly progressive reporter of political affairs, he had picked up a magisterial ponderosity which responded to abstractions like Honour and Justice as a minnow goes for a maggot, and he now proceeded to review Wodehouse's case with the hrmphs of a self-conscious impartiality:

> They have got hold of Mr P. G. Wodehouse, and what a fuss that is causing! Mr Wodehouse, it appears, was in a concentration camp and was thence transported to the luxuries of the Adlon Hotel in Berlin, and from the Adlon he has been broadcasting, announcing an invincible feeling of non-belligerency. This has caused a grave scandal. My morning newspaper, day after day, has letters from authors and clergymen and what not, denouncing Mr Wodehouse and some vowing never again to read his books. . . .
>
> The whole hullabaloo seems to me to be nonsensical and wrong-headed. Naturally we would all prefer that Mr Wodehouse should do nothing to help our enemies, but which of us can confidently declare what he would do with a revolver at his head or a knife at his neck? We might take the way of sacrifice; but don't let us too vociferously damn those who don't. . . . If we are to pursue Mr Wodehouse, do we go on to pursue that solid phalanx of British novelists who have taken care, by

timely removal to the United States, that they shall not find themselves in his predicament? I used to think we should, and I have said so publicly. I don't like this great Recessional. Authors are in the habit – and they should be in the habit – of claiming some nobility for their calling. Very well then. Noblesse Oblige. That was, and is, my feeling; but I am not prepared to make a case of it. Let them settle the matter with their own consciences. We do not know all the circumstances of those cases, any more than we know what, behind the deep veil of this war's mysteries, has happened in the case of Wodehouse.

We can almost hear the flaring of the match and the tiny detonations of the lips puffing life into the pipe-bowl; the voice of quiet sagacity murmuring through the cirrus clouds of plain-dealing, commonsensical decency. But having indulged himself just a little with the revolver and the knife and the concentration camp, Spring is suddenly visited by an alarming thought. Suppose this defence of a mere skylarker should mislead the reader into assuming that the judge approves of skylarking? Hastily Spring retrieves his error:

> I am not trying to make out a case for a friend. I do not know Mr Wodehouse. I have met him only once, and then spent no more than an hour in his company. Nor do I write because of excessive admiration for his books. Much nonsense about them, it seems to me, has been written by Hilaire Belloc and others; and if ever the University of Oxford made a fool of itself it did so when it conferred on Wodehouse the degree of Doctor of Letters. Wodehouse is a 'funny man' rather than a humorist, and even as a 'funny man' his range is narrow and shallow. But, I repeat, however funny he ever was, he is just that funny still; and I should find relief in one of his books from the condemnation of those who are so ready to stone him, those who, if they are without his alleged sin, are also, at the moment, without his danger and temptation.[6]

Notice that Spring never once says he believes Wodehouse to be innocent, or even that he hopes he may be. The call for justice appears to be based, not on a denial of the charges, but on the conspicuous lack of data. The Spring defence falls under three headings; first, that, even if Wodehouse is guilty of whatever charges the letter-writing clergymen have in mind, now is not the time to arraign him because the hard facts, to quote one of Spring's own titles, remain unknown; second, that none of us can say whether, in the same situation, we would have behaved any better; third, that, if Wodehouse has committed the crime of detaching himself from the war, he is by no means the only author to have done so, yet is the only one being pilloried for his crime. The third point in particular must have commended itself to Spring's unflinching sense of duty. While it was true that the United States was in some danger of congestion by British expatriates whose philosophical and aesthetic convictions seemed to require the ardours of American life just as war was about to erupt in Europe, almost nobody said so. It was an extremely touchy point with the intelligentsia, and Spring's determination to raise it is enough to make a cat laugh. He is also too honourable to deny that the commission by an author of misdemeanours can have no effect on the merits of his existing body of work. But it is not the buffoon who elicits Spring's compassion, only the abstraction of fair play. He takes a side-swipe at Wodehouse's work, and disowns him socially with comical haste. However, it says much for Spring that his sense of decency will not allow him to stand by and watch a fellow-writer torn to pieces to make a roman holiday for the mob.

That his defence was published, not in an engine of mass circulation, but in a slim volume of personal reflections, detracted from its propaganda effect without compromising by a single syllable the sturdiness of its argument. Even so, had all Wodehouse's defendants been as muted as Mackenzie, who could not get his letters published, and Spring, who confined himself to a page in a book, then the cause would surely have been lost. What the Wodehouse lobby now desperately required was some galvanic dialectical force to lift the debate up on to a plane elevated enough for light to break through. It was a forlorn hope, because not only was such an advocate unlikely to consider Wodehouse's case of sufficient importance in such troubled times, but it was also difficult to imagine where such a hero existed. It is at this point that the bizarre sequence of events took its most bizarre turn of all with the entry into the arena of the most unlikely of champions, a man widely regarded as the very antithesis of the Wooster–Jeeves manner and everything it represented, and yet perhaps the polemicist better equipped than any other to grasp the nature of the principles involved and beat them into coherence.

At first glance George Orwell appears to have less in common with Wodehouse than any other writer of the period. Indeed, the two of them might be said to represent the opposing polarities of political and literary thought: on one hand, an idealist who had fought in the Spanish Civil War; on the other the incorrigible schoolboy, the literary *flaneur* who poked facetious fun at the Soviets and had come to believe with perfect sincerity that the sporting fortunes of his old school were very nearly the most important things in life. No stranger bedfellows can ever have come together – Wodehouse, who represented the purely hedonistic role of literature, and Orwell, convinced that writing was no laughing matter. It had even been suggested by those who knew him well that Orwell was one of those curious inverted voluptuaries who actually enjoyed being miserable; one of his schoolfellows, Cyril Connolly, once said that he was not capable of blowing his nose without agonizing on working conditions in handkerchief factories. In book after book Orwell presented this image of stolid joylessness, and yet now, suddenly, this misanthrope was about to dash to the rescue of the most frivolous and politically irresponsible writer who had ever claimed the allegiance of the British reading public.

But beneath those craggy surfaces a perceptive observer might have deduced a more promising sentimental subsoil. In 1939 Orwell had begun the composition of extended essays which broke new ground by treating resolutely non-intellectual themes in a resolutely intellectual way. In the course of a curious career he had acquired the quaint conviction that what little virtue remained in the world resided in the working classes, and it followed from this that what interested the working classes must by definition be worthy of serious examination no matter how unfashionable those interests might be behind the bastions of critical orthodoxy. A hint of this populist approach may be found in a perceptive essay on Dickens (1939), in which Orwell concludes that Dickens is 'a free intelligence' who 'fights in the open'. In the same year he took the process very much further with the celebrated 'Boys' Weeklies', an analysis of the tuppenny bloods which then comprised the staple diet of the mass of schoolboys. Two years later came the equally famous examination of the saucy postcards of Donald McGill, and in 1944 a comparative assessment of *Raffles* and *No Orchids for Miss Blandish*. In such a context, fictitious characters as widely popular as Jeeves and the Earl of Emsworth would certainly not have been out of place. But apart from his deep interest in the art which commended itself to the world of the unschooled, Orwell revealed in one of these essays a chamber of his affections not generally associated with him, and it was in a corner of this chamber that the unlikely figure of P. G. Wodehouse resided.

In 'Boys' Weeklies', Orwell had argued the case that Billy Bunter and company, for all their apparent innocence, were in fact counter-revolutionary agents infiltrated by their wicked publishers across the frontiers of working-class youth in order to inculcate into readers a becoming subservience to their public-school masters. So far as Orwell's psychological understanding of the working classes is concerned, never did he disclose his own foolishness more completely than when pleading the case for something he described as 'a left-wing comic'. What was even more revealing was his evident inability, even in his paroxysm of wrath, to rinse the affection out of his writing. He is attempting to describe the idyll of public-school life to be found at Greyfriars School, the fictitious home of Bunter and company:

The year is 1910 – or 1940, but it is all the same. You are at Greyfriars, a rosy-cheeked boy of fourteen in posh tailor-made clothes, sitting down to tea in your study on the Remove passage after an exciting game of football which was won by an odd goal in the last half-minute. There is a cosy fire in the study, and outside the wind is whistling. The ivy clusters thickly around the old grey stones. The King is on his throne and the pound is worth a pound. Over in Europe the comic foreigners are jabbering and gesticulating, but the grim grey battleships of the British Fleet are steaming up the Channel and at the outposts of Empire the monocled Englishmen are holding the niggers at bay. Lord Mauleverer has just got another fiver and we are all settling down to a tremendous tea of sausages, sardines, crumpets, potted meat, jam and doughnuts. After tea we shall sit round the study fire having a good laugh at Billy Bunter and discussing the team for next week's match against Rookwood. Everything is safe, solid and unquestionable. Everything will be the same for ever and ever.[7]

The elements of paradise lost in that passage are too dominant to require underlining. Orwell's undoubted rage at the smugness of the tableau seems to be tempered with an incongruity of some kind; for so uncompromising a critic, that incongruity is dangerously close to wistfulness, as though the assailant scaling the walls in preparation for the destruction of the building cannot resist pressing his nose to the window for one last yearning glance at a haven so vividly imagined that he might once have experienced it himself.

And Orwell had experienced it, although not in the persona of the hard-headed critical enemy of Western capitalism. Before his political and aesthetic convictions had transmogrified him into Orwell the scourge of privilege and Empire, he had been Eric Blair, Etonian schoolboy and imperial watchdog with the Burma Police. The study he so bitterly described in 'Boys' Weeklies' was perhaps not so very unlike his own at Eton and, in defending Wodehouse, he was coming to the rescue, not just of a fellow public schoolboy, but of an old boy who had attended a college which paled into the comfortably second-rate when compared with the Etonian splendours of Blair's experience. Admittedly the evidence in the Greyfriars paragraph of ignorance of sporting affairs is worrying. A dedicated ex-athlete who cares deeply about victory for the Dulwich eleven is hardly likely to win the sympathy of a man so untutored in the sporting terminology he is deriding that he stoops to the solecism of 'an odd goal' when he means 'the odd goal'; the difference would have been microscopic to Orwell, multitudinous to Wodehouse, who understood the utterly different meanings of the two phrases. But it would be unwise to assume from this and other passages in his works that Orwell took a contemptuous view of the flannelled fools and muddied oafs of English life. An observation like 'Fishing certainly came first, but reading came a good second' sounds very much the view of one of that long succession of Wodehousean Bills and Toms and Sams who capture the heroine's heart and settle down to a life of cosily passionless domesticity in the purlieus of Valley Fields. In fact the remark is made by the hero of Orwell's *Coming Up for Air*, a young man called George Bowling, who, apart from the strikingly sporting overtone of his surname, is animated by the same deep love of angling which gave his creator so much pleasure. Orwell waxes eloquent on the pleasures of angling throughout the book, which includes one of the most mysterious remarks ever made by any sportsman: 'Fishing is the opposite of war.' The sportsman in Orwell may have lurked as deep below the surface as those fish whose scaly souls he so passionately coveted, but there the sportsman always remained, ready to rise to the surface should the occasion commend itself.

There were other reasons why the Wodehouse case should have attracted

Orwell. He was famous for his detestation of hypocrisy, and he loved a fight. He had only to raise his head to sniff the brimstone of corruption, and he now saw in the lineaments of the anti-Wodehouse brigade precisely those aspects of English political life he loathed so violently. Here was a perfect instance of how to enjoy oneself by being miserable. He had stumbled upon a large stone, and the fulcrum of his dialectical power would now enable him to turn it over.

In mounting his great defence of the beleaguered comedian,[8] Orwell drew together the tactics of Milne and Spring into a concerted strategy. Wodehouse was a monumental noodle too silly to be blamed for anything he did; one would no more arraign him than one would a little child. He could not be punished for anything because diminished responsibility had actually diminished to the point where it disappeared altogether. Such a man could not possibly have been a traitor because he lacked even the most rudimentary knowledge of the way the modern world worked; in order to switch allegiances, you have to know that those allegiances exist, and it was Orwell's argument that Wodehouse, preserved in the aspic of Edwardian gentility, knew too little of Hitlerite Germany to be capable of truckling to it. 'It is nonsense', says Orwell the man who knows what's what, briskly dismissing the fools and the literary *flaneurs*, 'to talk of fascist tendencies in Wodehouse's books. There are no post-1918 tendencies at all.' And again, 'Nowhere, so far as I know, does he so much as use the word "fascism" or 'Nazism".'

But if the case against Wodehouse is ridiculous, why has it attracted so much support? Here Orwell warms to his underlying theme, which is that there are a great many men much guiltier than Wodehouse who have been allowed to dance away from the scene of the crime without so much as a frown of disapproval:

> Wodehouse made an ideal whipping boy. For it was generally felt that the rich were treacherous, and Wodehouse – as Cassandra vigorously pointed out in his broadcast – was a rich man. But he was the kind of rich man who could be attacked with impunity and without risking any damage to the structure of society. To denounce Wodehouse was not like denouncing, say, Beaverbrook. A mere novelist, however large his earnings may happen to be, is not of the possessing class. . . . Consequently, Wodehouse's indiscretion gave a good propaganda opening. It was a chance to 'expose' a wealthy parasite without drawing attention to any of the parasites who really mattered. . . . In England the fiercest tirades against Quislings are uttered by English Conservatives who were practising appeasement in 1938 and Communists who were advocating it in 1940. I have striven to show how the wretched Wodehouse – just because success and expatriation had allowed him to remain mentally in the Edwardian age – became the *corpus vile* in a propaganda experiment, and I suggest that it is now time to regard the incident as closed.

Now this essay, which did much to clear Wodehouse's name – at the expense of branding him an idiot – first appeared in 1945, and almost everything of relevance has been said about it except the most important thing of all, which is that either Orwell did not have a very clear idea of what he was talking about, or that, having digested the facts in the case, he decided that the best way of presenting his argument was to excise those of them that obscured his argument. The crux comes with his remark that 'there are no post-1918 tendencies at all' in any of Wodehouse's novels, and that the reader will search in vain for any evidence of the existence of fascism or Nazism. The boldness of the assertion implies that Orwell knows the entire Wodehouse oeuvre, and indeed, in his preliminary analysis of Wodehouse's comic method, he shows a grasp of Woosterian principles which any resident of Blandings Castle would envy. He is virtually alone among critics, for instance, in noticing that Archie Moffam, besides being an ass, is also 'honest, kind-hearted, athletic and courageous'. Some of his other discoveries are less acceptable, particularly his belief that Mike Jackson has turned into Bertie Wooster. But he is perceptive on the theme of Wodehouse and the peerage, pointing out that Wodehouse 'is not attacking the social hierarchy . . . the Earl of Emsworth is funny because an earl ought to have more dignity'. Clearly Orwell has composed his defence from the vantage point of a dedicated reader; nobody who had simply mugged up the subject for the purposes of writing the essay would have achieved anything like so profound an understanding of Wodehouse's style, his characterizations, his attitudes.

Orwell's biographers stress repeatedly the degree of Orwell's attachment to the writing of Wodehouse; he was exposed to 'Dickens, Kipling and P. G. Wodehouse before he was twelve';[9] on arriving at his first boarding school, he was 'already an avid reader of P. G. Wodehouse's cheerful Public School novels, and he may innocently have imagined that life at boarding-school would be as glamorous as it is made to appear there';[10] his loyalty to Kipling, Wodehouse, Swift, Shaw and Thackeray was 'virtually unwavering throughout his life';[11] in the 1930s a friend remembers his habit of 'coming out into the garden to play cricket, to talk about books, Sherlock Holmes, P. G. Wodehouse'.[12] Which raises the vital question of precisely how far on into the 1930s Orwell extended his reading of Wodehouse. As the novels continued to appear in an unwavering stream, year after year, decade after decade, it would have been understandable if Orwell, like a great many other devotees, fell behind in the chase and contented himself with the occasional casual taking up of some random volume. Whatever the truth, the wisdom of his claim to know exactly what was and what was not to be found in the Wodehouse oeuvre is compromised heavily by one book in particular.

In 1938 there had first appeared a novel called *The Code of the Woosters*. It is one of the longer books and evidently gave Wodehouse a great deal of technical trouble. In his correspondence with Townend he describes how he has responded to the criticism of his paymasters at the *Saturday Evening Post* that the story contained 'too many stage waits'. Having come to see the justice of the complaint, he writes, 'Isn't it ghastly to think that after earning one's living as a writer for thirty-seven years one can make a blunder like that?' The blunder to which he is referring is the inclusion of fifteen pages later seen to be extraneous. On 4 January 1938 he writes from Low Wood: 'I am finding finishing *The Code of the Woosters* a ghastly sweat. I don't seem to have the drive and command of words I used to.' The reader, however, perceives nothing of Wodehouse's loss of faith; the intensely convoluted plot never runs out of control, and the language, for all its author's misgivings regarding the loss of stylistic flair, remains characteristically weightless. The story concerns a coveted cow-creamer, the maniacal maunderings of the magistrate Sir Watkyn Bassett and his whimsy-whamsy daughter Madeline, who thinks that 'the stars are God's daisy chain and that every time a little fairy hiccoughs a wee baby is born', the accomplishments of Aunt Dahlia's cook Anatole, the lunacies of Gussie Fink-Nottle, and various other familiar counters on the chequerboard of Wodehousean caprice.

But by far the most significant character in the book, or indeed in any book so far as Wodehouse's wartime fortunes are concerned, is Sir Watkyn's crony Roderick Spode, whose importance in the context of the Berlin broadcasts is profound indeed. We make our introduction in the opening chapter:

> He was, as I had already been able to perceive, a breathtaking cove. About seven feet in height, and swathed in a plaid ulster which made him look about six feet across, he caught the eye and arrested it. It was as if Nature had intended to make a gorilla, and had changed its mind at the last moment. But it wasn't merely the sheer expanse of the bird that impressed. Close to, what you noticed more was his face, which was square and powerful and slightly moustached towards the centre. His gaze was keen and piercing. I don't know if you have ever seen those pictures in the papers of Dictators with tilted chins and blazing eyes, inflaming the populace with fiery words on the occasion of the opening of a new skittle alley, but that was what he reminded me of.

Already we question the wisdom of Orwell's words regarding the absence of post-1918 tendencies in Wodehouse, and, having savoured the exactitude of Spode's description, begin to wonder exactly what E. C. Bentley had in mind when he cried out for 'serious' writing. As this opening scene progresses, Wodehouse strains every nerve to make sure we understand what Spode is:

> 'Oh, yes,' said the Dictator.
> 'Stealing umbrellas, apparently,' said the Dictator.
> The Dictator had to shove his oar in.
> The Dictator pursed his lips.
> 'Ha,' said the Dictator.
> They biffed off, the Dictator pausing at the door.

In Chapter Three Spode reappears holding up Wooster at gunpoint in the belief that he has snared a burglar. Again Wodehouse pushes home the striking resemblance of this hulking slob to a despot: 'He looked like a Dictator on the point of starting a purge.' An ugly customer, but the fault is Nature's rather than his own. It is not until the end of the chapter that Bertie discovers that he has been more percipient than he knows. Gussie, unutterably depressed by the knowledge that Sir Watkyn is demented enough to desire Madeline to marry Spode, finds consolation in the fact that Spode seems unlikely to take up the offer because 'he looks upon himself as a Man of Destiny, you see, and feels that marriage would interfere with his mission'. The theme of despotism, having been sustained with the unlikely comparison a few pages before of Gussie with Mussolini, is further driven home when Gussie see Spode as a latterday Napoleon. This baffles Wooster, who, for all his limitations, is far too sane to believe that anyone in real life would wish to behave with such paranoiac solemnity. So Gussie spells it out for him, leaving no lingering shadow of doubt in our minds as to what Wodehouse is up to:

> 'Don't you ever read the papers? Roderick Spode is the founder and head of the Saviours of Britain, a Fascist organization better known as the Black Shorts. His general idea, if he doesn't get knocked on the head with a bottle in one of the frequent brawls in which he and his followers indulge, is to make himself a Dictator.'

Bertie's initial prejudice against Spode having subsequently been borne out by the facts, he is flattered by the accuracy of his own deductions, but thinks he detects a slip of the tongue in Gussie's resume:

> 'Well, I'm dashed. I thought he was something of that sort. That chin . . . those eyes . . . and for the matter of that, that moustache. By the way, when you say "shorts" you mean "shirts", of course.'
> 'No. By the time Spode formed his association, there were no shirts left. He and his adherents wear black shorts.'
> 'Footer bags, you mean?'
> 'Yes.'
> 'How perfectly foul.'

In defiance of Orwell's argument, Wodehouse has mentioned the word 'fascist', named one of Europe's most odious dictators, and begun the process of sploshing custard pies into the face of Sir Oswald Mosley. The joke about shorts and shirts slyly insists on the feebly derivative style of Britain's would-be dictator, while Gussie's reference to the dialectics of bottle-breaking tells us that Spode can only ever hope to gain power by using brute force. In fact, as the story proceeds, Spode is revealed as a megalomaniac in whom the social graces can barely contain the lust for violence, a lust which is not so much a means to a political end as a source of gratification in itself. When warning Wooster what is likely to happen to him if the coveted cow-creamer should disappear, Spode says:

'If the thing disappears, however cunningly you and your female accomplice may have covered your traces, I shall know where it has gone, and I shall immediately beat you to a jelly. To a jelly,' he repeated, rolling the words round his tongue as if they were vintage port.

A little later Spode transfers his attentions to Gussie, explaining to Bertie in detail the programme he has in mind:

> 'Any message I can give him if he turns up?'
> 'Yes. You can tell him that I am going to break his neck.'
> 'Break his neck?'
> 'Yes. Are you deaf? Break his neck.'

Before long he has returned his attentions to Bertie, who is defended by his Aunt Dahlia. She informs Spode that he must not lay a finger on any nephew of hers, to which he responds with his plan to break every bone in Wooster's body. Frustrated in his aims, Spode then decides to shake Gussie 'like a rat', and before the end is trying to arrange circumstances so that he can get hold of Gussie and 'kick his spine up through his hat'. Any danger that the reader may not share the fear of Spode which animates all the other characters is dispelled by Wodehouse's ingenious comic device of making Spode grow steadily towards giantism as the story unfolds. When we first meet him, he seems to be seven feet tall, but soon his threats of physical violence add six inches to his stature. He continues growing, passes eight feet and, by the time he has announced his programme for rendering Gussie posthumous, 'he seemed to have grown a bit since our last meeting, being now about eight foot six'.

Then, with shocking abruptness, Spode disappears as an effective force, swept nonchalantly from the board by Jeeves, who informs his master that all that is required to reduce the despot to a jelly is to breathe the name of Eulalie. Wooster tries it out, and is much gratified by the effect, for he is now able to arraign his enemy on charges whose political exactitude might have surprised Orwell:

> 'The trouble with you, Spode, is that just because you have succeeded in inducing a handful of halfwits to disfigure the London scene by going about in black shorts, you think you're someone. You hear them shouting "Heil, Spode!" and you imagine it is the Voice of the People. That is where you make your bloomer. What the Voice of the People is saying is: "Look at that frightful ass Spode swanking about in footer bags! Did you ever in your puff see such a perfect perisher?" '

The guilty secret of Spode's past which Jeeves has uncovered turns out to be the Dictator's other life as a designer of ladies' underwear dispensed at a Bond Street emporium called 'Eulalie Sœurs'. As Wooster sagely observes,

'You can't be a successful dictator and design women's underclothing. One or the other. Not both.' To which Jeeves responds, 'Precisely, sir.'

Wodehouse and Spode grew old together; the old would-be dictator pops up intermittently in later novels, puffing faintly like an extinct but impenitent volcano. But what is the fate of such men, who have so foolishly misread the temperament of the British as to have placed themselves beyond the political pale? *The Code of the Woosters* had appeared in that uneasy summer which was sandwiched between the German invasion of Austria and the Munich Agreement. But one small consolation for dictators who never come to power is that they are allowed to survive; by 1970, by which time Spode's heroes on the continent had long since gone to perdition, there he still was, circulating in the same elevated society and still half-convinced that if only he could arrange for the kicking-in of a few spines, power might yet be his for the taking. *Much Obliged, Jeeves* was Wodehouse's ninetieth birthday present to himself, and offers a curious picture of a British by-election painted by a man who had not set foot in the country for forty years.

Bertie's friend Ginger Winship, having been weaned off roll-bunging habits at the Drones by a social-climbing wife, has now decided to contest Market Snodsbury in the Conservative interest, a course of action so incomprehensible to Wooster that he asks his friend, 'Why do you want to win the election? I'd have thought that you wouldn't have touched Parliament with a ten-foot pole', adding that he is well aware that the society there is very mixed. Ginger explains that it is all Mrs Winship's idea; Wooster, investigating the case, soon realizes that one of Ginger's greatest electioneering assets is Spode, who has by this time metamorphosed, through a few convenient funerals, into Lord Sidcup. Wooster remains unimpressed by the elevation, saying: 'I shall always think of him as Spode, no matter how many titles he may have inherited.' And although Wooster's sympathies lie with Ginger's political party if they lie anywhere at all, he cannot bring himself to take Spode as part of the Conservative package:

> 'Our views on each other were definite. His was that what England needed if it was to become a land fit for heroes to live in was fewer and better Woosters, while I had always felt that there was nothing wrong with England that a ton of bricks falling from a height on Spode's head wouldn't cure.'

It is Aunt Dahlia who explains to Wooster that, politics being the art of the possible, Ginger would be foolish not to accept the assistance of Spode:

> 'He needs all the help he can get, and Spode's one of those silver-tongued orators you read about. Extraordinary gift of the gab he has. He could get into Parliament without straining a sinew.'
> I dare say she was right, but I resented any praise of Spode. I made clear my displeasure by responding curtly, 'Then why doesn't he?'
> 'He can't, you poor chump. He's a lord.'

'Don't they allow lords in?'

'No, they don't.'

'I see,' I said, rather impressed by this proof that the House of Commons drew the line somewhere.

For all her cynicism, Aunt Dahlia acknowledges Spode's hideousness, dismissing him as 'a thug of the first order'. And it is certainly true that the years and the acquisition of a pair of supplementary chins have done little to temper Spode's moods of violence. Wooster finds him still 'likely to start trying to ascertain the colour of your insides', a feeling confirmed two pages later by Spode's threat to knock Wooster's teeth down his throat. Wooster then claims the immunity of his status as fellow-guest in Aunt Dahlia's house, but Spode will have none of this constitutional trifling:

'You probably think that being a guest in your aunt's house I would hesitate to butter you over the front lawn and dance on the fragments in hobnailed boots, but you are mistaken. It will be a genuine pleasure. By an odd coincidence, I brought a pair of hobnailed boots with me.'

Later, when it seems as if Wooster might become a temporary guest of Her Majesty, Spode warns him that on his emergence from Wormwood Scrubs, 'I shall tear you limb from limb'. The effect on Spode of his own political oratory soon has an alarming effect; hamstrung by his peerage, he decides to take steps to renounce it in an attempt to re-enter the mainstream of political life through the Commons. As Aunt Dahlia says, 'He sees himself holding the House of Commons spellbound':

'Why can't he hold the House of Lords spellbound?'

'It wouldn't be the same thing. It would be like playing in the Market Snodsbury tennis tournament instead of electrifying one and all on the Centre Court at Wimbledon.'

The world is saved from Spode's renascence by a fortuitous potato flung by one of Winship's opponents. Hitting Spode in the eye, it 'made him feel that if that was the sort of thing you have to go through to get elected to the House of Commons, he preferred to play it safe and stick to the House of Lords'. Instead, he marries Madeline Bassett, whose lifelong preoccupation with the mating habits of fairies has not altogether blinded her to the advantage of becoming the Countess of Sidcup. And so the would-be despot fades quietly into the tangled undergrowth of Debrett, his claws finally drawn by the matrimonial responsibilities he had always shunned. For the work of a man of ninety, *Much Obliged, Jeeves* has a surprising sharpness of claw itself, and the reader cannot help noticing the tincture of bitterness which has seeped into Wodehouse's view of British political life since the persiflage of *Psmith in the City*. When Bickersdyke was vilified, it was because he seemed incapable of living up to the high moral demands of Westminster; by the time Winship sets out on the same road it is not the traveller but the goal itself which is beneath contempt. Wooster has noticed that the society in the Commons is 'mixed', and is genuinely surprised to learn that even the Commons draws the line at peers of the realm; as for the Lords, it is no more than a sleepy backwater through whose shallows may cruise senescent despots like old Sidcup, harmlessly dissipating their fading seditious energies. It seems that at the end of his life, Wodehouse's once universal benevolence no longer extended to the Mother of Parliaments.

In the light of Spode's ugly exploits in *The Code of the Woosters*, Orwell's claim that there are 'no post-1918 tendencies' in Wodehouse's work may be seen either as a spectacular oversight or as the calculated disingenuousness of a shrewd political campaigner. It is possible that by 1938, when *The Code of the Woosters* first appeared, Orwell had long since relinquished his habit of reading the novels as they were published, and was genuinely unaware of the emergence in them of what sounds in retrospect very much like the cry of the liberal spirit. On the other hand, Orwell retained an abiding affection for Psmith, Archie Moffam and company, and, having settled on his strategy for the defence of their creator, may have decided that a plea of guilty but insane would be seriously compromised by the patent sanity of the characterization of Spode. A man who sees the potential danger posed by such a creature ought surely to have enough perception to realize that to broadcast from the enemy capital in wartime is to play into the hands of the Spodes of this world. We will never know which of the two explanations for Orwell's oversight was the real one, but in any case it is surprising that neither he nor any of the other participants in the debate felt that the real crux of the case lay not in the broadcasts themselves but in Wodehouse's presence in Berlin. Was he actually freed from internment by the Germans? Or was he removed to Berlin by their orders? If the former, then his foolishness was indeed monumental; if the latter, then the broadcasts may have been unavoidable.

In his defence, Orwell makes no mention of the origins of the campaign against Wodehouse. A writer like Connor, who could hardly have regarded himself as an arbiter of literary conduct, and who was too well acquainted with the laws of libel to have risked such an onslaught on his own initiative, was clearly a catspaw. But whose? The British Broadcasting Corporation had provided Connor with a stage for his performance, and, for some years after it, banned Wodehouse's lyrics from the air. But the Corporation later let it be known that it had mounted the attack most unwillingly, and had been coerced from on high, from the government itself, whose Minister of Information had insisted on the Connor attack. The precise apportioning of blame is difficult; in Asa Briggs' enormous and generally comprehensive history of the BBC,[13] there is no mention of the incident, and the victim himself makes things no clearer in his volumes of autobiography. But another writer who became involved at a later stage of Wodehouse's wartime crisis was bold enough to confront the minister responsible with a request for clarification:

Wodehouse's true offence was to have disinterested himself in the war. When I discussed his 'case' with Duff Cooper, then British Ambassador in Paris, this was the line he took. Wodehouse, he said, had always evaded reality and his responsibilities as a citizen.[14]

The charge, if it was true, was indeed grave in time of war. Let us see to what extent the Minister himself had contrived during the same period of time to meet reality and fulfil his responsibilities as a citizen.

Alfred Duff Cooper had entered the House of Commons in the Conservative interest in 1924, armoured against doubt by his conviction that his motives were purer than those of many of his colleagues, who were 'mostly business men who had recently made fortunes, often by methods that did not invite close inspection'. For the next thirteen years Cooper gallantly attempted to conquer his repugnance for his comrades in Mr Baldwin's unedifying army, succeeding so well that by 1931 his leader's eye had fallen upon him. The occasion was the notorious St George's by-election, for which Baldwin required a candidate who represented exactly his own view regarding the great controversy of the moment. This controversy was not, as a naïf might imagine, to do with unemployment, or education, or malnutrition, or peace, or even rearmament, but centred around the pressing question of whether politicians or newspaper owners had a monopoly of the nation's spirituality. This issue, which in retrospect may charitably be described as academic, inspired oratory not so very superior to that which later emerged in the great struggle for Market Snodsbury; it was during the St George's campaign that Mr Baldwin, campaigning on behalf of his young protégé, recited the famous lines composed by his cousin Rudyard Kipling to the effect that the Press barons, with whom Kipling had been known to consort now and then in the past, were aiming at power without responsibility, 'the prerogative of the harlot through the ages'.

Sustained by this judicious approach to the troubles of the British Empire, Cooper won the election comfortably enough, and, continuing to show conspicuous gallantry in the face of those party colleagues whose origins so troubled his sensibilities, rose swiftly through the ranks, thereby providing himself with ample opportunity to shoulder those responsibilities which he was later to reproach Wodehouse for having ignored. As Minister for War, Cooper was particularly conscientious in facing reality: when introducing the Army Estimates for 1936–7, he apologized for the mechanization of certain cavalry units, saying, 'It is like asking a great musical performer to throw away his violin and devote himself in future to a gramophone'. A few months after the publication of *The Code of the Woosters*, which, in its regrettable frivolity, could not hope to aspire to the intellectual heights of Cooper's reflections on the role of the horse in modern warfare, Baldwin's promising young man resigned in protest against Chamberlain's conduct at Munich, for which act he has often been praised by historians for his lack of culpability in the matter of Appeasement. But a Minister for War who serves under Baldwin, who foozles his army recruitment campaign, who then serves under

Chamberlain and who, having summed up the situation with the masterly phrase, 'The Germans are so beastly powerful', then calls for war, is no more than a Bluebeard who stops short at his sixth wife. In any case, Cooper's resignation after Munich is not after all quite the selfless act it was once thought to be. The whirligig of time brings in its revenges in political life as in all others, and one of those harlots of the Press so roundly abused at the St George's by-election gave the following account of how Cooper, on the occasion of his country's greatest diplomatic humiliation for a century, contrived to meet reality and fulfil his responsibilities as a citizen:

> When Chamberlain returned from Munich with 'Peace in Our Time', his colleagues, including Duff, were unanimous in their expression of joy and gladness. Duff stayed behind at the end of the meeting at Chamberlain's request. Duff was quite conciliatory and said he supposed his threat of resignation would be forgotten. Chamberlain refused, saying, 'I am afraid that at this stage that is impossible.' Duff was out.[15]

Whether Beaverbrook's account of the affair was animated by the dispassion of the historian or the animus of the victim remains unknown, but Cooper certainly had a gift for survival which innocents like Wodehouse might have envied. When war came he was appointed Minister of Information, and found himself with further opportunities to face reality and fulfil his responsibilities as a citizen. This he did in two ways; first, by subjecting Wodehouse to public humiliation, and second, by organizing troupes of investigators to circulate among the population in order to gauge the extent of national disaffection. This comic regiment became known, with the genial contempt which the British always bestow upon the public indiscretions of noodles, as 'Cooper's Snoopers', and deserves to figure prominently in any just assessment of how far their creator was prepared to face reality and fulfil his responsibilities as a citizen. Nor was Cooper's ingenuity quite exhausted. At one point, seeing that the beleaguered nation, debilitated by fifteen years of government by his political helpmates, desperately required the uplift of some tremendous gesture, Cooper provided it single-handed by going to Broadcasting House and reciting Macaulay's poem about the Armada. It is not known what practical effect this had on the respective war efforts of the contending dynasties, but it certainly showed what Cooper had in mind when he talked of facing reality and fulfilling one's responsibilities as a citizen. In retirement Cooper published a memoir entitled *Old Men Forget*. They do indeed, when it suits them; nowhere in this bulky work is there any mention of P. G. Wodehouse, from which posterity will be able to conclude that although the manifestations of facing reality and fulfilling one's responsibilities are numberless, the art of apology is not among them.

By the time Orwell's essay appeared, Wodehouse's wartime ordeal had progressed a great deal further, although not quite in the direction he would have wished. By 1944 he was living in Paris with Ethel anticipating the advance of the Allied invasion forces. At the time of the Liberation celebrations there arrived in the city a British journalist serving as liaison officer with the Gaullist 'Services Speciaux'. As there appeared to be no services to perform, speciaux or otherwise, the liaison officer was happy to pick up a remark by a colleague in MI6 that there existed a list of suspected traitors whose cases required investigation, and that one of the names on this list might appeal to the liaison officer as the pretext for a chore. The latter accepted, 'partly out of curiosity and partly from a feeling that no one who had made as elegant and original a contribution to contemporary letters and the general gaiety of living as Wodehouse had should be allowed to get caught up in the larger buffooneries of war'.[16] Thus began the friendship between Wodehouse and Malcolm Muggeridge.

The acquaintance began with Muggeridge's visit to the Bristol Hotel. He took with him no more than a vague idea what he would say or do, for he retained only the haziest recollection of the fuss over the broadcasts, 'nor was I to be counted among the more ardent Wodehouse aficionados, though I had greatly enjoyed some of his books, particularly his short stories and *Uncle Fred in the Springtime*'.[17] His first impression was of a schoolmaster: 'The encounter seemed so natural that it only occurred to me afterwards that Wodehouse may have thought that I had come to arrest him or something.'[18] Nothing was further from Muggeridge's thoughts. Throughout his career he was to display an admirable lack of charity when it came to the elastic ethics of the political life, and it may well be that he felt that there existed no higher endorsement of a man's morality than that a panjandrum like Cooper should disapprove of it. At any rate, Muggeridge confided that he felt the fuss over the broadcasts to be ludicrous, but went on to stress that others might not agree:

> In order to clear matters up, questions would have to be asked, and the legal position would have to be gone into. I slipped in the reference to the legal position (about which, of course, I knew nothing) in order to stress the gravity of Wodehouse's situation. In the circumstances then prevailing, it was decidedly serious.[19]

Muggeridge swiftly conceived a deep affection for both Plum and Ethel:

> I grew to love her, too, and it became increasingly hard for me to remember I was supposed to be probing a 'case' rather than just spending delightful hours with dear friends. All my endeavour was directed towards sparing them worry and discomfort, and relieving them of any apprehension they might have about their future fate. This, I know, is not the attitude Intelligence Officers are supposed to have in dealing with alleged traitors, but I have to admit that it was mine in dealing with the Wodehouses.[20]

Muggeridge's view was most untypical. On 22 November 1944, much to his astonishment, the Wodehouses were arrested by the French and taken to a police station on the Quai d'Orléans, where for the next five days they became pawns in a plot of Wodehousean extravagance. The British government, assuming that Wodehouse had broken French law, rushed a Home Office representative to Paris, only to discover that the French had no idea why they had arrested Wodehouse, who was entered in the charge book as Wodenhorse, except that in a vague sort of way they assumed they were doing their allies a favour. Muggeridge then contrived that the criminal be put in confinement, although not quite of the sort desired by some of the authorities; Wodehouse spent the next few weeks masquerading as an inmate in a maternity hospital. Meanwhile, in that club to whose membership Bickersdyke and Ginger Winship had so sedulously aspired, passions were rising to a climacteric. On 6 December, a Major Lucas asked the Foreign Secretary Anthony Eden if his attention had been drawn to Wodehouse's case; a Captain Gammans then asked why he had not been brought home for trial. Eden replied that the case 'was being closely watched',[21] and that Wodehouse had been released by the French on condition that he went into a hospital, Eden's legendary diplomatic mastery prevailing upon him not to say when the baby was expected. He did add that 'Mr Wodehouse had expressed no wish to go to England and that he, Mr Eden, was asking the French Government to state the legal grounds upon which the surveillance was being maintained'.[22] In response to further questions, the Minister said that there was no question of a trial, the Home Office having advised that there were no grounds upon which action could be taken. Mr Quintin Hogg asked if it was not obvious that anyone receiving a fee for broadcasting on the enemy wireless was trading with the enemy and was thereby punishable by law. Nine days later Hogg admitted in the House that no, it was not obvious, and that speaking on the enemy wireless in wartime was not an offence; he added that 'it very soon ought to be made one'. On 15 January 1945, the French authorities officially released the Wodehouses, who were now free to move as they pleased. They finally left for New York in April 1947, from which point Wodehouse ceased in any practical sense to be a British citizen, although it seems unlikely that anyone, least of all Wodehouse himself, realized this at the time. Certainly the British at large had no suspicion of what had happened, that charges of treason, just imprecise enough to be impossible to disprove, had been baseless, and that, as a result of his victimization at the hands of maladroit politicians, the victim felt disinclined to come home. His mood was best defined by Muggeridge, who, on the occasion of Wodehouse's ninetieth birthday, wrote:

Ethel has been back to England several times but Wodehouse never, though he is always theoretically planning to come. I doubt if he ever will. His attitude is like that of a man who has parted, in painful circumstances, from someone he loves and whom he both longs and dreads to see again.[23]

It was while Muggeridge was investigating the circumstances of Wodehouse's wartime indiscretions that he confronted the ex-Minister of Information, now Ambassador to France, with the question about the precise nature of the crime believed to have been committed. In reflecting on Cooper's Woosterian waffle about evading reality and fulfilling responsibilities, Muggeridge writes:

> Yet, after all, as I tried to indicate, there are different sorts of reality. Can we be so sure, for instance, that Hitler's ranting and Churchill's rhetoric and Roosevelt's Four Freedoms will seem more real to posterity than Jeeves and Bertie Wooster? I rather doubt it.[24]

Cooper ended his career by metamorphosing into Lord Norwich, although Wodehouse continued to regard him as Cooper, 'no matter how many titles he may have inherited'. As for Hogg, he subsequently inherited a title and ascended to the House of Lords, only to renounce that title and descend again to the House of Commons, only to receive another title and ascend back to the House of Lords, his yo-yo predilections no doubt having much to do with the conviction that to 'limit one's spellbinding operations to the House of Lords would be like playing in the Market Snodsbury tennis tournament instead of electrifying one and all on the Centre Court at Wimbledon'.

What was the truth of the affair? What exactly did Wodehouse do or not do in Europe during the war? Amid the chaos of claim and counterclaim, of bitter accusation and vehement denial, the charges without foundation, the political evasions and the hysteria of wartime propaganda, the half-truths, the garbled reports, the purblind eye-witness accounts, it was impossible for either Mackenzie or Hogg or Orwell or Cooper or Spring or Eden or any of the others who became enmeshed in the net of Wodehouse's dilemma to know exactly what had happened and why. Of the debaters, only Muggeridge knew the precise sequence of events and the circumstances in which they had occurred, and he evidently was disbarred by protocol from giving his account, although it is revealing that he, the one disinterested party to investigate the case, soon began speaking of Wodehouse in terms of endearment, just as had Jerome Kern, and Ira Gershwin, and Compton Mackenzie and William Townend and Florenz Ziegfeld and the regiments of chorus girls and editors long since gone to their reward. Ridiculous as it sounds, before the simple facts of Wodehouse's case could be disclosed, the world had to await the passing of the obligatory thirty-year lapse by which the British Establishment fondly hopes to escape the consequences of its own indiscretions, its evasions of reality, its failure to fulfil its responsibilities. In 1981, the centenary of Wodehouse's birth, the Conservative MP Iain Sproat, after some years of fruitless campaigning, finally persuaded the Home Office to allow him to examine the MI5 files which had remained inaccessible to the British even after the award of a knighthood to

Wodehouse in 1975, six weeks before his death.

After thirty years of fanciful guesswork whose cumulative effect was of a scenario blurred at the edges but unvarying in its central plot of sybaritism and betrayal, the actual account of what happened[25] sounds anti-climactic and yet curiously lurid in the very mildness with which it contradicts the testimonies of so many witnesses who were somewhere else at the time, much as, in a vintage Hollywood movie or a James Hilton best-seller, the final flashback, its ground carefully prepared by the earlier laying of false trails, achieves sensationalism through sheer innocuousness. In examining the file on Wodehouse, Sproat was opening a time-capsule coated with the dust of ages. Although only a generation had passed, the issues embodied in its folders now qualified as the gossip of antiquity. Most of the politicians were dead and gone, their thundering gasconades reduced to a distant squeak; the bureaucrats and the functionaries had long since risen in glory to Valhalla in triplicate, their ascent impeded only slightly by the encumbrance of lesser Birthday Honours. Half the population of Britain, including tens of thousands of dedicated Wodehouse readers, were still unborn when the Second World War began, and must have wondered idly about Sproat's campaign, if indeed they noticed it at all. But Justice, like Treason and Dishonour, is an abstraction of some relevance still, even though by the time he became its belated beneficiary, Wodehouse was beyond the reach of antagonists and defenders alike.

In the Wodehouse file Sproat found three documents of prime relevance. The first was a statement from Wodehouse telling of his activities between 1940 and 1944, ending with the sentence, 'I should like to conclude by saying that I never had any intention of assisting the enemy, and that I have suffered a great deal of mental pain as a result of my action.' The second document was an account by an officer in the Intelligence Corps, Major E. J. P. Cussen, describing the details of MI5's investigations. The third document, the one with the most relevance of all and yet the one least known, consisted of transcripts of the offending broadcasts. Among the other evidence were letters from Wodehouse to the Home Office and Foreign Office – 'I am a loyal subject of His Majesty' – telegrams, Civil Service memoranda, letters, bank statements and legal reports. From this confusion of previously unseen evidence, it was easy enough to piece together the exact sequence of events from the moment the war began to the day when Muggeridge walked into the Bristol Hotel.

When the Germans began their advance through the Low Countries, Wodehouse made arrangements with the officer commanding the British Military Hospital at Etaples that should the danger of capture become imminent, he would be warned to prepare for flight. He duplicated this arrangement with the British Consul at Le Touquet, who promised to tell the Wodehouses in good time should Guderian's soldiers look like reaching the coast. One day Wodehouse was listening to a BBC News bulletin describing how the enemy forces had been thrown back, when the Germans arrived. When MI5 questioned him about this period, Wodehouse said that to have fraternized with the enemy would have been difficult as he could not speak German. He later described the period at Le Touquet to Townend:

> What actually happened was that at the end of the second week of occupation, the house next door became full of German Labour Corps workers, and they seemed to have got me muddled up with Tennyson's Sir Walter Vivian, the gentleman who 'all a summer's day gave his broad lawns, until the set of sun, up to the people'. I suppose to a man fond of German Labour Corps workers, and liking to hear them singing in his bath, the conditions would have been ideal, but they didn't suit me. I chafed, and a fat lot of good chafing did me. They came again next day and brought their friends.

In one of the scandalous broadcasts he amplified his description of the early days of his interment in the following passage:

> Young men, starting out in life, have often asked me, 'How can I become an internee?' Well, there are several methods. My own was to buy a villa at Le Touquet and stay there till the Germans came along. This is probably the best and simplest system. You buy the villa and the Germans do the rest. . . . The proceedings were not marred by any vulgar brawling. All that happened, as far as I was concerned, was that I was strolling on the lawn with my wife one morning, when she lowered her voice and said, 'Don't look now, but there comes the German army'. And there they were, a fine body of men, rather prettily dressed in green, carrying machine guns.

After passing through assorted places of internment, Wodehouse ended up in the lunatic asylum at Tost, where one day the Lager Führer, Oberleutnant Buchelt, told Wodehouse how enjoyable he had found his recent article in the *Saturday Evening Post* called 'My War With Germany':

> The Lager Führer said, 'Why don't you do some broadcasts on similar lines for your American readers?' I said 'I should love to' or 'There's nothing I should like better', or some similar phrase. The inference I draw from this episode is either a) he had been told to sound me out on my willingness to broadcast, or b) that having been informed by me that I was willing, he reported to Berlin.

On the evening of 21 June 1941, Wodehouse was playing in a camp cricket match when he was told to pack his bags. He was then taken on the overnight train to Berlin and escorted to the Hotel Adlon, where to his surprise he was met by a visitation from out of the dim Schnellenhamerian past, a one-time San Francisco stockbroker called Raven von Barnikow, now a major in the German army. Unbeknown to Wodehouse, von Barnikow had been trying to get his old friend exchanged for a German screw manufacturer interned by the British. Barnikow said he had heard of Wodehouse's 'release' from another ex-Hollywood paragon, Werner Plack, now working in the German Foreign Office. Barnikow offered to lend Wodehouse some clothes, and as they were walking through the hotel lobby they met Plack:

> Plack asked me if I was tired after my journey and how I liked camp. It was in the course of this conversation that I mentioned the number of letters I'd received from American readers, and said it was maddening not to be able to answer them. Barnikow went to get the clothes, and Plack asked me if I would like to broadcast to America. I said 'Yes', and he said he would have me brought to his office next day to arrange details. He then hurried off. Shortly after this, before lunch, I met Buchelt in the lobby. He was in civilian clothes. He congratulated me on being released and I told him I was broadcasting my experiences. . . . On Wednesday June 25, I think I must have written and recorded my first talk. I was then driven with Plack to the broadcasting place where the manuscript was censored by three officials, each representing a branch of the authorities, and I then spoke it into a device. . . . Of course, I ought to have had the sense to see that it was a loony thing to do, to use the German radio for even the most harmless stuff. I suppose prison life saps the intellect.

In his report, Major Cussen noted that Wodehouse received the equivalent of £22 in payment for the broadcasts, which Connor may or may not have known when he spoke of 'a rich man trying to make his last and greatest sale'.

What emerges from this tragi-comic account of a man hopelessly out of his depth is that Wodehouse, the fine cutting edge of his perceptions blunted by isolation from Britain at just the psychological moment when the war was on the turn from a diplomatic hiatus to a fight to the death, displayed foolishness worthy of the most witless of his heroes. Through 1942–43 he and Ethel existed in the limbo of the official embarrassment of both sides, the Germans allowing them to leave for the country in the summer and return to Berlin in the winter on the understanding that the prisoners paid their own expenses. During this period Wodehouse asked his jailors for permission to come home to England in order to explain himself; the insane naïvety of the request is perhaps the most vivid example of the extent to which Wodehouse failed to understand the nature of the world he had tumbled into. In November 1942 he wrote to the British Foreign Office:

> It seemed to me at the time that there could be no harm in reading over the radio a short series of purely humorous and frivolous reminiscences, which, if I had been in England, would have appeared in *Punch*. I had written these talks while in camp and had read them to an audience of fellow internees, who were amused by them, which would not have been the case had they contained the slightest suggestion of German propaganda.

on 28 September 1944 Major Cussen submitted his report clearing Wodehouse of suspicion of treasonable acts; on 23 November 1944, the Director of Public Prosecutions informed MI5 that there was no sufficient evidence to call for prosecution: 'There is nothing to justify any action on my part.' More than a year before Cussen's report, the Germans, pressed by a housing shortage caused by air-raid damage, and requiring the services of Wodehouse's watchdogs for more arduous duties, had sent the English couple to Paris, where they remained until the day in 1944 when Muggeridge happened upon them, and perceived in a moment the less than shocking spectacle of a man whose only crime had been to behave like Wooster bereft of his Jeeves. Indeed, the worst that could be said of him was what Sir Oliver Lodge once said of Sir Arthur Conan Doyle, that he 'lacked the wisdom of the serpent'.

But if neither the Director of Public Prosecutions nor the Home Office nor MI5 nor the Foreign Secretary considered that a crime had been committed, why did investigators like Sproat a generation later encounter such intransigence on the part of the very bodies which had agreed so long ago that Wodehouse was innocent of anything more reprehensible than stupidity? The answer involves the most crushing irony of the whole affair, and seems better suited to the denouement of a Psmith novel than to the life of Psmith's creator. Those who had failed in their attempts to get at the files had understandably assumed that the rebuff was to do either with unspeakable crimes of Wodehouse's which still imperilled national morale or security, or perhaps with transactions involving prominent personages which the world was not yet ready to receive. As late in the day as 1971, the then Prime Minister Edward Heath rejected the idea of a Wodehouse knighthood on the grounds that the official files contained damaging material. Sproat's request to see the files was turned down, and he was told that the material 'was shocking and would remain classified for many years'. It is a classic example of political disingenuousness that Sproat was not told that the 'shocking' material might not really be quite what it seemed. The one possibility which had occurred to nobody until Sproat thought of it some years later, was that perhaps Wodehouse, instead of being the star of the melodrama, was, in the bureaucratic sense, a mere supporting player, and had all these years been unwittingly playing Catsmeat Potter-Pirbright to someone else's Bertie Wooster. In 1979, after the fall of Heath, after the knighthood bestowed by Sir Harold Wilson, after Wodehouse's death, Sproat reapplied to see the files and was again refused. But this time the official reaction was subtly different:

> 'I was led to believe – although I was never told in so many words – that there was one unnamed department in Whitehall that was blocking my application. . . . I came to the conclusion that somebody else was mentioned in the Wodehouse file, and that it was consequences arising from the mention of this other person that made the unnamed department anxious that the Wodehouse file remain secret. I therefore suggested that the name concerned be blanked out in the original papers. In the end this simple solution was adopted.'[26]

The blanked-out name proved to be that of another British internee who 'may or may not have been a traitor; what was clear was that those who originally compiled the file considered him of no consequence as far as any evidence for or against Wodehouse was concerned'.

It is a conventional and indubitably English story of political chicanery and bureaucratic moral imbecility reacting to bumbling foolishness, of madness in triplicate conspiring with intellecutal dishonesty to ruin a life. One wonders at the diplomatic silence of all those supernumeraries in Wodehouse's story who forgot their lines and melted away when their moment came: the officer commanding the British military hospital at Etaples, for instance, and the British Consul at Le Touquet, the underlings who received Wodehouse's letters to the Home and Foreign Offices, the nameless Spodes of a nameless Whitehall department who sacrificed an old man's reputation to an unnamed suspect. The British generally went in innocence of events. They continued to read Wodehouse with unwavering enthusiasm, they soon forgot dim rumours of perfidy, they thought that, by awarding knighthoods to Wodehouse and Charlie Chaplin on the same day, their rulers had for once displayed an admirable sense of values. But it is doubtful if they quite understood what Muggeridge was implying when he wrote of a man 'who has parted, in painful circumstances, from someone he loves and whom he both longs and dreads to see'. Perhaps the most succinct account of the affair is that provided by A. J. P. Taylor in his *English History, 1914–1945:*

> The novelist P. G. Wodehouse was captured by the Germans and interned. He gave a light-hearted talk over the German radio, describing life in an internment camp (where he continued to write novels under difficult conditions). The Germans released him when he reached the age of sixty, and he returned to France. At the liberation, orders were given to arrest him, and to send him to England for trial. A sensible British intelligence officer sheltered him until he could be smuggled into Switzerland. But for some years English publishers fought shy of Wodehouse's novels, and he never returned to his native country.[27]

What of Wodehouse's reaction to the events following the arrival in his garden of Guderian's emissaries? He maintained a public silence from then until his death. The BBC quietly reinstated his works, and the masterminds responsible for the affairs of Dulwich College, having expunged his name from the Roll of Honour, eventually put it back again. Wodehouse never pointed out that with *The Code of the Woosters* he had written a virulently anti-totalitarian novel at a time when such outspokenness in Chamberlain's England was not considered by his peers to be quite the done thing. Perhaps he derived a grim satisfaction from that moment at the Nazi War Crimes Trials at Nuremberg, when David Maxwell Fyfe, prosecuting one of the accused, was faced with the argument by the accused's counsel that the accused had been known to refrain from harming people when he had the power to persecute them:

> When it came to my turn again, I remarked that this greatly reminded me of a character in one of Mr P. G. Wodehouse's books, who was such a kindly man that days would go by during which he would wholly refrain from pulling the wings off flies. His friends would sit down and watch him not doing it.[28]

Prosecuting counsel's point was well made, even if he was careless with his quoting. When, in *Piccadilly Jim*, our hero is pleading on behalf of a friend accused of striking the odious Ogden, he says, 'In his normal state he wouldn't strike a lamb. I've known him do it.' Mrs Pett asks 'Do what?', and Jim replies, 'Not strike lambs.' A much bitterer irony is that the broadcasts, nominated for so long as texts of unspeakable pro-Nazi perfidy were, it appears, open to other interpretations, as Muggeridge disclosed:

> In the broadcasts there is not one phrase or word which can possibly be regarded as treasonable. Naturally, they were gone through minutely to confirm that this was so. Ironically enough, they were subsequently used at an American political warfare school as an example of how anti-German propaganda could subtly be put across by a skilful writer in the form of seemingly innocuous, light-hearted descriptive material. The fact is that Wodehouse is ill-fitted to live in an age of ideological conflict. He just does not react to human beings in that sort of way, and never seems to hate anyone – not even old friends who turned on him.[29]

But if he never actually hated them, he did at least do to them what he had been doing to everybody ever since that day when, having defaced the ledger at the Hong Kong and Shanghai Bank, he stepped out of Lombard Street into the sunset of the free-lance life. He extracted literary raw material from them. When A. A. Milne had so nauseated Sir Compton Mackenzie by mocking Wodehouse's non-existent accomplishments as a father of sons, he must mildly have upset Wodehouse too. Stepping one day into the generous estates of his imagination, Wodehouse wandered among its inhabitants searching for the poetasters, the precious versifiers, the perpetrators of the kind of literary excrescences which only a Rosie Banks could admire. Suddenly he came across the notorious Rodney Spelvin, last seen in 1924 settling down to the homely delights of marriage to Anastasia Bates. Spelvin, a hideous poet who had evolved into an even worse novelist, had been living ever since in a state of suspended animation, purified, it had been assumed, in the fires of Anastasia's tutelage. And then, in 1949, there appeared a short story called 'Rodney Has a Relapse', in which Spelvin, who for twenty-five years had trod the straight and narrow, suddenly erupts into his old, regrettable poetic ways, displaying in his comeback even worse aesthetic manners than ever. As Anastasia, saddened spouse, puts it, 'Rodney says he expects soon to have sufficient material for a slim volume.' Her brother William, whose small son is at the centre of the crisis, puts it more accurately:

> 'Do you know where Rodney is at this moment? Up in the nursery, bending over my son Timothy's cot, gathering material for a poem about the unfortunate little rat when asleep. Some bolony, no doubt, about how he hugs his teddy bear and dreams of angels. . . . When I tell you that he refers to him throughout as "Timothy Bobbin", you will appreciate what we are up against.'

The lampoon drifts much closer to the Hundred Acre Wood with Wodehouse, the master versifier, describing the contents of Spelvin's wastepaper basket:

> 'Timothy Bobbin has a puppy,
> A dear little puppy that goes bow-bow . . .'

> Beneath this were the words, 'Whoa, wait a minute!', followed, as though the writer had realized that this 'uppy' rhyming scheme was going to present difficulties, by some scattered notes:

> 'Safer to change to rabbit?
> (Habit . . . grab it . . . Stab it . . . Babbit).
> Rabbit looks tough too. How about canary?
> (Airy, dairy, fairy, hairy Mary, contrary, vary).
> Note: Canaries go tweet-tweet.
> (Beat, seat, feet, heat, meet, neat, repeat, sheet, complete, discreet).
> Yes, canary looks like goods.'

After sporting for a while in these poetic shallows, Spelvin finally commits himself to Pooh Corner with an emblematic composition:

> Timothy
>   Bobbin
>   Goes
>   Hoppity
>   Hoppity
>   Hoppity
>   Hoppity
>   Hop.

Underneath this Rodney has added 'Reminiscent?'. His misgivings are well justified, because what he has just composed is a mirror-image of Milne's poem 'Hoppity' in *When We Were Very Young* (1924). That Spelvin, in his resolution to return to his bad old ways, should have stooped so low was serious enough; after all, in his preoccupation with Bobbin's hops, he has even lapsed into the ultimate blasphemy of neglecting his golf. But what is far more serious is the corruption of young Timothy, whose role as a rhymester's guinea pig has caused so steep a decline that before long this once happy child is seen talking into a bluebell in the conviction that it is a fairy telephone. Spelvin is eventually restored to the clubhouse of righteousness by a vigilant wife, but the regeneration of Timothy is only effected by the threat of physical violence, at least vicariously. When his cousin and contemporary, Braid Bates, demands further poetic effusions within the family circle, his mother addresses to him a minatory rhetorical question: 'Does mother's little chickabiddy want his nose pushed sideways?'

There was one other small literary reprisal hidden deep in the enchanted wood of Wodehouse's imaginary world, and perhaps it can serve as the last word on his wartime misadventures. In a 1949 novel called *The Mating Season*, there is an early scene where Catsmeat Potter-Pirbright, having been implicated with Gussie Fink-Nottle in a bout of drunken rowdiness culminating in a dawn water ballet in the fountains of Trafalgar Square, is recounting to Wooster Gussie's awful fate in being sentenced to fourteen days in the coop. Wooster's first thought is that Gussie's betrothed, whimsy-whamsy Madeline Bassett, will be sure to cancel the nuptials the moment she reads in the newspapers of her future husband's disgrace. But Catsmeat quiets Wooster's fears, assuring him that Madeline will never know of the disgraceful fracas, 'because Gussie, showing unexpected intelligence, gave his name as Alfred Duff Cooper'.

Which may well prove to be that forgotten politician's best chance of immortality.

8

Knight
in
exile

THE AUNT, THE NANNY AND THE
governess, that unholy trinity of shuffled-off responsibilities, so dominate the
nineteenth-century landscape that the social historian, rummaging for an
epithet of definition, can only mourn the absence from the language of a
feminine equivalent to 'avuncular'. The callousness in this regard of the
Victorian British middle classes, whose sense of imperial mission persuaded
parents to suffer the little children to come unto somebody else, remains one
of the wonders of the civilized world. Throughout the imperial heyday, but
especially in the period between the Great Exhibition and the Great War, the
sons of the well-to-do were dumped on any person or institution willing to
accept money for the job. English literature is scattered with the bitter fruits
of this dereliction of parental duty: from Kipling and Saki, victimized by
relations whose stupidity was outdone only by their barbarism, to Kenneth
Grahame, who, placed in the custody of a grandmother of whom it was said,
'I don't suppose she could be described as a child-lover',[1] retired into a
self-preserving quietism in the face of that indifference which can sometimes be more hurtful than cruelty itself; or to Maugham, thrown by bereave-
ment upon the bleak shores of Victorian Whitstable and the mercies of a
reverend gentleman whose years of exposure to the Realpolitik of the
Church of England had taught him that its most expendable tenets were
Faith, Hope and Charity, and that the smallest of these was Charity. The
excuse of parents like the Kiplings – and it was the same excuse offered by
Mrs Jellyby when preferring the abstraction of the African coffee-berry to the
plight of her own child waiting with its head stuck between the area railings

– was that there was far more important work in this world than tending to
the needs of their own children. In Mr Kipling's case, this took the form of
teaching the art of architectural moulding to the citizens of Bombay. However, as there is no more important work in this world than tending to the
needs of your own children, neither the Kiplings' intelligence nor their
perceptions commend themselves to a posterity which knows what this kind
of excess of preoccupied patriotism can bring about. Like Mrs Jellyby, the
Kiplings were parenthood's absentee landlords, who professed to be dismayed when they found themselves emotionally dispossessed.

Angus Wilson, one of Kipling's most observant biographers, in wrestling
with this demon, performs the most wonderful contortions in a comically
misguided attempt to exonerate Kipling's parents from charges of wilful
neglect, and does not seem to understand the fundamental nature of the
issues at stake. Despite his encyclopedic knowledge of Kipling's art, he says
of the years of parentless hell, 'I do not think we can see it, as Edmund
Wilson did, as some lasting maiming of Kipling's genius', although he is
then obliged to add, somewhat ruefully, 'but Kipling himself clearly felt it as
a continual and frightening memory.'[2] In the case of Maugham, one of his
biographers, Ted Morgan, offers the feeble excuse that perhaps Maugham's
aunt and uncle were not as black as their nephew subsequently painted
them; however, as Maugham was there at the time and Morgan presumably
was not, the argument carries no weight.[3] H. H. Munro's case is even more
uncompromising. His father having taken up an appointment as Inspector-
General of the Burma Police, the son fell into the clutches of not one
monstrous aunt but two: Augusta, an accomplished sadist 'possessing no
brains to speak of, and the last person who should have been in charge of
children', and Charlotte, compared by Munro's sister without a flicker of
irony to Catherine of Russia.[4] Masquerading under the pseudonymous
disguise of Saki, Munro carried his detestation of surrogate parents to
lengths of homicidal paranoia in short stories like 'Sredni Vashtar'. As one of
Saki's critics asks, 'Of what other writer can it be said that his life could not be
written until his aunts had died?'[5]

To be sure, there were examples of victimized children who later tried
to rationalize the default of their parents, which is perfectly understandable; the forsaken child desperately requires some sort of explanation un-
connected with his own hypothetical unlovability. Apologists for the system
have argued that not all parents are fitted for the task expected of them, and
that sometimes the surrogate parent might be a great blessing. There is
nothing wrong with this argument except that its reverse applies equally
well. Churchill lived to bless his governess, Lord Curzon to damn his to
hellfire. On the credit side there must have been many Victorian hearties like
Charles Inglis Thornton, one of the cricketing heroes of Wodehouse's
boyhood.[6] Thornton was adopted by an uncle, Archdeacon Harrison of
Canterbury, and so tenderly nurtured that he was encouraged to Emsworth-
ian heights of self-indulgence culminating in his habit of stalking game
birds in the snow while camouflaged in a white night-shirt. Such a man

appears to have suffered very little emotional deprivation, living a life of rumbustious innocence, hitting cricket balls vast distances, and whiling away his retirement in travel.

To which group did Wodehouse belong, with the fortunate Thorntons or with the victimized Maughams? At first sight it seems that he was one of the lucky ones; in apologizing for never having published a formal auto-biography, he went out of his way to assure readers that his life had been pure bliss:

> The three essentials for an autobiography are that its compiler shall have had an eccentric father, a miserable misunderstood childhood and a hell of a time at his public school, and I enjoyed none of these advantages. My father was as normal as rice pudding, my childhood went like a breeze from start to finish, with everybody I met under-standing me perfectly, while as for my schooldays at Dulwich, they were just six years of unbroken bliss.

The claim may be taken as official Wodehouse policy regarding inquiries into his emotional background. He persistently rejected critical claims that there had ever been any shadows in his childhood, and even went out of his way to warn off any future literary psychologists who might be tempted to extrapolate from his texts the *storm und drang* of deprivation:

> I wish these critics wouldn't distort facts in order to make a point. George Orwell calls my stuff Edwardian (which God knows it is. No argument about that, George) and says the reason for it being Edwar-dian is that I did not set foot in England for sixteen years and so lost touch with conditions there. Sixteen years, mark you, during most of which I was living in London and was known as Beau Wodehouse of Norfolk Street. He is also apt to take some book which I wrote in 1907 and draw all sorts of portentous conclusions from it. Dash it, in 1907 I was practically in swaddling clothes, and it was extremely creditable to me that I was able to write at all.

But in his old age Wodehouse told one of his biographers, David Jasen, that school holidays in the years when his parents were away were not always idyllic:

> We would spend our holidays with various aunts, some of whom I liked but one or two of whom were very formidable Victorian women.

Even more to the point, the same biographer writes that 'the boys felt almost like orphans during their all-important formative years'. Wodehouse added that they 'looked upon mother more like an aunt. She came home very infrequently'. His Aunt Mary, in addition to being tyrannical, compounded the crime by publishing books, and may be somewhere at the root of that long succession of soppily literary ladies who flit so ominously through Wodehouse country; certainly it would not be committing the sin of portentousness to admit that it is Aunt Mary who was subsequently immortalized as Aunt Agatha:

> Aunt Agatha is one of those strong-minded women. She has an eye like a man-eating fish. . . . My experience is that when Aunt Agatha wants you to do a thing you do it, or else you find yourself wondering why those fellows in the olden days made such a fuss when they had trouble with the Spanish Inquisition.

> When I was a kid at school she was always able to turn me inside out with a single glance. There's about five foot nine of Aunt Agatha, topped off with a beaky nose, an eagle eye and a lot of grey hair, and the general effect is pretty formidable.

In *The Mating Season*, it is suggested by her nephew Wooster that Aunt Agatha eats broken bottles and kills rats with her teeth; in *Joy in the Morning* that she wears barbed wire next to her skin and conducts human sacrifices by the light of the full moon; in *Jeeves and the Feudal Spirit* that she periodically turns into a werewolf, and that the only reason she desists from devouring her young is that the said young are generally acknowledged to be inedible. It is only in the face of Agatha that the rest of the Wodehouse aunts are made to seem half-endurable.

The remark that he 'liked one or two' of his aunts probably explains the magnificently amoral but fudamentally lovable Aunt Dahlia, whose reaction to Wooster may be summed up as tolerance towards his idiocy; she knows all about his mental deficiency but is too doting to blame him for it. She is in the habit of greeting him with the words, 'Hello, ugly', a manifestation of familial affection to which he responds by claiming her as 'the old flesh and b', 'my good and deserving aunt', and 'the only decent aunt I've got'. But even she cannot tip the scales in favour of her breed. Wodehouse's world is littered with the bleached bones of aunts who have failed to measure up to the modest requirements of common decency. Wooster is actually convinced that they are the cause of all the trouble in the world, remarking that 'it has probably occurred to all thinking men that something drastic ought to be done about aunts', even stating his willingness to enrol in any society dedicated to their suppression. He tells Jeeves that 'behind every poor, innocent, harmless blighter who is going down for the third time in the soup, you will find, if you look carefully enough, the aunt who shoved him into it'. And when Jeeves plays devil's advocate, Wooster will have none of it, insisting, 'It is no good telling me there are good aunts and bad aunts. At the core, they are all alike. Sooner or later, out pops the cloven hoof.' This opinion understandably leaves Wooster with the revealing conviction that 'if I had my life to live again, Jeeves, I would start it as an orphan without any aunts. Don't they put aunts in Turkey in sacks and drop them in the

Bosphorus?'⁷ In *The Mating Season* it is not clear whether Wooster is retailing the objective truth or describing an hallucination:

> As far as the eye could reach, I found myself gazing on a surging sea of aunts. There were tall aunts, short aunts, stout aunts, thin aunts, and an aunt who was carrying on a conversation in a low voice to which nobody seemed to be paying the slightest attention.

But the most telling proof of the proposition that aunts have little to do with humanity comes, not in relation to Wooster, but to his protector. After all, it takes little to intimidate so genial a goof as Wooster; but when Jeeves himself bows to the auntly force, we know that it is one to be reckoned with. In *Right Ho, Jeeves*, the faithful retainer says:

> 'It is a recognized fact, sir, that there is nothing that so satisfactorily unites individuals who have been so unfortunate as to quarrel among themselves as a strong mutual dislike for some definite person. In my own family, if I may give a homely illustration, it was a generally accepted axiom that in times of domestic disagreement it was necessary only to invite my Aunt Annie for a visit to heal all breaches between the other members of the household.'

And in *Ring for Jeeves*, when the servant is told by his master that he is not interested in the late Aunt Emily, Jeeves remarks that in the course of her long life few people were.

This observation, coupled with Wooster's belief that 'in this life it is not aunts that matter, but the courage that one brings to them', calls to mind a writer not generally thought to have been conscripted in the Wodehousean cause. The gentlemen's gentlemen whose impassivity is so effective a sounding board for the levities of their employers in Wodehouse have often been seen as descendants of the admirable Crichton. But, as Owen Edwards has pointed out, Crichton, admirable or not, worshipped the social system much too abjectly to be taken for the progenitor of Jeeves, whose model had first been unveiled long before Barrie wrote his play. In *Company for Henry* there is a scene in the servants' hall between a valet and butler in which the conversation is enlivened by the following exchanges:

> 'You don't like Swedes?'
> 'I disapprove of them.'
> 'Why?'
> 'Their heads are too square.'
> 'And you disapprove of the Irish?'
> 'Precisely.'
> 'Why?'
> 'Because they are Irish.'

Abandoning this promising avenue, the two servants wander down the highway of conjugal theory:

> 'I should have thought that when two people love each other and want to get married. . . .'
> 'Marriage is not a process for prolonging the life of love. It merely mummifies the corpse.'
> 'But Mr Ferris, if there were no marriages, what would become of posterity?'
> 'I see no necessity for posterity, Mr Clarkson.'

The passage, untypical of Wodehouse because the joke is expressed in direct speech rather than in the commentary upon it, is one of those frequent moments in modern literature when Phipps, who so stoically plays Jeeves to Lord Goring's Wooster in Oscar Wilde's *An Ideal Husband*, might have been tempted to sue for plagiarism. Wildean epigram appears to have been well within Wodehouse's range, but only as part of a vast armoury of comic effects ranging from the list-joke of Jerome to the dese-an-dems-an-doze weisenheimers of Damon Runyon and the pastiche which S. J. Perelman converted into an industry. He also evinces an understanding almost unknown among the formally educated of what happens to the English language when it collides with the cockney sensibility; in a passage in a short story called 'The Passing of Ambrose', Wodehouse demonstrates the neglected truth that the dropping of an aspirate creates a vacuum into which the most improbable glottal shocks are impelled to dash:

> 'Here's your rat. A little the worse for wear, this sat is, I'm afraid, sir. A gentleman happened to step on it. You can't step on a nat, not without hurting it. That tat is not the yat it was.'

The supernumerary who utters that remarkable speech works as a commissionaire, hardly a station in life demanding lofty elocutionary standards. But at the heart of the Jeeves joke lies the fact that both the fastidiousness and the omniscience reside in a hired hand. Jeeves has been measured at various times against Sancho Panza and Sam Weller among others; but while the wisdom of Panza is rooted in his vulgarity, and that of Weller in his worldliness, the wisdom of Jeeves remains imperturbable, never failing to express itself in terms of his master's gentility. Jeeves has a far better taste than Wooster in shirts, cocktails, literature, music and manners and, when his master attempts to go his own way, is ready to make the supreme sacrifice of resignation rather than be a party to some particularly offensive neck-tie or ukelele. An interesting case has been argued that the true father of Jeeves was Littimer, valet of Steerforth in *David Copperfield*, and that Beach, butler at Blandings, derives from a Mrs Hominy in *Martin Chuzzlewit* who, although neither man nor manservant, shared with Beach the gift of making 'a procession of one'.[8] But the same writer, after arguing that Littimer was infallible, then suggests that Jeeves, for all his reputation, is really a clumsy bungler because he contrives to extricate Wooster from crises only at the expense of dubbing his master an imbecile, rather in the style of Orwell defending Wodehouse. But the point about Wooster is that he *is* an imbecile. Though Jeeves can save him, he cannot reconstitute him. And however thick the clay may be down at the lower extremities just beneath Jeeves' exquisitely creased trousers, he is at least as well-read as Wodehouse himself. In a brave attempt to identify the authors to be found on Jeeves' bookshelves, the most intrepid of all Wodehousean investigators has named Spinoza, Nietzsche, Dostoevsky, Lucretius, Pliny the Younger, Whittier, Sir Edward Fitzgerald, Pater, Shelley, Kipling, Keats, Scott, Wordsworth, Emerson, Marcus Aurelius, Shakespeare, Browning, Moore, Virgil, Horace, Dickens, Tennyson, Milton, Henley, Stevenson, Gray, Burns, Byron and 'whoever it was who wrote "The Wreck of the Hesperus" '.[9]

But if this finesse is not, to quote one of Jeeves' sources, to waste its sweetness on the desert air, its possessor must find employment with a master well-enough intentioned but also foolish enough to act as a foil. Before Jeeves there were several prototypes, but it took at least twenty years for the perfect model to emerge:

> I started writing in 1902, and every day I said to myself: 'I must get a character for a series.' In 1916 I wrote the first Jeeves story. About a year later I wrote another. But it wasn't till I had done about six at long intervals that I realized I had got a series-character.

In his introduction to *The World of Jeeves*, Wodehouse is more specific:

> I find it curious, now that I have written so much about him, to recall how softly and undramatically Jeeves first entered my little world. . . .
> On that occasion, he spoke just two lines.
> The first was:
> 'Mrs Gregson to see you, sir.'
> The second:
> 'Very good, sir, which suit will you wear?'
> That was in a story in a volume entitled *The Man With Two Left Feet*. It was only some time later, when I was going into the strange affair which is related under the title of 'The Artistic Career of Corky', that the man's qualities dawned upon me. I still blush to think of the off-hand way I treated him at our first encounter.

In a sense Jeeves begat Wooster as surely as Wodehouse begat Jeeves, because it is only by disclosing his own inadequacies that Wooster, in describing his adventures, comes to life as the abject honorary secretary of the Jeeves Appreciation Society. The master's foppish insularities go in inverse proportion to his servant's cerebral ingenuities. But Wooster must be able to afford a paragon like Jeeves, which means an independent income.

And he must be genteel enough to aspire to that gentlemanly perfection which Jeeves embodies. Wooster may be a fool, but he has to be an aristocratic fool. Where did Wodehouse find his landed peerage?

The names as well as their associations were real enough. In January 1904 he was living in a house called Threepwood, near Emsworth House, a preparatory school in the village of Emsworth on the borders of Hampshire and Sussex. If Threepwood never found its fictional apotheosis, Emsworth House certainly did; its topography is preserved in *The Little Nugget*. Long before this, when his fate as a bank clerk still hung in the balance, he had known the pleasures of life in a Shropshire home in the village of Stapleford. For three years the Wodehouses rented a house there, and in 1900, with the green lamps of Lombard Street looming, he spent the summer writing in a desperate attempt to acquire the free-lance's skills. These three years left Wodehouse with an affection for Shropshire so abiding that he bestowed upon it the most priceless patrimony at his disposal, Blandings Castle. Very much later, when the Castle was famous and beloved by a generation of readers, Wodehouse became himself the occupant of such a property, called Hunstanton Hall, in Norfolk. One biographer, in describing the lake, the park, the moat, the gardens which comprised the one thousand-acre estate, called it 'a real-life Blandings Castle'; it was here, in a punt on the moat, that the tenant sat with a typewriter ingeniously balanced on a small bedside table, apparently unable to convince himself that this was reality and not some kind of fairy story of the type in which he specialized. In time the two became confused:

> It's wonderful being back at Hunstanton Hall again, though things aren't so frightfully bright at the moment, as host has had a row with butler, who has given notice. The butler is a cheery soul who used to be the life and soul of the party, joining in the conversation at meals and laughing appreciatively if one made a joke, but now he hovers like a spectre, very strong and silent. I'm hoping peace will be declared soon. I think I like Hunstanton Hall as well in winter as in summer, though of course I don't get the moat in the winter months. I laid the scene for *Money for Nothing* at Hunstanton Hall.

Familiarity with a location like Hunstanton no doubt enlarged the possibilities of Blandings, and a butler who begged to differ so violently from his employer as to resign must surely have enriched the stockpot of ideas which nurtured Jeeves and Wooster, but the most vital element in this extraordinary world-making process had already been established for many years. In 1916, in a novel called *Something Fresh*, there had occurred one of the most famous entrances in popular fiction. It had been staged in a Piccadilly hotel bedroom occupied by the Hon. Frederick Threepwood:

> An elderly, thin-faced, bald-headed, amiably vacant man entered. He regarded the Hon. Freddie with a certain disfavour.

And well he might, for the Hon. Freddie is to plague the old coot with a depressing persistence for the next sixty years. We study the man in the doorway with some interest, taking due note of his ability to make the best clothes look ruffled, the most urban atmosphere to be faintly redolent of manure, the most literately constructed sentence to degenerate into nonsense. We are gazing at Clarence, ninth Earl of Emsworth, of Blandings Castle, Shropshire, a monument to the efficacy of inbreeding and congenital amnesia, the repository of more useless lore than can be found in a thousand country-house libraries. But for all the delicate imprecision of his thought processes, Clarence, ninth Earl of Emsworth retains a firm grip on the idea of heaven and hell, which for him takes the form of pigs and the Hon. Freddie respectively; when an incredulous relative asks him if 'a miserable pig' means more to him than young Threepwood's future, the old boy is shocked that anyone should need to ask the question at all: 'Of course it does.' As the saga of Blandings proceeds, supplementing its cast-list and increasing its acreage until in the end it becomes a boundless province of paradise itself, the Earl grows more bumbling, more confused, more endearing, eventually contriving to transmogrify himself by pure absence of will power into the essence of benevolent ascendency. There is no question that he is irresponsible, fails to shoulder his feudal responsibilities, represents an obsolete society, and will have to go. But not just yet. Clarence has much to be said for him, particularly in his desire for a quiet life. He can be bought off easily enough. Give him a pig, some swill, a sizeable sty and endless leisure, and he asks no more. He is gentle to young ladies, resents the hauteur of his sister Constance, and is absolutely convinced that the Hon. Freddie was sent to punish him for some ancient misdemeanour he cannot for the moment recall.

Is Clarence capable of any misdemeanour? His rake of a brother, the Hon. Galahad, has implied as much once or twice, hinting that when they were both young, Clarence was somewhere in the offing when Galahad was pursuing the holy grail of pink-tighted Dolly Henderson down the red plush labyrinth of Edwardian London. Admittedly this career as a boulevardier appears to have been limited to an ability to mix a wonderful salad, but there are moments of abstraction when Clarence pauses in his porcine labours to hum a snatch of some ancient melody half-remembered from a night out. Did Clarence ever attend the House of Lords? We know that he brackets David Lloyd George with the Hon. Freddie as one of the two blots on the national landscape, but he hardly seems the type to allow his political convictions to take precedence over his beliefs. In the constitutional crisis of 1911, had he elected to die in the dark, or just to lie in the park? It would have depended on the whim of that ornament of the twentieth-century fictional bestiary, the Empress of Blandings.

Where did Wodehouse encounter a character like Clarence? Did he bump into him on one of those summer holidays from Dulwich College? Or glimpse him disappearing into a childhood conservatory, there to bump into the potted plants and raise his hat to a bust of one of his ancestors? In disclosing the factual origins of Psmith, Wodehouse claimed to have built all his other creations from the ground up. While taking him at his word, it would be rash not to consider the case of the eighth Duke of Devonshire (1833–1908), who three times refused the office of Prime Minister, and once invited Edward VII to dinner only to go out to get a bite at the Turf Club because the invitation had, like most other things, slipped his mind. He was notorious for his mastery of the art of falling asleep at important junctures in public life, and would sometimes be seen walking past old political colleagues with 'his mouth wide open and his eyes half closed'.[10] He kept twenty revolvers at his stately home of Chatsworth, where, on days when he opened the house to the public, he would conceal himself among the tourists and be guided around his own property:

> He liked old, baggy, casual clothes, never took the slightest trouble with his guests, deliberately ignored those who might prove tiresome, and once, when a speaker in the House of Lords was declaiming on 'the greatest moments in life', the Duke opened his eyes long enough to remark to his neighbour, 'My greatest moment was when my pig won first prize at Skipton Fair'.[11]

The Duke may or may not have been the progenitor of Clarence Earl of Emsworth but, in the case of Clarence's brother Galahad, the annals of English social history are congested with his spiritual ancestors. Galahad is one of the last survivors of a vanished breed, whose occupational therapy consisted of scaling lamp-posts on Boat Race night, gambling through the day, coming home drunk by the light of dawn, philandering with broad-minded young ladies, frequenting racecourses, casinos, music halls, clubs and any other institution where the food was good, the furniture comfortable and the morality elastic. By the time he turns up at Blandings, in *Summer Lightning*, Galahad ought to be dead but mysteriously is not; as one of the young ladies at Blandings says,

> 'It really is an extraordinary thing that anyone who has had as good a time as he has can be so amazingly healthy. Everywhere you look, you see men leading model lives pegging out in their prime, while good old Uncle Gally, who apparently never went to bed till he was fifty, is still breezing along as fit and rosy as ever.'

A moment later, Galahad gives an impressive demonstration of this fine state of preservation by tripping over a spaniel and recovering his balance without spilling a drop of the whisky-and-soda in his hand, which he 'continued to bear aloft like some brave banner beneath which he had often fought and won'. Not that he is altogether without ethical standards. When he finds his niece drinking tea he is appalled: 'Don't tell me you are ruining your inside with that poison? You be very careful how you fool about with that stuff.'

Up to this point, Galahad is no more than a pretext for standing morality on its head. It is when he begins to illustrate his theme that we begin to see where Wodehouse has been delving:

> 'Did I ever tell you about poor Buffy Struggles back in 'ninety-three? Some misguided person lured poor old Buffy into one of those temperance lectures illustrated with coloured slides, and he called on me next day ashen, poor chap – ashen. "Gally," he said, "what would you say the procedure was when a fellow wants to buy tea? How would a fellow set about it?" "Tea?" I said. "What do you want tea for?" "To drink," said Buffy. "Pull yourself together, dear boy," I said, "you're talking wildly. You can't drink tea. Have a brandy-and-soda." "No more alcohol for me," said Buffy. "Look what it does to the common earthworm." "But you're not a common earthworm," I said, putting my finger on the flaw in his argument right away. "I dashed soon shall be if I go on drinking alcohol," said Buffy. Well, I begged him with tears in my eyes not to do anything rash, but I couldn't move him. He ordered in ten pounds of the muck, and was dead inside the year.'
>
> 'Good heavens! Really?'
>
> The Hon. Galahad nodded impressively. 'Dead as a door-nail. Got run over by a hansom cab, poor dear old chap, as he was crossing Piccadilly.'

Although blood-brother to the Earl, Galahad represents a side of London life utterly opposed to the rustic protocol of Blandings Castle. With his entry across its lawns, Wodehouse is introducing a new element into his Eden, the monied younger son without the encumbrances of responsibility, ambition or guilt. But he has his own sense of humour. It may not be the same as his brother's, but it exists, and he remains steadfast to it. Just as a bishop might list his ecclesiastical battle honours for the editor of *Who's Who*, so the Hon. Galahad Threepwood has remained proud of his own, rather different achievements:

> He had been a notable lad about town. A beau sabreur of Romano's. A Pink 'Un. A Pelican. A crony of Hughie Drummond and Fatty Coleman; a brother-in-arms of the Shifter, the Pitcher, Peter Blobbs and the rest of an interesting but not strait-laced circle. Bookmakers had called him by his pet name, barmaids had simpered beneath his gallant chaff. He had heard the chimes at midnight. And when he had looked in at the old Gardenia, commissionaires had fought for the privilege of throwing him out. A man, in a word, who should never have been taught to write, and who, if unhappily gifted with that ability, should have been restrained by Act of Parliament from writing Reminiscences.

In time, when the works of Wodehouse have become sufficiently ancient to require the annotations of literary archeologists, those remarks about Galahad will call for a weighty dissertation on the lines of the one written just before Wodehouse died by his most ingenious student, N. T. P. Murphy:

> A Pink 'Un was a member of the staff of *The Sporting Times* or one of its close associates, and a Pelican was one who belonged to the club of that name that flourished between 1887 and 1892. In many cases the terms are synonymous but had in their day the same cachet as, let us say, 'M.C. and bar'.[12]

Murphy goes on to quote from two once-famous books by Arthur Binstead,[13] *A Pink 'Un and a Pelican* and *Pitcher in Paradise*, saying that 'far from creating a never-never land, Wodehouse could justly claim, as he did latterly, to be a social historian as much as a novelist'. In fact, there is hardly a scandalous anecdote in Galahad's inexhaustible repertoire which is not an echo of something which once happened to the membership of the Pelican, whose supporters welshed on gambling debts, drove cabs through its front entrance, organized ratting matches, and, in moments of financial crisis, sold each other their moustaches at a fiver a time. The parallels between the Pelican and the Drones are so unmistakable that it is extraordinary that not until Wodehouse's ninety-third year, when Murphy's essay appeared, did anybody make the connection.

But in the case of the Hon. Galahad, as in all things, Wodehouse softens the outlines of history by applying to them the brush of the romantic novelist, making the point in book after book that, rake or not, Galahad adheres to a code of conduct at least as admirable as those in current usage on the ramparts of Blandings. For Galahad, like his creator, is an impenitent romantic. Having once learned the meaning of true love, he has remained constant to that nebulous ideal ever since and, as most of the plot-making which swirls about the purlieus of Market Snodsbury concerns the desirability in the dynastic sense of this or that marriage, he is clearly one of the heaviest crosses to be borne by snobs like his sister Lady Constance, whose only contribution to Western philosophy is the theory that chorus girls ought not to be allowed. Unfortunately for her, Galahad not only approves of professional entertainers, but has never ceased to reproach himself for his failure to marry one of them in particular, a weakness which transforms him from a detached spectator of his nephew Ronnie Fish's attempts to combat his own congenital idiocy into a fearless crusader on his behalf. The Blandings connection is effected through Fish's attachment to one Sue Brown, currently employed by an impresario named Mortimer Mason, who has

> always felt a fatherly fondness for this girl Sue Brown. He liked her for her own sake, for her unvarying cheerfulness and the honest way she worked. But what endeared her more particularly to him was the fact that she was Dolly Henderson's daughter. London was full of elderly gentlemen who became pleasantly maudlin when they thought of

Dolly Henderson and the dear old days when the heart was young and they had had waists.

At the head of that maudlin company stands Galahad himself, who, ever since he lost Dolly, has wandered the fleshpots of the earth inspired by a vision of amazonian thighs hidden under pink tights. The recollection of those tights, undimmed by the vicissitudes of a spectacular career, has sustained him in enough hours of crisis to keep the Emsworth line supplied for the next five generations, and, when he discovers that Fish wants to marry the daughter of a singer at the old Tivoli, he instantly allies himself with the lovers against Lady Constance. Soon he is explaining to Sue why he never married Dolly. Apparently she left the stage and – 'Oh, well, I was rather busy at the time – lot of heavy drinking to do, and so forth – and somehow we never met. The next thing I heard – two or three years ago – was that she was dead.' At this point Wodehouse is in grave danger of echoing Galahad's mawkishness whenever the subect of Dolly Henderson is raised. He also veers as close as his sensibilities will permit him to the vexed question of sex. To Lady Constance, Galahad's attachment to Sue Brown can only be explained by some sort of illicit blood-connection. In the sequel to *Summer Lightning*, a 1933 novel called *Heavy Weather*, Ronnie's mother, Lady Julia, second only to Agatha in auntly venom, asks Constance why Galahad should continue to be so loyal to the memory of Dolly, so heroic in the cause of her daughter Sue. Constance is not sure, but Julia wonders aloud if Galahad is Sue's father. Constance replies, with some lack of confidence, 'I believe not.' Eventually Julia puts the issue of Sue's parentage before Galahad:

> 'Tell me, Gally,' said Lady Julia, 'just as a matter of interest, *is* she your daughter?'
> The Hon. Galahad bristled. 'She is not. . . .'

Indeed, not only is she not, but it seems likely that Galahad's romantic recollection of Dolly is the recollection of one who admired her from afar. At any rate, his steadfast affection for the pink tights, and his insistence that even a chorus girl can sometimes be human, marks Galahad as one of nature's gentlemen. It may be regrettable that once, at a long-lost country-house party, he conspired with Puffy Benger to steal a pig and plant it in Plug Basham's bedroom, but there are more ways than one in which a man may prove his true nobility, a proposition further borne out by one of Gally's fellow-survivors from Pelican days, Frederick, fifth Earl of Ickenham, whose contribution to empirical philosophy incorporates the golden eugenic rule never to contemplate marriage to a girl unless you can tickle her.

The benignity of the peerage is not, however, unlimited, and it should not be thought that Wodehouse pandered to that myth. Faint alliterative echoes of the Duke of Devonshire pervade the figure of one of Emsworth's less welcome acquaintances, Alaric, sixth Duke of Dunstable, whose predatory nature is confirmed by Wodehouse when he compares the Duke's social standing with that 'of a shark at a bathing resort'. The Duke is not a pretty sight; whenever his moustache foams upwards, as it frequently does, it tends to break 'like a wave on the stern and rock-bound coast of the Dunstable nose'. Nor is his physical appearance misleading, for the Duke stands, with the possible exception of Spode, as the least savoury peer of the realm. He is mercenary, greedy, callous, stupid, insensitive and hopelessly vain, for which reasons he makes an irresistible foil for Clarence, so utterly unlike him in everything except an inability to follow the simplest argument. Emsworth loathes Alaric, while Galahad is naturally contemptuous of a man who has brought odiousness to such a fine art that back in the good old days the members of the Pelican had actually blackballed him. Perception is not the Duke's strong point, which is hardly surprising in one whose grandfather once rubbed the nose of a St James's club committee member in an unsatisfactory omelette. When confronted by the enigma of Emsworth's worship of the Empress of Blandings, Dunstable responds with all the forcefulness of a certifiable lunatic. Having peered into the Empress's sty and taken a long hard look, he sums up his reactions with masterly tactlessness:

> 'Disgusting!' he said at length.
> Lord Emsworth started violently. He could scarcely believe that he had heard aright. 'What?'
> 'That pig is too fat.'
> 'Too fat?'
> 'Much too fat. Look at her. Bulging.'
> 'But my dear Alaric, she is supposed to be fat.'
> 'Not as fat as that.'
> 'Yes, I assure you. She has already been given two medals for being fat.'
> 'Don't be silly, Clarence. What would a pig do with medals? It's no good trying to shirk the issue. There is only one word for that pig – gross. She reminds me of my Aunt Horatia, who died of apoplexy during Christmas dinner. Keeled over halfway through her second helping of plum pudding and never spoke again. This animal might be her double. And what do you expect? You stuff her and stuff her and stuff her, and I don't suppose she gets a lick of exercise from one week's end to another. What she wants is a cracking good gallop every morning and no starchy foods. That would get her into shape.'

Emsworth tries to defend everything he believes in by resorting to irony, asking the Duke if he is under the impression that the Empress is about to be entered for the Derby. But it is one of life's cardinal rules never to waste irony on mental defectives. Advising Clarence not to enter the Empress for the Derby or indeed any other race, Dunstable gives as his reason the fact that 'she might not win, and then you would have had all your trouble for nothing'. Any faint lingering doubt that somewhere underneath that man-

iacal exterior there may be lurking the last vestiges of a remembered sanity
are dispelled by the realization that in his youth the Duke suffered so serious
a breach of the sensibilities as to wish to marry Lady Constance.

The geographical scope afforded to Dunstable, Emsworth and company is
almost excessively constricted. These dotty peers with their rambling properties survive in only a few of the choicer, more verdant shires, just as their
younger sons limit their bread roll-throwing contests to the back streets of
Belgravia. There are virtually no provinces in their world, nor, surprisingly,
is there much Empire. To the inhabitants of Wodehouse's books, abroad
usually means America, which usually means either New York or Hollywood; the occasional spree on the Riviera is not unknown, but otherwise
Wooster and his friends live what Thomas Cook would have considered
stunted lives. A rare departure from this unwritten law is *Ring for Jeeves*, in
which the ethics of the Raj are sadly compromised by the wealth of the New
World when Major Tubby Frobisher marries the widow of Sigsbee Rockmeteller. Wooster, who has never heard of Kuala Lumpur, let alone Sigsbee
Rockmeteller, turns for enlightenment to that pin-striped gazetteer, Jeeves,
who ends a brisk résumé of recent Malayan history with the footnote, 'Mr
Somerset Maugham has written searchingly of life in these parts'.
Wodehouse writes of them rather less searchingly but with as little rever-
ence, ridiculing the convention of romance in the undergrowth:

> He had loved this woman from the very moment she had come into his
> life. How well he remembered that moment. The camp among the
> acacia trees. The boulder-strewn cliff. Old Simba the lion roaring in the
> distance. Old Tembo the elephant doing this and that in the *bimbo* or
> tall grass . . . as he sat listening to the hyenas and gazing at the snows of
> Kilimanjaro, it had brought him within an ace of writing poetry.

But Englishmen who go out to the tropics and nearly write poetry are
destined never to be the heroes of a Wodehouse story. That signal honour is
reserved for those modest young men inclined to wander no further afield in
search of true love than that suburban paradise which had first commended
itself in early adolescence. In the early novels he refers to Dulwich by its
proper name, but slowly, as the force of his imagination wrought changes in
the local topography, he recognized the need to rechristen it. The district
became transmuted into Valley Fields, where romance beckons over privet
hedges, burglars and policemen mingle contentedly, and any thoughts of
exile are dispelled by the comforting rumble of the No. 3 bus on its way to
Piccadilly. When good Wodehouseans retire, they go to Valley Fields, like
Keggs, who buys The Hook after retiring from the service of Lord Uffenham. Nobody could blame him, for Valley Fields is 'an island valley of
Avilion where a Drone can live on a clerk's salary'.[14] Whether there is
something in the air of the place, and whether, if there is, it is that same
something which inspired the daydreams of other inhabitants like A. E. W.
Mason, Chandler and C. S. Forester, Valley Fields is oddly conducive to

romance, as the eponymous hero of *Sam the Sudden* finds when he falls for Kay Derrick. No doubt, when he attended the college, Wodehouse had taken note of the regrettable latterday tendency to split up once-comfortable suburban villas into two separate properties. It is this practice, unsuspected by Sam, which makes it so difficult for him to find the two million pounds stolen from the New Asiatic Bank. In the final chapter, when the local estate agent Mr Cornelius enlightens us all, the mystery is solved and Valley Fields can revert once more to its customary mood of contented bliss:

> Clocks had been wound, cats put out of back doors, front doors bolted and chained. In a thousand homes a thousand good householders were restoring their tissues against the labours of another day. The silver-voiced clock on the big tower over the college struck the hour of two.

In college days Dulwich had retained its rustic vestiges, just as Valley Fields did in the novels. But even Wodehouse was aware that the chances were remote of the area escaping the touch of the later twentieth century. Once upon a time, Pritchett reminds us, Dulwich represented the best of both worlds:

> For all its rusticity, Dulwich was still virtually London; from the corner of the Parade one could see the dome of St Paul's only a few miles away, and a distant slit of the Thames. [15]

It was this contiguity which explained the popularity of the college with the professional classes. But it was a contiguity which rendered it dangerously vulnerable. In *Company for Henry*, the world has moved on, but Valley Fields holds grimly to the past. At first sight, all appears to be well:

> More lawns are cultivated, more green fly squirted with whale oil solution and more garden rollers borrowed there than anywhere else south of the Thames. Spreading trees line its thoroughfares.

The tranquillity is misleading. Satan, disguised as a property speculator, is edging up towards the trim hedges and the neatly barbered front gardens:

> I got into conversation with this bloke, and I found him in peevish mood. It seemed that he was an old inhabitant and it was his opinion that all these building operations that were going on in its midst were turning Valley Fields from a peaceful rural retreat into a sort of suburban Manchester. He said he was thankful that he was clearing out.

Later in the story, the hero, engaged in the customary Wodehousean pursuit of trying to win a female heart by stealing a paperweight, ruminates on what is happening to the suburb:

In holding up these Croxley Road building boffins he knew he was morally justified. They had no business coming defiling a charming oasis like Valley Fields with their beastly blocks of flats.

A strong case could be made out that in bowing in this way to progress or, at any rate, to change, Wodehouse was guilty of one of his very rare tactical solecisms, and that the novelist intent on constructing his own world, which was, of course, what Wodehouse spent his entire life doing, must ignore such incidentals as the despoliation of the landscape. It is an extremely delicate issue because, although the dream-existence of Emsworth, Wooster, Sam the Sudden and the rest of them is unique to Wodehouse, it does have its wellspring in reality. Psmith, Blumenfield and the Earl of Emsworth are by no means the only leading players to strike chords of realism. One of the most distinguished of all the inhabitants of their world, the great Stanley Featherstonehaugh Ukridge, can claim not one factual antecedent but two. Scholars have confirmed that Ukridge owes much to one Herbert W. Westbrook, whose friendship with Wodehouse dates back to the day in 1903 when he arrived at Plum's digs with a letter of introduction from a mutual friend at the Lombard Street bank. It was through Westbrook that Wodehouse found Emsworth House, where Westbrook was working as an assistant master; by 1904 he was considered worthy of an official acknowledgment of friendship, which he received in the form of the dedication to be found in *The Gold Bat*: 'To that Prince of Slackers, Herbert Westbrook.' Events now moved fast. By 1905 Wodehouse, aspiring to mastery of the banjo just as many years later Wooster was to do, purchased an instrument which Westbrook took the first opportunity to pawn. Soon afterwards, Townend wrote to his friend describing the tribulations of someone he knew in attempting to make a paying concern out of a chicken farm. The upshot was Ukridge's début, in *Love Among the Chickens*. In 1907 Westbrook actually collaborated with Wodehouse in the writing of one of the least known items in the oeuvre, *Not George Washington*, in which the two writers appear as Clyster and Eversleigh. Westbrook, who also shared duties with Wodehouse for a while on the 'By The Way' column, then fades out of the scenario – except that his peccadilloes and his generally felonious attitude towards life are perpetuated in the ambitions and piratical get-rich-quick schemes of Ukridge. In *Goodbye to All That*, Robert Graves says:

> The first distinguished writer I remember meeting after Swinburne was P. G. Wodehouse, a friend of my brother Perceval, whom he later gently caricatured as 'Ukridge'. Wodehouse was then in his early twenties, on the staff of *The Globe* and writing school stories for *The Captain* magazine. He gave me a penny, advising me to get marsh-mallows with it. Though too shy to express my gratitude at the time, I have never since permitted myself to be critical about his work. [16]

The same could not be said for Perceval Graves, who appeared to find the whole subject of Wodehouse distasteful, and could claim neither the close personal contact nor the mutual affection that Westbrook boasted, and it is surely affection which lies at the heart of Ukridge's genesis. He remains one of the greatest of all Wodehouse's creations, having suffered partial eclipse through no fault of his own but for the same unfortunate reason which afflicted Psmith, which is that their creator simply stopped thinking of things for them to do. It is in the Ukridge stories, even more than those featuring Kid Brady, that the reader may savour the fruits of a lifetime's appetite for prize-fighting; although Wilberforce 'Battling' Billson will clearly never contend for anything more elevated than the wooden spoon of the Ratcliff Highway, he remains one of the most memorable athletes of the century, and one whose Arthurian tendencies once inspired him to pull his punches after learning that his opponent had been up all night nursing his wife who had burned her hand at the local jam factory.

Whether Ukridge is Westbrook unalloyed, or with a dash of Graves, or whether he is pure Wodehouse, he is essentially ageless, just as Market Snodsbury is timeless, and Valley Fields ought to be but is no longer since the saddening information contained in *Company for Henry*. Property speculators do not fit into Wodehouse's dream of England, and it is after all a dream of England that he spent his life concocting. Whether in the padded cell at Tost or the punt in the moat at Hunstanton Hall or the room in Greenwich Village, that is what he was doing, using as his raw materials the clues provided by reality: a house called Threepwood, a village called Emsworth, a duke called Devonshire, a D'Oyly Carte heir called Rupert. All his schools were Dulwich, all his shires Shropshire, all his gentlemen's gentlemen a Brixtonian called Reginald Jeeves, so named because Wodehouse had noted the methods of one of his great heroes, Sir Arthur Conan Doyle, who had discovered the names Sherlock and Mycroft in the pages of *Wisden's Cricketers' Almanack*.

Wodehouse's exile from England, part self-imposed, part dictated by events beyond his control, was beneficial and perhaps in the end essential to his purpose. In his fictions, England slumbers through an Edwardian afternoon never to be disturbed. Beyond the walls of Blandings Castle and out beyond the railings of the Drones Club, Time proceeds, but curiously it has no effect on the dream. Archie Moffam has gone through Flanders Fields, motor cars race to and from Market Snodsbury, talking pictures obliterate the snorts of the Empress of Blandings, and modern musical comedy generously donates its daughters to the landed aristocracy. But the essential element, the sensibility of the characters, that is, the sensibility of their creator, remains irrevocably Edwardian. And although Wodehouse did live in England, at least in the physical sense, for many years after the Edwardians had disappeared into history, although he was perceptive enough to note modern trends in totalitarian insanity, he saw what he saw through an Edwardian window which, because of his detachment from events, remained unclouded by the decades. The first rule for those who wish to preserve an essence is to flee from it the moment it begins to change. Wodehouse's defender Sir Compton Mackenzie has described how, in his determination to maintain the Cornish town of Helston in the same state of perfect repair in which it had been during his youth, he achieved this end by staying away from the place for the rest of his life. In the same way, Wodehouse, who spent the last thirty years of his life in Long Island, never saw Dulwich encroached upon by London proper, never beheld the skyscrapers towering over the Mound Stand at Lord's, never stayed to witness the sale of the West End gentlemen's clubs to the highest bidder, or the extinction of the valet or a thousand other changes to his old homestead.

Of all the English writers of the century, the one who has the most in common with Wodehouse is perhaps Max Beerbohm, another incurable Edwardian who put style before environment. The Incorrigible Max once likened Wodehouse to the juggler Cinquevalli, no doubt because in comparing him with a music-hall artist instead of with a writer he was observing his own golden rule of never taking any of his contemporaries seriously. Yet it is the begetter of Zuleika Dobson more than anyone else who has something to tell us about the begetter of Bertie Wooster. For each man adopted the identical strategy, switching the location of his life in order to preserve intact the location of his art. No doubt Beerbohm's motives in settling for the Mediterranean were very different from Wodehouse's reasons for choosing Remsenburg, Long Island. But it is not cause but effect which will interest posterity. Max seems to have elected for the Riviera as an act of renunciation, Wodehouse for America because by then it had literally become his second home at a point in his life when his native land seemed to have disowned him.

It is perfectly understandable that few of his fellow-professionals appreciated what was happening to Wodehouse's art, any more than he himself did in any conscious way. On the contrary, it seems from his letters to Townend concerned with the structure of the novel that very often he struggled with the wrong problems, or rather, he struggled with irrelevancies after having solved the vital questions without even considering them. The riddle is well posed by Frank Swinnerton, the shrewdest assessor of current prices in the literary stock market. Having kept a close watch on Wodehouse's work over a long period, Swinnerton reached the following conclusion:

> He will show you exactly how young men of the brainless class might talk and think if they had been struck with the lunacy of genius, will phonetically record the speech of a man who has had pepper thrown in his face, will as readily give you the speech of a prize-fighter or a country policeman in pain or delight as the shrewd interchanges of a dashing young woman and the man of her heart or the subterfuges of a supposedly reformed character trying to turn an honest penny by means of begging letters. Whatever he does, he will make you believe that he does it upon the spur of the moment. His books have an irresistible air of improvisation. They continue from scene to scene as if there were nothing in life but preposterousness.[17]

Swinnerton concludes from this that the long novels are less satisfying than the short stories. But this is to assume that we read Wodehouse for the reasons which Wodehouse meant us to when he laboured with such terrible persistence to iron every last wrinkle out of his plots. What really endears him to his readers is not the working-out of the story, nor even the characters who carry it along, but the language in which the tale is told. Swinnerton's suggestion that Wodehouse can make us hear the smalltalk of a great gallimaufry of characters is a perceptive half-truth; what we do hear is the expression of this comic throng filtered through the sensibility of their creator. When Corky, narrator of the Ukridge anecdotes, witnesses the routing of a bellicose barman by Battling Billson, what he sees is an amorphous mass of beery unsociability flung out on its ear; what the reader is told is that the barman 'shot out as if impelled by some imperious force and did a sort of backwards foxtrot across the pavement'. The foxtrot metaphor remains with us long after the plot has faded, just as we can never forget that while Emsworth's remorse for having sired a cretin like Freddie is a commonplace emotion, Wodehouse elevates it to the realms of the unforgettable simply by the way in which he arranges his order of words:

> Years before, when a boy, and romantic as most boys are, his lordship had sometimes regretted that the Emsworths, though an ancient clan, did not possess a family curse. How little he had suspected that he was shortly to become the father of it.

Once again, the ramifications of the plot are forgotten in the face of such felicitous phrase-making. Emsworth himself could never express the idea in the way it has been expressed for him by an invisible chronicler, which is why over the years so many attempts to dramatize Wodehouse's fiction, that is, to render it into direct speech, have ended in disaster.

Swinnerton's anxiety about the plots, that 'reason may keep breaking in; actions may appear to have some fortuitousness; that significant form to which Clive Bell attaches such importance may vanish under scrutiny', is understandable but misplaced. In his finest work Wodehouse achieved convolutions of plot so dizzying that after a while even the most tenacious reader begins to lose his grip on things, and might be tempted, as Swinnerton suggests, to fling the book aside, were it not that by the time this stage is reached, usually about two-thirds the way through the narrative, he has been conditioned to the expectation of stylistic delights to tickle his fancy. The acute shrewdness of Swinnerton's appraisal cannot mask the fact that in rejecting the novels because of their confusing plots he is overlooking their true glory. In the sense that the structure of a Wodehouse novel is too baroque by far to be grasped at a single reading, or to be encompassed by a conventional dust-jacket précis, Swinnerton is right; a short story on the other hand is compact enough for us to hang on long enough for the working-out of the story. But this is to miss the point about Wodehouse which renders him unique, which is that alone among novelists, of either the comic or any other kind, he has, through the sheer virtuosity of his phrase-making, rendered everything else irrelevant. Plot becomes secondary, characterization utterly dependent on the narrator's voice, theme piffling, locale incidental. Nothing matters but the language, which sparkles and scintillates, twisting and turning down the most arcane byways of syntactical and exegetical mannerism, at last hypnotizing the reader, who is reduced, to borrow a Wodehouse epithet, to the status of an ostrich goggling at a brass doorknob. In effect, Wodehouse has reduced the Novel to pure style. What inevitably occurs in reading works like *The Code of the Woosters* or *A Pelican at Blandings* is that the reader, finally having lost his grasp of events, agrees to be led like a child down labyrinthine corridors of plot to the deep sigh of the denouement, having been beguiled on his journey by the exquisite beauty of the countryside, that is, the vocabulary. Very few readers can resist the temptation, when nearing the end of the journey, to race at triple speed through the last chapter, because the plot about the cow-creamer, or the scarab, or the paperweight, or the portrait, or the manuscript, which at first seemed so important to them and has, paradoxically, remained important to the author throughout, now hardly matters at all; which is why, without the text in front of him, the general reader finds it so difficult to distinguish *Summer Lightning* from *Heavy Weather*, *The Code of the Woosters* from *The Luck of the Bodkins*, *Galahad at Blandings* from *A Pelican at Blandings*. And yet, long after these books have been put aside, felicities continue to echo through the mind. The slamming of doors continues to raise the dust in the corridors of Blandings, and the abdominal rumblings of Beach reverberate dimly long after the pretext for his appearance has vanished from the mind. The point is well-made by A. J. P. Taylor:

> If plot were all, P. G. Wodehouse would count as an author of adventure stories. In fact, what mattered with Wodehouse was his style. He ranked with Congreve and Ronald Firbank as a master of exquisite, fantastic prose . . . the picture of the inter-war Englishman, particularly of the middle class, is incomplete unless we see him reading thrillers, detective stories, and P. G. Wodehouse.[18]

Taylor's nomination of 'inter-war' as the archetypal Wodehouse period is amplified by Wilfrid Sheed in the most perceptive of all critical essays on the subject.[19] Significantly, Sheed is a Briton living in America, as Wodehouse was, which helps him to take a more detached view of Emsworth and company than most of Wodehouse's British readers. Sheed, who deduces from photographic evidence that Wodehouse's mother made 'a perfect Lady Constance' and his father 'a sublime Lord Emsworth', sees the Great War as the 'incubation period', the time when the archetypal Wodehouse novel evolved from a light romance to the moonshine of his prime.[20] He also sees Wodehouse as a relentless bowdlerizer of unpleasantness, excising the pain from his own childhood, making a joke out of Duff Cooper, softening the asperities of the war between the classes:

The horrors of a class society, where dotty, monomaniac peers and their idiot sons littered the landscape and leeched off the rest of England, are magically made to vanish, to be replaced by the more manageable horrors of schoolboy convention. For instance, the only character outside the servants' hall who actually works for a living, namely the secretary, Baxter, is promoted into a monster, because he's too *serious*. Efficiency, which is good in Jeeves, is bad in Baxter. The author's commentary, which is as musically insistent as Jane Austen's, assures that we will feel this. Likewise, when the benighted Lady Constance does something decent like inviting a foreign poet to stay over, we know right away that this is potty and pretentious of her and that the poet will be a fraud. On the other hand, when Lord Emsworth, a ghastly bore, tells Psmith, a posturing wastrel, that the latter is all right because he doesn't look like a poet, we wholeheartedly agree that this is a good thing. Emsworth in fact can't follow a word Psmith says, but he knows a gentleman when he sees one.[21]

In nominating *Leave It to Psmith* (1923) as the watershed of Wodehouse's creative life, the moment where he is seen to abandon once and for all the light romantic novel in favour of diaphanous verbal sorcery, Sheed is selecting the stage in the author's life when Blandings Castle is finally established once and for all as the nerve-centre of the principality. The ex-public school, ex-bank clerk dasher breaches the walls of the landed aristocracy to win the hand of the beautiful Eve Halliday – after which he disappears for ever from the saga, his subsequent career as much a mystery to Wodehouse as it remains to the rest of us.

Sheed says of Psmith's creator that 'nobody ever struggled harder to suppress his genius in the interests of amiable tripe', but acknowledges the apparent contradiction that 'his only business was art'. That the contradiction was indeed only apparent is suggested by the probability that what the diffident, no-side Old Alleynian did was not to suppress his genius, but only its outward manifestations, so that the performer of Balzacian literary labours became concealed behind the façade of an old goof. It is certainly true that his only business was art. Wodehouse appears to have had no smalltalk except work, no relaxation except work, no religious conviction, no view of anything except through the distorting prism of his own art. When he died, on 14 February 1975, he left sixteen chapters of an unfinished novel which eventually appeared as *Sunset at Blandings*. There they all still were, trotting about their timeless world, Gally still flinging the morality of the Pelicans against the castle walls, Clarence still drooping over the Empress's sty 'like a wet sock and gazing at its occupant with a rapt expression', the Hon. Freddie still bravely attempting to cope with the consequences of his own imbecility. What had once seemed like interminable repetition had grown into a beloved ritual, as Wodehouse suspected it might. In 1929, in the preface to *Summer Lightning*, this mild-mannered man who all his life had poked fun at aesthetes without ever admitting that he was himself one, rounded on his reviewers in a typically facetious gesture of defiance:

> A certain critic – for such men, I regret to say, do exist – made the nasty
> remark about my last novel that it contained 'all the old Wodehouse
> characters under different names'. He has probably now been eaten by
> bears, like the children who made a mock of the prophet Elija; but if he
> still survives he will not be able to make a similar charge against
> *Summer Lightning*. With my superior intelligence, I have out-
> generalled the man this time by putting in all the old Wodehouse
> characters under the same name. Pretty silly it will make him feel, I
> rather fancy.

And so this gravely comic moralist, who preferred chorus girls to duchesses,
lyric writers to poets, most servants to most of their employers, and almost
anybody to bishops, headmasters, soldiers, politicians and aunts, having
quietly cast himself in the unlikely role of an Old Testament prophet, placed
himself beyond the reach of all critical canons except his own. He published
a hundred volumes of prose, wrote eighteen plays and contributed all or part
of thirty-three musical comedies. Happily married for sixty-one years to a
dedicated wife, he put what social talent he had into his life, wisely reserving
his genius for his work.

Epilogue

On the day after the death of P. G. Wodehouse, I was practising one of my favourite hobbies, which is getting comfortably lost in the back lanes of rustic south Hertfordshire, when it struck me, as we passed the ginger tom drowsing in the forecourt of 'The Cricketers' and the trusting donkey nibbling the ragged fringe of the hedgerow just beyond, that the England which Wodehouse must have remembered has changed a little less than in despondent moments we sometimes assume. We passed through a shallow valley overlooked by the turretted hauteur of just such a greystone country house whose corridors once echoed to the maladroit skitter of Gussie Fink-Nottle; up on the roof, where the flag was still flying, perhaps Madeline Bassett had once gazed into the night sky contemplating God's daisy chain. In the village at the end of the valley the eyes of china elephant bookends peeped out from behind the curtains of a semi-detached called 'Mon Repos', a name which will always stand for *Sam the Sudden*, whose entire plot hinges on the issue of where 'Mon Repos' ends and 'San Raphael' begins.

Since the day when he disclosed his dream of England, Wodehouse, in the course of one of the most fantastical of all literary careers, has inadvertently become an ideological battleground where the right-wing fanatics praise him with hysterical extravagance at the same time as left-wing doctrinaires positively froth at the mouth with loathing for him. In fact the innocuous, pipe-smoking, dog-and-cat-loving, abnormally normal Wodehouse has turned out to be the most catastrophic subject in the entire Eng.Lit. curriculum, seen invariably through either the red haze of Sean O'Casey's misty telescope – 'English Literature's performing flea' – or the milky opaqueness of Belloc's eccentric perspective – 'best writer of English now living . . . head of my profession'. And the moment one examines the relationship between the life and the work it becomes clear enough where the contradiction lies.

Wodehouse's critics, both for and against, having confused the social implications of his characters with the sober industry that created them, have tripped up over the most priceless of paradoxes, which is that Wodehouse contrived to build his towering monument to the efficacy of idling only by submitting himself all his life to a routine of grinding labour. This would presumably explain how Orwell, who is said to have lost so much sleep over the way others used the language, could misuse it himself so hilariously by describing as 'a wealthy parasite . . . almost incapable of imagining a desirable job' the author of one hundred and fifty literary works. Into his dream of England Wodehouse poured his brain-children, the most diversified gallery of eccentrics in comic fiction, ranging from the Pooteresque to the Runyonesque, inspired loons who think nothing of attributing *Hamlet* to Robert Burns or 'He is inebriated with the exhuberance of his own verbosity' to Jack Dempsey. Like every dedicated comedian, Wodehouse crammed his mind with as much useless knowledge as he could take on board, from the fact that the jazz musician Artie Shaw married nine times (see *The Mating Season*) to the fact that H. G. Wells once inscribed above the fireplace of a room in his mistress's home the announcement 'Two Lovers Built This House' (see *The Code of the Woosters*), from the Edwardian period in the development of Manchester United FC (see *Psmith in the City*) to the going rate for a photogenic gorilla in the emergent days of talking pictures (see the revelations of Mr Mulliner).

At various times critics have seen in all this relentless frivolity, and in the glorification of the peerage, an influence for the bad on the egalitarian spirit of the age. Neither Orwell nor O'Casey nor any of the others need have worried. The liberal spirit is not so susceptible to corruption that it is liable to collapse in the face of a funny earl or a deferential valet. In any case, there are always Sidcup and Dunstable to redress the balance against obsequiousness. Wodehouse made an infinite number of amusing remarks in his lifetime, invented a teeming population of clowns. The dream he dreamed of the England he preferred to the real one is an amusing dream, a vividly conceived and tightly constructed dream, but above all it is benign. Posterity may take the hint that the professional writers who have expressed a fondness for the dream or an admiration of the methods by which it was achieved, have been the hard workers in the fraternity: men like Arnold Bennett, who thanked Wodehouse for being the one humorist who 'can divert the whole town';[1] like Edmund Wilson, who, although not equipped to savour the joke, admitted that America had been pervaded by a kind of 'Anglo-American jargon in the insouciant British tradition, which I believe to be mainly the creation of the Englishman P. G. Wodehouse';[2] like Malcolm Muggeridge, who invoked the craft of letters, 'at which he has been so incomparable a practitioner. Something for which fellow practitioners must always honour and hope to emulate him'.[3] Perhaps the best summary of all, and the one which can stand as the last word on a very remarkable man, is Frank Swinnerton's. In the course of placing the creator of Wooster, Jeeves and company in the context of his time, Swinnerton wrote: 'In a period when laughter has been difficult, he has made men laugh without shame.'[4]

Notes to the text

Prologue
1 John Stuart Mill dismissed the British Empire as 'a system of outdoor relief for the upper classes'.

1 Schoolboy at Dulwich
1 G. M. Young, *Victorian Essays* (Oxford University Press, 1962), p. 136.
2 Thomas Hughes (1822–1896) was a jurist, radical reformer and writer whose life affords an interesting example of the ironies implicit in the methods of Dr Thomas Arnold of Rugby School, the most renowned and influential schoolmaster of the nineteenth century. Arnold's attempts to turn boys into gentlemen had the effect on Hughes of turning a gentleman into a boy, for Hughes remained a schoolboy all his life. His days at Rugby were the climacteric of his experience, and in 1858 he published *Tom Brown's Schooldays*, an attempt to convey to the 'simple readers' of the lower orders the spirit of public-school life; it was also a fictionalized autobiography of sorts, for there is no question that Hughes saw much of himself in the idealized Tom of the Brown clan 'who are scattered over the whole Empire, on which the sun never sets'. With reference to Wodehouse's approach to school fiction, it is revealing that Tom's father sends him to Rugby so that he might emerge as 'a brave, helpful, truth-telling Englishman, and a gentleman, and a Christian, that's all I want'.
3 Frederick Denison Maurice (1805–1872) was a Christian Socialist and free-thinking idealist who attempted to call the Victorian gentleman to his duty, which was to spread the gospel of education and enlightenment, or Platonism, among the lower orders. In 1848 he opened a night school which steadily developed into the Working Men's College, a development which breached his academic career when he was dismissed from his post of Professor of English Literature and Modern History at King's College, London. Among his disciples was Thomas Hughes and among his sympathizers Ruskin, Carlyle, Charles Kingsley and Thomas Arnold's son Matthew.
4 Reed was hopelessly at sea, however, the moment he attempted to break out of the quadrangle; his adult novel, *Give a Dog a Bad Name*, featuring a hero who strives to make amends after being implicated in a fatal accident on the football field, deserves its honoured niche in the Stuffed Owl room of the museum of Victorian literary culture.
5 Phil May (1864–1903) was the Leeds-born self-taught virtuoso who became the most renowned black-and-white comic illustrator of the Nineties. Dogged by a feeble constitution, he over-indulged bohemian tendencies, pushing himself beyond reasonable limits, but in his short life certainly achieved immortality. In 1885 he sailed to Australia to fill the post of cartoonist on the *Sydney Bulletin*. On his return five years later, he became a star of the popular illustrated press, especially at *Punch*. His cartoons of the life of the London poor are informed by personal experience, and are remarkable for an economy of line that he maintained even when straying outside his

usual province, as in his brilliant sketch of Mr Gladstone on the Treasury Bench, 1893. Once, when chided by an editor for not filling everything in, he replied, 'When I can leave out half the lines I now use, I shall want six times the money.'

6   *Vice Versa*, first published in 1882 by the comic novelist Thomas Anstey Guthrie (1856–1934), tells the fantastic story of the schoolboy Dick Bultitude whose father, in an attempt to lift his son's spirits at the end of the holidays when a return to school is imminent, says, 'I only wish I could be a boy again like you'. Because at the time of his utterance he is holding a magic stone, Bultitude Senior is taken at his word, after which he and his son find themselves living in each other's body.

7   Henry B. Farnie (d.1889) was the author and adaptor of musical farces. His heyday was around the time of Wodehouse's birth. By the time of publication of *A Prefect's Uncle*, his vogue was over. In 1893, Bernard Shaw, reviewing an old-fashioned operetta, criticized the libretto with the remark, 'The late H. B. Farnie was for an age, but not for all time.'

8   The assumption that his readers would be intimately familiar with the texts of the Savoy Operas was one which Wodehouse soon dropped after graduating from school stories to adult fiction.

9   Albert Trott (1873–1914), who played cricket for England *and* Australia, was one of the great off-break bowlers of the epoch, and the only man ever to hit a ball over the top of the Lord's pavilion. Trott took his own life at his Harlesden lodgings on the eve of the Great War.

10   The Aerated Bread Company had many branches in large cities, dispensing tea and light refreshments to the urban respectable poor.

11   William Yardley (1849–1900), who played cricket for Rugby, Cambridge, the Gentlemen and Kent, twice scored a century against Oxford at Lord's. He subsequently dabbled in dramatic criticism, and eventually enjoyed a highly successful career as a writer of farces and burlesques, notably for the Gaiety Theatre.

12   Thomas Arnold (1795–1842), educator, Fellow of Oriel College, Oxford, became headmaster of Rugby School in 1828, and, by concentrating less on academic distinction than on gentlemanly codes of conduct, raised Rugby to the heights among the public schools of England. Among his innovations was a reliance on prefects. His influence on all other schools of the period was profound.

13   *Cashel Byron's Profession*, a novel written by Bernard Shaw in the days of his obscurity and published in serial form in 1886, was well known to Wodehouse as the original of those pugilistic romances whose hero combines an infallible boxing technique with the manners of an exquisite.

14   Michael Colin Cowdrey, so named by a father zealous to echo the initials of the Marylebone Cricket Club, was one of the most gifted English cricketers of the post-Second-World-War period. Born in 1932, his career straddled the age in which the distinction between paid and unpaid players, or between Gentlemen and Players as it had always been known, was abolished. From 1963 until his retirement he, like all other ex-Amateurs, was a hired hand, a status wildly incongruous to a flower of the old school like Wodehouse, who never quite grasped the enormity of the social revolution which the altered situation of men like Cowdrey represented.

15   The Fosters were the seven sons of a Malvern parson, a brotherhood who so dominated the emergent years of the Worcestershire county side that it became known as Fostershire. The brothers were H.K. (1873–1950); W.L. (1874–1958); R.E. (1878–1914); B.S. (1882–1959); G.W. (1884–1971); M.K. (1889–1940); N.T. (1890–1978). The greatest was R.E.; the most Wodehousean H.K., Amateur Rackets Champion of England, who declined to play cricket for his country because he 'did not care for Test cricket'.

16   From an interview by Richard Usborne in *The Guardian*, September 1971.

17   Richard Usborne, *Wodehouse at Work to the End* (Barrie & Jenkins, 1976), p. 78.

18   Owen Dudley Edwards, *P. G. Wodehouse* (Martin Brian & O'Keeffe, 1977), p. 42.

19   *The World of Psmith* (Barrie & Jenkins, 1974), preface.

20   *Ibid.*

21   Barbara Tuchman, *The Proud Tower* (Macmillan, 1966), p. 360.

22   J. B. Priestley, *English Humour* (Heinemann, 1976), p. 108–9.

23   W. O. Lofts and D. J. Adley, *The World of Frank Richards* (Baker Press, 1975), p. 106.

24   S. C. Griffith, CBE, DFC (Dulwich, Cambridge, Sussex and England); Secretary, MCC 1962–74; President, MCC 1979–80. He named his son Mike after Wodehouse's character, Mike Jackson.

25   Frank MacShane, *The Life of Raymond Chandler* (Cape, 1976), p. 9.

26   *Ibid.*, p. 10.

27   *Ibid.*, p. 9.

28   Wilkie Bard (1874–1944) and George Robey (1869–1954) were among the most renowned comedians of the old music hall. Both specialized in 'dame' roles and the impersonation of formidable middle-aged women. One of Wodehouse's contemporaries, Sir Neville Cardus, shared with him an idolatry of Bard and Robey, being torn between Robey's Mother Goose and Bard's depiction of a cockney charwoman who, in mid-scrub, bursts into 'I Want to Sing in Opera'.

29   V. S. Pritchett, *A Cab at the Door* (Penguin, 1979), p. 88.

30   *Ibid.*

31   *Ibid.*, p. 114.

32   V. S. Pritchett, *London Perceived* (Chatto & Windus/Heinemann, 1962), p. 49.

2 Bank clerk in Lombard Street

1 Hall Caine (1853–1931) was the ponderous best-selling author of unreadable and very nearly unwriteable books with titles like *The Deemster*, *The Christian* and *The Manxman*. Of all Victorian literary lions, Caine shrank most quickly and most completely to the proportions of a pipsqueak. Arnold Bennett expressed a tolerance for Caine's books provided the proprietors of Mudie's circulating library did not force him at gunpoint to read one, and Shaw, writing in 1895 of *The Manxman*, said, 'I have not read the celebrated novel, and am prepared to go to the stake rather than face the least chapter of it.' There is contradictory evidence of Caine's appearance: Frank Swinnerton claims to have spotted Caine, 'black-coated, black-hatted, sweeping down the street like a giant black moth', but in Beerbohm's celebrated cartoon, 'Rossetti and his Circle', Caine is seen to be red-headed, red-moustached and goateed. Beerbohm also claimed that Caine was so ridiculous that at Edwardian parties you could raise a laugh simply by pronouncing his name.

2 Although Bickersdyke's drift to the Right is made to fling a dark shadow across his ethical stance, he was, after all, guilty of nothing more serious than the tactic adopted by dozens of Liberal Unionists in the wake of Mr Gladstone's Home Rule policy. It is revealing that the most notorious Liberal defector of all, Joseph Chamberlain, had in 1906 been the victim of Wodehouse's first successful song lyric (see chapter 4, p. 100).

3 Edwards, *P. G. Wodehouse*, pp. 45–6.

4 The Eatanswill election in chapter 13 of *Pickwick Papers*, contested by Messrs Slumkey and Sizkin, included among its features the locking-up of voters in coach-houses in order to keep them in a state of perpetual drunkenness without exposing them to the temptation of opposition bribes, the sobering-up of prospective supporters under the town pump at a shilling a head, and the dosing of the local brandy supply with laudanum. In Anthony Trollope's *Phineas Redux*, Phineas Finn is defeated at the Tankerville by-election when his Tory opponents buy votes at so much a head. These bought votes are subsequently declared void and Finn awarded a belated victory.

5 Wodehouse's collaborator in the genial musical lampooning of Joseph Chamberlain was Jerome Kern, who confessed, 'I had some European training in a small town outside of Heidelberg' (Gerald Bordman, *Jerome Kern: his Life and Music*, Oxford University Press, 1980, p. 23).

6 Samuel Hynes, *The Edwardian Turn of Mind* (Oxford University Press, 1968), p. 40.

7 *Ibid.*, pp. 48–9.

8 The first crime to be committed by Bickersdyke in *Psmith in the City*, establishing his irredeemable blackguardism once and for all, is to be instrumental in Mike Jackson's dismissal when the latter needs only two for his century, by walking in front of the sight screen.

9 Edwards expressed concern in his study of Wodehouse that the joke might later have offended Wodehouse's musical partner, Jerome Kern. However, as the partnership and resulting friendship between the two men had been struck long before publication of *The Swoop*, one assumes that Kern, if he knew of the text, would have laughed at it.

10 In Act I of *The Gondoliers*, Gilbert postulates a Republican Utopia bestowing parity on

The Aristocrat who banks with Coutts,
The Aristocrat who cleans the boots.

In Act II, the theme is developed with a description in a song called 'When Every One is Somebody, Then No-one's Anybody':

On every side Field-Marshals gleamed,
Small beer were Lords-Lieutenant deemed,
With Admirals the oceans teemed.

11 The 'child' was born in 1884, three years after Wodehouse, and, by one of those curious quirks of circumstance, was to follow Wodehouse into the gaseous world of musical comedy. At the end of the Edwardian era, Knox resigned from the Surrey side in order to become a musical comedy singer, and by 1910 had risen to the eminence of the cast of *The Dollar Princess* at Daly's Theatre, where he understudied Basil Foster – of Malvern, Middlesex and Worcestershire.

12 J. M. Barrie, *The Greenwood Hat* (Peter Davies, 1930), p. 19.

13 From an interview on BBC radio, 1970.

14 Janet Adam Smith, *John Buchan and His World* (Thames & Hudson, 1979), p. 27.

15 Barrie, *The Greenwood Hat*, p. 272.

16 Denis Mackail, *The Story of J.M.B.* (Peter Davies, 1941), p. 165.

17 H. G. Wells, *Experiment in Autobiography* (Gollancz, 1934), p. 371.

3 Free-lance in New York

1 James J. Corbett was World Heavyweight Champion, 1892–97.

2 James J. Jeffries was World Heavyweight Champion, 1899–1905.

3 Tom Sharkey was defeated by Jeffries in a championship match in 1899.

4 Norman Selby, alias Kid McCoy, won the World Welterweight title in 1896. Notorious as a cruel and devious fighter, he was married ten times to eight different women, and served eight years in a penitentiary after the death of one of them. He is the only boxing champion to have been challenged by Wodehouse (see chapter 3, pp. 66–7).

5 Corbett had knocked out the champion, John J. Sullivan, in 1892. After his retirement he went on the stage and in 1906 portrayed the hero in an adaptation of Bernard Shaw's novel, *Cashel Byron's Profession*. In connection with Wodehouse's knowledge of and interest in boxing, the fighter who fills the missing two-year gap between the reigns of Corbett and Jeffries is the Cornishman Bob Fitzsimmonds, who knocked out Corbett with his invention, the Solar Plexus punch, whose effect of inducing in the recipient a

temporary preoccupation with attempting to breathe was used by Wodehouse in *The Little Nugget* to describe the distress of the narrator: 'Of all cures for melancholy introspection a violent blow in the solar plexus is the most immediate. If Mr Corbett had any abstract worries that day in Carson City, I fancy they ceased to occupy his mind from the moment when Mr Fitzsimmonds administered that historic left jab.'

6   Philadelphia Jack O'Brien was the professional alias of John Hagen, a considerable fighter whose appreciation of his own eminence led him to travel to professional engagements accompanied by a valet and a private secretary. His appetite for the niceties of polite intercourse is conveyed by the fact that when a London boxing announcer described him as being from 'Americaw', O'Brien decided that the 'sonorousness of the effect compensates for the redundancy'. His ethics, however, did not always live up to his vocabulary. When, as the proprietor of a gymnasium, he was confronted for rent arrears by his landlord, a dropsical old German gentleman, he offered the old boy a free boxing lesson, in the course of which he pretended to be knocked unconscious, thus filling the landlord's heart with such contrition for having inflicted permanent injury that there were no more requests for rent. O'Brien's only other appearance in the annals of literature concerns his feat of knocking John O'Hara's father from one room to another, removing the door in the process.

7   Years later, perhaps in deference to the Kid's temporary retirement, Wodehouse wrote a lyric called 'When It's Tulip Time in Sing Sing', which included these affecting lines:

Oh, I'd give a lot to go there,
Life was never dull or slow there,
Every night there was a concert or a hop.
Or I'd sit discussing Coué
With my old friend bat-eared Louie,
Quite the nicest man that ever slugged a
   cop.

8   Among other incumbents during or just after Wodehouse's day were Clarence Rook, author of *The Hooligan Nights* and Bernard Shaw's favourite journalist–interviewer, and E. V. Lucas.

9   Thomas Hayward (1871–1939), Surrey cricketer who played thirty-five times for England and scored 104 centuries.

10   Frank Edward Woolley (1887–1978), Kent cricketer who played sixty-four times for England, scored 145 centuries, took 2,068 wickets and 1,015 catches.

11   Douglas Ward Carr (1872–1950), Kent cricketer who played once for England and who enjoyed the most amazing rise in the history of cricket. A schoolmaster by occupation, he was available for selection only during holidays. He made his county début in 1909 at the late age of thirty-seven. By August he was playing for his country against Australia, his first-class career then having lasted for only four months.

12   Christopher Mathewson (1880–1925), known as Matty, Christy and Big Six. Pitcher for the New York Giants, 1900–16, and for the Cincinnati Reds, 1916–18. Just as Carr won fame with the deception of the Googly, a ball which spins in an unexpected way, so Mathewson was famous for his Screwball, or Fadeaway, delivery. A man like Bingley Crocker would have rated Mathewson just above Moses and St Peter.

13   Tom Morris (1850–75) was the exemplar of the Scottish golfing dynasty which Wodehouse has in mind. The son of the greenkeeper to The Royal and Ancient Club at St Andrews who himself won four Open Championships, young Tom was born with a silver spoon in his mouth, to say nothing of a cleek and a baffy. He won his first Open at the age of sixteen and died eight years later from grief at the death of his wife. Those who are curious to see what he looked like should visit the churchyard of St Andrews Cathedral, where they will find a monument with the figure of Young Tom sculpted in relief, and paid for by public subscription.

14   The tradition of chucking custard pies at Russian art had been established by Stephen Leacock in 'Sorrows of a Super Soul', whose heroine, Marie Mushenough, writes that her lover, Otto Dinkenspiel, has touched her father: 'He touched him for ten roubles.' The tradition was later sustained by S. J. Perelman, whose 'A Farewell to Omsk' features a hero who 'dislodged a piece of horseradish from his tie, shied it at a passing Nihilist and slid forward into the fresh loam'.

4   Lyricist on Broadway

1   A character in *The Gondoliers*.

2   Farnie is quoting from *Patience*.

3   Wodehouse's response to his own stage début carries distinct echoes of Gilbert's behaviour on a similar occasion. When his translation of a song from *Manon Lescaut* was performed in London, he attended every performance of it, wondering what the audience would do if aware that, standing among them, was the very man whose words were thrilling them. Gilbert's biographer, Hesketh Pearson, adds: 'Later observation convinced him that they would not have leapt with ecstasy' (*Gilbert: His Life and Strife*, Methuen, 1957, p. 17).

4   Johnny Mercer, a lyricist who collaborated with Kern briefly and brilliantly in Hollywood in 1941, told me: 'Kern was a terribly smart man. I think he couldn't stand mediocrity, so he didn't have too much patience with people who didn't understand him. That's what I mean when I say he was autocratic. But he was really very gentle. And terribly curious about everything. He collected coins and first editions, and made a fortune out of both by selling later on. He wanted to know things. 'Exactly what do you mean by that?' he would ask. He'd check you up in conversation. And he was a marvellous

conversationalist who was just as interested in the dancing and the book and the lyrics of a show as he was in the music. And he was a great stickler for detail. He'd written with a lot of guys before me, and was enormously experienced in collaboration with Wodehouse, Hammerstein, Dorothy Fields, Harbach.'

5   Once, when requested by David Selznick to play a few prospective pieces, Kern is supposed to have walked out, saying 'I don't give samples'.

6   'Kern was the first composer who made me conscious that popular music was of inferior quality, and that musical comedy music was made of better material. I followed Kern's work and studied each song that he composed. I paid him the tribute of frank imitation, and many things that I wrote at this time, 1916, sounded as though Kern had written them himself.' Letter from George Gershwin to Isaac Goldberg, in the latter's *George Gershwin, a Study in American Music* (Simon & Schuster, 1931), p. 81.

7   His first full score was for *The Red Petticoat*, an undistinguished derivation of *The Girl of the Golden West*, in 1912.

8   Bordman, *Jerome Kern: His Life and Music*, p. 41.

9   The bewildering convolutions of his later, more famous ballads, exemplified by 'All the Things You Are' and 'Smoke Gets in Your Eyes', won for Kern a reputation for writing 'difficult' melodies, although this crass belief was cherished more by producers than by the public. Kern knew of these misgivings among the moguls, and never failed to take a perverse delight in jeering at their asininity. Once, when introduced to the English composer Vivian Ellis, who was at that time being told by his elders that his music was too complex for the popular market, Kern advised him: 'Go on being uncommercial, young man. There's a lot of money in it.'

10   Arthur Schwartz, composer of 'Dancing in the Dark' and 'By Myself', has defined 'They Didn't Believe Me' as 'the first colloquial American ballad'.

11   Wodehouse remained unimpressed by his successor and her friends. 'Those three-hour lunches at the Algonquin,' he said fifty years later, 'when did those slackers ever get any work done?'

12   The comic monstrousness of the Shuberts can hardly be exaggerated. They paid their artists so badly that one tenor, who spent most of his professional life touring in the Shubert patent money-making machine, *Blossom Time*, managed to save only at the expense of the hotels he stayed at: in his will he left 7,000 towels. It was Lee Shubert who dismissed the heritage of three centuries when he announced, 'Audiences don't like plays where people write letters with feathers.' When the son of one of the Shuberts was asked what his father might have achieved

with the benefit of more schooling, he replied, 'If my father had had an education, he could have been Hitler.'

13   Once, when his partner, Guy Bolton, in attempting to beguile Wodehouse into writing an adaptation of some forgotten Austrian turkey, said eagerly, 'It was a big hit in Vienna', Wodehouse replied wearily, 'What wouldn't be?'

14   Richard Rodgers, *Musical Stages* (W. H. Allen, 1975), p. 20

15   In a letter to Benny Green, 1962.

16   After Samuel Shipman, author of *East is West*, which is 'thought by some to be the ghastliest mess ever put on the American stage, but this is an opinion held only by those who did not see *The Rose of China*'.

17   William Anthony McGuire (1885–1940), librettist, director and drinker, worked with Wodehouse on two Broadway productions of Florenz Ziegfeld, *Rosalie* and *The Three Musketeers*. After most spectacularly mismanaging his duties while adapting Dumas to the muse of Rudolf Friml, he sent a cable to Ziegfeld reading, 'Congratulations in the darkest hour of your success'. This at least had the brevity of wit, which could not be said for the forty-two-page telegram he sent to Ziegfeld in 1927 which resulted in the genesis of *Rosalie*, the only show in Broadway history to be written by two composers, two librettists and two lyricists (see chapter 4, pp. 111–12). In 1931, working on the most spectacular disaster in the career of Fred Astaire, a show called *Smiles*, he was accused of delaying events by attempting to make love to the chorus girls in the balcony. His last and most comical practical joke was his script for the posthumous tribute to Ziegfeld perpetrated by MGM, *The Great Ziegfeld*. In the 1930s Wodehouse worked with him again in Hollywood, describing him as 'a wild Irishman who seems to be fighting the heads of the studio all the time. I get on very well with him myself'.

18   From a BBC radio interview, 1960.

19   Miles Kreuger, *Show Boat: the Story of a Classic American Musical* (Oxford University Press, 1977), p. 57.

20   A dummy is a succession of irrelevant words and sounds indicating where rhymes and rhythmic stresses fall, so that the lyricist unable to read musical notation can retain a record of what is required of him. Ira Gershwin's dummy for 'I Got Rhythm' begins: 'Roly poly, eating solely, ravioli, better watch your diet or bust.' Lorenz Hart's dummy for 'There's a Small Hotel' includes the passage: 'By and by, perhaps she'll die, perhaps she'll croak this summer. Her old man's a plumber, she's much dumber.' But the most famous dummy of all is the one which Irving Caesar claims he wrote for 'Tea For Two' only to have it mistaken for the finished lyric so emphatically by his fellow-workers that it was retained and is in use to this day.

21 *Punch*, 10 February 1965.
22 'A Fond Look at Days When Anything Went', *New York Herald Tribune*, 13 May 1962.
23 Ira Gershwin, *Lyrics on Several Occasions* (Elm Tree Books, 1977), p. 157.
24 Of those six lamented associates, the first four received the dubious accolade of a posthumous Hollywood tribute in, respectively, *The Great Ziegfeld* (1936); *Look For the Silver Lining* (1949); *Rhapsody in Blue* (1945); and *Till the Clouds Roll By* (1946).
25 Louis Hirsch (1887–1924) collaborated with Wodehouse in the Princess Theatre show, *Oh, My Dear!* (1918). His most famous composition was 'The Love Nest'.

5 Novelist in the stalls

1 Leslie Henson (1891–1957), actor, director, producer, frog-faced musical comedy performer, was especially admired by Wodehouse, and also incidentally by the Gershwins, in whose London productions he appeared more than once, much to the delight of Fred Astaire among others. Among the Wodehouse shows in which he appeared were *Kissing Time*, *The Cabaret Girl* and *The Beauty Prize*.
2 'Let's Have Another Cup of Coffee, Let's Have Another Piece of Pie' was written by Berlin for a 1932 Broadway show called *Face the Music*, based on a story about a man who backs a Broadway show. 'Not For All the Rice in China' appeared in the following season in a Berlin show called *Thousands Cheer*, starring the same Marilyn Miller who had led Ziegfeld such a dance during the run of *Rosalie*. Both Berlin shows attempted topical lampoon; in *Face the Music*, Albert Einstein was seen as a vaudeville comic; in *Thousands Cheer*, Clifton Webb impersonated Gandhi.
3 Berlin's 'I Want to Go Back to Michigan' was a popular song of the 1914 season.
4 Edna May (1878–1948) was an unknown performer recruited at the last minute for the title role of the Salvation Army lass who becomes *The Belle of New York*. The show opened in New York in 1897, ran for fifty-six performances and elevated Miss May to instant fame. In April 1898 it transferred to the Shaftesbury Theatre in London, becoming the first Broadway musical import ever to enjoy an extended London run. Miss May likewise was the first American musical-comedy heroine to win a London reputation.
5 The vogue for telephone songs had been established by Gustave Kerker, who, in the same year that he composed *The Belle of New York*, introduced another show called *The Telephone Girl*. Later, Berlin wrote a famous waltz beginning, 'All alone, by the telephone'. The tradition survived into the post-war era with the successful Comdon and Green musical, *Bells Are Ringing*.
6 'Break the News to Mother' was a failed ballad which enjoyed a belated success during the Spanish–American War in 1897. It was composed by one Charles K. Harris, who also had the distinction of writing the most idiotic telephone song ever published, 'Hello, Central, Give Me Heaven'.
7 From 1912, Ziegfeld produced a series of near-annual revues called *The Follies*. In 1915 he inaugurated a series of late-night supper shows called *The Frolics*. One of his designers for both these series was the word-mangler Urban (see chapter 4, p. 108).
8 'Sonny Boy', whose lyric represents the very crown of bathos in popular music, was perpetrated by the Three Musketeers of the 1920s Broadway musical, Ray Henderson (1896–1970), Buddy de Sylva (1895–1950) and Lew Brown (1893–1958). In 1928 the singer Al Jolson telephoned them from Hollywood, where he was filming *The Singing Fool*, telling them that he was desperate for a big song. The trio composed 'Sonny Boy' in ninety minutes and Jolson transformed it into the biggest hit of the day. Later on, Henderson, de Sylva and Brown attempted to exonerate themselves by claiming that the song was a practical joke which poor Jolson took seriously. Posterity should perhaps make allowances for Brown and Jolson, who had both been born in Tsarist Russia.
9 'Trees', a notorious instance of the confusion of God with arboriculture, had started life as a poem by one Joyce Kilmer. In 1922 a composer called Oscar Rasbach gave it a musical setting and it became famous. Rasbach subsequently attempted to corner the market in pantheism with 'The Red Woods', 'Mountains' and 'The Laughing Brook'.
10 The episode of Miss Vera Singleton and the hold-up is suspiciously reminiscent of a notorious episode in Ziegfeld's past which everyone on Broadway knew all about. In Wodehouse's story, Vera Singleton tries to get herself on the front page by suggesting to Moffam that they pretend that her jewels have been stolen. In 1907, Ziegfeld's leading lady and mistress, Anna Held, was the victim of a robbery involving jewels valued at $280,000. Ziegfeld's vague and unconvincing story about how he had recovered them led the police to suspect that he had arranged the theft for purposes of publicity, to which Ziegfeld had responded by pointing out, quite correctly, that Miss Held's show was already playing to capacity houses. Miss Held, who knew Ziegfeld better than the police did, was always convinced that Ziegfeld had stolen the jewels himself in order to collect the insurance and thereby raise the capital to finance a new show. Nobody was ever tried or arrested in connection with the crime, and from then on Miss Held's relationship with Ziegfeld deteriorated, never to recover.
11 In *Carnival* (Martin Secker, 1912), Mackenzie tells the tragic tale of a West End dancer who marries into retirement in Cornwall. Among his other dance novels are *The Vanity Girl* (1920) and *Figure of Eight* (1936).
12 Between his 'Mr Chamberlain' song of 1906, and his final acceptance as a composer

with 'They Didn't Believe Me' nine years later, Kern contributed interpolated numbers to more than forty Broadway productions.
13   In *Bring on the Girls*, Wodehouse says that *Oh, Boy!* ran for 475 performances in New York, during which time there were four additional companies on the road. It cost $30,000 to produce and made a profit of $181,641.
14   Usborne, *Wodehouse at Work to the End*, p. 115.
15   Edwards, *P. G. Wodehouse*, p. 184.
16   The biggest fiasco in Wodehouse's career had been the aforementioned *The Rose of China*.
17   The choreographer employed by Erlanger on Bolton and Wodehouse's *Miss Springtime*, Julian Mitchell, 'was very nearly stone-deaf. His method of hearing a melody was to press his ear closely to the back of the piano. If the piano was in the pit, he would seat himself on top of it like a sort of Buddha. For some reason which aurists may be able to explain he could hear a little better in this position.'
18   Ira Gershwin, in a letter to Benny Green, 1962.
19   *The Cabaret Girl* ran for 462 performances, which made it, apart from the Kern musical, *Sally*, the most successful musical comedy in which Wodehouse had a hand.
20   Mackenzie, *Carnival*.

6   Scriptwriter in Hollywood

1   B. Rosenberg and H. Silverstein, *The Real Tinsel* (Collier Macmillan, 1970), p. 187.
2   *Ibid.*
3   Roland Flamini, *Scarlett, Rhett and a Cast of Thousands* (André Deutsch, 1976), p. 3.
4   Edmund Wilson, *The Shores of Light* (Farrar, Straus & Giroux, 1952), p. 633.
5   Edmund Wilson, 'The Playwright in Paradise', *Note-books of Night* (Secker & Warburg, 1945), p. 40.
6   Flamini, *Scarlett, Rhett and a Cast of Thousands*, p. 3.
7   It may well be that there was a god of moonshine and that deity took Selznick's action as a propitiatory gesture. At the height of the burning, Selznick was confronted by an apparition in the form of his own brother accompanied by an English actress called Vivien Leigh, her beautiful face lit by the glow of the flames. Selznick had found his Scarlett at last.

7   Novelist in a padded cell

1   Frank Sullivan was an American humorous essayist who joined *The New Yorker* in 1931 and became well-known for the Arbuthnot dialogues, which disclosed a standard cliché in every response. His collections tended to have felicitous titles like *A Pearl in Every Oyster* and *The Night the Old Nostalgia Burned Down*. In August 1940, at about the time Wodehouse was being removed to the Citadel at Huy, Sullivan indulged in a cliché worthy of Arbuthnot

when he said that 'England could not be licked'.
2   Sir Compton Mackenzie, *My Life and Times*, octave 8 (Chatto & Windus, 1969), p. 129.
3   *Ibid.*
4   *Ibid.*, pp. 129–30.
5   James Ramsay MacDonald (1866–1937), whose life was a steady descent from the lofty heights of youthful idealism to the potholes of Cabinet office. Leader of the Labour Party, he is remembered as the inventor of a political manœuvre of startling originality, being the first Prime Minister in British history to join the Opposition while in office. He died while on an ocean voyage, hence the remark, 'MacDonald died at sea – where he was all his life'.
6   Howard Spring, *In the Meantime* (Constable, 1942), pp. 77–9.
7   George Orwell, 'Boys' Weeklies', *The Collected Essays of George Orwell* (Secker & Warburg, 1961).
8   Orwell, 'In Defence of P. G. Wodehouse', *Collected Essays*.
9   P. Stansky and W. Abrahams, *The Unknown Orwell* (Constable, 1972), p. 16.
10   *Ibid.*, p. 28.
11   *Ibid.*, p. 49.
12   P. Stansky and W. Abrahams, *Orwell – The Transformation* (Constable, 1979), p. 108.
13   Asa Briggs, *The History of Broadcasting in the United Kingdom* (Oxford University Press).
14   Malcolm Muggeridge, 'Wodehouse in Distress', *Homage to P. G. Wodehouse*, ed. Thelma Cazalet-Keir (Barrie & Jenkins, 1973), p. 97.
15   A. J. P. Taylor, *Beaverbrook* (Penguin, 1974), p. 501.
16   Muggeridge, 'Wodehouse in Distress', p. 89.
17   *Ibid.*, p. 90.
18   *Ibid.*
19   *Ibid.*, p. 91.
20   *Ibid.*, p. 94.
21   David A. Jasen, *P. G. Wodehouse: A Portrait of a Master* (Garnstone Press, 1975), p. 185.
22   *Ibid.*
23   Muggeridge, 'Wodehouse in Distress', p. 97.
24   *Ibid.*, pp. 97–8.
25   Iain Sproat, 'The Evidence that Clears P. G. Wodehouse', *Now! Magazine*, 6 February 1981.
26   *Ibid.*
27   A. J. P. Taylor, *English History, 1914–1945* (Penguin, 1970), p. 648.
28   Geoffrey Jaggard, *Wooster's World* (Macdonald, 1967).
29   Muggeridge, 'Wodehouse in Distress', pp. 92–3.

8   Knight in exile

1   Peter Green, *Kenneth Grahame* (John Murray, 1959), p. 16.
2   Angus Wilson, *The Strange Ride of*

Rudyard Kipling (Secker & Warburg, 1977), p. 342.

3 Ted Morgan, *Somerset Maugham* (Cape, 1980), pp. 13–14.

4 *The Complete Short Stories of Saki* (Bodley Head, 1930), pp. 639–40.

5 Christopher Morley, introduction to *The Complete Short Stories of Saki*.

6 Charles Inglis Thornton (1850–1929), Eton, Cambridge University, Kent and England; big hitter who in 1871, at Hove, drove a cricket ball a distance of 168 yards 2 feet.

7 The ferocity of this idea is matched by the sadistic dispatch of a hated aunt in Saki's 'Sredni Vashtar'; interestingly, when Saki's sister attempted to justify her brother's cruel fantasies, she claimed that his childhood had been animated by constant warfare with 'aunt calling to aunt like mastodons bellowing across primeval swamps' – a simile taken from *The Inimitable Jeeves*.

8 Honor Tracy, 'Jeeves: No Hero He', *Daily Telegraph*.

9 Usborne, *Wodehouse at Work to the End*, p. 213.

10 Tuchman, *The Proud Tower*, p. 40.

11 *Ibid*., p. 42.

12 N. T. P. Murphy, 'The Real Drones Club', *Blackwood's Magazine*, August 1975.

13 Arthur M. Binstead was an author and late-Victorian man-about-town who published several volumes of reminiscence concerning symbols of a vanished night life like Romano's Restaurant and the promenade at the Empire Theatre. His best-known works are *A Pink 'Un and a Pelican*, *Pitcher in Paradise* and *Gal's Gossip*. Binstead was a prominent contributor to the 'Pink 'Un', as the *Sporting Times* was known. His most memorable phrase was the one he coined for the ceremony of flinging a bill in the air to see on whose plate it would fall, which he defined as 'the hazard of the gentle flutter'.

14 Usborne, *Wodehouse at Work to the End*, p. 154.

15 Pritchett, *A Cab at the Door*, p. 88.

16 Robert Graves, *Goodbye to All That* (Cassell, 1929), p. 18.

17 Frank Swinnerton, *The Georgian Literary Scene* (Dent, 1938), p. 348.

18 Taylor, *English History, 1914–1945*, p. 390–91.

19 Wilfrid Sheed, 'P. G. Wodehouse: "Leave It to Psmith"', *The Good Word* (Sidgwick and Jackson, 1968).

20 *Ibid*.

21 *Ibid*.

Epilogue

1 Andrew Mylett (ed.), *Arnold Bennett: The Evening Standard Years* (Chatto & Windus, 1974), p. 344.

2 Wilson, *The Shores of Light*, p. 633.

3 Muggeridge, 'Wodehouse in Distress', p. 99.

4 Swinnerton, *The Georgian Literary Scene*, p. 348.

Chronology

15 October 1881
Born Guildford, Surrey
18 May 1894
Enters Dulwich College
February 1900
First published piece, in *The Public School Magazine*
September 1900
Joins Hong Kong and Shanghai Bank, Lombard Street, London
August 1901
Début in 'By The Way' column of *The Globe*
September 1902
Resigns from bank. Publishes first school novel, *The Pothunters*
August 1903
Regular appointment to 'By The Way'
April 1904
First trip to America
December 1904
First song lyric performed in *Sergeant Brue*, Strand Theatre
March 1906
Meets Jerome Kern. Song, 'Mr Chamberlain', performed in *The Beauty of Bath*, Aldwych Theatre
June 1906
First adult novel published, *Love Among the Chickens*, introducing Stanley Featherstonehaugh Ukridge
January 1908
Serial, 'The Lost Lambs', introduces Rupert Psmith
May 1909
Second trip to America

August 1914
Meets Ethel Newton Rowley in New York
September 1914
Marries her
September 1915
Short story, 'Extricating Young Gussie', introduces Jeeves and Wooster. First Blandings novel, *Something Fresh* (US *Something New*)
February 1916
First Broadway musical, *Pom Pom*
September 1916
First musical with Kern, *Miss Spring-time*
February 1917
First Princess Theatre musical, *Oh, Boy!*
March 1928
Last musical as lyricist, *The Three Musketeers*
May 1930–May 1931
Contract writer with MGM
November 1934
Last musical as librettist, *Anything Goes*
October 1936–April 1937
Return to Hollywood for MGM
June 1939
Honorary D.Litt. Oxon. Leaves Britain for last time
May 1940
Captured by Germans at Le Touquet
July 1940
Interned
June 1941
Broadcasts from Berlin
September 1943
Removed to Paris

January 1945
Released from detention in Paris hospital
April 1947
Returns to New York

January 1975
Knight Commander of the British Empire
14 February 1975
Dies in Long Island, New York

Bibliography

The dates refer to the year of publication of the edition used by the author.

Anstey, F.
Vice Versa (1882)
Barrie, J. M.
When a Man's Single (1892); *The Green-wood Hat* (1930)
Behrman, S. N.
Conversations with Max (1960)
Bordman, G.
Jerome Kern: his Life and Music (1980)
Briggs, A.
Victorian People (1954); *The History of Broadcasting in the United Kingdom*
Cardus, N.
Autobiography (1947); *Final Score* (1970)
Cazalet-Keir, T. (ed.)
Homage to P.G. Wodehouse (1973)
Childers, E.
The Riddle of the Sands (1903)
Collins, W.
The Moonstone (1868)
Cooper, D.
Old Men Forget (1953)
Dickens, C.
Pickwick Papers (1836–7); *Martin Chuzzlewit* (1843–4); *David Copperfield* (1849–50)
Dietz, H.
Dancing in the Dark (1974)
Edwards, O. D.
P.G. Wodehouse (1977)
Ellis, V.
I'm on a See-Saw (1953)
Farrar, D.

Eric, or Little by Little (1858)
Ferber, E.
Show Boat (1925)
Fitzgerald, F. S.
The Great Gatsby (1926)
Flamini, R.
Scarlett, Rhett and a Cast of Thousands (1976)
Gershwin, I.
Lyrics on Several Occasions (1977)
Gilbert, W. S.
The Savoy Operas
Goldberg, I.
George Gershwin, a Study in American Music (1931)
Graves, R.
Goodbye to All That (1929)
Green, P.
Kenneth Grahame (1959)
Higham, C.
Ziegfeld (1973); *The Adventures of Conan Doyle* (1976)
Howarth, P.
Play Up and Play the Game (1973)
Hughes, T.
Tom Brown's Schooldays (1857)
Hynes, S.
The Edwardian Turn of Mind (1968)
Jaggard, G.
Wooster's World (1967)
James, R. R.
The British Revolution (1977)
Jerome, J. K.
Three Men in a Boat (1889)

Kaufman, G. and Hart, M.
Once in a Lifetime (1931)
Kreuger, M.
Show Boat: the Story of a Classic American Musical (1977)
Leacock, S.
Literary Lapses (1910)
Le Queux, W.
The Invasion of 1910 (1894)
Lerner, A. J.
The Street Where I Live (1978)
Lofts, W. O. and Adley, D. J.
The World of Frank Richards (1975)
Mackail, D.
The Story of J.M.B. (1941)
Mackenzie, C.
Carnival (1912); *My Life and Times*, octave 8 (1969)
MacShane, F.
The Life of Raymond Chandler (1976); *The Life of John O'Hara* (1980)
Mason, A. E. W.
The Four Feathers (1902)
Maugham, W. S.
Of Human Bondage (1915)
Milne, A. A.
When We Were Very Young (1924)
Morgan, T.
Somerset Maugham (1980)
Morris, J.
Pax Britannica (1968)
Murphy, N. T. P.
'The Real Drones Club', *Blackwood's Magazine* (August, 1975)
Mylett, A. (ed.)
Arnold Bennett: the Evening Standard Years (1974)
O'Hara, J.
Sermons and Soda Water (1960)
Orwell, G.
The Collected Essays of George Orwell (1961)
Pearson, H.
Gilbert, his Life and Strife (1957)
Perelman, S. J.
Crazy Like a Fox (1945)
Priestley, J. B.
English Humour (1976)
Pritchett, V. S.
London Perceived (1962); *A Cab at the Door* (1979)
Reed, T. B.
The Fifth Form at St Dominic's (1885); *The Willoughby Captains* (1887)
Rodgers, R.
Musical Stages (1975)

Rosenberg, B. and Silverstein, H.
The Real Tinsel (1970)
Runyon, D.
More Than Somewhat (1937); *Furthermore* (1938)
Saki
The Complete Short Stories of Saki (1930)
Schwartz, C.
Cole Porter, a Biography (1977)
Shaw, G. B.
Cashel Byron's Profession (1882); *Our Theatres in the Nineties* (1931)
Sheed, W.
The Good Word (1968)
Smith, J. A.
John Buchan and his World (1979)
Spring, H.
In the Meantime (1942)
Sproat, I.
'The Evidence that Clears P.G. Wodehouse', *Now! Magazine*, 6 February 1981
Stansky, P. and Abrahams, W.
The Unknown Orwell (1972); *Orwell – The Transformation* (1979)
Swinnerton, F.
The Georgian Literary Scene (1938); *Background with Chorus* (1956)
Taylor, A. J. P.
English History, 1914–1945 (1970); *Beaverbrook* (1974)
Tracy, H.
'Jeeves: No Hero He', *Daily Telegraph*
Trollope, A.
Phineas Redux (1874)
Tuchman, B.
The Proud Tower (1966)
Turner, E. S.
Boys Will Be Boys (1948)
Usborne, R.
Wodehouse at Work to the End (1976)
Wells, H. G.
Kipps (1905); *Experiment in Autobiography* (1934)
Wilde, O.
An Ideal Husband (1895)
Wilson, A.
The Strange Ride of Rudyard Kipling (1977)
Wilson, E.
Note-books of Night (1945); *The Shores of Light* (1952)
Wisden's Cricketers' Almanack
Young, G. M.
Victorian Essays (1962)

Index

Works by P. G. Wodehouse or to which he contributed are followed by (PGW)

Adventures of Sally, The (PGW), 150–1
Aerated Bread Company (ABC), 20
Agatha, Aunt, 216
Alsop, Wilfred, 128
America, 64–5, 227; tycoons, 76–9; *see also* Hollywood; New York
American, The (magazine), 173
Andrews, Dana, 178–9
Anstey, Thomas, *see* Guthrie, Thomas Anstey
Anything Goes (PGW), 120–1, 151
'Archibald's Benefit' (PGW), 88
Arnold, Dr Thomas, 20, 240
'Artistic Career of Corky, The' (PGW), 219
Ashby Hall, 91–2
Asquith, H. H., 50
Astaire, Fred, 176, 177–8, 243
'At Geisenheimer's' (PGW), 128–9
aunts, 9, 215–17

Bachelors Anonymous (PGW), 128, 151–2
Baden-Powell, General, 47
Baerman, A. E., 69–70
Balcon, Michael, 179
Baldwin, Stanley, 200
Balfour, Arthur, 45
Banks, Cuthbert, *see* Cuthbert Banks
Bard, Wilkie, 34
Barmy in Wonderland (PGW), 37, 151
Barnikow, Raven von, 206–7
Barrie, J. M., 28, 55, 60–3, 217
baseball, 82, 93
Bassett, Madeline, 194, 195, 198, 212
Bassett, Sir Watkyn, 194, 195

Bassingham-Bassingham, Cyril, 137
Bates, Anastasia, 90, 210–12
Bates, William, 90
Beach, Sebastian, 129, 131, 218
Beamish, Rosalie, 155
Beauty of Bath, The (PGW), 100
Beaverbrook, Lord, 201
Beckford College, 17
Beerbohm, Max, 231, 241
Belle of New York, The, 129
Bellinger, Cora, 133
Bennett, Arnold, 237, 241
Bentley, E. C., 185
Berlin, Irving, 103, 108, 111, 128–9, 244
'Best Seller' (PGW), 130
Belloc, Hilaire, 238
Bevan, George, 142–5
Bickersdyke, John, 38–9, 43–4, 51, 52, 241
'Bill' (lyric; PGW), 116–19, 136, 151
'Bill the Bloodhound' (PGW), 140–2
Billson, Wilberforce 'Battling', 230, 232
Bingley, Johnny, 156, 157
Binstead, Arthur, 224
Blakeney, Felicia, 89–90
Blandings Castle, 145, 220, 221, 234
Blandings, Empress of, 221, 226, 234
Blizzard, 91
Blumenfield, 137–8
Blumenthal, 137
Bolton, Guy, 102–3, 110, 111–12, 114, 120–1, 123, 183
Bordoni, Irene, 112
Bott, J. Gladstone, 91
boxing, 21, 64–7, 230
Boy's Own Paper, The, 15
Brady, Kid, 67, 73, 74

Brewster, 134, 135, 137
Brian, Donald, 108
Briggs, Asa, 199
Briggs, Sir Eustace, 19–20
Bring on the Girls (PGW), 138
Brinkmeyer, 160–1, 175
British Broadcasting Corporation, 199, 209
Broadway, New York theatre, 99–123, 124–5
Brooke-Haven, P. (PGW pseudonym), 101
Brown, Lew, 244
Brown, Sue, 224–5
Brusiloff, Vladimir, 88–9
Buchan, John, 58
Bulpitt, Samuel, 78–9, 127–8
Bunter, Billy, 29, 190–1
'By The Way' (newspaper column), 67–9, 70, 97, 106, 229

Cabaret Girl, The (PGW), 150
Caesar, Irving, 243
Caffyn, George, 137–8
Cagney, James, 174
Caine, Hall, 41
Carr, Douglas Ward, 81
Carroll, Lewis, 28
Carson, Sir Edward, 46–7
'Cassandra', *see* Connor, William
Castaways, The (PGW), 173
Chamberlain, Joseph, 100, 241
Chamberlain, Neville, 200–1
Chandler, Florence, 33
Chandler, Raymond, 33–4, 227
Chaplin, Charlie, 174, 209
Chatsworth, 222
'Chester Forgets Himself' (PGW), 89–90
Childers, Erskine, 45
chorus girls, 129, 224–5
Chugwater, Clarence, 47–50
Churchill, Winston, 167, 214
cinema, *see* Hollywood
Clapham Common, 42
classics, classical education, 12, 18–19, 54
Clicking of Cuthbert, The (PGW), 85, 88–9
Clifford, Martin, *see* Hamilton, Charles
Code of the Woosters, The (PGW), 193–7, 199, 209, 237
Cohan, George M., 99
Collier's Weekly (magazine), 70
Collins, Wilkie, 80
Colossal-Exquisite, 154
Columbia Broadcasting System, 183
Coming Up for Air, 191
Company for Henry (PGW), 91–4, 217–18, 228–9
Comstock, Ray, 108
Connolly, Cyril, 189
Connor, William ('Cassandra'), 184–5, 199, 207
Cooley, Joey, 160, 175
Cooper, Alfred Duff (Lord Norwich), 200–1, 204, 212
Cooper, Jackie, 173–4, 175
Corbett, James J., 65
Cosmopolitan (magazine), 70
Cosy Moments (magazine), 67, 73
Cowdrey, Michael Colin, 22
Crichton, the Admirable, 217
cricket, 12, 22, 23, 27, 35–6, 52, 80–1, 84–5, 86–7, 92–4

Crocker, Bingley, 80–4
Crocker, Mrs Bingley, 82–4
Crocker, Eugenia, 80
Crocker, Jimmy, 80, 82–3, 83, 84
Crouse, Russell, 120–1
Crowninshield, Frank, 101
Curzon, Lord, 214
Cussen, Major E. J. P., 205, 207, 208
Cuthbert Banks, 88–9

Dahlia, Aunt, 196, 197–8, 216
Daily Mail, 45–6
Daily Mirror, *see* Connor, William
Daily Telegraph, 185, 186
Damsel in Distress, A (PGW), 142–5, 176–8; film version, 122, 176–8
Davies, Marion, 144, 167
Dawlish, Bill (Lord), 79, 129
De Mille, Cecil B., 179
de Sylva, Buddy, 244
'Deep Waters' (PGW), 70
Delancy, Cabot, 158
Denison, Ray, 139
Derrick, Kay, 228
Devine, Raymond Parsloe, 88, 89
Devonshire, eighth Duke of, 222, 225
Dickens, Charles, 49
Dietz, Howard, 103, 105
Dillingham, Charles, 108
Donahue, Jack, 112
Dore, Billie, 143, 144–5
Doyle, Sir Arthur Conan, 230
D'Oyly Carte, Rupert, 27
Duff, J. Buchanan, 133
Dulwich, Valley Fields, 34–6, 92, 227–9
Dulwich College, 9–10, 11–13, 32–6, 52–3, 58, 209, 215
Duncan Sisters, 111
Dunstable, Alaric, sixth Duke of, 225–7

Eatanswill election, 44
Eden, Anthony, 203
Edith, Aunt, 9
Edwards, Owen Dudley, 145, 217
Elizabeth College, 9
Ellis, Vivian, 243
Emsworth, Clarence, ninth Earl of, 26, 78, 128, 130–1, 193, 220–2, 226, 232, 234
Emsworth House, 220, 229
Engaged, 26
Eric, or Little by Little, *see* Farrar, Frederick
Erlanger, Abraham, 107, 138
Experiment with Autobiography, 62
'Extricating Young Gussie' (PGW), 138–40

Fairbanks, Douglas, 71
Fairmile, Sally, 133–4
Farnie, 17–18, 26, 96
Farnie, Henry B., 240
Farrar, Frederick, 14–15, 16, 23, 31
fascism, 195; *see also* Spode, Roderick
Fenn, Robert, 20, 99
Ferber, Edna, 117
Fifth Form at St Dominic's, The, 16
Fink-Nottle, Gussie, 194, 195, 196, 212
Fish, Ronnie, 129, 224–5
Fishbein, Isadore, 154, 162
Fitzgerald, Scott, 127
Fitzsimmonds, Bob, 241–2

Flamini, Roland, 175
Flannery, Harry, 183
Flicker Film Company, 89
Follow the Girl, 142–3, 144–5
Fontaine, Joan, 177–8, 178
football, 85
Ford, Ogden, 80
Forester, C. S., 227
Foster brothers, 22
Fotheringay-Phipps, Barmy, 151
Four Feathers, The, 21
Franklin, Packy, 77
Freedley, Vincent, 112, 120–1
Frobisher, Major Tubby, 227
Frohman, Charles, 115
Funny Face, 150
Fyfe, David Maxwell, 209–10

Galahad at Blandings (PGW), 128
Gans, Joe, 65–6
Gedge, J. Wellington, 76–7
Gentleman of Leisure, A (US title *The Intrusion of Jimmy*; PGW), 70–2
German invasion threat, 44–51
Gershwin, George, 99, 103, 112, 123, 136, 176, 177, 179
Gershwin, Ira, 103, 106, 112, 113, 122–3, 136, 150, 178, 243
Gilbert, W. S., 13, 18, 19, 26, 49, 95–8, 113, 242
Gilkes, Dr A. H., 12–13, 33
Girl on the Boat, The (PGW), 79
Girl from Brighton, The, 140–1
Gladstone, Herbert, 50
Globe, The, 67–8, 70
Glossop, Tuppy, 133, 139
Glutz, Sigismund, 154, 156
'Goalkeeper and the Plutocrat, The' (PGW), 85
Goble, Isaac, 146–9
Gold Bat, The (PGW), 19–20, 31, 98, 229
Goldwyn, Samuel, 168, 178–9, 179
golf, 85–91
Golf Omnibus, The (PGW), 85, 87–8
'Good Angels, The' (PGW), 70
Grahame, Kenneth, 28, 213
Graves, Perceval, 229–30
Graves, Robert, 229
Great Gatsby, The, 127
Great Neck Golf Club, 113
Grenville, Pelham (PGW pseudonym), 101
Grey, Clifford, 115
Greyfriars School, 29–30, 190–2
Griffo, Young, 65
Grim's Dyke, 95
Grossmith, George, 112, 150
Guderian, General Heinz, 181
Guthrie, Thomas Anstey, 17, 21

Haddock, Esmond, 129
Hailsham, Lord, *see* Hogg, Quintin
Haldane, Richard, 50–1
Hall, Owen, 98
Hamilton, Charles ('Frank Richards', 'Martin Clifford'), 29–32
Hammerstein, Oscar, 103, 117, 118–19
Hardy, Bill, 92
Harris, Sir Augustus, 97
Harris, Charles K., 244
Harris, Frank, 62
Hart, Lorenz, 103, 105, 131, 243

Have a Heart, 105
Havershot, third Earl of, 162–3
Hayward, Thomas, 81
Head of Kay's, The (PGW), 17, 20, 35
Heart of a Goof, The (PGW), 87
Heath, Edward, 208
Heavy Weather (PGW), 129, 225
Held, Anna, 244
Henderson, Dolly, 130, 224–5
Henderson, Ray, 244
Henson, Leslie, 125
Hicks, Seymour, 50, 98, 99–100
Higgs, 99–100
'High Stakes' (PGW), 91
Hignett, Arthur, 40, 58
Hignett, Eustace, 79
Hignett, Mrs Horace, 79
Hirsch, Louis, 123
Hobbs, Sir Jack, 52
Hogg, Quintin (later Lord Hailsham), 203, 204
Holbeton, Lord, 133–4
Hollywood, cinema, 153–80, 227
Hong Kong, 8, 65
Hong Kong and Shanghai Bank, 54–7, 63
Hot Water (PGW), 76–7, 171
'How's That, Umpire?' (PGW), 80
Hughes, Thomas, 15, 16
Hunstanton Hall, Norfolk, 220
Hutchings, Kenneth, 52
Hymack, Wilson, 135–7
Hyndman, Henry Mayers, 27

Ickenham, Frederick, fifth Earl of, 225
'In Alcala' (PGW), 57
Indiscretions of Archie, The (PGW), 68
Inimitable Jeeves, The (PGW), 137–8
Intrusion of Jimmy, The, see *Gentleman of Leisure, A*
Invasion of 1910, The, 45–7
'It's a Long Way Back to Mother's Knee', 135–6

Jackson, Mike, 22, 23–5, 27, 28, 34–6, 38–44 *passim*, 56, 72, 74, 86–7
Jarvis, Bat, 73–4
Jasen, David, 215
Jeeves (PGW), 121–2
Jeeves, Reginald, 26, 133, 155, 196–7, 217, 218–20, 227, 230
Jeeves and the Feudal Spirit (PGW), 216
'Jeeves and the Song of Songs' (PGW), 133
Jeffries, James J., 65
Jerome, Jerome K., 51–2
Jill the Reckless (PGW), 37, 145–50
Johnstone, Justine, 108, 144
Jolson, Al, 244
Joy in the Morning (PGW), 216
'Juice of an Orange, The' (PGW), 174–5
Julia, Aunt, 129, 139–40, 225

Keggs, 227
Kellett, E. E., 15
Kelly, Aunt, 92
Kenningford, 42–4
Kerker, Gustave, 244
Kern, Jerome, 98–101, 119, 123, 136, 244–5; collaboration with PGW, 68, 98–101, 102–4, 107, 110, 111, 114–19, 241

Kipling, Rudyard, 13, 23, 213–14
Kitty Darlin' (PGW), 105
Knox, N. A., 52

landed gentry, peerage, 76, 91–2, 220–7
Lassie, 180
Laughing Gas (PGW), 175
Le Queux, William, 45–7, 50
Leacock, Stephen, 242
Leave It to Jane, 105, 110
Leave It to Psmith (PGW), 127, 234
Lerner, Alan, 123
Levitsky, Mr, 157, 158
Lindsay, Howard, 120–1
literature, poets, 84, 88–90
Little Nugget, The (PGW), 28, 37, 80, 129, 220, 242
Lord Emsworth and Others (PGW), 128, 129
Love Among the Chickens (PGW), 69–70, 229
Loy, Myrna, 174
Lucas, E. V., 242

McCoy, Kid, 65, 66–7
MacDonald, James Ramsay, 187
McEachern, John, 71–2, 75
McGuire, William Anthony, 109, 111–12, 113, 176
Mackail, Denis, 62
Mackenzie, Sir Compton, 129, 142, 151, 185, 186, 230–1
magazines, Edwardian, 59–60, 63
Maloney, Pugsy, 128
'Man I Love, The', 136
Man With Two Left Feet, The (PGW), 138, 219
Manchester United FC, 41–2, 237
Mannering-Phipps, Gussie, 131, 139–40
Marberry, Elizabeth, 102
Margaret Milsom, 88
Mariner, Jill, 145–50
Market Snodsbury, 197, 198, 200
Markham Square, 59
Marsh, Mae, 178
Marshmoreton, Lord, 142, 144–5
Martin Chuzzlewit, 218
Mary, Aunt, 215–16
Mason, A. E. W., 21, 227
Mason, Mortimer, 224
Mason, Wally, 145–6, 148–50
Mathewson, Christopher ('Matty'), 82
Mating Season, The (PGW), 128, 129, 131, 155, 212, 216, 217, 237
Maud, Lady Patricia, 142–5
Maugham, W. Somerset, 213, 214, 227
Maurice, F. D., 16
Maxwell, Rutherford, 57
May, Edna, 129
May, Phil, 17
Mayer, Louis B., 167, 173–4, 175, 176, 179
Medulla-Oblongata, 154, 156
Mercer, Johnny, 105, 242
Meredith, Chester, 89–90
Metro-Goldwyn-Mayer Studios (MGM), 167–9, 171–2, 173–4, 176
MI5, 51, 205
Mike (PGW), 23, 31; *see also* Jackson, Mike
Mill, John Stuart, 239
Miller, Jeff, 182
Miller, Johnson, 147
Miller, Marilyn, 111–12, 123, 144

Milne, A. A., 28, 186, 210–12
Miss 1917 (PGW), 105
Miss Springtime (PGW), 109
Mitchell, Julian, 245
'Mixed Threesome, A' (PGW), 87
Moffam, Archie, 132, 134–7, 193
Money in the Bank (PGW), 182
Money for Nothing (PGW), 220
Morgan, Helen, 117
Morgan, Ted, 214
Morris, Tom, 86
Morro Castle, 120
Mosley, Sir Oswald, 195
'Mr Chamberlain' (lyric; PGW), 100–1
Much Obliged, Jeeves (PGW), 197–9
Muggeridge, Malcolm, 199–200 ('another writer'), 202–4, 210, 237–8
Mulliner, Mr, 159
Mulliner, Bulstrode, 159
Mulliner, Montrose, 155–7, 163
Mulliner, Wilmot, 157, 158
Mullins, Spike, 71
Munich, 200–1
Munro, H. H., *see* Saki
Murphy, N. T. P., 224
musical theatre, 98–123, 124–5; *see also under* Wodehouse
'My War With Germany' (PGW), 206

Nagel, Conrad, 173
Nast, Condé, 101
National Service League, 45
Nesbit, E., 28
New Asiatic Bank, 38–41, 51, 57
New York, 64–7, 70–5, 227; *see also* Broadway
Nichols, Jerry, 128
Ninety in the Shade (PGW), 104
Northcliffe, Lord, 45–6, 51
Not George Washington (PGW), 229
Nutcombe, Ira J., 79, 85

O'Brien, Jack, 66
O'Casey, Sean, 185, 236–7
O'Hara, John, 127
Oh, Boy! (PGW), 105, 110, 245
Oh, Lady! Lady! (PGW), 109–10, 116–17, 131–2
'Ole Man River', 133
Once in a Lifetime, 179–80
Opal, Senator Ambrose, 77
Orwell, George, 189–99, 215, 237
Oxford University, 32, 53, 185

Packard, Jane, 90
'Packet of Seeds, A' (lyric; PGW), 104–5
Pain, Barry, 13
Paradene, Henry, 91–2, 94
Paramount Studios, 175
Parker, Dorothy, 101, 109–10
'Passing of Ambrose, The' (PGW), 218
Payn, James, 13
Peavey, Miss, 127
peerage, *see* landed gentry
Pelican Club, 224
Perelman, S. J., 218, 242
Perfecto-Zizzbaum Corporation, 154, 155–60, 173, 179
Pett, Nesta Ford, 80, 83–4
Pett, Peter, 80, 81–2, 83, 84

Phybus, George, 155, 156
Piccadilly Jim (PGW), 80–4, 94, 105, 210
Pickering, Mr, 127
Pickwick Papers, *see* Eatanswill election
Pigs Have Wings (PGW), 127
Pilbeam, Percy, 131
Pilkington, Otis, 145–9
Pitt, Jimmy, 70–2, 75
Plack, Werner, 207
Plum, J. (PGW pseudonym), 101
poets, *see* literature
police, 71–2, 74–5
politics, 43–4; *see also* fascism; German
    invasion threat; *and* German broadcasts
    under Wodehouse
Polk, J. B., 78
Pope-Hennessy, John, 8
Porgy and Bess, 179
Porter, Cole, 120–1
Pothunters, The (PGW), 13–14, 30, 63, 71, 96
Potter-Pirbright, Catsmeat, 154, 212
Potter-Pirbright, Corky (Cora Starr), 154–5,
    164
Prefect's Uncle, A (PGW), 17–18, 25–6, 96
Priestley, J. B., 28–9, 33–4
Princess Theatre, 101–2, 105–6, 108
Pritchett, V. S., 35, 36, 228
Psmith, Rupert, 23–8, 38–44 *passim*, 52, 56,
    67, 72–5, 126, 129–30, 234
Psmith, Journalist (PGW), 72–5, 128
Psmith in the City (PGW), 37–44, 51, 56, 57, 58,
    63, 85, 237, 241
Public School Magazine, The, 58, 63
'Put Me in My Little Cell' (lyric; PGW), 98

Quhayne brothers, 49
Quick Service (PGW), 76, 133–4

'Rag of Paper, A', 60
Rasbach, Oscar, 244
Reed, Talbot Baines, 15–17, 31
Religious Tract Society, 15, 16
Remsenburg, Long Island, 34
Rice, Henry Pifield, 140–2
Richards, Frank, *see* Hamilton, Charles
Riddle of the Sands, The, 45
Right Ho, Jeeves (PGW), 217
Ring for Jeeves (PGW), 217, 227
Rivers, Alston, 50
Riviera Girl, The (PGW), 105
RKO, 176–7
Roberts, Field-Marshal Earl, 45–7, 50
Robey, George, 34
Rockmeteller, Sigsbee, 227
Rodgers, Richard, 105–6, 131
'Rodney Fails to Qualify' (PGW), 90
'Rodney Has a Relapse' (PGW), 210–12
Rogers, Ginger, 177
Romberg, Sigmund, 112, 113
Rook, Clarence, 242
Rooke, Freddie, 146
Roper, Miss, 9
Rosalie (PGW), 111–14, 170, 171, 243
Rose of America, The, 146–50
Rose of China, The, 108–9
Rowley, Ethel Newton, *see* Wodehouse,
    Ethel
Runyon, Damon, 218

St Austin's School, 13, 26, 29, 30
St George's by-election, 200
St Jim's, 29, 30
Saki (H. H. Munro), 213, 214, 246
Sally (PGW), 114–15
Sam Goldwyn (dog), 154–5
Sam the Sudden (PGW), 228, 236
Savage, Colonel Henry, 108
Savoy Operas, *see* Gilbert, W. S.
Scented Sinners, 159–60
Schnellenhamer, Jacob Z., 153–66, 173,
    174–5, 180
school stories, 14–17; *see also under*
    Wodehouse
Schoonmaker, James, 78
Schwartz, Arthur, 243
Sedleigh, 23, 28
Seldes, Gilbert, 110
Selznick, David, 175, 179, 179–80, 243
Sergeant Brue (PGW), 98
Sermons and Soda Water (PGW), 127
Shackleton, Sir Ernest, 12
Sharkey, Tom, 65
Shaw, Artie, 237
Shaw, George Bernard, 21, 27, 241
Sheed, Wilfrid, 233–4
Shipman, Samuel, 109
Show Boat (PGW), 100, 117–19, 124
Shropshire, 220
Shubert brothers, 102, 138
Sidcup, Lord, *see* Spode, Roderick
Singh, Huree Jamset Ram, 30
Singleton, Vera, 134–5
Sitting Pretty (PGW), 111
Smith, Harry B., 104, 105
socialism, 27, 42–3, 44, 46
Something Fresh (PGW), 145, 220–1
'Sonny Boy', 133
Spelvin, Rodney, 88, 90–1, 210–12
Spode, Roderick (Lord Sidcup), 194–9
Spring, Howard, 186–9
Sproat, Iain, 204–5, 208
Stalky and Co., 23
Stapleford, Shropshire, 220
Starr, Cora, *see* Potter-Pirbright, Corky
Steptoe, Mrs Howard, 76
Stevens, George, 176
Stickney, J. Wendell, 92
Strand Magazine, The, 59
Strand Theatre, 98
Sturgis, Mortimer, 87
Sullivan, Frank, 184
Summer Lightning (PGW), 129, 131, 222,
    234–5
Summer Moonshine (PGW), 77, 78, 127–8
Sun Yat Sen, 8
Sunset at Blandings (PGW), 130–1, 234
Swinnerton, Frank, 231–2, 232, 238, 241
Swoop, The (PGW), 47–50

Tales of St Austin's (PGW), 18–19
Tankerville election, 44
Taylor, A. J. P., 209, 233
Taylor, Robert, 174
team games, 7, 12, 85; *see also* cricket
Thalberg, Irving, 170
Thank You, Jeeves (PGW), 128
'They Didn't Believe Me', 101
'Things Are Looking Up', 122

Thomas, William Beach, 67–8
Thomson, Jim, 13
Thornton, Charles Inglis, 214–15
Those Three French Girls (PGW), 170–1
Three Musketeers, The (PGW), 112, 114, 243
Threepwood (house), 220
Threepwood, Hon. Frederick, 77, 127, 220–1, 232, 234
Threepwood, Hon. Galahad, 130, 221, 222–5, 226, 234
Thuermer, Angus, 182–3
'Till the Clouds Roll By' (lyric; PGW), 118
Tom Brown's Schooldays, *see* Hughes, Thomas
Topsy and Eva, 111
Townend, William, 11, 13, 32, 34, 53, 69, 125, 172, 229
Trevis, Roland, 147
Trollope, Anthony, *see* Tankerville election
Trott, Albert, 19
Trout, Ephraim, 151–2
Trout, Wilbur, 78
Tulse Hill Parliament, 43–4, 56
'Tuppenny Millionaire, The' (PGW), 57
Twentieth Century-Fox studios, 174

Uffenham, George, Viscount, 182
Ukridge, Stanley Featherstonehaugh, 109, 229–30
Uncle Fred in the Springtime (PGW), 202
Uneasy Money (PGW), 79, 105, 127, 129
upbringing, parental shortcomings in respect of, 8–9, 213–15
Urban, Joe, 108
Usborne, Richard, 25, 131, 145, 151

Valley Fields, *see* Dulwich
Vanderbilt, Eustiss, 158
Vanity Fair (magazine), 75, 101, 109
Variety (magazine), 171
Venner, Sir Alfred, 13
Vernon-Smith, Herbert, 29
Very Good Eddie, 102–3, 104
Very Good, Jeeves (PGW), 133
Vosper, Orlo, 127

Waddesley-Davenport, Cyril, 156
Walker, Mayor James, 113
Waller, Mr, 42–4, 51
Warner Brothers, 174
Warner, Jack, 179
Weatherby, Joss, 134
Wells, H. G., 62–3, 237
West, 40, 58
West, C. P., (PGW pseudonym), 101
Westbrook, Herbert W., 229
Weston, Alice, 140–2
Wharton, Colonel, 29
Wharton, Harry, 30
When a Man's Single, 60–3
'When It's Tulip Time in Sing Sing' (lyric; PGW), 242
Whitaker, Alma, 171–2
White Feather, The (PGW), 21
Widgeon, Freddie, 128
Wilde, Oscar, 26, 218
Willoughby Captains, The, 16–17
Wilson, Angus, 214
Wilson, Edmund, 101, 179, 237

Wilson, Sir Harold, 208
Windsor, Billy, 74, 75
Winship, Ginger, 197
Wodehouse, Eleanor (*née* Deane; mother of PGW), 8–9, 11, 233
Wodehouse, Ernest Armine (brother of PGW), 8, 9, 53
Wodehouse, Ethel (*née* Rowley; wife of PGW), 101, 167, 169, 183, 201–2, 202, 207, 235
Wodehouse, Henry Ernest (father of PGW), 8–9, 11, 53–4, 57–9, 215, 233
Wodehouse, Hugh (uncle of PGW), 65
Wodehouse, Pelham Grenville
　birth, childhood, 8–9, 31, 215–16
　and Dulwich, *see* Dulwich
　first literary composition, 9
　as writer, 13, 58–60, 63, 69–70, 110, 171, 180, 193–4, 231–5, 236–8
　as reader, 13, 113
　first book, 13
　school stories, 14, 17, 20–2, 23, 29, 30
　transition to adult novels, 23–8
　use of language, 24, 25–6, 232, 233
　real-life origins of his characters, 26–7, 220–2, 229–30
　schoolboys in adult world as key to his work, 28–9
　banking not understood by, 34, 55–7
　most autobiographical of his books, 37
　between school and writing, 38, 52–60, 63
　to America, 64–5, 70
　in Fleet St, *see* 'By The Way'
　as lyricist, 68, 84, 98, 100, 101, 104–23, 124–5, 151–2, 243
　mid-Atlantic style, 75–6, 80, 84
　Englishness, 93
　lunch with Gilbert, 95–7
　as theatre critic, 101
　theatre's effect on his fiction, 107, 109, 125–52
　early to bed, 113
　in Hollywood, 166–8, 169–73, 175–8, 180
　modest needs, 175
　German broadcasts, 181–212
　exile from England, 203, 209, 230–1
　knighthood, 208
　geography of his works, 227–9
　plots, 232–3
　death, 234
Wodehouse, Philip Peveril (brother of PGW), 8, 9
Wood Hills Literary and Debating Society, 88
Woolley, Frank Edward, 81
Wooster, Bertie, 122, 128, 129, 131, 131–2, 133, 137–8, 139–40, 154–5, 164, 194–9 *passim*, 212, 216–20 *passim*, 227
work, distasteful necessity of, 37–8
World of Jeeves, The (PGW), 219
Wrykyn, 11, 19, 21, 22, 23, 26, 29–30

Yardley, William, 240
'You Never Knew About Me' (lyric; PGW), 105

Zagorin, Elmer Z., 79
Zanuck, Daryll F., 174
Ziegfeld, Florenz, 111–14, 117, 123, 132, 243, 244
Ziegfeld, Mrs Florenz, 101
Zizzbaum, Benjamin, 154